HANNAH ARENDT AND ISAIAH BERLIN

Hannah Arendt and Isaiah Berlin

FREEDOM, POLITICS AND HUMANITY

KEI HIRUTA

PRINCETON UNIVERSITY PRESS
PRINCETON & OXFORD

Published by Princeton University Press
41 William Street, Princeton, New Jersey 08540
6 Oxford Street, Woodstock, Oxfordshire OX20 1TR

press.princeton.edu

All Rights Reserved

Library of Congress Cataloging-in-Publication Data

Names: Hiruta, Kei, 1981– author.
Title: Hannah Arendt and Isaiah Berlin : freedom, politics and
    humanity / Kei Hiruta.
Description: Princeton, New Jersey : Princeton University Press, 2021. |
    Includes bibliographical references and index.
Identifiers: LCCN 2021011347 (print) | LCCN 2021011348 (ebook) |
    ISBN 9780691182261 (hardback) | ISBN 9780691226132 (ebook)
Subjects: LCSH: Political science—Philosophy. | Arendt, Hannah, 1906–1975. |
    Berlin, Isaiah, 1909–1997.
Classification: LCC JA71 .H58 2021 (print) | LCC JA71 (ebook) | DDC 320.01–dc23
LC record available at https://lccn.loc.gov/2021011347
LC ebook record available at https://lccn.loc.gov/2021011348

British Library Cataloging-in-Publication Data is available

Editorial: Ben Tate and Josh Drake
Production Editorial: Kathleen Cioffi
Jacket Design: Lauren Smith
Production: Danielle Amatucci
Publicity: Alyssa Sanford and Amy Stewart
Copyeditor: Francis Eaves

Jacket images: (top left) Hannah Arendt, 1949 / dpa Picture Alliance / Alamy; (bottom right) Isaiah Berlin, 1995 / Agence Opale / Alamy

This book has been composed in Arno

Printed on acid-free paper. ∞

Printed in the United States of America

10 9 8 7 6 5 4 3 2 1

CONTENTS

1   Introduction   1

2   A Real Bête Noire   9

3   Freedom   48

4   Inhumanity   87

5   Evil and Judgement   124

6   Islands of Freedom   161

7   Conclusion   199

Acknowledgements   205

Appendix   209

Abbreviations   211

Notes   215

Index   267

HANNAH ARENDT AND ISAIAH BERLIN

1

Introduction

Years ago, I brought Hannah and Isaiah together. [. . .] The meeting was a
disaster from the start. She was too solemn, portentous, Teutonic, Hegelian for
him. She mistook his wit for frivolousness and thought him inadequately serious.
—ARTHUR SCHLESINGER JR.[1]

IN 1991, the American philosopher Norman Oliver Brown wrote to his friend
and former tutor Isaiah Berlin,[2] and favourably mentioned a recently published book entitled *Republic of Fear*.[3] A pioneering study of Saddam Hussein
and his Ba'ath Party, the book drew comparisons between the 'Kafkaesque'
world of Saddam's Iraq and its purported precursors in the twentieth century.
In so doing, it drew on some of the anti-totalitarian classics, including Berlin's
Four Essays on Liberty and Hannah Arendt's *The Origins of Totalitarianism*.[4]
Berlin was not pleased with this pairing. He wrote to Brown, 'I assume that
[*Republic of Fear*] is about the horrors of Iraq, etc., but what deeply offends
me is the linking of my name with that of Miss Hannah Arendt [. . .]. [D]o tell
me that you do see some radical differences between Miss Arendt and
myself—otherwise how can we go on knowing each other?'[5]

The strong dislike for Arendt that Berlin expressed in his 1991 letter to
Brown has a long history. It began a half-century earlier, when the two thinkers
were introduced to each other in wartime New York. Not much is known
about this meeting, but their opinions were certainly different and their personal chemistry evidently bad. The relationship between the two thinkers did
not improve, to say the least, when they spoke again at Harvard University
about a decade later, probably in 1949. Arthur Schlesinger Jr., the political scientist who arranged this meeting, would later recall the occasion as a 'disaster
from the start'.[6] Their paths did not cross again for more than fifteen years, as
Berlin continued to build his dazzling academic career in Britain, while Arendt
established herself as an influential public intellectual in the United States.

Nevertheless, they were not far apart socially, culturally or intellectually. They not only shared various research interests but also had many mutual friends, academic contacts and collaborators. Some of them, most notably the British political theorist Bernard Crick, attempted to persuade Berlin of the importance of Arendt's work. The Oxford philosopher was never persuaded. On the contrary, enhanced by his deep scepticism about the phenomenological tradition in philosophy, Berlin dismissed her theoretical work such as *The Human Condition* as an assemblage of 'free metaphysical association'.[7] His contempt subsequently evolved into a lifelong hatred with the publication of *Eichmann in Jerusalem: A Report on the Banality of Evil* in 1963. He wholeheartedly endorsed the widespread accusation that Arendt arrogantly and patronisingly blamed the victims of the Holocaust and that she proposed a deeply flawed account of evil.

Curiously, despite his disdain for Arendt and her work, Berlin kept reading—or, more precisely, skimming through—her books and articles, including neglected works such as *Rahel Varnhagen: The Life of a Jewess* as well as more major writings such as *The Human Condition* and *On Revolution*.[8] The more he read, however, the more convinced he was that his assessment of Arendt's work had been sound. The late Berlin summarised his considered opinion as follows: Arendt 'produces no arguments, no evidence of serious philosophical or historical thought'.[9] In addition, Berlin's animosity towards Arendt was never softened either by her death or by the ensuing passage of time. In the 1991 letter to Brown cited above, Berlin described Arendt as 'a real bête noire to me—in life, and after her death'. He continued, 'I really do look upon her as everything that I detest most'.[10]

Arendt was aware of Berlin's hostility towards her. This was thanks in no small part to the writer Mary McCarthy, who repeatedly disputed Berlin's dismissal of Arendt, so much so that her friendship with him came to be 'destroyed' as a result.[11] Meanwhile, Arendt herself never quite reciprocated Berlin's hostility. For one thing, she was, and was proud to be, a controversial figure, attracting many embittered critics especially after the publication of *Eichmann in Jerusalem*. She could not possibly respond to all of them, and from her point of view Berlin did not stand out as an especially important or worthy one. She was aware of his standing and connections in Britain, Israel and the USA, but she hardly considered him to be an original thinker.[12] This was partly because Arendt took the superiority of German philosophy over its Anglo-American counterpart for granted. Although she respected Hobbes, she generally saw Britain as something of a philosophical desert and saw little merit in the analytic movement inaugurated by Russell, Moore and others. In this respect, our protagonists' prejudices were symmetrical: just as Berlin was unable to appreciate German phenomenology, Arendt was unable to appreciate British empiricism.

Nevertheless, Arendt regarded Berlin as a learned scholar, especially when it came to Russian intellectual history. She sometimes used his writings in her classes;[13] and her surviving personal library contains a copy of Berlin's first book, *Karl Marx: His Life and Environment*, and four essays by him.[14] It is, however, indicative that the only piece by Berlin that Arendt seems to have read carefully was his introduction to Franco Venturi's *Roots of Revolution*. In fact, it is as the author of this introduction that Berlin makes his one and only appearance (in a footnote) in Arendt's published work.[15] For her, Berlin was a respectable intellectual historian and a moderately important member of what she called the 'Jewish establishment'. His animosity towards her was met by her indifference to him, accompanied by occasional suspicion.

Things could have been different. They were contemporaries, Arendt born in 1906 and Berlin in 1909. They belonged to the group of twentieth-century Jewish émigré intellectuals whose thoughts and life stories were intertwined with each other.[16] Born into German-Jewish and Baltic-Jewish families respectively, Arendt and Berlin alike experienced their share of antisemitism in their formative years. Both came to be preoccupied with Europe's looming crises in the 1930s, decided to abandon a promising career in pure philosophy by the end of World War II and thereafter devoted much of their time and energy to understanding the roots of totalitarianism, containing its growth and preempting its resurgence. Both of them had friends and relatives murdered or driven to death by the totalitarian regimes that they came to study in their academic work. Moreover, they themselves lived in the emerging totalitarian world and were consequently in a position to do something akin to what anthropologists call 'participatory observation': data collection by way of actually living in the society one aims to study. As is well known, the young Isaiah Berlin witnessed in horror both the February and October Revolutions in Petrograd. He subsequently returned to Soviet Russia to serve in the British Embassy in 1945–46, after having 'a recurring nightmare of being arrested' and giving thought to the prospect of suicide in the event of an arrest.[17] For her part, Arendt *was* arrested and endured an eight-day interrogation in Nazified Germany, followed by a five-week detention in an internment camp in occupied France (where she too gave thought to taking her own life) before migrating to the United States to write *The Origins of Totalitarianism*. Oppression, domination, inhumanity and the subversion of politics were their existential as well as intellectual issues; so were freedom, humanity and politics.

———

The twin goals of this study are to trace the development of the unfortunate relationship between the historical figures of Hannah Arendt and Isaiah

Berlin, and to bring their ideas into conversation. The former goal is historical
and biographical in nature; the latter, theoretical. The former involves the following questions:

> When and where did Arendt and Berlin meet, and what happened
> during those meetings?
> How did the personal conflict between the two emerge?
> How did Berlin develop his animosity towards Arendt, and she her
> indifference and suspicion towards him?
> What other interactions did they have apart from their actual meetings?

These questions are worth asking not only because they form a fascinating part
of twentieth-century intellectual, literary and cultural history. They are worth
asking also because the personal, the political and the intellectual were hardly
separable in both Arendt's and Berlin's lives and works. I take seriously what I
believe to be an elementary truth about them both: political theory for them
was more than a job or paid work. It was a vocation in the Weberian sense, and
each led the life of a political thinker, embodying a distinct theoretical outlook.[18] Deeply concerned with urgent issues of their times, both of our protagonists attempted to exercise, albeit in differing ways, influence on the 'real
world' they inhabited. As I shall show, this mode of living and thinking has its
own downsides and consequently is not unequivocally superior to the more
detached and institutionalised mode of political theorising that has become
the norm today. Still, we have some good reason to feel nostalgic about the
time when political theorists took themselves more seriously because their
'ideas really did have consequences.'[19]

The other, theoretical side of this study concerns a set of fundamental issues
that simultaneously connected and divided our protagonists. They connected
in that they were central to both Arendt's and Berlin's thought; and they divided in that they were answered by the two thinkers in conflicting ways.
Those central issues may be formally and schematically stated as follows:

> What does it mean for human beings to be free?
> What is it like for a person to be denied his or her freedom, and deprived
> of his or her humanity?[20] What are the central features of the worst
> form of unfree and inhumane society, known as totalitarianism, and
> how does this paradigmatically emerge?
> How should we assess the apparent failure to resist or confront the evil of
> totalitarianism, such as when one is coerced into cooperating with a
> state-sponsored mass murderer?
> What kind of society or polity ought we to aim to build if we want as
> many people as possible to be free and live a genuinely human life?

Arendt's and Berlin's sometimes overlapping and sometimes conflicting reflections on these questions will be considered in Chapters 3–6. These chapters are thematically organised, although each is loosely tied to a chronological phase. The third chapter, on 'Freedom', focuses on the late 1950s and early 1960s, when both of our protagonists fully matured as political thinkers and presented their rival theories of freedom, underpinned by competing views of the human condition. The fourth chapter, on 'Inhumanity', covers a longer period and traces the protagonists' lifelong engagement with totalitarianism. It mainly examines two distinct bodies of work: their wartime and immediate post-war analyses of totalitarian politics and society; and their later attempts to reconsider the history of Western political thought in light of the reality of Nazism and Stalinism. Chapter 5, on 'Evil and Judgement', focuses on Arendt's *Eichmann in Jerusalem* and Berlin's commentary on it. As their dispute is tied to their disagreement over central moral and political concepts, such as responsibility, judgement, power and agency, this chapter also covers the relevant work on these concepts. Chapter 6, on 'Islands of Freedom', delves more deeply into the two thinkers' middle and late works to tease out their competing visions of an ideal polity. Along the way, it considers their rival perspectives on a range of real-world politics and societies, including Britain's liberal present and its imperial past, the United States in the turbulent 1960s and Central and East European resistance to Soviet domination. In the Conclusion (Chapter 7), I briefly restate my main arguments and consider their implications for political thought and political philosophy today.

Although the story I tell in this book has many twists and turns, its backbone is simple and may be programmatically stated as follows. First, at the heart of the theoretical disagreement between Arendt and Berlin lie competing views of what it means to be human (Chapter 3). If, as Miller and Dagger observe, contemporary political theory is characterised by its dismissal of 'deep metaphysical questions', such as that of 'the human condition', as irrelevant to 'discover[ing] how people should live in societies and order their common affairs', both Arendt and Berlin belonged to an earlier era, when political theory was less 'shallow'.[21] Second, the two thinkers' disagreement over freedom and humanity is anchored in their differing perspectives on totalitarianism. Although both took totalitarianism to be the ultimate form of inhumanity and unfreedom, they theorised it differently, as a result of focusing on competing models of it: the Nazi model in Arendt's case, and the Bolshevik model in Berlin's (Chapter 4). These differences—over freedom and humanity on the one hand, and the unfreedom and inhumanity of totalitarianism on the other—gave rise to further points of disagreement over a number of issues. These included the possibility of resistance under totalitarian conditions (Chapter 5), and the shape of an ideal polity, where men and women have a decent chance to live a free and fulfilling life (Chapter 6). Arendt's and Berlin's experiences and life stories provide an important backdrop to all of those major points of comparison, although their ideas are not reducible to their biographies. Thus, the historical-biographical story told in Chapter 2 informs the rest of the book that focuses on the theoretical disagreement between the two thinkers.

———

Hannah Arendt and Isaiah Berlin is the first comprehensive study of the Arendt–Berlin conflict in all its personal, political and theoretical aspects. Needless to say, however, it builds on the existing literature that has illuminated the conflict from more specific angles. While each such contribution will be discussed (often in notes) in the pages that follow, what needs to be highlighted in this introductory chapter is the scarcity and late emergence of the relevant literature. True, those who knew Arendt and/or Berlin personally began writing on their conflict as early as the 1970s;[22] and yet scholarly works on it have appeared only recently.[23] This is no accident. In fact, Berlin's determination to distance himself from the woman he 'detested most' played a significant role in this context.[24] As those who have examined his unpublished papers will know, Berlin had much to say on Arendt and her work, but he hardly ever expressed his views in print because he disliked her so much that he was unwilling 'to enter into any relations with [her], not even those of hostility'.[25] It is true that there was one exception to this rule in his lifetime: he let one substantial commentary on Arendt appear in 1991, as part of his interviews with Ramin Jahanbegloo.[26] Except for this, however, he kept his public silence on his 'bête noire'.[27] As a result, it was only after his death in 1997 that Berlin's hostile comments on Arendt began to appear in print. Michael Ignatieff's authorised biography was an important turning point in this regard.[28] Nevertheless, it still gave an incomplete picture, attracting some insightful, but largely speculative remarks by scholars.[29] A fair sample of Berlin's full commentary on Arendt's work and personality only appeared in 2004–15, when Henry Hardy, Jennifer Holmes and Mark Pottle published his select letters in four volumes.[30] This is why the Arendt–Berlin conflict, especially his hostility towards her, has been a topic largely neglected until recently; and why the telling of the whole story of this conflict has never been attempted, until now.

Finally, I would like to make some remarks to indicate at the outset what this book is *not* about. First, as should already be clear, this study is a piece neither of undiluted political philosophy nor of undiluted intellectual history. It mobilises methodological tools taken from both disciplines. On the one hand, it carefully examines Arendt's and Berlin's life stories and reconstructs the relevant contexts to illuminate the two thinkers' ideas and their comparative strengths and weaknesses. On the other hand, it often discusses their ideas in the abstract, bracketing the contexts in which these were produced, circulated and consumed. Sceptics might say that such juxtaposition of the two approaches is of necessity incoherent. They might say that political philosophy and intellectual history are entirely separate enterprises, and one must choose which approach to use before applying either of them to the object of study. I beg to differ. In my opinion, in the study of political thought broadly construed, the choice of a method should follow the object and goal of study, not vice versa. And this study requires both philosophical and historical approaches. To borrow the words of a recent historian of philosophy, to complain of academic research such as mine 'as neither properly philosophical nor properly historical is like complaining of a bridge that it is neither on one bank nor the other'.[31] That said, I shall not dwell on methodological issues at a general and abstract level, because the present study is not a contribution to the methodological debate in political thought. The proof of the pudding is in the eating. The following chapters show *what* my research found; after reading the book, each reader may draw his or her own conclusions as to whether the *way* I conducted my research has been successful or not.

Second, this study is not a defence of one of our protagonists against the other. It is, on the contrary, a decidedly non-partisan book. Needless to say, this does not mean that I am or attempt to be neutral vis-à-vis the Arendt–Berlin conflict. It means, rather, that I assess the two thinkers' individual arguments on their own merits, instead of supporting either of them indiscriminately. I know this is likely to disappoint some readers. In this context it is worth recalling that Arendt, if not Berlin, remains a highly divisive figure, commanding blind loyalty among some and inciting strong hostility among others. The former would like to see an unflinching defence of their master against her critics; the latter, a wholesale attack on their nemesis. This book is of no use to either party. As I hope to show in the pages that follow, both Arendt and Berlin got many things right and many things wrong, albeit in differing ways. The point of juxtaposing the two is not to decide which side 'won', for disagreement between thinkers is not a sporting competition, a beauty contest or any other such game. The point, rather, is to *appreciate* Arendt's and Berlin's ideas better, reading their works against each other, so that the tacit assumptions each theorist made and the hidden biases each had can be teased out and critically scrutinised.

If this sounds evasive, and if I am asked to 'confess' my preferences and prejudices, the only thing I can honestly say is as follows: I know I have prejudices in favour of *both* Arendt *and* Berlin. I know that my intellectual formation has been inseparable from my compulsive interest in the works of both, and that my outlook has been fundamentally shaped by my sustained critical engagement with them both. Arendt and Berlin are *equally* my intellectual heroes.

The two heroes, however, failed disastrously to get along with each other. The next chapter tells the story of this failure.

2

A Real Bête Noire

Animosity

'I do indeed have views on Miss Arendt. I am a profound non-admirer of both her work and her personality (she knew this).'[1] This is how, in the winter of 1992, then eighty-two-year-old Isaiah Berlin began his reply to a writer who was preparing a monograph on Hannah Arendt and Martin Heidegger.[2] The writer, the late Elżbieta Ettinger, was naturally intrigued. She sent several more letters to ask Berlin to elaborate on his views, share anecdotes and arrange a meeting with her. Unfortunately for Ettinger, a meeting did not materialise due to Berlin's illness; fortunately for later historians, he responded to her requests in writing, and reiterated at once what he had told others on various occasions. He said, among other things, that Arendt was pretentious, self-important and unsympathetic; that her 1958 book *The Human Condition* showed her 'wide ignorance [. . .] of Greek classics', just as her 1951 book *The Origins of Totalitarianism* displayed comparable ignorance of modern Russian history; that she sharply and irresponsibly changed her mind about Zionism; and that she expressed 'unbelievable arrogance in telling the Jewish victims of the Nazis how they should have behaved' in *Eichmann in Jerusalem*.[3] Along the way, Berlin referred to Arendt as 'my bête noire', as he did repeatedly, on various occasions.[4]

How did he develop such animosity towards Arendt? This chapter charts the key stages of this development, which will shed light on my discussion of the two thinkers' political and intellectual disagreement in later chapters. To this end, a brief overview of their lives is in order.

The Life of Hannah Arendt

Hannah Arendt was born in 1906 near Hanover and grew up in Königsberg, then capital of East Prussia, now the Russian city of Kaliningrad. The only child of secular, middle-class, politically socialist and fully assimilated parents, she attended a German kindergarten, a mandatory Christian Sunday school and German schools, with a vague awareness of her identity as a Jew. Her mother Martha was devoted to the Goethean ideal of *Bildung* or character formation, and her parental and pedagogic efforts were richly rewarded by the young Hannah's love of classical and modern European philosophy and literature. Having spent a few semesters at the University of Berlin before an official university enrolment, Hannah Arendt studied philosophy at the University of Marburg, where she had a now well-known romantic affair with her teacher Martin Heidegger. She was not particularly impressed by Heidegger's former mentor Edmund Husserl, whose lectures on 'Introduction to Phenomenology' she attended in the winter semester of 1926/27.[5] However, she found an ideal teacher in Karl Jaspers in Heidelberg, where she completed her doctoral dissertation on 'The Concept of Love in Augustine' in 1929.[6]

A deepening crisis in Germany interrupted Arendt's subsequent academic career. Spectacularly exploiting the economic and political crises of the late 1920s and early 1930s, the Nazi Party won 18.3% of the vote at the September 1930 national election, and 37.4% at the following July 1932 election to become the largest party in the Reichstag. Arendt had a sense of what was to come, observing, 'Today in Germany it seems Jewish assimilation must declare bankruptcy.'[7] The shock of the Reichstag Fire on 27 February 1933 completed her turn to politics; she could no longer 'be a bystander.'[8] She now abandoned any hope for piecemeal reform, hid communists in her apartment and, most dramatically, accepted a request by members of the Zionist Federation of Germany to illicitly collect evidence of rising antisemitism in Nazified Germany. This resulted in her arrest and an eight-day interrogation. Released, but knowing that 'she was unlikely to be twice blessed', she left Germany illegally for Paris.[9]

Her involvement in Zionism intensified during her first few years in the French capital. She formally joined the World Zionist Organization; worked for an office of another Zionist organisation, France-Palestine; advocated Labour Zionist ideas in print; was drawn to the Buberian idea of Jewish cultural renaissance; and began working for Youth Aliyah, an organisation supporting young Jews' migration to Palestine as Zionist pioneers.[10] But her Zionist outlook came to incorporate a broadly Marxian perspective from 1936, partly due to the influence of her future (and second) husband, Heinrich Blücher. This self-educated German communist belonged to a group of Weimar intellectuals in exile, including Walter Benjamin, Arnold Zweig and Erich Cohn-Bendit, whom Arendt regularly met in Paris. Their situations drastically changed once the war broke out in September 1939. The French authorities now began interning 'enemy aliens', sending Arendt to a women's camp in Gurs and Blücher to a male equivalent in Colombes.[11] Released, and reunited by sheer chance, the now married couple emigrated to the United States in May 1941.

Having settled in New York, Arendt wrote columns for the German-language newspaper *Aufbau* over the next few years, while seeking to re-launch her career as a scholar and an intellectual.[12] This does not mean that she devoted all of her time and energy to purely intellectual pursuits. On the contrary, she worked tirelessly in the mid- and late 1940s for the Commission on European Jewish Cultural Reconstruction and its successor organisation Jewish Cultural Reconstruction, Inc. to restore, inspect, organise and distribute looted Jewish cultural artefacts from post-war Europe to various institutions in Palestine/Israel, the United States and elsewhere. Meanwhile, she made a major scholarly breakthrough in 1951 with the publication of *The Origins of Totalitarianism*. This was followed by further studies on Marxism and the tradition of Western political thought behind it, resulting in *The Human Condition*, *Between Past and Future* and *On Revolution*. Her thought subsequently developed in a new direction, when she covered the trial of the Nazi criminal Adolf Eichmann. Published in 1963, *Eichmann in Jerusalem: A Report on the Banality of Evil* provoked intense controversy, sometimes referred to as 'a civil war [. . .] among New York intellectuals'.[13] Her preliminary idea that Eichmann's evil might be accounted for by his sheer inability to think eventually developed into a full-fledged enquiry into the 'life of the mind'; that is, human capacities for thinking, willing and judging. Arendt in her later years also continued to write on contemporary social and political issues, confirming her reputation as one of the most influential public intellectuals of the twentieth century. She died in 1975 at the relatively young age of sixty-nine.

The Life of Isaiah Berlin

Isaiah Berlin was born in 1909 in the Latvian city of Riga, then a provincial capital in the Russian Empire, into a wealthy Russian-speaking Jewish family. The city was relatively stable until the outbreak of war in 1914, which triggered a new wave of antisemitism, prompting the family to move to Russia proper.[14] The Berlins eventually found a temporary home in Petrograd, where the young Isaiah, at the ages of seven and eight respectively, witnessed the February and October Revolutions of 1917. His father, Mendel, managed his timber business despite the upheavals, but he felt 'imprisoned' in the Bolshevik-controlled city, and the family ultimately decided to migrate to England.[15]

Having settled in London in 1921, Isaiah Berlin attended St Paul's School between 1922 and 1928. He then went to Corpus Christi College, Oxford, to read Greats (a course in philosophy and ancient history) and Politics, Philosophy and Economics, attaining Firsts in both courses. In 1932, immediately after graduation, with 'no application, no interview', Berlin became a philosophy lecturer at New College.[16] This was soon followed by his admission as a prize fellow to All Souls College, at the age of twenty-three, the first Jew to hold the position in the five-hundred-year history of Britain's most prestigious academic institution.[17] The weekly meetings of young philosophers, including A. J. Ayer, J. L. Austin and Stuart Hampshire, hosted by Berlin in his rooms in the mid-1930s would become an academic legend, and he played an important role in the resurgence and renewal of empiricist philosophy in inter- and post-war Oxford and Britain. During the same period, Berlin developed an interest in political thought, not least because of the deepening crises in 1930s Europe. Having accepted an offer to write an introductory monograph on Karl Marx in 1933, he ferociously read and built 'the intellectual capital on which he was to depend for the rest of his life'.[18] He submitted the final manuscript of *Karl Marx: His Life and Environment* on 12 September 1938, less than three weeks before the Munich Agreement, which mandated the German occupation of the Sudetenland.[19] Once war broke out, he began seeking ways to contribute to the war effort of his adopted country against Nazi Germany.

Berlin's foreign origins, and a physical disability in his left arm, caused him to be denied official war work, frustrating his 'wish to help to win the war'.[20] But he was eventually offered a post in New York analysing public opinion in the United States and helping London to challenge America's isolationism. The philosopher-turned-diplomat quickly mobilised his enormous personal charm and elite institutional connections to build an impressive network of friends and contacts. Having proved his worth, he was offered another job in public service, this time at the British Embassy in Washington, drafting weekly summaries of American public opinion which were dispatched to Whitehall.[21] After the war, Berlin worked for the British Embassy in Moscow between September 1945 and January 1946. He had a glimpse of both life under Stalinist rule and what he regarded as the residue of the great Russian cultural tradition from the pre-Bolshevik era, incarnated in the persons of the poet Anna Akhmatova and Boris Pasternak, the author of *Doctor Zhivago*.

Berlin finally returned to Oxford in April 1946 to resume his academic career, which he decided to devote to the study of political ideas and their history. Among the many issues he addressed in the following half-century were the following: differing understandings of the meaning of liberty/freedom; the competing developments of rationalism and romanticism in modern European culture; Russian thought and intellectual history; contemporary figures of extraordinary gifts, from J. L. Austin to Chaim Weizmann; and the nature of human and social studies (*Geisteswissenschaften*) as distinct from the natural sciences (*Naturwissenschaften*). Berlin became a much sought-after public intellectual in post-war Britain and beyond; travelled widely, and especially to the United States, where he held various visiting positions; and was in correspondence with an impressive array of friends, students, scholars, journalists, writers, artists, diplomats and politicians across the world. He also proved himself to be an imaginative university reformer and a brilliant academic administrator, serving as the founding president of Wolfson College, Oxford, between 1966 and 1975, and as the President of the British Academy between 1974 and 1978. By the time of his death in 1997 at the age of eighty-eight, he was, in the memorable words of the literary critic Stefan Collini, considered very close to 'the academic equivalent of a saint'.[22]

Conversations on Zionism

Arendt and Berlin only held substantive conversations twice in their lives, although they were present in the same room on at least one and possibly other occasions.[23] The first conversation took place in wartime New York, probably in late 1941; the second in Harvard, probably during the first half of 1949.[24] The two meetings marked the disastrous beginnings of our protagonists' mutual story.

New York, 1941

Both thinkers arrived in New York City within a year or so before their first meeting. Berlin initially arrived there in the summer of 1940 and, after a three-month return to England in winter, properly settled in the city in January 1941.[25] Arendt arrived four months later, in May. Their situations then were very different. He was a public servant, a specialist attaché to the British Press Service, working at 30 Rockefeller Plaza and receiving a salary as a government employee. She was a stateless refugee, renting two small rooms with a shared kitchen with her husband and mother, initially dependent on financial support from the Zionist Organization of America.[26] He suspended his academic career in 1940 out of choice; she did so in 1933 out of sheer necessity. In the United States, he, needless to say, spoke English fluently, while Arendt had to spend the summer of 1941 learning the new language with a host family in Winchester, Massachusetts, arranged by Self-Help for Refugees.[27] But they had much in common also, including a sense of responsibility—or of a mission, even—to do something to alleviate the unfolding catastrophe. Both were eagerly and ambitiously remaking themselves in the new country, believing that they could exercise some influence over the course of history.

Their styles of engagement were different, however, reflecting their differing temperaments and anticipating their later work. Berlin was a part of the team of government employees. He had his own political agenda and informally pursued it, and he once, in 1943, abused his office to leak confidential information about a UK policy to protect Zionist interests.[28] Yet he always attempted to make his and Britain's goals coincide, both by influencing the country's policy-makers and by compromising as much as he could to keep the official line. In short, Berlin 'strove to be "one of us"' in his adopted homeland.[29] Arendt, by contrast, always sought to be an independent voice, 'fellow travelling with larger political movements', while keeping a critical distance from them.[30] She wrote for various media, from weeklies to highbrow magazines and academic journals; regardless, her preferred mode of engagement was publication. She was not, unlike Berlin, 'Machiavellian' in one sense of the term: she was not interested in whispering to a prince; she was more concerned to persuade the *demos*. Consider what each was doing in the spring of 1942, by way of illustration. While Berlin sent a telegram to Chaim Weizmann to ask 'if there [is] anything I could conceivably do', Arendt was discussing publication plans with Waldemar Gurian, editor of the *Review of Politics*. She assured him of her commitment in the following terms: 'as I am of the opinion that nothing is as important as fighting the Nazis, I would naturally never pretend to be busy with something else.'[31] The two thinkers' shared commitment to 'fighting the Nazis' manifested itself very differently.

How did the *Aufbau* columnist and the British official meet each other? Through Kurt Blumenfeld, is the answer. Born in 1884 in Marggrabowa, East Prussia, Blumenfeld encountered Zionism while studying law in the city of Berlin. He soon began playing an active role in what was then still an insignificant political movement. Having abandoned his prospective career in law by 1909, Blumenfeld was eventually elected as the president of the Zionist Federation of Germany in 1924.[32] He met Arendt in Heidelberg in 1926, when he gave a lecture at the invitation of her friend Hans Jonas, acting on behalf of the local Zionist student club.[33] The lecture, which she attended out of her friendship with Jonas rather than her interest in Zionism, had little immediate impact on her. Her preoccupation would remain philosophical until the early 1930s. Nevertheless, Arendt and Blumenfeld instantly became friends, and this proved important as she was becoming politicised after completing her dissertation in 1929.[34] In fact, it was Blumenfeld who, in the summer of 1933, asked Arendt to undertake the illegal work for the Zionists that led to her arrest. Both of them left Germany soon afterwards—Arendt westward for Paris and Blumenfeld eastward for Palestine. But they were reunited in 1941 in New York, where Blumenfeld had been representing the Keren Hayesod (Foundation Fund), the Zionist Organization's primary vehicle for fundraising for settlement and economic development in Palestine.[35] Although Arendt never became an activist within the organisation, the two German Jews remained personally close and collaborated when they shared political goals in 1940s America.

How the German Zionist leader came to know Isaiah Berlin is less clear. It is possible that Blumenfeld met the adolescent Isaiah in 1920s London, where

the Berlins probably 'moved [. . .] in the same circle as leading Zionists', including members of Keren Hayesod, then based in the British capital.[36] However,
given the young Berlin's relatively limited connections to Zionists outside Britain, it is more likely that he met Blumenfeld in wartime New York. There, as
early as 1940–41, Berlin in his capacity as a British official made contact with
key Zionist leaders and supporters, including the founders of the American
Jewish Congress Stephen Wise and Louis Lipsky, Supreme Court Justice Louis
Brandeis, theologian Reinhold Niebuhr and the publisher—and Arendt's
future employer (1946–48)—Salman Schocken.[37] Some of the wartime correspondence between Blumenfeld and Berlin is lost, but one surviving item,
dated 12 January 1945, shows what kind of relations they had.[38] Addressing the
correspondent as 'Mr. Berlin', Blumenfeld enclosed a copy of his recently published essay on Chaim Weizmann. Brief, businesslike and written in a formal
style, Blumenfeld's letter to Berlin indicates that the correspondents were not
personally close but had been in professional contact with each other.

Blumenfeld introduced Berlin to Arendt in late 1941, apparently in his own
rooms.[39] The only surviving records of this meeting are Berlin's later recollections, which focus on one issue: the intensity of Arendt's Zionist commitment.
'At that time', Berlin recalled, 'she seemed to me a hundred per cent Zionist.'[40]
He put it even more strongly elsewhere: 'her fanatical Jewish nationalism [. . .]
was, I remember, too much for me.'[41] These words might strike us as surprising
today, when Arendt is often portrayed as a post-Zionist *avant la lettre*. But this
popular image tells us little about her stance on Zionism in the early 1940s.
Timing is of prime importance in this context, for Arendt's thinking about
Zionism evolved drastically and discontinuously during the 1930s and 1940s,
responding to the dramatic turns of events in Europe and the Middle East.
What, then, was her stance on Zionism in late 1941, when she met Berlin? At
that time, she had been fiercely arguing for the formation of a Jewish army to
'battle Hitler with weapons in our hands'.[42] She hoped that the extremity of
the situation would compel ordinary Jews to arm themselves, build solidarity,
acquire a political consciousness and exercise collective agency. She advocated
a 'return to the original national, revolutionary slogans of the [Zionist] movement', including 'a national recuperation of the Jewish people'.[43] The impression of Arendt that Berlin formed at their first meeting was not groundless.

In fact, Arendt's position in late 1941 came rather close to that of the Revisionists, a group of radical Zionists more confrontational and more uncom-
promising than the official Zionists led by Weizmann. While Arendt was
explicitly critical of what she regarded as the Revisionists' excessive reliance
on violence,[44] the tone and rhetoric of her impassioned call for the formation
of a Jewish army was scarcely less militant. Indeed, for the historian Derek
Penslar, they were 'reminiscent of the Revisionist Zionist leader Vladimir

Jabotinsky'.[45] Moreover, initially unaware that the Committee for a Jewish Army (CJA) was linked to the Revisionist Party, Arendt actively supported it for several months until she became aware of the connection in March 1942.[46] In the meantime, Isaiah Berlin was firmly on the other side of the Zionist split: the faithful Weizmannite that he had always been and would remain. Interestingly, around the time when Arendt supported the CJA, Berlin was affiliated with the Emergency Committee for Zionist Affairs that was attempting to persuade the CJA to stay in line with the official Zionist goals.[47] It is thus possible that Blumenfeld introduced Arendt and Berlin as associates, respectively, of these two rival Zionist groups. Speculation aside, the strand of Zionism Arendt supported in late 1941 and the alternative strand that Berlin supported in the same period certainly conflicted with each other. This was not to be the only time when they found themselves standing at the opposing ends of a political spectrum.

Harvard, 1949

The second meeting took place at Harvard University approximately ten years later. The precise date is unknown, although the best guess would be sometime during the spring or early summer of 1949.[48] What we know with certainty is that it was Arthur Schlesinger Jr. who brought Arendt and Berlin together this time. Now best remembered for his role as special assistant to President Kennedy (1961–63) and for his Pulitzer Prize-winning book *A Thousand Days: John F. Kennedy in the White House*, Schlesinger was a lifelong friend and political ally of Isaiah Berlin. The two men met in Washington, DC, in winter 1943–44. The Harvard historian then worked for the Office of Strategic Services, a precursor to the CIA, located at 2430 E Street, Foggy Bottom, while the Oxford philosopher worked for the British Embassy, approximately two miles north-west of the OSS headquarters.[49] The friendship that the two men had formed in wartime Washington developed in early 1949 when Berlin was a visiting lecturer at Harvard, teaching 'The Development of Revolutionary Ideas in Russia'.[50] By the time Berlin arrived in Harvard in January, Schlesinger had already completed his Cold War liberal manifesto *The Vital Center: The Politics of Freedom*, which by the author's own account was indebted to Berlin.[51] But the two men's closeness was not only political or intellectual, but also personal. The late Berlin would describe Schlesinger as 'an extremely nice man; [. . .] perfectly decent, upright and honest'.[52] Schlesinger would reciprocate even more generously, describing Berlin as endowed with 'an enormous generosity of spirit, an unparalleled sense of fun' and 'the marvellous quality of *intensifying* life so that one perceived more and thought more and understood more'.[53]

Schlesinger enjoyed no comparable friendship with Hannah Arendt. Again, it is hard to determine when they met for the first time. The earliest possible date is May 1948, when both participated in a conference in New York on 'Jewish Experience in America', organised by *Commentary* magazine. The list of twenty-eight attendees is highly impressive: Daniel Bell, Nathan Glazer and Sidney Hook, as well as Arendt and Schlesinger, were present. The chair of the conference, Oscar Handlin, felt positive about the occasion, at which '[m]any participants met each other for the first time and found the opportunity, in free and candid discussion, to become acquainted with a diversity of attitudes and of current lines of research.'[54] If this conference was where Arendt and Schlesinger came to know each other, however, the meeting did not develop into an enduring friendship. No correspondence between the two is found in the Hannah Arendt Papers, archived in the Library of Congress, or in the Arthur M. Schlesinger Personal Papers, archived in the John F. Kennedy Library. Moreover, Schlesinger's *Journals 1952–2000* refers to Arendt only once, and he echoes Berlin's disparaging remarks about her. He wrote on 7 April 1977, 'Isaiah [Berlin] was in New York on his way to Japan. I called him and expressed particular pleasure over his listing Hannah Arendt in the *Times Literary Supplement* as one of the most overrated writers of the century.'[55]

This, however, was hardly an opinion that Schlesinger had held three decades earlier. According to his younger self, Arendt had 'brilliantly argued' that the 'image of twentieth-century totalitarianism is [...] the concentration camp', and *The Vital Center* owed a good deal to Arendt's 1948 essay 'The Concentration Camps'.[56] Furthermore, in 1953, Schlesinger and Arendt, together with Dwight Macdonald, Alfred Kazin, Mary McCarthy, Harold Rosenberg and Richard Rovere, discussed the idea of launching a new magazine in opposition to the (Senator Joseph) McCarthyite threat to civil liberties. The plan came to naught due to a lack of funding.[57] But this episode indicates that the relationship between Arendt and Schlesinger was cordial when they met Berlin in 1949.

What Schlesinger would remember about this meeting is the sheer difference between the personalities and dispositions of Arendt and Berlin. According to Schlesinger, '[s]he was too solemn, portentous, Teutonic, Hegelian for him. She mistook his wit for frivolousness and thought him inadequately serious.'[58] Berlin would remember something else, more consequential: it was Arendt's (purportedly) complete change of mind about Zionism that left a lasting impression on him. '[When] I met her in New York in 1941', Berlin recalled, 'she seemed to me a hundred per cent Zionist. On the second occasion when I met her, about ten years later, she attacked Israel.'[59]

It is a matter of debate whether Arendt had changed her mind as sharply as Berlin thought she did. Given the specific timing of his two meetings with her, however, it is not difficult to see why Berlin should have *perceived* Arendt's complex shift of allegiance as a straightforward 180-degree turn. Already in March 1942, just a few months after her first meeting with Berlin, Arendt broke with the CJA and began working with the *Aufbau* editor Joseph Maier to launch what turned out to be a short-lived grassroots Jewish national liberation movement to challenge the overly diplomatic approach characteristic of official Zionism. Her feeling towards Zionism at this point was one of strong frustration rather than disillusionment. This, however, began to change soon afterwards. A decisive event was the Extraordinary Zionist Conference, which Arendt attended as an observer, at the Biltmore Hotel in New York on 6–11 May 1942. The carefully worded Biltmore programme that the delegates adopted 'symbolized the Zionists' resolve to establish a Jewish state in Palestine', while tactfully bypassing the intractable question of territorial boundaries, so as to prevent the internal discord among different Zionist groups from developing into an open conflict.[60] Historians of Zionism often portray Biltmore positively, as marking a significant step in the right direction, paving the way for the establishment of the State of Israel in 1948.[61] To Arendt's eyes, by contrast, it marked a wrong turn, partly because it frustrated her proposal for the creation of a Jewish army, but more fundamentally because it adopted, if cautiously, a nation-state nationalism, of which she had *always* been sceptical. After Biltmore, the ambivalent sympathy she had held for official Zionism evaporated.

Scholars disagree as to what Arendt opted for after Biltmore. According to some, she effectively endorsed Ihud's advocacy for the establishment of a binational state, and constitutional parity between Jews and Arabs, in Palestine.[62] According to others, she advocated her distinct brand of Arab–Jewish federalism, in principle rejecting nation-state Zionism and binationalism alike, despite her tactical eleventh-hour support for Ihud's programme in early 1948.[63] According to others still, Arendt herself may have been unsure of exactly what she wanted, although she found none of the options on the table satisfactory and was 'intent on showing that everyone else was wrong'.[64] We do not need to settle this controversy here. The relevant point is that Arendt's opposition to official Zionism became more intense and more vocal after Biltmore, when her sense of urgency was intensified as news about the destruction of European Jewry kept flowing into the United States. Her indignation climaxed in late 1944, when she published her now famous essay 'Zionism Reconsidered'.[65] This was followed by 'To Save the Jewish Homeland' (5 May 1948) and the widely read ninth chapter of *The Origins of Totalitarianism*, 'The Decline of the Nation-State and the End of the Rights of Man' (1951). It is above all these three pieces of writing that commentators today cite when they, approvingly or disapprovingly, present Arendt as a proto-post-Zionist or even an anti-Zionist.[66]

Observe, however, that those three pieces of writing registered rather different sentiments. The 1944 essay, 'Zionism Reconsidered', was a particularly argumentative piece. It was written in response to the resolution adopted by the Zionist Organization of America in Atlantic City on 15 October. This resolution not only reaffirmed the Biltmore programme but also, in Arendt's words, '[went] even a step further' in the direction of nation-state Zionism.[67] It is therefore hardly surprising that 'Zionism Reconsidered' should be animated by 'irony, sarcasm, condemnation, scorn, and blunt denunciation' of the Zionist movement and its leadership.[68] But this explosive tone would progressively change to the more restrained tenor of regret and a sense of powerlessness in the later essays, published in the late 1940s and early 1950s, as Arendt's emphasis shifted from what Zionists *ought to do* to what they *ought to have done*. Berlin never specified how she 'attacked Israel' at their second meeting in 1949. But it is safe to assume that her tone was similar to that of her writings from this period, saturated by a profound sense of disappointment. Her tone was indeed bitter; yet that did not derive from anti-Zionism per se. In fact, as late as in 1951, she did not forget to acknowledge that the creation of the State of Israel achieved 'the restoration of human rights [. . .] through the restoration or the establishment of national rights'.[69] Rather, the bitterness had more to do with *resentment*, for the political movement with which she had at least half-identified irretrievably drifted away between May 1942 and May 1948. From Arendt's perspective, she never betrayed Zionism; it was Zionism that betrayed itself.

Zionism: Politics and Identity

Berlin found his meetings with Arendt unforgettably *annoying* rather than boring or unfruitful. On the first occasion, he was annoyed because he found her opinionated and dogmatic. Arendt, Berlin recalled, 'preached Zionism at me, *as if I needed it*'.[70] On the second occasion, he was annoyed because he thought she had shifted from a fanatical Zionism to its opposite pole. But it is worth asking why he *should* have been annoyed. To begin with, Berlin was a moderate, a sceptic and, paradoxical though it may sound, a committed anti-fanatic. He claimed for his own the French statesman Charles-Maurice de Talleyrand's maxim: *Surtout, Messieurs, point de zèle* (Above all, gentlemen, no zeal whatsoever).[71] If so, why should Berlin be annoyed when he felt his commitment to a political ideology, rather than his loyalty to his family or friends, was in doubt?[72] Similarly, it is far from clear why Berlin should be annoyed by Arendt's change of mind over Zionism. Is it not part of what it is to be a liberal, especially a Millian liberal, as Berlin identified himself, to encourage people constantly to examine their own convictions and change their minds as they grow and mature? Was this not precisely what Arendt did vis-à-vis Zionism? It is as though the Mill in Berlin had to go into hiding every time he spoke of Arendt. Or was there something further behind Berlin's seemingly illiberal attitude?[73]

This is one area where the personal intersected with the political and the intellectual. Of course, Berlin's lifelong support for liberal Zionism was partly a matter of theoretical commitment. He believed that the human need to belong to one's own group was universal, and that a certain form of nationalism, whose chief function was to provide a home for the collective life of a people, was a legitimate means of meeting that need. As a consequence, he defended a liberal Zionism conceptualised as a particular manifestation of that form of nationalism. He was a Zionist because he endorsed universal principles of liberalism and nationality (see further Chapter 6). Be that as it may, his liberal Zionist commitment was more than a theoretical issue. It was also a matter of identity. This is best illustrated by the manner in which he related his various life stories to his political convictions. Consider the following exemplary case: in the aftermath of the Russian Revolution, the Berlins left Petrograd and stayed in Riga before migrating to England. In the Baltic city, the family suffered antisemitic verbal assaults and harassment. The philosopher summarised the lesson that he had learned as a boy in Riga thus:

> We were Jews. . . . We were not Russian. We were not Letts. We were something else. We had to have a home. There was no point living in a perpetual *qui vive*. Above all there was no point denying it, concealing it. To do so was undignified and unsuccessful.[74]

This, needless to say, does not by itself amount to a commitment to Zionism, usually understood as an ideology or a movement aiming to build a Jewish state in Palestine. But it registers important elements of it, including a recognition of the failure of assimilationism. Berlin's memory stored many such episodes, including, to mention but one more, his walking around with a blue and white flag in a synagogue basement in Petrograd celebrating the Balfour Declaration, at the age of eight.[75] Together, these memories made his Zionist commitment part of who he was. If, as is often suggested, one's sense of oneself crucially depends on the stories one tells about oneself, stories about Zionism constituted an essential part of Berlin's 'narrative self'. Given this, it is not difficult to see why he should take exception to what he took to be Arendt's shifting stance on Zionism. Changing one's mind over *this* issue was, in his view, more than a change of opinion; it must be a conversion, entailing a fundamental alteration to one's identity. To this we must add the fact, of which Berlin was well aware, that it was easy to be a Zionist in the 1940s and 1950s, and hard to *remain* one later. To his credit, Berlin held firm to the end of his life in 1997, despite his increasing disappointment in subsequent developments in Israeli politics. A sense of pride is discernible in the remark he made as a seventy-nine-year-old man: 'I was a Zionist even as a schoolboy.'[76] He did not need a Hannah Arendt to 'preach Zionism' at him.

The story was different with Arendt. Unlike Berlin, she did not grow up as a Zionist. She was not a Zionist as a schoolgirl, to adapt Berlin's expression. From her point of view, she was not only entitled but also morally required to adjust her stance on Zionism, depending on the movement's differing merits at different stages of development. This was precisely what she attempted to do. In 1933 in Germany, she did what she could to assist Blumenfeld's group; having been exiled to Paris, she criticised the Zionist leadership *from within* for its overly reconciliatory approach, while working for Youth Aliyah;[77] in 1940s America, she continued to express similar internal dissent, even though the gap between what she wanted Zionism to be and how it actually developed kept widening; and once the gap became too wide, she lapsed into silence (until the capture of Adolf Eichmann prompted her to revisit Zionist politics, but this is a different story that will be discussed below). To her credit, Arendt's involvement with Zionist politics was by no means transitory. The resentful tone of her late 1940s/early 1950s essays was a result of her intense fifteen-year-long political engagement and its ultimate failure. Berlin, however, was not in a position to know the full complexity and subtlety of Arendt's attitude towards Zionism. He saw her shift as a shocking instance of betrayal.

One wonders what might have happened if the timing of the two thinkers' meetings had been different—if, for example, their first meeting had occurred a year later than it did. In other words, what would have happened if the first meeting had taken place a few months *after* Biltmore, when Arendt had already become highly critical of the Zionist movement? Or if Berlin had been unable to come to the second meeting, due to the flu from which he had just recovered? In either scenario, Berlin might not have considered Arendt irresponsible and untrustworthy, capable of changing her mind over an issue of fundamental, and indeed existential, importance. But these are counterfactuals, and what did happen was something less fortunate. Soon after their second meeting in 1949, Berlin developed a good deal of what psychologists call 'epistemological bias' against Arendt. She was not yet his 'bête noire', but it was likely that Berlin would react more negatively than neutrally should there be another chance for their paths to cross. Such an occasion did not arise for several years. Berlin resumed his academic career in Oxford, as Arendt did in New York. However, in 1958, seventeen years after their first meeting, their paths did cross again—not physically but intellectually.[78] This time the encounter occurred on the other side of the Atlantic, in England, and the battleground shifted from politics to the other shared preoccupation of theirs: philosophy.

'Metaphysical Free Association'

Berlin repeatedly used the phrase 'metaphysical free association' to dismiss Arendt's theoretical work. The phrase is loaded with historical and philosophical significance, rooted in the rivalry between the competing intellectual traditions out of which the two thinkers respectively emerged. Moreover, Berlin's dismissal of her concerned not so much Arendt's specific ideas as her entire mode or style of thinking and writing. What is wrong with her intellectual style, according to Berlin? And did Arendt reciprocate his wholesale dismissal? These questions will be considered here before I turn to individual points of disagreement between the two thinkers in later chapters.

'A Relentlessly Negative Report'

In 1958, the London-based publisher Faber & Faber was considering whether to buy UK publication rights to Hannah Arendt's *The Human Condition*, due to appear in the United States from the University of Chicago Press. The British company contacted Sir Isaiah Berlin, recently elected Chichele professor of social and political theory at Oxford, to act as an external reviewer. The choice was natural enough. Arendt's book was what we today call 'interdisciplinary' work, covering issues in political theory, social theory, social and cultural criticism, philosophy, intellectual history and the history of philosophy. The reviewer's proficiency was no less wide-ranging. He had been a full-time philosophy lecturer, a full-time diplomat, a famed analyst of American politics and society, a trusted Russianist and an idiosyncratic Sovietologist, a multilingual historian of modern European political thought, a biographer of Karl Marx, an occasional cultural and music critic and a brilliant essayist and broadcaster. Recently knighted and elected as a fellow of the British Academy, his standing in Anglophone academia was solidly established. While Arendt was not showered with honours as Berlin was, she too had gained well-deserved recognition as one of the most influential writers of her generation with the publication of *The Origins of Totalitarianism*. Their 1958 encounter, then, was different from their earlier meetings in 1941 and 1949. Their paths now crossed as fully matured thinkers. And it was Arendt the thinker that Berlin firmly denounced in what Henry Hardy and Jennifer Holmes described as his 'relentlessly negative report' for Faber & Faber.[79]

Berlin raised 'two objections' to *The Human Condition*: 'it will not sell, and it is no good.'[80] His first objection was to prove conclusively wrong. Now regarded as canonical, Arendt's 1958 book has never been out of print and has sold many more copies than most academic titles. Whether Berlin's second objection was right is, of course, a matter of opinion. His basic objection was that *The Human Condition* addressed a set of misconceived questions. According to Berlin, the author drew implausibly rigid and ultimately arbitrary distinctions between work and labour, between action and behaviour and so on, assigning to herself the pointless task of elucidating false distinctions. On the surface, Berlin's opinion is similar to those of Arendt's more sympathetic critics such as Bhikhu Parekh and Hanna Pitkin, who argue that her conceptual distinctions are so rigid that they not only fail to do justice to ordinary usage but also are incapable of being consistently adhered to, even by Arendt herself.[81] However, while Arendt's sympathetic critics argue that her categories illuminate something important despite their excessive rigidity, Berlin saw no merit in her distinction-making. He, in fact, expressed the suspicion that her flawed reasoning might have stemmed from 'her inadequate command of English (a language she appears to have learned only in mature years, as a refugee in America from Germany)'.[82] This is a harsh statement, especially coming from someone who was acutely aware of the pain of being treated as an outsider. Nearly four decades earlier, when he was a newly arrived migrant in England, the young Isaiah came back from school crying, having been unable to understand a word of what others were saying.[83] Now, the mature Sir Isaiah, a comfortable insider in the male-dominated Anglophone academic community and a famed wordsmith who wrote 'as well as Conrad',[84] delivered from his power base in Oxford a forbidding message to Hannah Arendt: 'You do not belong here.'

Seyla Benhabib is one of Arendt's sympathetic readers who find Berlin's dismissal of Arendt's work 'offensive'.[85] Although her comments on Berlin predated the appearance of the second volume of Berlin's collected letters that made the existence of the Faber & Faber report public,[86] Benhabib had a perceptive sense of what Berlin had to say about *The Human Condition*, having read Ramin Jahanbegloo's interview with him.[87] Benhabib wrote that 'to any careful reader of Hannah Arendt, [Berlin's] criticism of her work in this interview and his rather off-the-cuff remarks about Greek and Jewish attitudes toward work in *The Human Condition* exhibit neither a deep understanding of nor an engagement with Arendt's thought.'[88] Benhabib was certainly right in one respect. It is unlikely that Berlin had the patience to finish reading the book he was reviewing. Much later, he said that he had stopped reading *The Human Condition* after the first two chapters (out of six)—that is, 78 out of 325 pages—as he found 'that everything she said [in those chapters] was historically nonsense'.[89] These words might involve a lapse of memory on Berlin's part, because he in fact cited from the fifth chapter (p. 230) of *The Human Condition* in his Faber & Faber report. Nevertheless, it indeed remains true that his relentlessly negative report was based, as Benhabib put it, on 'neither a deep understanding of nor an engagement with Arendt's thought'.[90]

Does this mean that Berlin was lazy and did not do his job as a reviewer for Faber & Faber? Certainly, those who consider *The Human Condition* to be a serious piece of scholarship have every reason to think so. But Berlin himself would not agree with such critics' opinions, for he was convinced that *The Human Condition* was not worth taking seriously, that it did not deserve to be read carefully. He was aware that his was a minority opinion. Favourable book reviews appeared in various papers, many of his friends praised it, and he himself had been requested to write a review of it for at least *five* periodicals.[91] He asked some of his trusted friends for their opinions of the book and encouraged them to challenge his negative verdict.[92] But his view never changed. Berlin most probably never read the book from cover to cover, and reiterated the assessment that he had reached in the late 1950s for the rest of his life: *The Human Condition* was 'no good' and 'absolutely unreadable', and the author's arguments were 'historically nonsense' and reflected her 'wide ignorance'.[93] In short, he found *The Human Condition* '"not true, not new and not amusing", as Trotsky once said about a speech by Stalin'.[94]

Did Berlin's inability to appreciate Arendt's now classic work stem from his disapproval of her stance on Zionism, as some critics have alleged?[95] I doubt it. As I discussed earlier, it is true that their political differences generated a degree of epistemological bias on Berlin's part. Yet this cannot account entirely for his denunciation of Arendt's philosophical work, not least because he bluntly condemned other thinkers of a phenomenological orientation in similar terms. Let me cite a few examples. According to Berlin, Arendt's doctoral supervisor Karl Jaspers 'talks dim rubbish & is a façade with an interior partly hollow, partly squalid, too bogus even for Continental metaphysicians';[96] Theodor Adorno was, like Arendt, incomprehensible and 'produced endless clouds of black smoke in place of ideas';[97] and David Riesman, Erich Fromm, Maurice Merleau-Ponty and Jean-Paul Sartre as well as Arendt were 'sincere and muddleheaded'.[98] As for Heidegger, Berlin could not make up his mind, calling him variously 'a major thinker of some kind' and 'some kind of gifted charlatan'.[99] He had kinder things to say about Edmund Husserl, admiring his Kantian challenge to 'the rather dreary and rather vulgar empiricism of Mill and Comte and Wundt'. Yet, when it came to Husserl's weaknesses, Berlin's terms of denunciation struck a familiar note: 'Husserl was obscure, pompous, metaphysical'.[100]

To his credit, Berlin criticised his *own* work in similar terms when he was not happy with what he had written. Consider his description of his draft essay, 'Political Ideas in the Twentieth Century', eventually published in *Foreign Affairs* in April 1950 and later reprinted in *Four Essays on Liberty*—which means that the essay, translated into more than twenty languages, has never been out of print for seven decades. The author himself had the following to say to the magazine editor about his now classic piece:

The article is of a monstrous length [. . .]; its sentences are inelegant, its style turgid, its grammar uncertain. The treatment of the subject [. . .] is all [. . .] too abstract, large, vague, metaphysical. It does not deal with the events and views of the past 50 years either seriatim or in some lucid, coherent, detailed fashion, as behoves an expert sufficiently qualified to appear in your pages. It oscillates between the obvious and the obscure; in short it is a Carlylian monstrosity.[101]

In Berlin's book, terms such as 'obscure', 'muddled' and 'metaphysical' designated *general* philosophical weaknesses. His standards were clearly demanding to an extreme degree, but when he considered that a thinker did not live up to those standards, he consistently mobilised these terms to criticise him or her, irrespective of the target's gender, cultural background or political allegiances. True, his personal dislike for and political disagreement with Arendt magnified the intensity of his disapproval of *The Human Condition*. But it is foolish to speculate that Berlin might have admired the book if the author had been a male Zionist from somewhere outside Germany. His philosophical complaints about Arendt's work were in essence philosophical, not political.

A Revolution in Philosophy

Berlin's standards, by which Arendt's work ranked lowest, were to a large extent a product of his time, and more specifically, of two revolutions in philosophy. One was the emergence of phenomenology in Germany. Initially announced by Husserl in his *Logical Investigations* (1900–1901),[102] the new philosophical movement would develop throughout the twentieth century and beyond, attracting a number of highly gifted thinkers, from Heidegger and Jaspers to Sartre, Merleau-Ponty and Levinas. While the creativity of these individual contributors would make phenomenology an internally diverse and 'pluralistic tradition', they nevertheless shared 'a certain style and methodological commitment'.[103] Central to this was the determination to analyse whatever appears to the experiencer in the manner in which it appears to him or her, unclouded by worn-out philosophical concepts and theories. As Sophie Loidolt writes, '[t]he famous dicta "To the things themselves!" (Husserl) and "No theories!" (Heidegger) have become paradigmatic for the resolve to refrain from construction in thought and only to rely on intuition with respect to what is given in experience.'[104] Phenomenology thus presented itself as a radical challenge to traditional philosophical schools of all stripes, which it dismissed as overly theoretical, abstract and devoid of any experiential ground. It was an ambitious movement, and its allure was hard to resist. With 'its theme of renewal' it captivated a new generation of students in Germany in the turbulent years of World War I and its aftermath.[105]

The young Arendt was one of those students. She was a beneficiary of what she would later describe as the 'liberation of philosophy' initiated by Husserl.[106] But the figure that truly drew her to the new philosophical movement was not Husserl but his unruly successor, Martin Heidegger. The latter was then developing his own brand of phenomenology, often characterised as 'existential', drawing on an eclectic group of thinkers, including Dilthey, Nietzsche, Kierkegaard, Kant and Aristotle. Unwilling to remain a mere disciple of Husserl, he was ready to mount an attack on his former mentor's project from within, to assert his own originality, creativity and superiority. It was this *enfant terrible* of phenomenology who fascinated the young Arendt at the University of Marburg in 1924–26. She attended his courses on 'Plato's *Sophist*' (winter semester 1924), 'History of the Concept of Time' (summer semester 1925) and 'Logic: The Question of Truth' (winter semester 1925).[107] Her formal enrolments were complemented by her meetings with her teacher, who soon became her lover, and she had access to Heidegger's more political work such as his 1924 lectures on Aristotle's *Rhetoric* and *Nicomachean Ethics*.[108] His impact on Arendt's intellectual development would prove to be literally lifelong. Although the mature Arendt (rather like Berlin) claimed to have left philosophy, and identified herself as a political theorist,[109] her basic approach remained broadly phenomenological, and much of her work may be read as a continuous attempt at internally criticising and overcoming the crowning achievement of the phenomenological tradition: Heidegger's existential phenomenology. Her most important work in this context is *The Human Condition*, which simultaneously contains a deep appreciation of, and a fundamental challenge to, Heidegger's philosophy (see further Chapter 3). It simultaneously inherits *and* subverts his categories. It is with this duality in mind that we should read a letter of Arendt's to Heidegger from 1960: *The Human Condition*, she told her former teacher, 'owes practically everything to you in every aspect'.[110]

In her contribution to Heidegger's *Festschrift* entitled 'Heidegger at Eighty',[111] Arendt recounts her experience as a student in the Weimar Republic. Among her contemporaries there was 'widespread discontent' with traditional research and teaching, with the 'academic talk *about* philosophy' as opposed to philosophy proper.[112] But the students did not know what they wanted instead. Then came the rumour of a brilliant young thinker. He had published little and yet his 'name travelled all over Germany like the rumor of the hidden king'.[113] Arendt continues,

> The rumor about Heidegger put it quite simply: Thinking has come to life again; the cultural treasures of the past, believed to be dead, are being made

to speak, in the course of which it turns out that they propose things altogether different from the familiar, worn-out trivialities they had been presumed to say. There is a teacher; one can perhaps learn to think.[114]

In 'Heidegger at Eighty', those recollections are followed by a substantial analysis of Heidegger's mode of thinking, a concise assessment of his achievement and a brief discussion of the philosopher's political misadventures during the Nazis' rise to power. Understandably, the literature on Arendt's essay largely focused on the last part, the central question being whether her discussion is too charitable to her former teacher and lover, even amounting to the 'whitewashing' of Heidegger's disgraceful Nazi past.[115] For our present purpose, however, we must direct our attention to the less discussed, middle part of the essay.[116] Perhaps evoking the image of a hermeneutic circle, Arendt characterises Heidegger's thinking as a ceaseless and relentless questioning and re-questioning, moving in no particular direction and yet undermining both the foundations of traditional philosophical theories and the results of Heidegger's own thinking. The 'single immediate result' of such thinking, Arendt argues, was the 'collapse' of 'the edifice of traditional metaphysics'.[117] Heidegger did not, and (contrary to Husserl) did not intend to, find a secure ultimate foundation on which a new philosophy and new sciences might be built. Rather, his thinking left no foundations secure.

Arendt's assessment is in a way unoriginal. It echoes various commentators' emphasis on the significance of Heidegger's dismantling of 'metaphysics', in this context referring generically to all traditional forms of enquiry in which the most fundamental question of philosophy, the meaning of Being, is obscured. Nevertheless, while many consider Heidegger to have *begun* the dismantling, followed by self-styled anti-metaphysicians such as Jacques Derrida, Arendt regarded Heidegger's work much more highly, seeing him as essentially *completing* the task of ending metaphysics. According to her, 'what we owe [Heidegger], *and only him*, is that this collapse [of metaphysics] took place in a manner worthy of what had preceded it; that metaphysics was *thought* through to its end'.[118] In Arendt's opinion, the most important event in the history of philosophy since Kant unfolded before her own eyes in inter-war Germany.

Another Revolution in Philosophy

This is hardly how a new generation of empiricists across the English Channel saw what was happening in German philosophy. Of particular relevance here is A. J. Ayer's famous attack on Heidegger in his 1936 book *Language, Truth and Logic,* which he began writing at his friend Isaiah Berlin's suggestion.[119] The twenty-six-year-old author drew a now familiar contrast between allegedly obscure, clumsy and ultimately nonsensical 'German' metaphysics, and rational, rigorous and clear-headed 'British' philosophy. This is a curious contrast, for many of Ayer's ideas actually originated from the un-British city of Vienna, where he spent four months in 1932–33 to study with Moritz Schlick, Otto Neurath, Rudolf Carnap, Kurt Gödel and other members of the Vienna Circle.[120] But Ayer's contrast between the 'German' and the 'British' concerned intellectual traditions rather than geographical locations. He saw the new empiricism of the Vienna Circle as a continuation and radicalisation of the classical empiricism of Berkeley, Locke and Hume, handed down in Ayer's time to Russell, Moore and the early Wittgenstein. Thus, in the first chapter of *Language, Truth and Logic*, polemically entitled 'The Elimination of Metaphysics', Ayer subjected one German philosopher—Heidegger—and one pre-Russell/Moore/Wittgenstein British philosopher—Bradley—to the *same* criticism. Ayer's attack was characteristically simple, quick and drastic. He claimed that Heidegger failed to understand the working of language and was consequently 'devoted to the production of nonsense'.[121] Similarly, he mentioned Bradley's then highly regarded *Appearance and Reality* as a storehouse of 'pseudo-propositions', and briefly discussed a sentence 'taken at random' from the book to illustrate what nonsensical philosophical chatter looked like.[122] My concern here is not the intrinsic merit of Ayer's savage criticism, but his intended message vis-à-vis the phenomenological revolution. That message is clear enough: in spite of Husserl's and Heidegger's talk about renewing philosophy—'thinking [...] come to life again', in Arendt's words—the phenomenologists were every bit as tradition-bound, metaphysical and obsolete as Bradley was. Contrary to Arendt's assessment, Heidegger did not end bad philosophy; rather, he was the latest example of bad philosophy deserving of demolition. If one was to end metaphysics, Ayer contended, one must end Heidegger, too.

Berlin never wholeheartedly endorsed Ayer's positivist project. In fact, his early philosophical work included important criticisms of the latter's central principles.[123] On the issue of 'German metaphysics', however, it is not their differences but their similarities that truly stand out. As Ayer's contemporary at Oxford, Berlin also studied as part of his undergraduate education the work of British idealists such as Bradley, Bosanquet, Green and McTaggart.[124] He too found their work uninspiring and felt a greater sympathy for the renewal of the empiricist tradition occurring in Cambridge and Vienna.[125] Again like Ayer, Berlin saw more similarities than differences between the allegedly new philosophy of Husserl and Heidegger and the old one of Kant, Hegel and Green. He too saw the emergence of phenomenology as a negligible tremor in comparison to the real revolution beginning with Russell and Moore. Like Ayer, Berlin belonged to the generation of British philosophers who dismissed their idealist precursors as muddled, nonsensical, metaphysical and 'Germanic'. Iris Murdoch nicely captures this generational clash by way of discussing how the idealist McTaggart and the empiricist Moore might talk past each other: 'McTaggart says that time is unreal. Moore replies that he has just eaten his breakfast.'[126] Berlin could certainly appreciate the 1933 letter he received from Ayer, then studying in Vienna. According to Ayer, '"metaphysical" is the ultimate term of abuse', and '[e]ven to think of Heidegger makes [members of the Vienna Circle] sick.'[127]

As must already be clear, we may discern a close proximity between the tropes Ayer mobilised to attack Heidegger and Bradley and the tropes Berlin used to dismiss Arendt's 'metaphysical free association'. Of course, Berlin was hardly a typical Anglophone analytic philosopher. The mature Berlin became, in fact, something like an internal dissident among his anti-Continental colleagues at Oxford. Nevertheless, he remained broadly faithful to the empiricist tradition and never abandoned his Ayeresque hostility towards 'German metaphysicians' and their lesser followers in France, North America and elsewhere. Thus, the late Berlin indiscriminately dismissed 'the French philosophers of the 1940–80 variety' as 'exactly what the French call *fumiste*', and attacked 'the disciples of both Heidegger and the Frankfurt School, e.g. Miss Hannah Arendt', on the grounds that they were 'liable to produce [. . .] professional patter'.[128] While Berlin disliked everything Arendt wrote, he expressed particular dislike for her more philosophical work. In retrospect, he called *The Human Condition* '[t]he book that shocked me most'.[129]

Let me be more precise. Berlin's attitude towards twentieth-century Continental philosophy is a complex and somewhat paradoxical one. On the one hand, he generally lacked the willingness to engage seriously with *contemporary* European thinkers such as Arendt, Adorno, Heidegger, Jaspers and Sartre, not because their ideas were 'beyond his comfort zone' but because he thought they were bogus, hollow and 'metaphysical', albeit to differing degrees.[130] On the other hand, Berlin mobilised his famed capacity for empathetic understanding to make sense of European thinkers *prior to* the twentieth century, making difficult and often idiosyncratic ideas of Giambattista Vico, the young Hegelians, Johann Georg Hamann and others not only comprehensible but also relevant and alive to his twentieth-century Anglophone readers. Moreover, he often drew on those European ideas to criticise what he considered to be the excessively ahistorical and simplistic tendency in twentieth-century empiricist projects, including Ayer's logical positivism. In other words, Berlin often played the European card to keep his empiricist colleagues in their place, while playing the empiricist card to highlight what he regarded as the characteristic weaknesses of contemporary European philosophers. He repeatedly played the latter card to dismiss Arendt as 'unreadable' and 'incomprehensible', although he also had more concrete, and ultimately more interesting, things to say about her specific ideas.

It must be noted, however, that Berlin's unwillingness to concede the significance of phenomenologists' work was matched by Arendt's unwillingness to appreciate the Anglophone empiricist tradition and its vigorous reassertions in the twentieth century. There is little evidence to show that she tried to familiarise herself with the work of Russell, Moore, Ayer, Austin, Quine, Hart or Rawls. An interesting, though hardly reassuring, exception to this rule was her brief discussion of P. F. Strawson in *The Life of the Mind*. Letting Strawson stand as typical of 'the Oxford school of criticism', she mocked the Oxonians' romance of clarity and analytic rigour as follows:

> It is characteristic of the Oxford school of criticism to understand [. . .] fallacies as logical non sequiturs—as though philosophers throughout the centuries had been, for reasons unknown, just a bit too stupid to discover the elementary flaw in their arguments. The truth of the matter is that elementary logical mistakes are quite rare in the history of philosophy.[131]

Arendt turned Oxford philosophers' sense of superiority on its head. The reason that they often felt past philosophers to have been 'just a bit too stupid' to make coherent arguments was not that past philosophers had *in fact* been stupid. Rather, it was that the Oxford philosophers themselves were unable to understand why some of the philosophical arguments of the past *appeared to them* to be incoherent. The real fool is he or she who hastily calls others foolish. This, in Arendt's view, accounted for the Oxonians' propensity for 'uncritically dismiss[ing]' philosophical arguments as 'meaningless'.[132] Although Arendt did not specify who, besides Strawson, belonged to this group of allegedly foolish Oxford philosophers, it is safe to assume that the 'Oxford' she had in mind was her contemporary, post-idealist Oxford. The author of *Language, Truth and Logic* was likely to exemplify this type of foolishness. Not only was he known for his habit of declaring various arguments nonsensical or literally meaningless; he was also utterly incapable of appreciating Heidegger's contributions to philosophy. What more would one need to confirm Ayer's incompetence as a philosopher?

And what, then, of Ayer's friend and contemporary, Isaiah Berlin? A revealing, albeit brief, remark by Arendt is found in her lecture notes dated 1963, when she taught a course entitled 'Introduction into Politics' at the University of Chicago. Discussing Berlin's essay 'Does Political Theory Still Exist?', Arendt noted (correctly) that he conceptualised philosophical questions as those 'which "puzzle us" and to which "no wide agreement exists on the meaning of the concepts involved"'. Then, in her characteristic way, she added a critical observation to highlight the difference, as she saw it, between philosophy as it used to be in ancient Greece and what it had become by the mid-twentieth century in the Anglophone world. She wrote, 'This [Berlinian] being puzzled [is] certainly a far cry from the original wonder—*thaumadzein* from *theasthai*—which according to Plato and Aristotle was the beginning of all philosophy. What is left is a feeling of unease, of *malaise* that there exist things about which no increase of knowledge will ever dispel our ignorance.'[133] In other words, Arendt detected something superficial in Berlin's mode of philosophy, one which could hardly be motivated by the disorientating 'original wonder' that had once provoked the Greeks to philosophise. Her assessment of the Oxonian contrasted starkly with her view of existential philosophers in continental Europe such as Kierkegaard, Heidegger, Jaspers, Sartre and Camus. The latter (like the Greeks, and unlike Berlin) were not merely 'puzzled' by the beings of various entities, but were *shocked* by Being as such.[134] In Arendt's view, then, Berlin differed little from Strawson and Ayer. His sweeping dismissal of 'Continental metaphysicians' merely indicated his own incompetence as a philosopher. Similarly, when he 'uncritically dismissed' the phenomenologists' entire mode of thinking and writing as metaphysical and obscure, he too failed to consider adequately why their works *appeared to him* as such. If so, from Arendt's point of view, he too would qualify as a member of the fools' party that she called the 'Oxford school of criticism'.

Berlin once characterised 'the great [empiricist] revolution inaugurated by Bertrand Russell' as 'perhaps the greatest since the seventeenth century'.[135] Arendt could not disagree more. She saw it as a minor tremor in comparison to the real philosophical earthquake that occurred in early twentieth-century Germany. It is erroneous to think, as William Phillips did, that Berlin 'had too much of a systematic education and mind' to appreciate Arendt.[136] Her education was no less systematic than Berlin's, to say the least (she, after all, had a doctorate, and he did not). The real issue was that their minds were nurtured in very different cultures and schools of thought. Arendt to some extent shared nineteenth- and early twentieth-century German thinkers' presumption that their philosophy and culture were superior to their British and 'Anglo-American' counterparts, which were supposed to be superficial, materialistic and utilitarian. Nietzsche gave the best expression to this snobbery in one of his aphorisms, fired at the 'offensive clarity' of J. S. Mill. 'Man does *not* strive for happiness,' Nietzsche declared, 'only the English do that.'[137] Arendt was more fair-minded, but she was by no means free from Nietzschean prejudices. For example, when the name of John Locke came up at a small dinner party, Norman Podhoretz recalls, Arendt quipped, 'Ach, these English, they think they have philosophers.'[138] Similarly, when asked by a graduate student at The New School 'what philosopher who wrote in English [...] would be deserving of a [doctoral] dissertation', Arendt managed to mention Hobbes but then, after 'a long pause', could not think of any other British name.[139] One might say she at least named *one* British philosopher. If so, however, one may be reminded that, in *The Origins of Totalitarianism*, she acerbically labelled Hobbes 'the true [. . .] philosopher of the bourgeoisie'.[140] Such, for her, was Britain's contribution to philosophy.

In short, the absence of direct intellectual engagement between Arendt and Berlin was not due only to their unfortunate personal chemistry and political differences, but also to the widening chasm that came to be known as the 'analytic–Continental divide' in philosophy.[141] It is irrelevant in this context that the 'analytic–Continental' dichotomy is crude in many ways and that rivalries between different strands *within* each of the two traditions could be as fierce as the broader rivalry *between* the analytic and Continental traditions. What is relevant is that Arendt belonged, and saw herself as belonging, to a particular strand of Continental philosophy whose identity partly depended on its hostility towards purportedly shallow British empiricism. To rephrase her own oft-cited remark, if she may be said to have come from anywhere, Arendt came from an exceptionally vibrant period of German philosophy, in which its own tradition was vigorously contested, drastically renewed and given a new lease of life.[142] In her view, the new twin epicentres of philosophy were not Vienna and Cambridge (let alone Oxford). They were, rather, Marburg and Freiburg.

I shall in the following chapters build interpretative bridges to let Arendt's and Berlin's ideas speak to each other, minimising their stylistic differences to concentrate on their substantive disagreements. Of course, as Bernard Williams said, the matter of style and that of substance are often inseparable in philosophy.[143] However, removing stylistic differences from the discussion *where possible* may be rewarding, as I hope to show throughout this study. My present point, though, is more limited: Hannah Arendt was well on her way to becoming Berlin's 'real bête noire' by 1958. He had already developed political and philosophical aversions to her. Then, with the publication of her 'report' on the trial of Adolf Eichmann, yet another layer of dislike was added. This layer was distinctly *moral* in nature.

A 'Civil War' in New York

Berlin's critical comments on *Eichmann in Jerusalem* deserve detailed examination, and I shall take up the task in Chapter 5. As a preliminary to the later discussion, this section will give an overview of the Eichmann controversy and its historical background, and review Berlin's initial response to Arendt's controversial work. In so doing, I shall substantiate the argument I have implicitly made already: although it is tempting to inflate the significance of Berlin's hostility to *Eichmann in Jerusalem*, this accounts for only a part of his animosity towards Arendt and her work.

The Mass Murderer

First, a sketch of Eichmann's career and crimes is in order. Hannah Arendt's exact contemporary, Adolf Eichmann (b. 1906) joined the Nazi Party and the SS in 1932, at the age of twenty-six. While his initial motive for joining was a mixture of chance, opportunism and moderate political sympathies,[144] he began to play an active role soon afterwards, becoming a member of the Nazi Security Service (SD) in late 1934. Having invented himself as an expert on Jewish issues, Eichmann built a successful career within the Nazi system, devising and implementing a number of anti-Jewish measures in subsequent years. A breakthrough came in 1938 when he was assigned the task of overseeing mass migration from the newly 'unified' Austria. The Central Office for Jewish Migration in Vienna would coerce an estimated 128,000 Jews into leaving the country by the time of the border closure in November 1941.[145] Once he had successfully replicated the 'Vienna model' in occupied Prague, Eichmann's reputation grew, and he was promoted in October 1939 to a Gestapo department in the city of Berlin in charge of Jewish migration from the Reich at large.

Within the next few years, the meaning of the 'removal' of the Jews would develop from mass migration into forced expulsion and ultimately into extermination. Eichmann's ideas evolved and his role grew accordingly until the end of the war. Later, in Jerusalem, his defence lawyer would claim that Eichmann had been no more than a 'small cog' in the Nazi apparatus, merely playing a replaceable role as a bureaucrat. In truth, Eichmann had been an often imaginative leader of the 'Final Solution', in addition to being multiple cogs, energetically working to operate the killing machine in Austria, Belgium, France, Germany, Greece, Hungary, Italy, the Netherlands, Poland, Slovakia and elsewhere.[146] His devotion did not necessarily mean inflexibility. As the Reich's strategic need to secure resources to continue the war came to claim priority over the ideological requirement to annihilate the Jews, Eichmann participated in various ransom negotiations, including the famous 'blood for goods' case in Hungary, to which I shall return in Chapter 5. As German defeat became more likely, he began devising a complex plan to secure his post-war escape, while lying to his colleagues about his determination to fight on to the bitter end. It was around this time that he apparently made the infamous remark, made public by his former right-hand man Dieter Wisliceny during the Nuremberg trials, that 'he would leap laughing into the grave because the feeling that he had 5 million people on his conscience would be for him a source of extraordinary satisfaction.'[147]

Eichmann did not leap into the grave, however. He hid his identity in the POW camps where he was interned after the war. He then fled to Lüneburg Heath in northern Germany, where he forged a new identity as Otto Heninger and lived as a logger and subsequently a chicken farmer. His safety was momentarily threatened in 1947, when his loyal wife's deceitful attempt to obtain a death certificate for her husband failed and backfired, prompting operations to search for the notorious Nazi criminal. However, assisted by a network of Nazi sympathisers and human traffickers, Eichmann forged yet another identity as Ricardo Klement and left Germany for Buenos Aires in the summer of 1950.[148] In his new country, he lived more contentedly, finding himself in a community of Nazi expats, securing various managerial jobs and receiving a stable salary, to be joined in 1952 by his wife and three children (soon followed by a fourth).[149] No longer feeling that they needed to be as anonymous and secretive as they had been, Eichmann and his fellow Nazis chattered about their shared past and future ambitions. The chatter developed into a project in the late 1950s, when they began collaborating with the former Dutch SS volunteer-turned-writer Willem Sassen to publish their views. Eichmann's motive for joining this project remains obscure. He surely had petty motives, such as the prospect of monetary gain and his desire to impress his Nazi peers. But he also had more serious reasons, including his strong desire, even a perverse sense of a duty, to get the 'facts' straight amid the 'lies' of both 'world Jewry' and some of his former colleagues, who had exaggerated Eichmann's role in the mass killing to deflate their share of responsibility. He may also have wished to assist the neo-Nazi attempt to undermine Adenauer's government and by implication the post-war order itself. He knew he risked his safety, but he was willing to take the risk to make himself heard.

Rumours about Eichmann's whereabouts appeared throughout the 1950s, locating him variously in Europe, the Middle East and South America. Nevertheless, the willingness to hunt, try and punish the notorious Nazi criminal in hiding was not particularly strong in the Bundesrepublik, where too many people inside as well as outside the government had reasons to fear what might come out of an Eichmann trial.[150] Willingness had also waned elsewhere by the mid-1950s. More concerned with fighting communism than rectifying past injustices, Western governments were anxious not to alienate their German ally, while Israel was busy tackling more urgent problems, including existential threats. Historians have in fact debated whether Eichmann could have been arrested earlier if Germany, the United States and/or Argentina had had the will to fully utilise the information gathered by their intelligence agencies.[151] Some historians have also noted that even the Israeli intelligence service, Mossad, responded rather slowly to the initial pieces of information eventually leading to Eichmann's capture.[152] Nevertheless, the increasing inflow of information linking Eichmann to Argentina eventually persuaded Mossad to take robust action, resulting in one of the organisation's best-known operations. On 11 May 1960, a team of Israeli 'volunteers' in Argentina captured Ricardo Klement, interrogated him and confirmed his identity as Adolf Eichmann. They thence abducted him and successfully brought him to Israel by the morning of 23 May.[153] Soon afterwards, the Israeli prime minister David Ben-Gurion announced the news of the capture. This, according to the American television network CBS, 'electrified the world [. . .] as though Hitler himself had been found'.[154]

Berlin's and Arendt's Responses

The news intrigued both Isaiah Berlin and Hannah Arendt, prompting them to respond in different ways. The Oxford philosopher commented on the capture as if he had been an Israeli political strategist. Many then questioned Israel's legal right to try the accused, whose alleged crimes were committed before the establishment of the state in 1948. If the newly founded state tried, judged and punished him, critics wondered, would that not amount to an ex post facto law? But the legal issue did not bother Berlin. What interested him was the political question: would the impending trial benefit the Jewish state on balance? Berlin expressed his reservations from early on. Israel might hope to 'remind the world about the slaughter', but the reminder was likely to fall on deaf ears. It might also hope to 'nail down the guilt of the guilty', but that would be 'politically unwise for a state'. It is not clear from the surviving papers in what specific sense Berlin considered the 'nailing down' politically unwise. A likely explanation is that he was echoing the then widespread worry about the potential backlash against Israel—a worry, incidentally, that Karl Jaspers repeatedly expressed in his letters to Arendt before the beginning of the trial.[155] Besides, Berlin continued, Israel's other motive might be to turn the trial into a call for unity among the Jews, but this too would be ineffective, for those who would hear the call had already been united, and those who needed to be unified would not respond to the call. In short, the attempt '[wouldn't] convert anyone'.[156]

Regardless, Berlin foresaw that a trial in Israel was bound to take place. Once it began, he took advantage of his trip to Jerusalem in the spring of 1962 to see the accused with his own eyes. Having watched the trial 'for half an hour or so',[157] he wrote down his impressions in a letter to his wife, Aline. His immediate response scarcely differed from that of Arendt and many others who witnessed Eichmann at Beit Ha'am, a cultural centre converted into a courtroom. That is, Berlin was struck by the apparent ordinariness and mediocrity— 'banality' in Arendt's expression—of the man inside the glass booth. Eichmann,

Berlin recorded, 'looked like a slightly cancerous rat: like any little Austro-German booking office clerk'.[158] In subsequent months and years, Berlin would give further thought to the man he saw in Jerusalem. But his opinion about the trial itself hardly changed. He remained convinced that it served the Jewish state badly. He also came to the conclusion during the trial that the likely verdict, a death penalty, would worsen Israel's international standing. He even considered intervening in a characteristically Berlinian manner: whispering to the prince, that is, writing to Ben-Gurion directly.[159] Berlin appears to have abandoned this idea, but he at least 'wrote to a high Israeli official, intending it, of course, to reach the Prime Minister of Israel'.[160] However, even Berlin himself did not believe that his intervention would change Ben-Gurion's mind, or Eichmann's fate for that matter. He conceded the is/ought distinction: 'I am sure they should not hang him, and yet I fear they will.'[161] The convict was indeed executed, on 31 May 1962, to Berlin's disappointment.

In retrospect, one may wonder if Berlin's worry was exaggerated. Perhaps, in the long run, Israel's determination and ability to bring Eichmann to justice served the state better than the philosopher had anticipated. But his worry was by no means groundless. The capture of Eichmann stirred much talk about 'vengeful Jews' in contrast to 'forgiving Christians' in the international media.[162] It also provoked antisemitic attacks on Jewish communities in the diaspora. An especially shocking incident occurred in Buenos Aires, where three men, professing to be acting 'in revenge for Eichmann', kidnapped a nineteen-year-old Jewish female university student, tortured her and tattooed a swastika on her chest.[163] The Eichmann capture further sparked a diplomatic row between Israel and Argentina, the latter lodging a formal complaint with the UN Security Council.[164] Besides, Berlin may have feared that the trial would give Eichmann the opportunity to propagate in public what we today call a Holocaust denial. As it turned out, the accused concentrated his efforts on denying *his part* in the genocide, rather than the genocide itself.

Hannah Arendt's response to the news of Eichmann's capture was more personal than Berlin's. This may not come as a surprise. Eichmann had his share of responsibility for the fate of Arendt's fellow inmates at the Gurs internment camp who, unlike Arendt, could not flee and subsequently perished in Auschwitz.[165] After arriving in America, she closely followed the news of the plight of European Jewry, unlike Berlin, who claimed rather questionably that he had not read or heard about the extermination until 1944 or even 1945 (see further Chapter 5).[166] Arendt's first published commentary on Eichmann's lethal work, by contrast, dates back to as early as 3 September 1943; since at least this date she had closely studied both primary and secondary sources relating to Eichmann's crimes.[167] Of course, she could not rely on the wealth of archival materials and historical scholarship readily available to us today when she wrote on the nature and origins of Nazism. But the author of *The Origins of Totalitarianism*, which briefly introduced Eichmann as the head of 'Himmler's special Gestapo department for the liquidation (not merely the study) of the Jewish question', was certainly more qualified than most of her contemporaries to discuss the impending trial.[168] Her offer to act as a trial reporter for the *New Yorker* was gladly accepted by the magazine's editor, William Shawn.[169] Arendt had to cancel or rearrange her various commitments to make time for a trip to Jerusalem. She found the rescheduling 'dreadful', not least because the beginning of the trial was repeatedly postponed. Yet, she wrote to Jaspers, 'I would never be able to forgive myself if I didn't go and look at this walking disaster face to face in all his [i.e., Eichmann's] bizarre vacuousness'.[170] She put it even more starkly elsewhere: 'To attend this trial is somehow, I feel, an obligation I owe my past'.[171]

Arendt initially saw herself as no more than 'a simple reporter' of the trial, and her original plan was to 'write a single article for the *New Yorker*'.[172] In other words, when she set foot in Jerusalem, she did not know she was going to write a series of five magazine articles that would develop into a monograph. Nor was she (contrary to an allegation by David Cesarani[173]) preparing to fit Eichmann into the pre-formed theory of totalitarianism that she had presented in *Origins*. Rather, she unexpectedly found herself writing far more than she had intended because, firstly, she found everything written on the trial so far highly unsatisfactory; secondly, the *New Yorker* editors let her take as much time as she needed and write as much as she wanted; and thirdly—most importantly—she was genuinely puzzled by the figure of Adolf Eichmann and the nature of his evil. This unexpected origin of *Eichmann in Jerusalem* is worth keeping in mind, for it explains the hybrid nature of the book, which is neither a conventional trial report nor a theoretical treatise. She did not write her 'report' *from* Jerusalem for the American audience; she wrote most of the texts *in* New York where she studied the interrogation and trial transcripts. Nor did she intend to develop a general theory of evil in the book. Rather, she wrote down her provisional reflections on the nature of evil prompted by what she saw in Jerusalem. In fact, in her fertile mind a new train of thought about evil *began* in 1961–63 and continued to the end of her life.

The Eichmann Controversy

The most controversial part of *Eichmann in Jerusalem* concerned what the author called 'the darkest chapter of the whole dark story', namely, the 'role of the Jewish leaders in the destruction of their own people'.[174] Challenging the then clear-cut distinction between the guilty Germans and the innocent Jews, Arendt sharply criticised what she regarded as failures on the part of the Jewish leaders dealing with the Nazis. It is not quite accurate to say that she broke a taboo. The initial arrival of survivors in Palestine in late 1942 had already, and quite naturally, provoked discussion as to whether Jewish leaders had done enough to mitigate the catastrophe; the disturbed Ben-Gurion called this a '"sadistic campaign" of mutual accusations'.[175] After the war, in the mid-1950s, the issue was raised anew and in a more dramatic form by the so-called 'Kastner trial', when the Israeli judge Benjamin Halevi accused the wartime Hungarian-Jewish leader Rudolf Kastner of 'selling his soul to the devil', that is, collaborating with the Nazis (see further Chapter 5). The issue of 'collaboration' had been a subject of scholarly discussion for some time, too: for example, in Léon Poliakov's *Bréviaire de la haine* (1951), which Arendt cited in *The Origins of Totalitarianism*, and Raul Hilberg's landmark *The Destruction of the European Jews* (1961), which Arendt drew heavily upon in *Eichmann in Jerusalem*.[176] Moreover, Arendt herself had previously considered the dilemmas with which Jewish leaders were confronted in Nazified Europe, albeit more sympathetically than in the comparable discussion in her 1963 'report'.[177]

The explosive nature of Arendt's divisive work thus stemmed not so much from the fact that she confronted the controversial issue as from the *manner* in which she confronted it. In many of her readers' eyes, Arendt's tone was utterly inappropriate, showing disrespect for and even cruelty towards the victims of the Holocaust. The following lines of *Eichmann in Jerusalem* were the most controversial:

> Wherever Jews lived, there were recognized Jewish leaders, and this leadership, almost without exception, cooperated in one way or another, for one reason or another, with the Nazis. The whole truth was that if the Jewish people had really been unorganized and leaderless, there would have been chaos and plenty of misery but the total number of victims would hardly have been between four and a half and six million people.[178]

One does not need to be unsympathetic to Arendt's work to see why words like these should have proved explosive in the early 1960s, when the memory of the extermination was painfully vivid and yet was rarely expressed in the popular media. Her tone significantly differed from that of later works tackling similar moral and historical issues, such as Yehuda Bauer's *Jews for Sale*, written in a highly scientific style drawing on hard statistics, and Bernard Wasserstein's *The Ambiguity of Virtue*, permeated by sympathy, humane warmth and a determination to be *non-judgemental*.[179] In contrast to both of these works, the empirical side of Arendt's *Eichmann* was more episodic than systematic and scientific, and the non-empirical side was animated by her characteristic willingness to exercise the faculty of judgement. Her critics have attacked *Eichmann* on both fronts. For example, Jacob Robinson in his four-hundred-page refutation of Arendt's 'report' made the exaggerated claim that he had found four hundred 'factual errors' in *Eichmann in Jerusalem*,[180] while virtually all of her critics, including Berlin, accused her of moralising about the behaviour of the victims of the Shoah. As we shall see, she had her reasons for approaching the controversial issue as she did, but her critics did not bother to consider her reasons carefully. On the contrary, some simply returned in kind what they took to be Arendt's cruelty, calling her a 'devil's representative', charging her with 'digging future Jewish graves', and so on.[181]

The other major issue on which the initial round of the Eichmann controversy focused concerned the all-too-famous phrase in the subtitle of Arendt's book: 'the banality of evil'. In retrospect, her basic idea was not nearly as controversial as her critics took it to be. Her main message was that one did not need to be an extraordinarily evil person to commit an extraordinarily evil deed; on the contrary, a mediocre person with no profound motives (such as Eichmann, in Arendt's view) could play a significant role in horrendous crimes, so long as he or she failed to think about the true significance of his or her behaviour. As Luke Russell succinctly puts it, Arendt's 'banality' is intended to 'denote ordinariness of type of motive and type of agent, rather than ordinariness of action'.[182] Today, even those who have reservations about *Eichmann in Jerusalem* concede a degree of persuasive force in the 'banality' argument.[183] However, Arendt's contemporary readers responded differently, being genuinely unable to understand what she meant by 'banality'. While her defenders like to blame her readers for making insufficient effort to understand her message, I believe she was partly to blame for causing confusion. Notwithstanding her decision to use 'the banality of evil' in the book's subtitle, she did not elucidate what she meant by the provocative phrase: it appeared only once in the book version, where the author did not provide a definition;[184] and it did not appear at all in the original *New Yorker* articles. True, Arendt's idea becomes reasonably clear if *Eichmann in Jerusalem* is read together with her other, especially later, texts.[185] But *Eichmann* by itself does little to explain the author's thoughts on evil, and it is hardly unreasonable for many of her contemporary readers to have found the book confusing. Unfortunately, some frustrated readers then projected what they *wanted* to see into 'banality', claiming that Arendt devalued the seriousness of Eichmann's crimes, often forgetting that she unambiguously supported the execution of the mass murderer.

Arendt was genuinely taken aback by the scale and intensity of the controversy her work provoked. She not only felt gravely misunderstood but also came to be convinced that the 'Jewish establishment' carried out an organised campaign to distort her work and control its perception. The campaign had been so successful that 'a good part of the discussion', according to Arendt, 'deal[t] with a book that *no one wrote*'.[186] Her suspicion of an organised campaign was exaggerated, but not groundless. Several groups did mobilise to counter what they considered to be Arendt's poisonous work.[187] For example, the Anti-Defamation League of B'nai B'rith issued a public denunciation of *Eichmann in Jerusalem* and distributed a pamphlet called *Arendt Nonsense*; Siegfried Moses of the Council of Jews from Germany attempted to stop the publication of Arendt's 'report' in book form; and the Israeli prosecutor Gideon Hausner and the president of the World Zionist Organization Nahum Goldmann both spoke at a meeting of the Bergen-Belsen Survivors Association in New York to denounce Arendt's alleged desire to 'rewrite history' (Hausner) and to 'throw [...] stones at the victims of the Nazis' (Goldmann).[188] She felt powerless in the face of the 'money, personnel, time, connections, etc.' of her adversaries, claiming that the *image* of her book that they created clouded her readers' eyes so efficiently that even the finest minds such as Gershom Scholem could no longer see clearly what was written in her book.[189]

Of course, Arendt had her defenders. Writers such as Mary McCarthy, Hans Morgenthau, Daniel Bell and Dwight Macdonald did what they could to support what they saw as valid in *Eichmann in Jerusalem*.[190] However, their efforts did little to transform the impassioned furore into reasoned discussion. On the contrary, they often provoked violent responses, such as when Alfred Kazin—a somewhat ambivalent defender of Arendt—attempted to speak for her in a public forum, only to be silenced by Lionel Abel roaring, 'Who asked you to come up here? Who asked your opinion?'[191] The controversial author herself became wary in the meantime. On a rare occasion when she defended herself in public, she called the debates 'meaningless and mindless', further infuriating critics who had accused her of arrogance.[192] So it continued until 1966, when 'everyone seemed to have burned out'.[193] If the Eichmann controversy was a 'civil war' among New York intellectuals, it was akin more to Thomas Hobbes's hypothetical state of nature than to the real-world counterpart in the nineteenth-century United States of America: it degenerated into a chaotic assemblage of multiple fights fought over short-term goals, no longer moving towards peace and reconciliation, which is what a civil war ought to aim at, at least in theory.

Isaiah Berlin and the Eichmann Controversy

Isaiah Berlin was not a central player in the Eichmann controversy. Yet he followed it with interest and played a small part in it. As in the case of *The Human Condition*, he had been asked to write a review of *Eichmann in Jerusalem*. He declined the request, and stated his rationale with admirable candour in a letter to William Phillips, editor of the *Partisan Review*: 'I feel a curious allergy about all that [Arendt] writes—and I am quite sure that I should be more than reasonably unfair. [. . .] The book on Eichmann may well be excellent, but I should probably not perceive that.'[194] He said something similar in a letter to Mary McCarthy:

> As it is—although I have not read the book [*Eichmann in Jerusalem*] properly, it seems to me one of her clearer, better argued, more incisive works—not the dark, Teutonic, cloud of irrelevancy and free association that the other works seemed to me to be (the book on revolutions takes us straight back to the old German metaphysical trough, and I cannot take it). [. . .] Miss A. is certainly more entitled to her views about Eichmann than to her views about the Greeks, the Hebrews, or the eighteenth and nineteenth century, which have so upset the more factual and scrupulous amongst my colleagues.[195]

Taming his hostility towards Arendt and her work, Berlin thus conceded that *Eichmann in Jerusalem* could be 'excellent', consistent with his long-held view that her discussion of Nazism in *Origins* was the least bad of her works. However, as historians such as Arie Dubnov and Lotte Houwink ten Cate have recently shown, Berlin did play a role in the publication of the English translation of the famous Arendt–Scholem exchange in *Encounter*. His role was twofold: first, he encouraged Scholem to publish an English translation of the exchange;[196] second, he 'acted as a go-between' for Scholem and the London-based assistant editor of *Encounter*, John Mander.[197] This means, on the one hand, Berlin played no role in the original publication of the exchange (in German) in the Tel Aviv-based magazine *Mitteilungsblatt*. Nor did he play a part in the reprinting of the exchange in the Swiss journal *Neue Zürcher Zeitung*. In both these cases, the person who took the initiative was Scholem himself.[198] On the other hand, Berlin played a significant role when it came to the English translation. He brought the Arendt–Scholem exchange to the attention of the *Encounter* editors, and 'suggested that [the journal] might be interested in it'.[199]

When Arendt heard from Mander that his magazine wanted to publish her exchange with Scholem, she was concerned that what she had originally conceived of as a private discussion with a friend was now reaching an unduly large audience. In spite of her reservations, however, she gave *Encounter* permission to publish the exchange, on condition that she would have a say in the English translation.[200] She would soon regret this decision, feeling like she 'had stumbled into an ambush' or 'a trap'.[201] It is not known whether she was aware of Berlin's involvement in the *Encounter* episode, although she was by then developing the suspicion that Berlin, as someone 'on the closest of terms with the government in Israel', had been a part of what she considered to be an organised campaign against *Eichmann in Jerusalem*.[202] At any rate, the English translation of the Arendt–Scholem exchange duly appeared in the January 1964 issue of *Encounter*, much to Arendt's regret.

Given this background, it is indicative that Berlin occasionally expressed mischievous delight in the spectacle of devastation amid the intellectuals' civil war across the Atlantic. He told his friend Stephen Spender in July 1963, 'I love the fearful scandal about Miss Arendt's book.'[203] In fairness to Berlin, he did not exploit the opportunity to mount a wholesale attack on Arendt during the Eichmann controversy, when she was most vulnerable and 'became a pariah among her own people.'[204] Nevertheless, as the *Encounter* episode indicates, he morally supported her critics and was willing to give his assistance to those condemning *Eichmann in Jerusalem*. This is hardly surprising, for her critics were now echoing Berlin's long-held view that Arendt was intellectually superficial and morally arrogant. He was thus glad to see Robinson's refutation of Arendt's four hundred 'factual errors', thinking that it 'contain[ed] enough material [. . .] to expose [Arendt's] feeble grasp of fact.'[205] Additionally, Berlin may have helped John Sparrow, warden of All Souls College, to write an anonymous and highly critical review of Arendt's book for the *Times Literary Supplement*. David Caute, a former fellow of All Souls, puts forward the following suggestion: 'We can surmise that they talked long into the night [. . .], Berlin updating Sparrow on the controversy in American Jewish circles.'[206]

While Berlin thought highly of Sparrow's review, it was Scholem's exchange with Arendt that left a deeper impression on him in the long run. Scholem's two key allegations struck Berlin as just and right: first, Arendt lacked 'the love of the Jewish people'; and second, her discussion of Jewish leadership was characterised by a 'heartless, frequently almost sneering and malicious tone.'[207] Berlin would for the rest of his life appeal to Scholem's authority and refer to 'the terrible lack of heart of which Scholem rightly accused Hannah Arendt', to support his own opinion of her.[208]

It is notable, however, that Berlin was willing to go further than Scholem when criticising Arendt. Even before *Eichmann in Jerusalem* was published, Scholem and Arendt had quarrelled with each other, most notably over the latter's 1944 essay 'Zionism Reconsidered', which 'disappointed [Scholem] so profoundly and [. . .] somewhat embittered' him.[209] Nevertheless, they had been personal friends since the 1930s, collaborated closely in the late 1940s and early 1950s, and continued to treat each other *respectfully* even as the Eichmann controversy strained their friendship and ultimately ended it.[210] As Arendt was aware, Scholem did not accept or reiterate some of the harshest charges that others levelled against her, including Arendt's purported 'self-hatred', during the controversy.[211] Berlin, by contrast, fully accepted this charge.[212] He made arguably his cruellest remark on Arendt in July 1963, at the height of the Eichmann controversy. Arendt's 'own unconscious is filled with most fearful monsters', Berlin alleged, 'and if anyone needs deep, deep analysis it is Miss A.'[213]

By the time the initial round of the Eichmann controversy came to an end in the late 1960s, 'Arendt' had become a general noun in Berlin's book to designate something like perversity and deformation.[214] The seeds of dislike for Hannah Arendt that had been sown in Berlin's heart and mind in 1941 had matured into fully blooming animosity by the end of the 1960s. It never wilted, to the end of his life.

A Conference on Revolutionary Russia

Arendt's and Berlin's paths crossed one last time in April 1967, when Richard Pipes organised a conference at the Russian Research Center at Harvard University to mark the fiftieth anniversary of the Russian Revolution. The participants, twenty-seven in total, represented 'the great and the good in the profession', and included George Kennan, Merle Fainsod, Adam Ulam, Leonard Schapiro, E. H. Carr and Marc Ferro.[215] Arendt's presence might be surprising, for she was by no means a Sovietologist or an expert on Russian Studies. But her role was to respond to Ulam's presentation on 'The Uses of Revolution', and the task seemed appropriate for the author of *On Revolution*. Ever a nonconformist, Arendt herself was flattered to be the only non-specialist at the conference. ('Characteristically', Young-Bruehl writes, 'she noted to Jaspers that she was the only one *nicht vom Fach*, not from the profession, and did not say she was the only one not male.'[216]) Berlin, by contrast, was an insider to the Russian Studies community in the US in general and to Harvard's Russian Research Center in particular. He had been affiliated with the latter on and off since 1949, and had been on close terms with Richard Pipes, who dedicated his 1970 book to him.[217] The Harvard historian in fact visited Berlin in Oxford while travelling to the UK in June 1966, and the two frequently corresponded with each other to discuss the conference plan.[218] In one of the letters, Berlin expressed his reservations about Arendt, but did not veto her participation in the conference. He told Pipes, 'I have no opinion of the lady. Still, we shall be none the poorer for her.'[219]

The conference duly took place on 4–9 April.[220] The proceedings, which included a summary of the discussions following the formal presentations, were published as a 350-page volume, *Revolutionary Russia*.[221] Did Arendt and Berlin cross swords at the conference? Not quite. They exchanged words twice, but the image of sword-crossing is hardly appropriate to describe these interactions. The first exchange occurred during the session devoted to Kennan's paper on 'The Breakdown of the Tsarist Autocracy'. Towards the end of the discussion, Arendt suggested that 'Russian nationalism was fundamentally different from nationalism in Western Europe and that from the middle of the nineteenth century Russian nationalism was actually Pan-Slavism'. This suggestion was not well received by the specialists in the room. Kennan challenged Arendt with the remark that 'Russian nationalism was only in part Pan-Slav'. This was echoed by Berlin, who added that political pan-Slavism was a short-term phenomenon and no longer 'in existence by 1900'. The subsequent comments by others did not support Arendt, either, and the discussion soon developed in a different direction. *Revolutionary Russia* records no counterargument by Arendt directed at the Kennan–Berlin alliance.[222]

The next brief exchange between Arendt and Berlin occurred during the discussion following Pipes's paper on 'The Origins of Bolshevism', to which Berlin was a designated respondent. Again, Arendt initiated the exchange. Reiterating her observations in *On Revolution*,[223] she highlighted the deep tension between Lenin the man of action and Lenin the Communist Party leader. The former, according to Arendt, recognised the significance of spontaneity and free action thanks to his first-hand experience of revolutionary movements, while the latter subscribed doctrinally to a determinist ideology and one-party rule. Her comments were appropriate, for the aim of Pipes's paper was to trace the young Lenin's intellectual evolution that culminated in Bolshevism by the turn of the century. Berlin, however, did not quite respond to Arendt's claims. Instead, he again made a very brief comment to question the historical accuracy of Arendt's remarks, this time pointing out that 'most of the activists did not become Marxists but Social Revolutionaries or terrorists'. The subsequent discussion again developed in a different direction, and the session ended with the platitude, stated by Pipes, that the subject of the young Lenin 'deserves intense study'.[224]

What sense should we make of these exchanges of words between Arendt and Berlin in April 1967? One interpretation, suggested by Ilya Winham, is to see Berlin as choosing to fight a defensive war employing the strategy of manoeuvre.[225] He was aware that Arendt was the only non-specialist in the room. His superiority over Arendt was secure as long as the discussion focused on Russian history, whereas his supremacy could be in doubt had the discussion expanded to include wider issues in political theory. On this interpretation, Harvard's Russian Research Center was an ideal battlefield for Berlin. All he needed to do was to wait for Arendt to enter *his* territory; once she did, he could strike to expose 'her wide ignorance of [. . .] modern Russian history'.[226] But there is another, and ultimately more plausible, interpretation, which better accounts for the brevity of Berlin's comments on Arendt. That is, he confined his response to her to a bare minimum because he did not want to engage with her. He did not ignore her altogether, but that was only because he was unable to tolerate 'her wide ignorance'. The central feature of their 1967 interaction, then, was not so much 'Berlin's pedantic zeal to correct' Arendt's errors as his reluctance to speak to her in the first place.[227] This interpretation is

supported by some of his letters, in one of which he expressed his unwillingness 'to enter into any relations with [Arendt], not even those of hostility'.[228]

We do not have sufficient evidence to pin down exactly what Berlin was
thinking or feeling when he briefly interacted with Arendt twice at the Harvard conference. For her part, Arendt did not seem to care much about Berlin's
thoughts or feelings. She found the conference 'very interesting', as she excitedly told Karl Jaspers.[229] Her remarks on Ulam's paper were indeed well appreciated by the speaker, and she actively participated in the conference from
beginning to end. Perhaps her non-specialist status made her feel more relaxed
than usual. She knew she belonged 'in the category of layman', as she told her
audience at the beginning of her response to Ulam.[230] She may not have
minded much if she was told that she did not know some facts about Russian
history. This possibly explains why she found the Harvard conference particularly stimulating, as she could test her ideas in the presence of twenty-six qualified fact gatherers, including Berlin.

More might be said about the Harvard conference had there been a better
record of it. But the limited information available to us is sufficient to show
that, from the perspective of the present study, it was something of a missed
opportunity. Arendt and Berlin hardly crossed swords on this occasion. A
more appropriate metaphor to describe their interaction is one of a prolonged
stalemate in a pointless trench warfare. Each side fired a couple of times from
the trench, but they missed the target, and neither side was ready to launch an
all-out offensive. And how else could it be? Arguing with Berlin was never
Arendt's priority, not least because she had many more adversaries than he
ever faced. For his part, Berlin had already made up his mind about Arendt by
the time he arrived in Cambridge, Massachusetts, in April 1967. Once the conference began, he did what he had said he would do vis-à-vis Arendt: stayed
away from her as much as possible.

It was at the same university, Harvard, that the two thinkers had met nearly
two decades earlier, in 1949, on Arthur Schlesinger's initiative. The meeting
had turned out to be a 'disaster', but they at least spoke to each other.[231] A
further disaster was avoided in 1967; but only because the distance between
Arendt and Berlin had become so vast that a clash, or crossing of swords, was
no longer possible. Such was the last encounter between them—eight years
and eight months before Arendt's untimely death.

'In Life, and after Her Death'

In the spring of 1972, Berlin expressed his now firmly established animosity
towards Arendt in the following terms: 'my allergy vis-à-vis Miss Arendt is
absolute and her mere presence in a room gives me goose-flesh.'[232] He avoided

her in print as well as physically, expressing his unwillingness to 'wash[. . .] even the cleanest linen in public'.[233] The implication is that he would be embarrassed to have public discussion with her, even if he had been spotlessly in the right. He did not, however, need to be careful to avoid her in person or in print for long, as Arendt died in December 1975, a year after he wrote those harsh words. Berlin, by contrast, had more than two decades to live to see the growth of her posthumous reputation. This, he thought, would diminish sooner or later, because he saw nothing of lasting value in Arendt's work. In this respect, he has turned out to be wrong (so far at least), as Arendt's fame has shown no sign of decline. On the contrary, both *The Origins of Totalitarianism* and *The Human Condition* have come to be recognised as 'modern classics', and 'Arendt studies' had become a subdiscipline and a minor industry by the time of Berlin's death in 1997.

Arendt's undiminishing posthumous renown added a further layer to Berlin's attitude towards her. Much to his annoyance, new generations of scholars came to associate the two thinkers in various ways. An instance occurred in 1983, when Berlin received a request from his younger Oxford colleagues Zbigniew Pełczyński and John Gray to write an introduction to their planned edited volume entitled 'Conceptions of Liberty in Political Philosophy'.[234] The invitation was entirely appropriate. Berlin had been Britain's foremost theorist of liberty over the past two decades, was on good terms with both Gray and Pełczyński and had in fact attended the conference from which their edited volume emerged. Nevertheless, he declined the invitation on the grounds that he 'hated' one of the thinkers discussed in the book: Hannah Arendt. He was unwilling to see his name appearing on the same page as hers. 'Much though I dislike Miss A.,' he told one of the co-editors, 'I don't want her to *rotate* in her grave.'[235]

And so it continued. For example, when Ramin Jahanbegloo conducted a series of recorded interviews with Berlin in December 1988, he suggested some points of proximity between Berlin's and Arendt's work. Unaware of his interviewee's intense dislike for Arendt, Jahanbegloo inadvertently provoked in him deep indignation. Berlin said in response, 'You frighten me when you say that she is close to me.'[236] Something similar occurred a couple of years later when, as I noted in my Introduction, Norman Oliver Brown mentioned *Republic of Fear* by Kanan Makiya, alias Samir al-Khalil, to Berlin.[237] The latter replied with a sense of exasperation, 'Down with al-Khalil, and do tell me that you [i.e., Brown] do see some radical differences between Miss Arendt and myself—otherwise how can we go on knowing each other?' Never mind that *Republic of Fear* did not discuss Arendt and Berlin on the same page, or even in the same chapter;[238] Berlin reacted strongly all the same: 'She is a real bête noire to me—*in life, and after her death*.'[239] The passage of time clearly did not assuage Berlin's hostility towards Arendt.

Was Berlin right to insist on 'some radical differences' between him and the woman he 'detested most'? The answer is, yes and no. On the one hand, he was undoubtedly wide of the mark when he said he '[could not] conceive of any issue that could bring me to the same platform as Miss Hannah Arendt'.[240] Among the shared issues that could and did bring them to 'the same platform' were, needless to say, the twin evils of Nazism and Stalinism as the ultimate enemy to respond to, and the defence of human freedom in the age of mass killing and total war. In addition, both thinkers were highly sceptical of consequentialist reasoning and its maxim, 'You can't make an omelette without breaking eggs', which each interpreted as justification for state-sponsored terror to achieve ideological goals. Moreover, they both echoed what appears to be their generation's discontent (shared in differing ways by Michael Oakeshott, Friedrich Hayek, Leo Strauss, Theodor Adorno and Max Horkheimer, among others) with the main, rationalist current of Western political thought and its failure to do justice to the complexity of human life. They further shared deep scepticism about what both regarded as a recent manifestation of that rationalist tendency, namely, the over-application of scientific methods to the study of human affairs. These are but a sample of the issues that could bring Arendt and Berlin to 'the same platform'.[241]

On the other hand, Berlin was right in insisting that there were 'some radical differences' between himself and Arendt—not in that their ideas did not share common ground, but in that the ground which they had in common was also a battlefield, as it were, upon which they faced each other as opponents. One is reminded here that an enemy's enemy is not always a friend. The two thinkers certainly shared a perception of Nazism and Stalinism as the archenemy. Yet their ideas conflicted, sometimes irreconcilably, over several key issues. This made their mutual dislike far more than a merely personal quarrel. It is time to examine each of these points of *theoretical* conflict, beginning with the most fundamental: what it means for human beings to be free.

3

Freedom

ON 22 MAY 1958, Hannah Arendt delivered a lecture in Zurich on 'Freiheit und Politik' ('Freedom and Politics'),[1] later revised and published in English under the title 'What Is Freedom?'[2] Simultaneously historical and philosophical, the twenty-five-page essay gives a panoramic view of differing understandings of freedom, from the pre-Socratics to the present. It also defends one particular understanding Arendt calls 'political freedom', whose essence she summarises in a proverbial form: 'The *raison d'être* of politics is freedom, and its field of experience is action.'[3] According to Arendt, this idea is so deeply rooted in our culture that her discussion of the intricate connection between politics, freedom and action would strike her readers as immediately intelligible. In this sense, she claims, her discussion amounts to 'no more than to reflect on [an] old truism.'[4]

As Arendt's lecture was going to press, to appear in the winter issue of the German journal *Neue Rundschau*, Isaiah Berlin, on the other side of the English Channel, gave a lecture on 31 October on 'Two Concepts of Liberty', to inaugurate his Chichele professorship of social and political theory at Oxford. He was almost certainly unaware of Arendt's lecture five months earlier. He had not attended it, and he had drafted and revised 'Two Concepts' *before* the publication of Arendt's piece.[5] At first glance, his lecture has several points of proximity to Arendt's. Blending historical scholarship and philosophical argument, the fifty-seven-page text gives an overview of competing understandings of freedom, from ancient civilisations to the twentieth century, and defends one particular understanding Berlin calls 'negative liberty'. He relies on some of the standard distinctions Arendt also uses in 'What Is Freedom?', including those between the ancient and the modern, and between freedom as a political concept and freedom as free will. He discusses key figures who are considered in Arendt's text as well, including the Stoics, Hobbes, Rousseau, Kant, Montesquieu and Mill. And, again like Arendt, he considers his preferred conception of freedom to be commonplace and immediately intelligible to his readers. In spite of these surface similarities, however, the substance of their arguments could scarcely be more different.

The aim of this chapter is to examine Arendt's and Berlin's rival theories of freedom. This is by no means the only point of disagreement between the two thinkers. However, it is the most fundamental of all their disagreements because, for both of our protagonists, to be free is to be *human* in the full sense of the term, and to deprive one of freedom is to deny one's humanity. Consequently, to examine their disagreement over freedom is not only to consider what they meant by the term 'liberty' or 'freedom' and what value they saw in it. It is also to tease out their competing conceptions of the human condition, which ultimately underpin their respective theories of freedom and of political thought as a whole. To anticipate my main argument, I hope to show in this chapter that the following observation by the British philosopher Martin Hollis was true when it came to Arendt and Berlin: 'all political and social theorists, I venture to claim, depend on some model of man in explaining what moves people and accounts for institutions. Such models are sometimes hidden but never absent [. . .]. There is no more central or pervasive topic in the study of politics.'[6]

A further advantage of beginning our enquiry into Arendt's and Berlin's political thought with freedom is that both thinkers had reached a certain intellectual maturity by the time they presented their respective theories of freedom. Of course, they had many more years to live, and neither's intellectual development stopped in the 1950s or the 1960s. Nevertheless, the backbone of each theorist's thought was formed by the time Arendt published *The Human Condition* (1958), *Between Past and Future* (1961) and *On Revolution* (1963), and by the time Berlin published 'Two Concepts of Liberty' in 1958 and its revised version in 1969. To put it differently, both thinkers were still very much in the making even in the early 1950s. For example, although *The Origins of Totalitarianism*, published in 1951, was undoubtedly a groundbreaking book, some of Arendt's key ideas such as her flagship distinctions between force, violence and power, and between labour, work and action, were still missing from this early masterpiece. Similarly, while Berlin had been writing extensively on liberty and freedom since the early 1950s, it was only later in the decade that he came to formulate his flagship distinction between negative and positive liberty. Although both thinkers would add to, refine and develop their ideas on freedom and other issues subsequently, their mid-career writings serve as an ideal starting point for our enquiry in the rest of this book.

This chapter is in four main sections (besides this introductory one). The first introduces some basic analytic tools and terminological distinctions on which my subsequent discussion relies. I explicate how I use the terms 'liberty' and 'freedom', and differentiate between 'conceptions', 'concepts', 'ideas' and 'theories'. Next, I turn to Berlin's theory of freedom. While he is best known for his dichotomous division between negative and positive liberty, each of these concepts may be subdivided. Consequently, his theory of freedom can be shown to be richer, more complex and more ambiguous than is commonly supposed. Nevertheless, all things considered, Berlin prioritises negative liberty over its positive rival—or, more precisely, rivals—on the basis of his conviction that the negative concept is truer to the essential aspect of the human condition: that the human being is a choice-making creature.

The following section turns to Arendt's theory of freedom. It analyses this in comparison to Berlin's theory on the one hand, and the neo-republican theory proposed by Quentin Skinner and Philip Pettit on the other. It will be shown that Arendt's political freedom is distinct from the negative, positive and neo-republican concepts, and is based on an alternative view of the human condition, whereby the human being is conceptualised as a political animal conditioned by plurality and natality. Finally, I examine Arendt's and Berlin's competing histories of freedom, especially their conflicting perspectives on ancient philosophy, to explicate further the central point of disagreement between the two thinkers.

Terms and Distinctions

First, a brief discussion of terminology is in order. There has been a long debate as to whether the words 'liberty' and 'freedom' are, or should be used as, exact synonyms. No single attempt is likely to bring an end to this dispute, and this book is not intended to do so. To minimise confusion and avoid misunderstanding, however, I shall use the following terminological devices in the pages that follow. First, I reject the idea that 'liberty' and 'freedom' ought to be strictly distinguished from each other. True, the two terms register slightly different nuances and connotations, elusively conveying 'older tensions of meaning persist[ing] in the folk memory of English-speaking people'.[7] Etymologically, 'liberty' originates from Latin and Old French, and 'freedom' from Germanic languages. One was brought into the English language by the Normans; the other, by the Anglo-Saxons. Consequently, it is more conventional to speak of Kant's, Hegel's or Marx's theory of freedom than of liberty, as it is more straightforward to use 'freedom', rather than 'liberty', to translate or discuss what these German-speaking authors wrote about *Freiheit*. Similarly, one can at least make sense of, if not agree with, David Ritchie's hyperbolic remark that liberty is 'something French, foolish and frivolous', whereas freedom is 'English, solid and sensible, if just a trifle dull'.[8] One may list many other instances in which 'liberty' and 'freedom' convey, or are said to convey, different connotations. However, as Hanna Pitkin demonstrates in her seminal essay 'Are Freedom and Liberty Twins?', such differences are very subtle and ultimately incoherent, and they get immensely more complex as we turn to the verbs 'to free' and 'to liberate', the adjectives 'free' and 'liberal' and the adverbs 'freely' and 'liberally'.[9] To follow the overly rigid terminological distinction between 'liberty' and 'freedom' hardly helps to capture these complexities, and it is advisable that we abandon the vain hope that clarity might be achieved if and only if the two terms are strictly distinguished from each other.

My present point is substantiated by none other than Hannah Arendt herself. As is well known, she underlines differences between 'liberty' and 'freedom' in the first chapter of *On Revolution*, challenging the modern convention that the two terms may be used as exact synonyms.[10] But she does not follow her own distinction later in the same book.[11] For example, she uses 'liberty' and 'freedom' interchangeably in its last chapter, entitled 'The Revolutionary Tradition and its Lost Treasure', characterising 'the *freedom* of movement' as 'the greatest and most elementary of all negative *liberties*'.[12] Similarly in other texts, for example in a piece composed in the late 1960s and published posthumously as '"The Freedom to Be Free"', Arendt observes that '*liberty* [in the late eighteenth century] meant no more than *freedom* from unjustifiable restraint'.[13] A persistent pattern is discernible in her usage of the terms 'liberty' and 'freedom'. On the one hand, she repeatedly uses them interchangeably, especially in their adjectival and adverbial forms. On the other, she repeatedly attempts to highlight different nuances conveyed by the two terms. In short, Arendt is inconsistent, at least as inconsistent as ordinary language is, as to whether 'liberty' and 'freedom' are exact synonyms. This is hardly surprising, because the simplistic liberty/freedom dichotomy cannot do justice to the complexity of Arendt's thought, or to the untidiness of ordinary language. A more promising approach, then, is to accept this untidiness, acknowledge the semantic overlap as well as differences between 'liberty' and 'freedom' and introduce a range of terminological distinctions to specify the precise sense of liberty or freedom under consideration.

For this purpose it is useful to build on H.L.A. Hart's and John Rawls's work and distinguish between a conception, a concept, an idea and a theory.[14] The distinction between the first two is familiar enough. *Concepts* are basic units or 'building blocks of thoughts',[15] whereas *conceptions* designate differing interpretations of a given concept when its meaning is open to contestation. For example, distributive justice is a highly contested *concept* and may be interpreted differently, giving rise to a range of *conceptions*, such as liberal egalitarian, welfare-based and desert-based, for example. Helpful though it is, however, the concept/conception dichotomy is still too crude to let us navigate through the highly complex debate over liberty and freedom (or over justice, for that matter). Two further terms may thus be added to enrich the dichotomy. One is *idea*, which is used as a generic category to group relevant concepts together. For example, while distributive justice and criminal justice may be seen as independent concepts, they may be grouped together as emanating from a more abstract idea of justice. To put it another way, the *idea* of justice breaks down into multiple *concepts*, such as distributive justice and criminal justice, each of which in turn breaks down into multiple *conceptions*, such as the welfare-based and desert-based conceptions of distributive justice, and the retributivist and consequentialist conceptions of criminal justice. Finally, I use the term *theory* to refer to a pattern of thought, rigidly systematic or relatively unsystematic, centring on a given concept and its conception, and accompanied by relevant considerations.[16] For example, it is normally the case that one's specific conception of distributive justice is accompanied by considerations on the appropriate role of the state, on the permissible level of socio-economic inequality, and so on. When one combines one's conception of distributive justice with one's conceptions of authority, equality and so on in this way, one is said to have a theory of distributive justice.

Let me emphasise that these terminological distinctions are no more than a heuristic device. Their value consists solely in their ability to help adjust one's focus to see clearly what one would like to see; to assign greater value than this is to fetishise the heuristic device, that is, to misrecognise its instrumental worth as an intrinsic one. Let me draw an analogy by way of illustration. Consider a conversation you may have with a friend who recently moved to London. You may wish to ask him or her the precise address, or the nearest train station, or the neighbourhood, depending on what you would like to do with that information. For example, you would need to know the exact address if you are planning to send your friend a parcel, while you would only need to know his or her neighbourhood if you would like to meet him or her at a nearby café. A similarly pragmatic approach is advisable when fine-tuning the analytic lens with which to examine ideas. For example, I shall focus on the *concept* of negative liberty when outlining a way of thinking about freedom on a relatively general level, whereas I shall zoom in on one's *conception* of negative liberty to analyse one's particular interpretation of the concept. I am not concerned as to whether the conception/concept/idea/theory distinction is useful for considering general issues in linguistic philosophy or the philosophy of language. What matters in the present context is that the distinction is useful for the task at hand: to examine Arendt's and Berlin's competing theories of freedom.

Berlin's Theory of Liberty

Isaiah Berlin's interest in liberty/freedom lasted a lifetime. The evolution of this interest has been extensively studied, most notably in Joshua Cherniss's intellectual biography of the young Berlin.[17] It goes back at least to 1928, when the future philosopher wrote his earliest surviving essay on freedom at St Paul's School.[18] This was to be followed by his first book, *Karl Marx* (1939), which contained an analysis of Marx's 'purely Hegelian view of freedom';[19] by his immediate post-war writings on Soviet Russia, which analysed oppression, coercion, persecution and other forms of unfreedom;[20] and by his various writings during the 1950s, when he struggled to form a satisfactory theory of liberty.[21] This effort came to fruition in 1958, when he preliminarily presented his mature theory in 'Two Concepts of Liberty'.[22] Although he continued to develop his ideas in subsequent years, the fundamentals of Berlin's mature theory had solidified by 1969, when a revised version of 'Two Concepts' was published together with other essays in *Four Essays on Liberty*.[23] In this chapter, I focus on those fundamentals.

Negative Liberty

Let me begin with negative liberty. Berlin characterises this as a concept that has been variously formulated by a group of theorists, including Hobbes, Bentham, Constant, Tocqueville and Mill. Part of Berlin's goal in 'Two Concepts of Liberty' is to give an overview of this intellectual tradition. But another part, which is more relevant to the current discussion, is to present what Berlin takes to be the most defensible conception of negative liberty, to show its superiority over its positive counterpart. This specifically Berlinian conception of negative liberty is conventionally characterised as 'freedom as non-interference'. This is a good starting point, but it is not as illuminating as is often supposed, because interference is not a self-explanatory concept and may be interpreted in a variety of ways. One consequently needs to analyse what kind of interference and other pertinent concepts such as prevention, constraints, oppression and obstacles are relevant to Berlin's freedom as non-interference. Some progress may be made on this issue if we characterise Berlin's negative liberty as follows: one is negatively free if one is not prevented by others from doing what one could otherwise do. One type of prevention is physical. For example, one is negatively free to stroll if nobody physically prevents one from strolling when one wants to; whereas one is unfree to stroll if someone shoots one in the leg when one attempts to go for a stroll. But relevant prevention can also be psychological. One's freedom to stroll may be negated if one is told by someone else that one will be shot in the leg if one goes for a stroll. Whether the shooting is actually undertaken is irrelevant, so long as the threat is taken to be serious and credible. To the extent that psychological constraints can in this way be no less effective than physical constraints, negative liberty 'consists in not being prevented from *choosing* as I do by other men'.[24] While the existence of negative liberty 'depends ultimately on causal interactions among bodies', some bodily interactions, for example A's pointing a gun at B, can make B's desired action ineligible and negate B's negative liberty.[25]

To be negatively free in Berlin's sense is more than feeling free. One feels free if one's desires are not frustrated, but this may be achieved 'as effectively by eliminating desires as by satisfying them'.[26] For example, a would-be writer who finds it difficult to complete his or her novel may end his or her frustration as well by abandoning his or her ambitions altogether as by getting his or her work published. Of course, some philosophers, such as the Stoics, have exploited this idea and conceptualised freedom as self-control, seeing the elimination of desires as a genuine path to freedom. According to this view, one is free if one masters the art of living such as to lead a peaceful and pleasant life regardless of the external circumstances in which one finds oneself. Berlin concedes that this view is coherent and intelligible. Yet he firmly rejects it as false, as amounting to an 'unmistakable [. . .] form of the doctrine of sour grapes'.[27] The allusion here is to Aesop's fable, in which a fox rationalises its inability to reach ripe grapes on a lofty branch by telling itself that the grapes *must* be sour and unworthy of attaining or even pursuing. Negative liberty rejects such rationalisation. To be negatively free is to *be* free; it is not to *feel* free.

To be negatively free to do or be X is different from being capable of doing or being X. One may not be able to fly, but this does not mean that one is unfree to fly. One may not be able to cross a road that has been destroyed by an earthquake, but this does not mean that one is unfree to cross the road. One is said to be unfree if and only if one's desires are frustrated as a result of 'alterable human practices'.[28] Paradigmatically, one is made unfree by somebody's *deliberate* interference; in this case one is said to be oppressed. But one may also be made unfree as an *unintended* consequence of 'the operation of human agencies'.[29] Consider poverty.[30] One is unfree to obtain, as well as incapable of obtaining, food, water and other basic necessities if one's poverty is caused by human-made arrangements. Such a situation is different from a food crisis directly caused by a natural disaster (provided that the disaster is not caused by human activities). In the latter situation, the victims are incapable of obtaining, but are neither unfree nor free to obtain, basic necessities. The concept of negative liberty is simply irrelevant here.

To substantiate this point, Berlin famously underlines the difference between negative liberty and 'the conditions of its exercise'.[31] A sick and starving citizen who has no shoes or clothes to wear is unlikely to go to a voting booth until his or her basic needs are fulfilled. This, however, does not mean that the citizen does not have the freedom to vote. What he or she lacks is a set of conditions for exercising that freedom; the citizen will, if he or she so wishes, exercise the freedom to vote that he or she *already* has once his or her more basic needs, such as food, shelter and security, are fulfilled. Is this a plausible claim? Not everyone thinks so. Berlin's strict separation between freedom and its conditions has been criticised for amounting to 'an unfortunate reversion' towards libertarianism; that is, towards the inflation of the value of negative liberty at the expense of other considerations, especially economic equality.[32] On this critical reading, Berlin is a marginally left-wing version of Friedrich Hayek, whose seemingly rigorous analysis of liberty effectively disguises the denial of liberty to the economically disadvantaged.

Is this a valid criticism? Is Berlin a libertarian pretending to be a liberal? On the one hand, this criticism is one-sided to the extent that Berlin's endorsement of negative liberty is not unconditional. On the contrary, he concedes that negative liberty must be balanced against, and at times compromised by, other values such as equality, justice and solidarity. This means that Berlin's distinction between liberty and its conditions is intended to be analytic, rather than social or political. He underlines this distinction because he believes that 'nothing is gained by a confusion of terms'.[33] On the other hand, however, critics are right to note that Berlin has little to say on economic inequality in general and the destructive forces of what we today call neoliberalism in particular. Although he acknowledges the importance of the latter issue and even warns of 'the evils of unrestricted laissez-faire' in his 1969 'Introduction' to *Four Essays on Liberty*, Berlin does not discuss in detail how the unregulated exercise of negative liberty, especially in the economic sphere, could result in the violation of 'basic human rights' and of negative liberty itself.[34] Nor does he have much to say on how 'the evils of unrestricted laissez-faire' might be contained. He came to regret this insufficiency of attention, and highlighted his awareness of the perils of neoliberal economy on later occasions, especially in interviews.[35] The late Berlin's effort has been assisted by similar efforts by his friendly readers, who insist on the difference between Berlin and libertarians on the value of negative liberty.[36] Yet Berlin's critics have never been persuaded, and some continue to claim that he was blind to, and indeed complicit in, the harm done by neoliberalism.[37] A tone of resignation is discernible in a remark Berlin made in 1986: 'What I'm accused of is always the same, which is some kind of dry, negative individualism.'[38]

Non-Interference and the Ability to Choose

To complicate the matter further, Berlin does not always characterise his conception of negative liberty as non-interference. According to an alternative account he repeatedly provides, to be negatively free is to have opportunities. This is different from exercising or realising them. Berlin highlights this difference by repeatedly invoking the image of 'open doors'. A free person has many open doors of various sorts in front of him or her. He or she may not be walking through a door, or may not have decided which door to walk through, but these do not make him or her unfree or less free. To be free consists first and foremost in one's ability to choose between multiple options. Note that both the number and quality of options matter to Berlin's negative liberty. By way of illustration, consider hypothetical detainees under four different situations, assuming that no one likes or wants to be detained:

> α will be held in detention for thirty days.
> β may choose between thirty- and thirty-one-day detention.
> γ may choose between thirty-, thirty-one- and thirty-two-day detention.
> δ may choose between thirty-day detention and immediate release.

According to Berlin, β and γ (as well as δ) are freer than α because they have more options; and δ is freer than β and γ (as well as α) because δ's options are qualitatively better than the others', although, numerically speaking, δ does not have more options than β or γ. Unfortunately, he does not specify exactly how the numerical and qualitative aspects of negative liberty may be compared with each other.[39] Contrary to his critics' allegations, however, he does not focus exclusively on the numerical dimension.[40] He is certainly aware that immediate release is better than one fewer day in detention. Nevertheless, he places relatively strong emphasis on the numerical dimension, underlining that the availability of an additional option necessarily increases negative liberty, even if the option is not desirable. To have more options is one thing; whether the options are desirable is another; and both matter to negative liberty. Thus, in my example, β is not *much* freer than α but β is freer nonetheless. To cite Berlin's more humorous example, to 'stand on my head and crow like a cock if I feel so inclined' may be wholly worthless; and yet to be able to do so is a genuine freedom.[41]

The image of open doors is a vivid and forceful one, but it invites important ambiguity. In fact, it may be said that Berlin unintentionally presents two conceptions of negative liberty: non-interference and the ability to choose. Of course, the two have significant areas of overlap and sometimes even coincide, as in the case of the detainee, for example. A detainee's ability to choose is limited because he or she is detained by an external interferer. In this case, liberty as non-interference and liberty as the ability to choose coincide. They do not *necessarily* coincide, however. For example, if one is monolingual, one is unable to do various things that a bilingual person can do, such as reading foreign language books in the original. Other things being equal, the monolingual person has many fewer options or open doors to choose from than the bilingual. This, however, does not necessarily mean that the former was subjected to external interference. Of course, such interference is in principle possible. If, for example, a child is prohibited from learning a foreign language by his or her eccentric ethno-nationalist parents, who believe that bilingualism amounts to national betrayal, then the child is negatively unfree in both senses of the term. First, the child is unfree, or at least less free than a bilingual person, in the 'open door' sense, because he or she has fewer options than the latter. Second, the child is also unfree in the 'non-interference' sense, for he or she has been prevented from acquiring a second language by external interferers, that is, the ethno-nationalist parents. Nevertheless, in other and more mundane cases, a monolingual person's relative lack of options may not be due to external interference. One may, for example, be simply unable to acquire a second language in spite of one's best efforts. In this case, one is negatively *unfree* in the 'open door' sense and yet negatively *free* in the 'non-interference' sense. Berlin's two conceptions of negative liberty part company.

Which, then, is Berlin's *true* conception of negative liberty? Is it non-interference, or the ability to choose? The former is often presented as shorthand for Berlinian negative liberty. It has the advantage of being consistent with the aforementioned distinction Berlin draws between freedom and power. If his conception of negative liberty is a pure choice or 'open door' conception, it is not clear why a person who is unable to fly should not be seen as unfree, for if one could fly one would surely have an additional option, another 'open door' to walk through (or fly through), and to this extent be 'freer'. Does Berlin's rejection of this reasoning indicate that his true conception of negative liberty is non-interference? Perhaps. But the problem with excluding the 'open door' definition altogether from Berlinian negative liberty is that his texts are in fact characterised by deep ambiguity, and his numerous accounts of negative liberty constantly oscillate between non-interference and the ability to choose.[42] A more candid assessment of the matter, then, acknowledges this ambiguity and asks why it exists in the first place. To this question there is an unequivocal answer: although they are conceptually distinct, the two senses of negative liberty often coincide in empirical reality; and Berlin is concerned with those instances where individuals' ability to choose is diminished *as a result of* external interference. This is nicely captured by one of his numerous formulations of negative liberty. 'To be free', he writes, 'is to be able to make an *unforced choice*; and choice entails competing possibilities.'[43] This may be analytically frustrating, because it encompasses both liberty as non-interference and liberty as the ability to choose. It arguably indicates, however, that Berlin's priority is not analytic clarity, pure and simple. It is, rather, to underline the indispensability of *both* non-interference *and* the presence of multiple options to human liberty in its most basic sense.

Positive Liberty

On a general level, Berlin characterises positive liberty as a reply to the question, 'By whom am I to be governed?' To this the advocate of positive liberty replies, 'Myself.'[44] Again, however, to define positive liberty as self-mastery does not illuminate much, because, like interference, mastery is not a self-explanatory concept, may be variously interpreted and can consequently generate a wide range of conceptions. Berlin is not interested in compiling a comprehensive list of these diverse conceptions. Instead, he focuses on two in particular—the Stoic and the rationalist—to underline the vulnerability of positive liberty to political abuse to discredit its normative appeal. There is thus asymmetry between his discussions of negative and of positive liberty. When he discusses the former, he is concerned to articulate and defend *his own* conception; when he discusses the latter, he considers various conceptions *suggested by others*, and criticises them.[45]

The first conception of positive liberty Berlin focuses on is the Stoic one, which associates self-mastery with self-control, abstinence, discipline and, ultimately, self-abnegation. Stoics and negative liberty theorists agree that A is not free to do X if A is prevented by others from doing X. But they disagree as to how A may be freed in this situation. According to negative liberty theorists, the *only* way to end A's unfreedom is to remove or override the relevant obstacles. According to the Stoics, by contrast, A's unfreedom ends 1) if the relevant obstacles are removed or overridden; *or* 2) if A gives up his or her desire to do X. The distinct claim of the Stoic conception, according to Berlin, is that it considers those two options *equally* valid. The logical conclusion of this claim is the equation of absolute freedom and total self-abnegation—that is, suicide. As one's desires can always be frustrated and one 'can never be wholly secure' so long as one is alive, '[t]otal liberation in this sense [. . .] is conferred only by death.'[46] This idea is coherent, but strikes Berlin as highly unappealing. As I noted earlier, it reminds him of Aesop's self-deceiving fox.

The other conception of positive liberty Berlin focuses on is the rationalist one, which associates self-mastery with self-direction guided by the reflexive use of reason. This conception holds that to do something freely is not merely to satisfy the preferences one *happens* to have. 'Freedom is not freedom to do what is irrational, or stupid, or wrong.'[47] To do X freely in the positive sense consists in *knowing* that X is worth doing, as well as in actually doing it. One advantage of this reasoning is that it can account for the sense of 'false liberty' one may have when one reflects on something one did to one's later regret, or when one is doing something while being vaguely aware that one will later regret the action that one is currently undertaking. Consider a smoker who has been unable to quit smoking, while he or she knows he or she must quit because smoking is bad.[48] The smoker is not unfree to quit smoking in the negative sense because, first, he or she has the option of quitting as well as that of not quitting and, second, he or she is not externally prevented by others from doing what he or she could otherwise do, that is, quit smoking. By contrast, the smoker is unfree to quit smoking in the positive sense because he or she is internally prevented by his or her uncontrolled desires from doing what he or she knows is the right thing to do, that is, quit smoking. Negative liberty theorists can of course concede that it is unfortunate, bad and so on that the smoker should keep doing what he or she later regrets; but they are unable to call the smoker *unfree*, for neither external interference nor the absence of multiple options is involved in this case. The concept of positive liberty sees internal constraints as a genuine obstacle to human liberty. Its negative counterpart does not.

'Mythology of the Real Self'

Why does Berlin consider positive liberty to be susceptible to political abuse? Wherein lies its weakness? His answer is that it contains within itself a vulnerable component that he calls the 'mythology of the real self'.[49] To conceptualise liberty as self-mastery entails the distinction between 'higher' and 'lower' ends of action, pursued by two corresponding selves, because the idea of one's being a master of *oneself* would otherwise be unintelligible. Berlin concedes that this idea could be politically risk-free. In the case of Stoicism, for example, the self is divided between one that pursues frustratable desires and the other that has the prudence and the strength of will to abandon them. Here, the division is strictly individualist and occurs *within* a single person. It entails no obvious political implications.

Nevertheless, Berlin continues, a highly undesirable development occurred in Kant's moral philosophy, in which the division between the two selves took a stronger form. As self-mastery came to be conceptualised as rational self-direction, the two selves were equated with the rational–irrational pair. Consider the case of the smoker again. From the Kantian point of view, the smoker is divided between his or her 'rational self' that knows he or she should quit smoking and his or her 'irrational self' that is unable to do what its rational counterpart knows he or she ought to do. To be free, then, means to *subordinate* one's irrational desires to the demands of one's rational self, so as to achieve self-mastery. Herein lies, according to Berlin, the vulnerability of positive liberty. Notwithstanding the aforementioned advantage of being able to account for the sense of 'false liberty', the rationalist version of the mythology of the real self has the disadvantage of allowing the deprivation of the fulfilment of one's actually held desires to be seen as compatible with freedom. In fact, such deprivation may be seen as liberating, so long as the desires are deemed irrational or otherwise unworthy of pursuit. This reasoning allows would-be interferers, including tyrants, to claim that they are helping one realise one's 'true freedom' when they in fact coerce one into doing something one would not otherwise do. Similarly, it allows interferers to claim that they are merely blocking the exercise of one's 'false liberty' when they in fact prevent one from doing what one actually and expressly wants to do. The concept of positive liberty can in this way be appropriated by external interferers to deprive one of negative liberty in the name of 'true freedom'. Self-mastery gives way to mastery by others.

According to Berlin's controversial interpretation, the seeds of tyrannical oppression sown in Kant's moral philosophy fully matured in Rousseau's political theory. Both thinkers conceptualised freedom as 'obedience to self-imposed injunctions'.[50] However, while Kant's conception of freedom remained individualist, Rousseau *collectivised* it by integrating the rational self into a larger whole of the general will, dismissing the irrational self as merely pursuing one's private and particular interests. Expressed in his well-known phrase in *The Social Contract*, 'forcing men to be free', Rousseau offered a theoretical justification for the subordination of individuals' actually held wishes and desires to the collective demands of the state. This Berlin criticises in the strongest possible terms, going so far as to write that 'there is not a dictator in the West who in the years after Rousseau did not use this monstrous paradox in order to justify his behaviour'.[51] Berlin's genealogy of positive liberty beginning with the Stoics thus culminates in Rousseau via Kant, paving the way for positive liberty-based tyrants and totalitarian leaders, including Lenin and Stalin. This might strike readers today as exaggerated, even ridiculously so, for Berlin effectively suggests that Kant anticipated Stalin. Nevertheless, his argument is based on two ideas that were popular in the mid-twentieth century, if not today: first, that Rousseau, Hegel and Marx were precursors to twentieth-century totalitarians; and second, that Rousseau bridged Kant and Hegel (and by implication Marx) theoretically. Both claims were indeed made by Bertrand Russell, who wrote that 'Hitler is an outcome of Rousseau' and that Rousseau and Kant unintentionally 'gave rise to' both Hitler and Stalin.[52] Berlin's genealogy of positive liberty works out the full implications of those two claims combined.

The Primacy of Negative Liberty

As must already be clear, one important line of argument Berlin deploys in defence of negative liberty is an indirect one: negative liberty is *less* vulnerable to abuse than its positive counterpart. He makes the historical observation that, *as a matter of fact*, tyrants and dictators have appropriated positive liberty to such an extent that the concept by the mid-twentieth century had morphed into 'something close to a pure totalitarian doctrine'.[53] Here, Berlin undoubtedly has Soviet leaders in mind as his principal target of criticism, and commentators are right in detecting a hint of 'the "us" and "them" logic animating the Cold War' on the relevant pages.[54] Berlin himself is candid about his political commitment. For example, he acknowledges in a later interview that, when he wrote 'Two Concepts', he 'was maddened by all the marxist cheating which went on, all the things that were said about "true liberty", Stalinist and communist patter about "true freedom"'.[55] This is hardly a projection of his later interests onto his past. His 1969 'Introduction' already made it clear that his strong emphasis on the downside of positive liberty was to a significant extent circumstantial, writing that 'whereas liberal ultra-individualism could scarcely be said to be a rising force at present, the rhetoric of "positive" liberty [. . .] continues to play its historic role [. . .] as a cloak for despotism in the name of a wider freedom'.[56] To this extent, 'Two Concepts' is indeed what its readers often take it to be: a Cold War text.

This, however, does not mean that the negative/positive distinction corresponds to the liberal/communist distinction or even the liberal/illiberal one. While Berlin's list of positive liberty theorists includes 'the last disciples of Hegel and Marx' as well as their politically dubious predecessors, including Fichte and Rousseau, it also includes the politically quietist Stoics, Kierkegaard and 'Buddhist sages', and Kantian liberals such as T. H. Green, F. H. Bradley and Bernard Bosanquet.[57] In fact, Berlin goes so far as to argue that positive liberty via Kant 'enters into the tradition of liberal individualism at least as deeply as the "negative" concept of freedom'.[58] In short, some advocates of positive liberty are anti-liberal; others are not. Berlin's list of negative liberty theorists is similarly a mixed bag, containing authoritarian Hobbes and the liberal-authoritarian hybrid Jeremy Bentham, as well as classical liberals such as Constant, Mill and Tocqueville. It is notable in this context that Berlin used the liberal/romantic dichotomy to classify various conceptions of liberty in his work prior to 'Two Concepts'.[59] But he came to realise by 1958 that not all liberals endorsed negative liberty (consider Green), and that not all negative liberty theorists were liberals (consider Hobbes). Consequently, he abandoned the liberal/romantic distinction for the negative/positive pair, to which he adhered for the rest of his life.

Observe, further, that Berlin's theoretical critique of positive liberty is not predicated on his historical observations about the abuses of this concept in empirical reality. Of course, the force of his critique would have been significantly diminished if his historical observations were inaccurate. However, even if he were wrong about the historical connections between positive liberty and actually existing tyrannies, dictatorships and totalitarianisms, the central argument he makes would be valid as a stand-alone theoretical argument: positive liberty as self-mastery is vulnerable to political abuse to the extent that it contains within itself the idea of a divided self that may be appropriated by external interferers. Negative liberty is superior to its positive counterpart at least insofar as it is exempted from the risk of such abuse. 'To stress negative freedom', he later said, 'is never to deny positive freedom. To stress positive freedom is often to deny negative.'[60]

Nevertheless, the more important argument Berlin makes in defence of negative liberty is distinct from his claims about the vulnerability of positive liberty. It is anchored in his flagship idea that has come to be known as 'value pluralism'. The core of this idea consists in the observations that the number of ultimate and objective values that human beings pursue and live by is neither one nor infinite, but plural; and that those values are not always harmonisable or commensurable with each other, so that conflict between good and good (apart from conflict between good and evil) often necessarily takes place and loss is sometimes inevitable.[61] In Berlin's words,

> The world that we encounter in ordinary experience is one in which we are faced with choices between ends equally ultimate, and claims equally absolute, the realisation of some of which must inevitably involve the sacrifice of others. Indeed, it is because this is their situation that men place such immense value upon the freedom to choose [. . .]. If, as I believe, the ends of men are many, and not all of them are in principle compatible with each other, then the possibility of conflict—and of tragedy—can never wholly be eliminated from human life, either personal or social. The necessity of choosing between absolute claims is then an inescapable characteristic of the human condition. This gives its value to freedom as Acton conceived of it—as an end in itself, and not as a temporary need.[62]

If pluralism in this sense is true and not all values are in principle compatible or commensurable with each other, human beings must of necessity choose between objective and ultimate values: for example, between liberty and equality, and between efficiency and spontaneity. Since negative liberty (unlike its positive counterpart) assigns fundamental normative significance to the freedom of the individual to choose for him- or herself what is good for him or her, it is better attuned to the unavoidability of value conflict and must therefore be considered a 'truer and more humane ideal' than positive liberty.[63] While Berlin would have more to say on his conception of pluralism in his subsequent career, 'Two Concepts' already makes it clear that the value of negative liberty is ultimately grounded in the key implication of what he takes to be the truth of value pluralism: that the human being is a choice-making creature.[64] As he puts it

later, 'making choices is intrinsic to being a human being'.[65] Conversely, to 'refrain from choosing [...] would make you *inhuman*'.[66]

Berlin's value pluralist defence of negative liberty may be seen more clearly
if we turn to his critique and appropriation of Mill's work.[67] He draws a sharp
contrast between the liberal and consequentialist sides of Mill's thought to
downplay the significance of the latter. *Pace* Mill the consequentialist, Berlin
argues, the primary reason why negative liberty is valuable is not that it is instrumental in the development of men and women's individuality, which in
turn promotes the diversity of interests and opinions that is supposed to be
instrumental in the collective progress of civilised society. Berlin's objection
is twofold. First, the consequentialist reasoning is empirically unfounded,
because individuality can flourish to the highest degree in 'severely disciplined
communities' as well as in 'more tolerant or indifferent societies'.[68] Berlin believed that he saw strong, possibly conclusive, evidence to demonstrate this
during his visit to the Soviet Union in 1945–46, when he met the poet Anna
Akhmatova, the writer Boris Pasternak and others who defended their artistic
integrity under Stalinist rule.[69] Their freedom of expression was significantly
restricted and yet their creative powers remained undiminished. The vitality
of these Russian artists showed that Mill had overstated his case when he
wrote that '[g]enius can only breathe freely in an *atmosphere* of freedom'.[70]
Second, Mill's consequentialist argument is redundant, because what ultimately makes negative liberty intrinsically valuable is the implication of value
pluralism for human life: that human beings are destined to choose between
ultimate and objective values. This makes the freedom of choice an essential
part of what it means to be human. Mill the defender of liberty saw this, Berlin
suggests, although Mill the consequentialist failed to see it. This is why Berlin
presents his defence of negative liberty as a restatement of Mill's argument in
On Liberty. The truth that the human being is a choice-making creature is the
ultimate foundation of the value of negative liberty.

As Berlin himself acknowledges, his discussion of Mill's conception of liberty is not an impartial explanation. Rather, it is a reconstruction of Mill's main
argument, which he incorporates into his own theory of freedom. However,
he does not explicate precisely where he departs from Mill. Nor does he fully
acknowledge the degree of interpretive violence that he inflicts on Mill's work.
In fact, while Berlin gives the impression that he does not alter the substance
of Mill's conception of liberty while modifying Mill's justification for it, his
own conception of negative liberty is not as Millian as he presents it to be. It
is certainly true that Mill has Berlinian negative liberty partly in mind when
he characterises freedom as consisting in 'pursuing our own good in our own
way'.[71] Nevertheless, as Michael Freeden observes, Mill's emphasis is not only
on the ability to choose but also on the exercise of the chosen act, and his

conception of liberty is 'not merely the passive condition of not being inter-
fered with, but the active one of cultivating valuable behaviour and purposes'.[72]
In short, it integrates both negative and positive components.[73] Berlin's negative liberty, by contrast, is more unequivocally negative. True, as I have discussed, it displays important ambiguities and complexities, as his emphasis
oscillates between the number and quality of options available to the liberty-
holder on the one hand and the absence of relevant interference on the other.
This oscillation does not stem from his ambivalence towards negative liberty,
however, but from his ambition to form the most satisfactory conception of
it, grounded in the idea that the human being is a choice-making creature.

Finally, let me emphasise that Berlin does not dismiss positive liberty as
invalid or worthless. It is true that 'Two Concepts' on its own is a rather partisan piece, concerned to highlight the susceptibility of the positive concept
to appropriation and political abuse. Nevertheless, responding to his critics'
charges, Berlin repeatedly emphasised in his post-1958 work that he was aware
of the validity of positive liberty. He said, for example, that '[p]ositive liberty
[. . .] is a valid universal goal' and that it 'is fundamentally a metaphor based
on the idea of negative freedom, but it's a metaphor for something *absolutely
genuine*.'[74] One should not take remarks such as these as mere afterthoughts
that occurred to the author under attack. Berlin's unpublished and posthumously published papers in fact show that, prior to 1958, he had felt even *stronger* ambivalence towards what he would later call positive liberty.[75] This is not
to say, however, that Berlin appreciates positive and negative liberty equally.
Rather, he sees the former as one option, and the latter as that on the basis of
which one may choose between multiple options. To extend his own imagery,
positive liberty is one of the many open doors one may walk through if one
chooses to, whereas negative liberty designates the prior condition of having
various open doors in the first place. The life of a person who does not exercise
positive liberty may be impoverished. But the life of a person who does not
have a measure of negative liberty is unbearable—in fact, it is *inhuman*. To this
extent, negative liberty has primacy over positive liberty.

Arendt's Theory of Freedom

Hannah Arendt was fifty-two years old when she gave her lecture on 'Freiheit
und Politik' in Zurich in 1958. It is only to be expected that she would have
more to say on freedom, both before and after the lecture. Still, the durability
of her interest in the topic may surprise us. Her first substantive discussion of
freedom is found in her doctoral dissertation on Augustine, completed in
1929.[76] Her initial interest in the specifically political concept of freedom
emerged in the turbulent 1930s.[77] Her wartime essays repeatedly discussed the

'struggle for freedom' against Nazism;[78] and her subsequent work contained important analyses of various forms of unfreedom under totalitarian rule, culminating in *The Origins of Totalitarianism*.[79] As I shall elaborate in the next chapter, this was followed by her extensive study of the history of Western political thought during the 1950s, when she worked towards a book on Marx and Marxism that she never completed. This effort, however, gave rise to her mature political theory, at the heart of which lies her view of politics, freedom and action and their intricate connections. It is to this view that I now turn.

Arendt on Negative Liberty

It is not known whether Hannah Arendt ever read Berlin's 'Two Concepts of Liberty'.[80] The Stevenson Library of Bard College preserves a part—consisting of four thousand items—of her personal library. This contains a highly abridged version of 'Two Concepts', included in Anthony Quinton's anthology of essays, *Political Philosophy*, published in 1967.[81] But Arendt's copy of this book shows no sign of extensive use: in fact, it could be sold as 'very good' at a second-hand bookstore notwithstanding being over fifty years old.[82] Of course, it is possible that Arendt read a library copy of Berlin's *Four Essays on Liberty* or had a copy of it that has been lost. Nevertheless, there is no known evidence to indicate that she was familiar with Berlin's 'Two Concepts'. She never mentioned the essay. Nor did she ever refer to other writing by Berlin on liberty/freedom. While she relied on his work to navigate her way through Russian intellectual history, she chose other interlocutors when it came to liberty/freedom.

This is not to say that Arendt was unfamiliar with the distinction between negative and positive liberty. As many scholars have noted, Berlin did not invent, but appropriated, this distinction, which dates back at least to the late eighteenth century.[83] Arendt herself contrasted 'psychologically negative' and 'psychologically positive' freedom in a *Denktagebuch* entry dated as early as June 1951—that is, seven years before Berlin's delivery of 'Two Concepts' as a lecture.[84] More interesting still is her *Denktagebuch* entry of July 1953, in which she contrasts the Christian and Greek conceptions of freedom, characterising the former as 'negative', as 'frei von . . .' (free from . . .), and the latter as 'positive', in terms of 'ein πολίτης sein, nicht Sklave sein' (to be a citizen, not be a slave).[85] In addition, she was familiar with other pre-Berlinian uses of the negative/positive distinction, including Martin Heidegger's in 'On the Essence of Truth', originally composed as a lecture in 1930 and later published in 1943.[86] Freedom, Heidegger writes, is not what 'common sense' would have us believe. It is neither 'negative' nor 'positive', neither the 'mere absence of constraint with respect to what we can or cannot do' nor 'mere readiness for what is required and necessary'. Prior to these two concepts, Heidegger declares, is a third concept of freedom. This is ontological freedom as 'engagement in the disclosure of beings as such'.[87]

How Arendt appropriated Heidegger's discussion of 'the disclosure of beings' in her theory of freedom will be discussed shortly. For now, consider her comments on negative liberty. One thing to note is that she typically uses 'negative liberties' in the plural to designate specific items such as the 'freedom of movement' and 'free[dom] from want and fear'.[88] But this does not mean that she never discusses negative liberty in the singular. She occasionally does so to refer to something akin to Benjamin Constant's 'liberty of the moderns', associating it with 'freedom from unjustified restraint', and seeing the state as the principal entity liable to impose such restraint.[89] Importantly, she is not hostile to either negative liberty in the singular or negative liberties in the plural. Her tone of discussion is more or less neutral, attributing the negative concept to thinkers to whom she is broadly sympathetic, such as William Blackstone, Montesquieu and the American Framers. Nevertheless, she considers negative liberty or liberties to be *inadequate*, and sees them in instrumental terms, as something that is necessary for pursuing higher goals or ideals. Among these is what she calls 'political freedom', which she claims as her own conception.

Political Freedom

What, then, is Arendt's political freedom, and wherein lies its value? On a general level, one is politically free in Arendt's sense when one is acting and interacting, and speaking and deliberating with others about matters of public concern in a formally or informally institutionalised public realm. To be free is to exercise an opportunity for political participation. To use Berlin's imagery, a free person in Arendt's sense is not somebody standing in front of numerous attractive open doors, but somebody actually walking through a door *to* politics. Freedom, for her, is 'a state of being manifest in action'.[90]

To be politically free requires a set of preconditions. One needs to eat, drink, sleep and satisfy basic biological needs prior to participating in politics. In addition, political participation typically assumes the existence of a network of fairly stable and durable institutions, from the constitution and other laws of the land to non-legal customs and practices, regulating political conduct, governing the deliberative process and decision-making procedures and overseeing the proper implementation of agreed policies.[91] Men and women enter such a network of institutions as citizens. Citizenship makes people equal for political purposes, abstracting various natural differences that they have as human beings. It enables citizens to construct public *personae* to appear before and among their fellow citizens. Those who do not have citizenship—slaves, women and manual labourers in antiquity and refugees and the stateless in modern times, among others—are excluded from an established public realm and hence lack an elementary condition for political freedom. Arendt consequently uses the term 'liberation' to refer to the lifting of both biological and legal barriers to entering the public realm. To be 'liberated' is to have a status for political participation. To be free is to make use of that status.[92]

However, the significance of *formal* institutions for Arendt's conception of political freedom should not be overstated. For one thing, she argues that one could be politically free even when formal institutions are not (yet) in place. For example, those who revolted against British rule in colonial America enjoyed limited legal protection to exercise their freedom to act, but this did not prevent them from acting freely to declare independence, write and ratify a new constitution and lay the foundation for a new free republic. Similarly, those who rose against Soviet domination in Hungary in 1956 had no legal right to do so, but this did not prevent them from exercising their political freedom to act in concert to protest against communist rule (see further Chapter 6). Besides, Arendt is insistent on the defectiveness of laws unsupported by a matching political culture, echoing the wisdom of sociologically oriented mid-twentieth-century political scientists such as Robert Dahl, Gabriel Almond and Sidney Verba.[93] This is not to say that this body of work *directly* influenced Arendt. She was too hostile to the idea of applying scientific methods to the study of politics to appreciate these political scientists' contributions in an impartial manner. Nevertheless, her view was closer to theirs than she cared to admit, not least because both looked to aspects of American practices to theorise democratic politics. She cites John Adams to make her point: 'a constitution is a standard, a pillar, and a bond when it is understood, approved and beloved. But without this intelligence and attachment, it might as well be a kite or balloon, flying in the air.'[94] While political freedom is significantly promoted by formal institutions, it is not guaranteed by them and can sometimes manifest itself without them.

What ultimately enables political freedom, then, is what Arendt calls the 'in-between', or the space that simultaneously 'relates and separates' people.[95] More specifically, it is the politicised 'in-between', or the 'space of appearance', where men and women as citizens gather together, show the courage to speak and act in public, express the willingness to hear what others have to say and see what others have to do, and form and exchange opinions about others' words and deeds. Arendt repeatedly claims that human beings have the built-in potential to speak and act to bring the space of appearance into being in this way, and calls this potential 'human plurality'. This is, in Arendt's words, 'specifically *the* condition—not only the *conditio sine qua non*, but the *conditio per quam*—of all political life'.[96]

To see her conception of political freedom in more detail, consider the analogy that Arendt repeatedly draws between performing arts and freedom experienced in political action. She claims that the analogy is hardly new because 'Greeks always used such metaphors as flute-playing, dancing, healing, and sea-faring to distinguish political from other activities'.[97] That said, she still proposes a recognisably 'Arendtian' interpretation of the Greek past to present her conception of political freedom. Consider by way of illustration an artist whose life is devoted to dance. Wherein lies his or her freedom? The dancer is free, according to the Berlinian negative conception, if he or she is not prevented, physically or psychologically, or directly or indirectly, by others from dancing when he or she chooses to dance. According to Arendt's Greek-inspired conception, by contrast, the dancer is free when he or she is actually dancing in such a way that he or she may be meaningfully described as realising what his or her life is for, namely, dance. This normally requires certain preconditions and settings, from a proper pair of shoes to a stage and an audience. Similarly, Arendtian political action takes place in 'a kind of theater' regulated by laws, citizenship and other institutional settings.[98] In both performing arts and politics, Arendt observes, excellence or 'virtuosity of performance' is 'decisive'.[99]

Like all analogies, that of Arendt between politics and performing arts is not without limitations. In fact, it is misleading in one respect: while a dancer may be able to dance alone, an Arendtian freedom-holder cannot be alone to make use of his or her freedom and take political action. This is the case because to act politically in Arendt's sense is always to act in concert with others. The image of the artist that Arendt tacitly assumes is that not of a lone performer, but of a member of a company. Notwithstanding this limitation, however, her analogy effectively highlights one central feature that political freedom shares with performing arts: namely, that 'the accomplishment lies in the performance itself and not in an end product'.[100] Of course, a great dancer's or a flute-player's performance may be instrumental in improving individuals' wellbeing, enriching human culture, stimulating the economy and so on. But it seems perverse to say that these results or end products exhaust the value of performing arts. The same is true of Arendtian politics. She does not deny that it is ideal if one's exercise of political freedom results in desirable consequences, such as a written constitution, but she refuses to equate the significance of an action with the consequences of it. That is why she praises stillborn revolutions such as the Hungarian uprising no less than the more successful American Revolution. Commenting on the 'most glorious hours' of the 'Hungarian people' in 1956, she writes that the 'stature' of the revolutionary uprising 'will not depend upon victory or defeat'.[101] Whether an action is successful is one thing; whether it is great is another. The former depends on the consequences; the latter, on virtuosity.

Political Freedom and Positive Liberty

Should Arendt's political freedom be seen as a subspecies of positive liberty? The answer is an unambiguous 'no' if we mean by 'positive liberty' Berlinian freedom as self-mastery. This, as I discussed earlier, may be interpreted in various ways and yet always refers to mastery over one's *internal* desires, wishes and preferences. Contrary to some critics' allegations, Arendt's conception of political freedom is emphatically not this type of self-mastery.[102] This is the case because the exercise of Arendtian political freedom is possible only in the sphere of intersubjectivity. If one is to be an Arendtian political actor, one needs *others* before and among whom one exercises freedom. The Arendtian actor never attains self-mastery, firstly because what he or she can do depends on the deeds of others (fellow citizens qua co-actors), and secondly because what his or her action means depends on the opinions and judgements of others (fellow citizens qua spectators). Berlinian positive liberty, by contrast, may be exercised in complete solitude. One does not rely on others to be a master of oneself. Moreover, one does not even need oneself to be one's own master because, as I have discussed, the surest way of controlling one's frustratable desires is suicide.[103] It is no coincidence that Arendt thinks poorly of Berlinian positive liberty theorists from the Stoics to Hegel and Marx. Among this group of thinkers Kant alone attracts Arendt's sympathy and admiration, but the aspect of his work she appreciates is not his moral philosophy but his aesthetics and theory of judgement.[104] Although Arendt does not use the term 'self-mastery' to challenge Berlinian positive liberty, she effectively challenges it by way of criticising what she calls 'sovereignty' or 'sovereign freedom', understood as the ability of an individual or a collectivity to exercise exclusive control over oneself or itself.[105] Slight differences of emphasis notwithstanding, what is wrong with freedom as sovereignty and with freedom as self-mastery *alike* is the failure to see that freedom is crucially dependent on the presence of others. 'If men wish to be free', Arendt writes, 'it is precisely sovereignty they must renounce.'[106] To rephrase this in Berlinian terms, if men wish to be free, it is positive liberty as self-mastery they must renounce.[107]

This, however, is not to say that Arendt's conception of political freedom may not be called 'positive' in a broader, non-Berlinian sense. In fact, it is a positive conception to the extent that it cannot be adequately characterised (negatively) as the *absence* of unfreedom, as *non*-X. Furthermore, it might be seen as a highly idiosyncratic member of the family of conceptions known as 'freedom as self-realisation'. This family conceptualises freedom in terms of 'a pattern of action of a certain kind', rather than the absence of constraint or interference by others.[108] In its strong form, it equates freedom with 'the fulfilment of one's possibilities'.[109] More specifically still, the subspecies—or, perhaps, cousin—of self-realisation integral to Arendt's political freedom is *self-disclosure*. She herself uses this and related terms, including the 'disclosure of who somebody is', the 'disclosure of the subject' and the 'disclosure of the agent'.[110] Her rationale for preferring the term 'self-disclosure' to 'self-realisation' seems to be that the former, unlike the latter, implies the presence of others. To disclose oneself is always to disclose oneself *to somebody else*. It is worth noting in this context that Arendt discusses performing arts in stark contrast with craftsmanship, associating the former with 'acting' and the latter with 'making'. A carpenter absorbed in his or her work *alone* may be realising him- or herself. But he or she cannot be said to be disclosing him- or herself because there is nobody *to whom* the carpenter discloses him- or herself. By contrast, a dancer performing in the presence of an audience is disclosing as well as realising him- or herself. The same is true of the Arendtian political actor. Whenever one exercises the political freedom to act, one discloses oneself *to* those who witness what one does and who one is. 'Speech and action', Arendt writes, 'are the modes in which human beings appear to each other [. . .] *qua* men.'[111]

A further advantage of 'self-disclosure', from Arendt's point of view, is that it is not tainted by deterministic connotations that the term 'self-realisation' might evoke. Consider the classic teleological metaphor of the acorn and the oak tree, applied to the idea of self-realisation. According to Arendt, human beings are like acorns to the extent that they have the potentiality to develop and flourish under suitable conditions; and if they do, she writes, they flourish in 'the shining brightness we once called glory'.[112] But human beings differ from teleologically conceptualised acorns in two crucial respects. One concerns individuality. When a human being exercises his or her freedom to act and realises his or her potentiality in full, he or she discloses his or her *unique identity*. By contrast, when an acorn matures into an oak tree, it remains an anonymous member of the species, indistinguishable from and interchangeable with other oak trees. Second, while we know in advance that an acorn will mature into an oak tree if it realises its potentiality, nobody knows in advance who an Arendtian actor will be until he or she discloses him- or herself. Only after the fulfilment of one's potential does one find, in retrospect, who one (potentially) was and now is. As Bonnie Honig perceptively writes, paraphrasing Arendt, the unique identity one acquires as a result of free action is a 'reward' for one's performance.[113]

Political Freedom and Republican Liberty

Although it is sometimes described as 'republican',[114] Arendt's political freedom should also be distinguished from the neo-republican concept of liberty recently developed by Quentin Skinner, Philip Pettit and others.[115] According to this group of theorists, liberty should be conceptualised as non-domination, rather than non-interference. The former is more satisfactory than the latter because one may be made unfree even if one is entirely free from *actual* interference, so long as one is aware that someone else is in a position (potentially) to interfere with one—so long as, that is, somebody else is in a position to dominate. On this understanding, one's awareness that somebody *can* exercise arbitrary power over one is enough for one to stop acting or thinking freely, for this awareness prevents one from thinking or acting in ways that could trigger actual interference by one's master. Freedom as non-domination is a social ideal that demands a degree of equality among relevant parties.

It is true that Arendt and neo-republicans can be meaningfully contrasted with negative liberty theorists, such as Berlin, to the extent that both see an essential connection between political participation and individual freedom. Nevertheless, they differ from each other in two crucial respects. First, Arendt criticises both the substance of negative liberty and the means of securing it, whereas neo-republicans protest solely at the means. Arendt (unlike neo-republicans) sees intrinsic value in political participation. Neo-republicans (unlike Arendt) consider political participation important only insofar as it is instrumental in 'avoiding the evils associated with interference'.[116] It may be said that Arendt makes a positive-incentive argument for political participation, emphasising how rewarding it is to act in concert with others. As Jeremy Arnold nicely puts it, Arendtian freedom experienced in political participation 'often induce[s] the feeling or thought that one would rather not be anywhere else or doing anything else than just being where one is or doing what one is doing'.[117] Neo-republicans, by contrast, make a negative-incentive argument for political participation. They warn us about the risk that the relations of domination may arise if we do not take part in politics to a sufficient extent.

The other major point of disagreement between Arendt and contemporary neo-republicans concerns who should or would participate in politics. The latter generally think that *all* citizens should serve the republic if they wish to secure individual liberty, because a failure to do so would provide room for the rise of dominating power. Arendt, by contrast, suggests that the self-chosen *few* would voluntarily participate in politics because they 'have a taste for public freedom and cannot be "happy" without it'.[118] She believes that everyone should be given the opportunity to participate in politics. But she is aware that some people will choose not to make use of that opportunity, and insists that they ought *not* to be coerced into political life. Arendt's political theory may be less realistic than its neo-republican counterpart to the extent that it assumes that political participation can make people 'happy' in a strong, eudaemonic sense. Nevertheless, her theory is more realistic in another respect, in that she does not, unlike Machiavelli and his successors, demand that unwilling citizens perform public duties.[119] In Arendt's view, 'the task of good government' is no more than 'to assure [the self-chosen few] of their rightful place in the public realm'.[120] Exclusion from the public realm should always be self-exclusion.

This means that Arendt, like Berlin and other liberals, recognises the negative liberty 'to choose *not* to engage in politics' as an important option.[121] To have no such liberty is to live under tyranny, and she does not fail to underline the significant difference between tyranny and 'constitutional, limited government', where citizens have the right, but are under no legal obligation, to participate in politics.[122] Recall in this context my earlier discussion about Arendt's appreciation of the (instrumental) value of negative liberty/liberties. According to her, 'freedom from politics' is 'one of the most important negative liberties we have enjoyed since the end of the ancient world'.[123] It is no small achievement for people to liberate themselves from tyrannical rule, and Arendt does not belittle the significance of such liberation. This, however, hardly makes her a supporter of the anti-perfectionist liberalism running from Berlin to Rawls. On the contrary, she departs from the liberal conventions in insisting that freedom from politics is normatively inadequate and in claiming that human beings can realise their potential in full only in political action. To use Berlin's imagery again, on Arendt's view, a person in liberal society must be able to have many open doors of various kinds in front of him or her, including the bourgeois door to withdrawal from politics and enjoyment of privacy and family life. However, there is only one door to choose to walk through if a person is to be genuinely free and to lead a fulfilling life. That is the door leading *to* 'the political way of life'.[124] This is the case because, according to Arendt, to be human is to be free, and to be free is to act.[125]

Political Freedom and Natality

Why does Arendt privilege politics over other human activities? Why does she repeatedly underline the intrinsic connection between political freedom and 'a truly human life'?[126] The answer is found in her understanding of the human condition—of what it means to be human. True, she is reluctant to discuss 'human nature' in general or 'Man' in the abstract.[127] But what she rejects is a static conception of human nature. She does not refrain from making important general claims about human beings, so long as the claims are about a stable and yet changeable, '*quasi*-transcendental' set of conditions.[128] These conditions reveal a general, albeit non-absolute, structure of human beings' concrete existence.

To some extent, it is a matter of mere semantics whether the term 'human nature' should be avoided due to its unfortunately essentialist connotations.

Few serious thinkers in modernity, and surely none after Darwin, have considered nature—let alone human nature—to be static, fixed or unchangeable.[129] Nevertheless, the term 'human nature' is often seen as implying such essentialism, and Arendt proposes, in *The Human Condition*, to use the term 'human condition' to pre-empt confusion. Her terminological preference, however, is more than a simple effort to pre-empt confusion. It also signals her broadly Heideggerian orientation that draws our attention to 'conditions' understood as defining limits. At every moment of their lives men and women find themselves amid a set of conditions that they neither created nor are able to overcome or transcend. This does not only mean that they, as bodily beings, cannot escape certain physical conditions and cannot, for example, release themselves from gravity. It also means, more importantly, that each and every human being at the moment of birth enters a world that is already inhabited by other human beings, permeated by their relationships and filled with human-made objects, institutions, cultures and so on. This texture of human life exists not because of what one does but because of what generations before one was born have done. Whatever one does in one's life cannot undo this pre-existing texture; it can only add new threads of meaning to it. In this sense, Arendt writes, 'human existence is conditioned existence'.[130] It is important to keep in mind in this context that conditions are not the same as constraints, and limits are not the same as limitations.[131] On the contrary, conditionality in Arendt's sense demarcates the realm of possibility; what men and women can do, as well as cannot do, depends on the human condition. To understand how men and women are conditioned in this sense is to understand what it means to be human.

Arendt builds on Heidegger and Aristotle to theorise the human condition. To begin with, consider her characterisation of the human being in quasi-Heideggerian terms as a 'natal'. This is a direct and explicit response to Heidegger's conception of mortality as a fundamental existential condition of 'man', or *Dasein* in Heidegger's terminology. According to Heidegger, three central features of death make mortality, or the possibility of death, differ from all other possibilities open to human beings. First, mortality is omnipresent, in that one may die literally at any moment. Second, it is unavoidable, in that each and every one of us must die one day. Third, however, death is unrealisable or '*distinctly* impending', in that one is no longer there to experience it when the possibility of one's own death materialises.[132] So understood, mortality informs human beings of their fundamental finitude: that '[o]ur birth was not necessary; the course of our life could have been otherwise; its continuation from moment to moment is no more than a fact; and it will come to an end at some point.'[133] This being so, it is difficult for human beings to face and bear their own mortality. However, one does not live authentically unless one comes to terms with one's own limits and becomes appropriately responsive to one's being-unto-death. In this sense, as Peter Gordon puts it, Heidegger's 'normative image of humanity' consists above all in finitude and responsiveness.[134]

Arendt inherits this theme from Heidegger and subverts it to develop her own understanding of the human condition. She certainly does not deny that mortality is a fundamental human condition. Nevertheless, she has remarkably little to say on death or mortality per se, and the little she has to say often concerns the *immortality* of the great deeds and words that outlast the relevant actor's own death.[135] The reason for this apparent omission is that mortality is *irrelevant* to the political mode of being to which much of her work is devoted.[136] To understand *this* mode, she draws our attention to the other end of the human life that terminates with death: to birth. According to Arendt, natality, the possibility of birth, sets a defining limit no less fundamental than mortality to the being of human beings. Simply put, each and every one had to be born in order to *be*. Like Heidegger, Arendt considers human beings to be fundamentally conditioned, and (again like him) she wants men and women to become appropriately responsive to human finitude. But the responsiveness she wants them to cultivate is the responsiveness to natality, rather than to mortality. This requires men and women to become attuned to their capacity for action because to 'actualiz[e] the human condition of natality' means 'to act [. . .], to take an initiative, to begin [. . .], to set something into motion'.[137] To refrain from acting is not like refraining from taking up any other random option available to human beings. On the contrary, it means a *failure* to properly appreciate the human condition. In this sense, she writes, 'no human being can refrain [from acting] and still be human.'[138]

In this way, Arendt extracts a highly un-Heideggerian lesson from her critical engagement with Heidegger's work. On her view, action qua the actualisation of the human condition of natality is not one of many (of what Heidegger termed) existentiell possibilities that the world has to offer us. On the contrary, she writes,

> With words and deeds we insert ourselves into the human world, and this insertion is like a second birth, in which we confirm and take upon ourselves the naked fact of our original physical appearance. [. . . The] impulse [of this insertion] springs from the beginning which came into the world when we were born and to which we respond by beginning something new on our own initiative. [. . .] Because they are *initium*, newcomers and beginners by virtue of birth, men take initiative, are prompted into action.[139]

Arendt has a specific type of beginning in mind when she discusses beginning in relation to natality: beginning as interruption. Here again, she relentlessly appropriates her former teacher's work, firstly reiterating Heidegger's cyclical conception of nature. All creatures in nature, including plants, animals and *Homo sapiens* as biological species, endlessly reproduce themselves, following their own species-wise instincts and behavioural patterns. We cannot in a proper sense speak of 'individual' flowers, 'individual' bees or even 'individual' members of *Homo sapiens*, because these are mere instantiations of their respective species-beings. They are essentially replaceable with other members of the same species.[140] Human beings qua human beings, by contrast, are 'unique, unexchangeable, and unrepeatable entities'.[141] Each and every one of them leads his or her own life *linearly*, beginning with his or her own singular birth and ending with his or her own singular death. When a human being is born, the cycle of nature is interrupted by the physical appearance of an irreplaceable being who lives such a linear life; and when this being acts to begin something new and to interrupt the cycle of nature, he or she is said to have responded to his or her human condition of natality qua the original fact of physical appearance. To recall, it is the appreciation of the omnipresent, unavoidable and yet unrealisable possibility of death that allows Heidegger's *Dasein* to be aware of his or her own finitude, to take responsibility for his or her own life, and to give him or her the chance to lead an authentic life. By contrast, it is the appreciation of the necessity of birth that allows Arendt's 'natal' to be aware of his or her conditionedness, to recognise his or her ability to act and to take part in political life to respond to his or her natality. If one is to live authentically, one must respond to the call of natality and its demand for actualisation. In this sense, Arendt writes, 'men, though they must die, are not born in order to die but in order to begin.'[142]

Political Freedom and Plurality

Let me turn to another crucial instance of Arendt's appropriation of Heidegger's philosophy, which informs her discussion of *plurality*. She basically accepts his analysis of *Dasein* as a being-in-the-world and being-with. That is, first, one always already finds oneself in a web of relations within which one encounters entities as they present themselves to one, such as benches to sit on and cutlery with which to eat. Second, one always already finds oneself in a world inhabited by others like oneself, because otherwise such a web of relations would be inconceivable. Even that which one supposedly does 'by oneself' presupposes one's being-with-others, such as when one sits on a bench maintained *by somebody else* (the relevant city authority, for example), or uses cutlery manufactured *by somebody else* (a private company that produces household goods, for example). Arendt, in short, shares Heidegger's anti-Cartesian ontology. Furthermore, she partially agrees with his view that 'man' in his average everydayness shows no individuality, conforming to and being lost in the collective and unanimous 'they'. In fact, according to Arendt, Heidegger's hermeneutic phenomenology of average everyday life in terms of the 'they' 'offer[s] most penetrating insights into one of the basic aspects of society'.[143]

This, however, is not to say that she uncritically accepts his diagnosis. On the contrary, she modifies and complements it in a variety of ways—for example, by bringing her own critical perspective to show how 'man' in his average everydayness is increasingly lost in socio-economic activities, rather than in 'idle talk, curiosity and ambiguity', as Heidegger originally suggested in *Being and Time*.[144] In other words, she introduces an innovative conception of 'the social' to enrich Heidegger's analysis of the 'they'.[145] But the point at which Arendt departs from Heidegger most decisively concerns not so much diagnosis as prescription. Heidegger's response to the problem of the inauthenticity of the 'they' is to encourage *Dasein* to step back from the everyday environment, appreciate his or her finitude, hear the call of conscience and resolutely confront his or her being-unto-death. What this precisely means and practically demands is a matter of much debate, which need not concern us here. The relevant point is that Arendt finds Heidegger's suggestions solipsistic. In her view, he at best reiterates philosophy's age-old (Platonic) hostility towards living among and thinking with others,[146] and at worst gives philosophical licence to groundless decisionism, for 'no idea of man guides the selection of the modes of being' in Heidegger's philosophy.[147]

Arendt's critical engagement with Heidegger's being-in-the-world and being-with spanned several decades. Unsurprisingly, she had varying things to say, and she explicitly asked herself in 1970 if she had been right to criticise Heidegger for solipsism in her earlier work.[148] Subsequent scholars have been confronted with a number of interpretive difficulties as a result. Some, such as Seyla Benhabib and Richard Bernstein, have underlined Arendt's harsher comments on Heidegger's supposed solipsism. According to them, Heidegger's existential analytic is solely concerned with forms of 'relating-oneself-to-oneself', and 'there is [nothing] in Heidegger that even approximates what Arendt means by plurality'.[149] Others, such as Dana Villa, argue that even Arendt's most charitable comments on Heidegger do not do justice to the full complexity of Heidegger's attitude towards the 'they'. Contrary to Benhabib and Bernstein, Villa argues that Heidegger's proposal for 'the "transcendence" of fallen everydayness [. . .] can imply the achievement of a more authentic form of *community life*'.[150] Important though it is, this interpretive debate may be set aside for our present purpose, for much of the debate concerns Heidegger's work rather than Arendt's attitude towards it. As for the latter, she on balance expressed rather strong reservations about Heidegger's purported solipsistic tendencies, notwithstanding the aforementioned self-doubt that she came to entertain during the final years of her life. In much of her academic career, she made a sustained effort to appropriate Heideggerian themes to develop her own phenomenology of plurality 'to break with [Heidegger's] own philosophy'.[151]

Of particular relevance to the theme of plurality are the two theoretical moves Arendt makes in opposition to Heidegger. First, she suggests that men and women should embrace their being-in-the-world-with-others: that they should recognise that the world consists not only in useful, 'ready-to-hand' things and their functional relations but also in the 'in-between' of acting men and women; and that they should act together to create such an in-between amid the public-ness of the 'they'. Second, she identifies the political realm as *the* space in which men and women can relate to each other as human beings, disclose their identi-ties to each other and act together not only to create, but also to preserve and institutionalise, the in-between. In short, if one is to live authentically, one ought not to confront death alone and run 'into existential solitude'; rather, one ought to move 'into the light of the public'.[152] In making these suggestions, Arendt follows Karl Jaspers and, behind him, the Kant of the third *Critique*. Her charac-terisation of Jaspers's philosophy indeed strikes an autobiographical note. It at-tempts, Arendt writes, to 'accommodate [...] the modern desire to create, in a world that is no longer a home to us, a human world that could become our home'.[153] Arendt agrees with Heidegger that one could be lost in one's being-with. But she insists, challenging Heidegger and building on Jaspers, that the loss could be remedied by learning to respond properly to the human condition of plurality. In other words, she proposes that we should appreciate the fact that 'men, not Man, live on the earth and inhabit the world'.[154]

The Political Animal

It is against this background of critical inheritance of Heidegger's insights that Arendt's restatement of the Aristotelian notion of the political animal should be understood. As Jeremy Waldron observes, what Arendt means by 'political animal' is very different from some of the major senses that the term signifies in ordinary language, such as a person who relentlessly seeks power, or one who turns everything into an issue of political dispute, or one who likes to talk about politics in order to show off his or her oratorical talent.[155] Rather, what Arendt means is the ideal of a person who comes to the public realm out of a concern for the world, and deliberates and exchanges opinions with his or her fellow citizens about the common good—about *what* a polity should strive for as well as *how* to achieve agreed ends. In engaging in this kind of activity, men and women are rewarded with self-disclosure and the happiness of living with and among their fellow political animals. A person who chooses to with-draw from politics altogether, by contrast, lives an impoverished life. Such a person fails to respond appropriately to his or her natality and plurality, and leaves his or her full potentiality unrealised and his or her identity un-disclosed. Judith Butler's summary of Arendt's thought is to the point: 'No human can be human alone. And no human can be human without acting in concert with others and on conditions of equality.'[156]

Let me return to Mill's discussion of liberty to see in more detail how Arendt's Aristotle-inspired notion of the political animal underpins her conception of political freedom. As I discussed earlier, Mill is more sympathetic to non-negative conceptions of liberty than Berlin is, effectively endorsing aspects of freedom as self-realisation. But he is still strongly committed to a liberal individualism that affirms the multiplicity of ways in which men and women develop their individuality, conceptualise valuable goals and reconceptualise them in light of new experiences, and lead fulfilling lives accordingly. To use Rawlsian terminology, Mill is a pluralist with respect to the competing conceptions of the good. Arendt, by contrast, shows no comparable commitment to liberal moral pluralism.[157] Rather, her conception of the political animal tacitly assumes a monist view of the good, giving normative authority to the political mode of being over the alternative modes. The political mode is conceptualised as the privileged mode of being in which men and women, both as individuals and as a collective 'we', may realise their highest possibilities.[158] Conversely, to be thoroughly apolitical is to have one's natality and plurality dormant. It is to be deprived of the opportunity to lead a truly meaningful life, in which one lives with others 'as a distinct and unique being' with a fully disclosed identity.[159]

It is worth recalling in this context that Arendt makes a highly controversial claim that a 'life with no speech and action' is *less human* than 'the life of an exploiter or a slaveholder'.[160] As we all know today, the ability of ancient Athenian citizens to participate in politics depended on the exploitation of women on the one hand, and the appropriation of slave labour on the other. This, Arendt concedes, makes Athenian citizens' lives 'unjust', but she insists that the unjust lives 'certainly are human'.[161] They are different from the life of a person who never takes the initiative to act and speak in public because 'no human being can refrain [from this initiative] and still be human'.[162] On Arendt's view, to own a slave is to commit a grave injustice, but to refrain from speech and action altogether amounts to a failure of an entirely different order: it is to renounce humanity. She writes, 'A life without speech and action is literally dead to the world; it has ceased to be a human life because it is no longer lived among men.'[163] In her words, 'to be human and to be free are one and the same.'[164]

Let me add a word of caution to avoid misunderstanding. I am aware that my use of the term 'monism' to characterise an important aspect of Arendt's political thought is likely to make some scholars feel uneasy, because much of her work is devoted to the affirmation of plurality. This, together with natality, may be seen as a master concept of Arendt's thought.[165] If so, one may wonder, how can *any* aspect of her work be described as monist? This is an understandable reaction, but it is based on a confusion. It stems from the unfortunate and yet unalterable fact that terms such as 'monism', 'pluralism' and 'plurality' have a number of meanings, some of which have nothing to do with each other. Although Arendt is certainly a pluralist in many senses, she (or anybody else, for that matter) is not a pluralist in each and every known sense of the word.[166] For example, she is committed to what might be called an ontological pluralism that affirms the irreducible differences among human beings, their perspectives and the ways in which they relate to the world. She is also committed to a political (Tocquevillian) pluralism that highlights the significance of vibrant civil society and associational life for democratic politics; and she is additionally committed to another type of political (Schmittian) pluralism that challenges the idea of a homogenising world government and affirms the multiplicity of political units comprising global politics. One could add more items to this list to specify the multiple senses in which Arendt *is* a pluralist.

However, those types of pluralism to which Arendt is committed are distinct from the liberal moral pluralism at issue here: the affirmation of the plurality of conceptions of the good, entailing the categorical denial of the idea that one particular way of life is more human or more fulfilling than others. Arendt is not committed to *this* type of pluralism. She does not believe that the life of a consumer who chooses to do nothing but maximise his or her hedonistic pleasure is as valuable as the life of a citizen who at least occasionally participates in politics. Similarly, Arendt does not think that the life of a risk-taking and initiative-taking entrepreneur, endowed with heroism and the frontier spirit, can be on a par with the life of a citizen who channels his or her energy into politics. As Margaret Canovan observes, if Arendt thought that such an entrepreneur—an energetic and imaginative *homo economicus*—could be as *free* as the active citizen enjoying public happiness, her theory would have shown important similarities to that of Ayn Rand.[167] But Arendt is not an Ayn Rand. She defends a hierarchical division between the political and the economic.[168]

For liberal moral pluralists, what gives worth and dignity to the life of the consumer or that of the entrepreneur is the sheer fact that it is the life that he or she *chose* to live. Arendt does not accept this. In her theoretical framework, the only mode of being that could possibly match the active, political mode is the contemplative one. Her assessment of this mode is deeply ambivalent, for it changes considerably as her career progresses. While the early Arendt was rather hostile to the *bios theoretikos*, the late Arendt came to 'reassess[...] some of her harsh rejections' of it, especially in *The Life of the Mind*.[169] Consequently, it is possible that the late Arendt was moving in the direction of dualism (rather than pluralism), to recognise the *vita contemplativa* and the *vita activa* as equally valuable, equally fulfilling and equally *human*. But I doubt that she ever completely abandoned her ambition to subvert, rather than simply to flatten, the traditional hierarchy in which the *vita contemplativa* is given supremacy over the *vita activa*. I doubt, in other words, that she ever gave up her project to restore the dignity of the *vita activa* against the weight of the tradition. As Dana Villa writes, Arendt 'does want a world in which strong citizenship, and the "free *moeurs*" that sustain it (Tocqueville), have *a clear and distinct moral priority*.'[170]

———

To summarise my argument so far, Arendt endorses political freedom because it is only in political action and speech that the human being can appropriately respond to the human conditions of natality and plurality, realise his or her potential in full, disclose him- or herself, acquire his or her unique identity and have his or her being-in-the-world-with-others reaffirmed. Berlin, by contrast, considers negative liberty to be 'a truer and more humane ideal' because the human being, due to the truth of value pluralism, is a choice-making creature and cannot be otherwise. According to Arendt, freedom in her distinctly political sense 'is the quintessence of the human condition'; according to Berlin, it is the liberty to make unforced choices between multiple options that 'is intrinsic to being a human being'.[171] The two thinkers agree that freedom is essential to humanity. But they disagree on the most satisfactory meaning of freedom, as their views of the human condition significantly differ from each other. What lies beneath their dispute over freedom is therefore a deeper disagreement over the human condition itself—over, that is, what it means to be human. One proposes the vision of the human being as a political animal conditioned by natality and plurality. The other proposes an alternative vision of the human being as a choice-making creature. This is the most fundamental theoretical difference that divides Hannah Arendt and Isaiah Berlin.

Negative Liberty, Political Freedom and Individuality

One scholar who spent much time reflecting on and responding to both of our protagonists' work was Bernard Crick. Thirteen and ten years younger than Arendt and Berlin respectively, Crick was one of the first British scholars to recognise the originality and importance of Arendt's work. Berlin liked and admired Crick, despite the latter's explicit intellectual debt to Arendt, especially in his influential 1962 book *In Defence of Politics*.[172] The two men regularly corresponded with each other in the early 1960s, when Berlin helped

Crick to find an academic job in the UK. When Crick was appointed in 1965 as professor of political theory at the University of Sheffield, he gave an inaugural lecture entitled 'Freedom as Politics', in which he respectfully and yet vigorously challenged Berlin's endorsement of negative liberty and defended an Arendtian conception of 'freedom as politics'.[173] Berlin received a copy of Crick's lecture, to which he responded critically in both his private letters and his 1969 'Introduction' to *Four Essays on Liberty*.[174] As Berlin hardly made any direct comments on Arendt's own writings on freedom, it is worth considering his response to Crick as a proxy for his opinion on Arendt. This allows us to put Arendt's and Berlin's ideas into further conversation.

One interesting question Berlin asks Crick in one of his letters concerns Aristotle's *Politics*. He asks whether Crick 'would not wish to distinguish [his] view from Aristotle's' because the Greek philosopher is more monist than Crick appears to think. Berlin writes that

> when [Aristotle] says [. . .] that liberty (or freedom) *is* doing as one likes [. . .] he condemns it and recommends states in which men are educated by the State to pursue virtuous ends: men are imperfect; there *are* classes, with differing interests; so equilibrium has to be powerful; but there is only *one* end proper to men; eudaimonia (happiness) and human nature is *one* and definable, and so the differences between men and groups are, if not actually regretted, not regarded as either natural or sources of vitality and pleasing variety. Variety is a *very* late ideal![175]

Berlin was probably unaware that Arendt in 'What Is Freedom?' referred to the same part of Aristotle's *Politics* to illustrate the idea of political freedom.[176] At first glance, her reading differs little from Berlin's. She writes that 'the statement "Freedom means the doing what a man likes" is put [by Aristotle] in the mouths of those who do not know what freedom is'.[177] But the lessons Arendt and Berlin extract from Aristotle could scarcely be more different. Whereas Arendt *approvingly* refers to the *Politics* to remind her readers that the 'original field' where freedom was experienced was 'the realm of politics and human affairs',[178] Berlin *disapprovingly* cites Aristotle to question whether Crick is or would like to be as Aristotelian as he says he is. Then, in the same letter, Berlin contrasts Aristotle with Diogenes and Epicurus, who dismissed the significance of the polis, refused to take part in public life and yet, on Berlin's view, remained free. The fact that men like Diogenes and Epicurus did not use their freedom to participate in politics by no means meant that they were unfree, on Berlin's view (though not on Aristotle's). Freedom is a precondition for politics—not vice versa. Berlin's comments on Crick may be read as his comments on Arendt too: 'why are creativity, self-realization etc, *liberty*?'[179]

The contrast between Aristotle on the one hand, and Diogenes and Epicurus on the other, is an issue that Berlin discusses in detail in his 1962 lecture entitled 'The Birth of Greek Individualism'.[180] One might say that this is an archaeological piece, as distinct from the genealogical 'Two Concepts of Liberty'. The latter tracks the evolution of two rival concepts of liberty over centuries. The former, by contrast, focuses on a more limited period when a major change, or a Nietzschean 'transvaluation of values', took place.[181] The period in question is the fourth century BCE. At this 'turning-point in the history of political thought', the classical outlook of Plato, Aristotle, Sophocles, Aeschylus, Thucydides and Herodotus came to be eclipsed by the Hellenistic outlook of Epicurus, Zeno of Citium, Chrysippus and Carneades.[182] Berlin's analysis of this shift is rich and complex, but on the issue of freedom he makes three historical observations reminiscent of Arendt's comparable analysis in 'What Is Freedom?'. First, Arendt and Berlin agree that the concept of negative liberty as something to cherish, rather than to condemn, was entirely unknown in the classical period. Both concur with Benjamin Constant's view that the liberty of the ancients was essentially collectivist, 'consist[ing] in an active and constant participation in collective power'.[183] If Athens was freer than Sparta, Berlin observes, it was freer strictly in this classical sense: Athenians were more willing to 'perform their civic duties [without being coerced into doing so] out of love for their *polis*'.[184] Arendt similarly characterises the classical conception of freedom as 'an exclusively political concept, indeed the quintessence of the city-state and of citizenship'.[185] Second, both Arendt and Berlin downgrade the differences between Stoicism and Epicureanism to contrast these together with their classical rival. Moreover, they paraphrase Epictetus almost verbatim to illustrate the anti-classical and subjectivist conception of 'freedom as self-abnegation' (Berlin) or 'inner freedom' (Arendt): to be free, according to this conception, consists in limiting oneself to what is in one's power.[186] Finally, both Arendt and Berlin insist on the uniqueness of Hellenistic liberty. They similarly characterise this as 'a total reversal' (Berlin) or 'the very opposite' (Arendt) of the classical concept on the one hand; and they both contrast it with the modern concept represented by Mill's *On Liberty* on the other.[187] They agree, in other words, that the Hellenistic concept is neither the liberty of the ancients nor that of the moderns; it is neither collectivist nor negative.

Behind those points of historical agreement, however, lies profound *normative* disagreement. Berlin, for his part, shows deep ambivalence towards the legacy of Hellenism, and more specifically towards the Stoic conception of freedom. As I discussed earlier, he interprets this as a form of positive liberty in 'Two Concepts', in which the Stoics are presented as precursors to Kant and Rousseau and, by extension, Lenin and Stalin. 'The Birth of Greek Individualism', by contrast, discusses the Stoic conception more approvingly. It highlights the ability of the Stoic conception to subvert what Berlin considers to be the excessive moralism of the classical outlook, which 'today is called an *engagé* attitude to politics'.[188] In this outlook, the life of the individual was always considered in functional relation to the life of the polis, and politics as a means of pursuing private goals simply did not exist. A defender of negative liberty, concerned with the excessive power of the state to interfere with individual conduct, Berlin finds the classical outlook hardly appealing and expresses his doubt that 'the decline of the "organic" community' in the fourth century BCE was 'an unmixed disaster'. On the contrary, he suggests, it may have liberated individuals from 'a sense of suffocation in the *polis*'.[189] Arendt, by contrast, finds no such positivity in the Hellenistic outlook. She dismisses the subjectivist or inner conception of freedom as 'derivative', as little more than a reflection of 'estrangement from the world' following the decline of Greek city-states.[190] Central to *her* history of freedom are the twin achievements of classical Greece and republican Rome, in which 'freedom was an exclusively political concept'.[191] Compared to these two periods, Hellenistic Greece was a dark age, when freedom came to be dislocated from its proper place, that is, the polis. Where Berlin sees the birth of a new individualism and indeed 'a new conception of life', Arendt sees nothing other than freedom's retreat from the world to the self—safe and comforting but solitary, invisible and inauthentic.[192]

The two thinkers' normative disagreement entails what might be called their 'methodological' differences. Berlin, on the one hand, challenges the materialist approach that explains the transvaluational change in the fourth century BCE as straightforwardly reflecting the decline of Greek city-states following the battle of Chaeronea. Ever insistent on the autonomous power of ideas irreducible to external factors, Berlin argues that the materialist view is not adequate to 'explain so abrupt, swift and total a transformation of political outlook'.[193] He consequently speculates that anti-classical ideas might have been more widespread than the surviving historical evidence would have us believe, highlighting the fact that '[t]he vast bulk of our information' comes from the enemies of the anti-classical camp, namely, Plato and Aristotle.[194] Having to rely solely on them to learn about Sophists, Cynics, Sceptics and 'other so-called minor sects' is, Berlin humorously writes, analogous to having to rely solely on Bertrand Russell's *History of Western Philosophy* to learn about medieval thought.[195] Berlin thus discusses anti-classical thinkers, such as Diogenes, Crates of Thebes, Antisthenes, Aristippus and the Aristophanic Socrates, at considerable length and with evident fascination in 'The Birth of Greek Individualism'. Arendt, on the other hand, shows no comparable interest in these marginalised figures. She summarily dismisses Stoics and Epicureans as mere 'popular and popularizing sectarians of late antiquity'.[196] In her eyes they are insignificant figures who made modest contributions to the philosophical tradition that 'has distorted, instead of clarifying, the very idea of freedom'.[197] To study Stoicism and Epicureanism, in her view, would help us little to understand what freedom is. A more promising approach is to 'go back' to classical antiquity and 'pre-philosophical' experiences, so as to restore the original meaning of freedom, which had sunk into oblivion with the decline of Greek city-states.[198]

Finally, Berlin's appreciation of Greek individualism does not necessarily mean that he is more deeply committed than Arendt to the normative value of individuality. Arendt's point is precisely that individuality cannot be fully realised if one assigns excessive value to 'freedom from politics' and stays outside the public realm. If men and women wish to 'show who they really and inexchangeably' are, they *must* enter the public realm to take the initiative to act in concert with others.[199] Only in the specifically political mode of being can the human condition be truly appreciated; and only through such appreciation can men and women express their individuality to the full. On her view, it is not liberal individualism, but the Aristotelian defence of the public realm that provides a route to the agonistic individuality that was more common among the ancients than among the moderns. Berlin profoundly disagrees. He believes that the political is but one sphere of human life, and that the political way of life is but one way of leading a truly human life. The ways in which men and women express their individuality must be manifold, because human values are irreducibly many and not all of them are political. The incapacity to appreciate such deep pluralism is, in Berlin's view, one of the chief weaknesses of 'the *engagé* attitude to politics', to which Arendt's political theory (and Crick's) is susceptible. To the extent that Hellenism challenged this attitude and made room for individuals to choose 'freely'—in the negative sense of the term—what ends to pursue and what life to live, Berlin welcomes the Hellenistic contributions to human liberty. In his view, a monist conception of the good, Aristotelian or otherwise, does not provide a route to Millian individuality, 'diversity, versatility [and] fullness of life'.[200] Only liberal individualism, anchored in value pluralism, does so. In short, what Arendt and Berlin disagree over is not the value of individuality as such, but *what kind* of individuality humanity should strive for.

Conclusion

In 1986, in response to a question by Beata Polanowska-Sygulska, Berlin expressed his belief that 'at the base of ethical, political and every other normative idea is always one's [...] conception of man'.[201] This proposition, so long as 'man' (or human) is understood in non-essentialist terms, is true when it comes to Arendt and Berlin: their rival theories of freedom are indeed anchored in their conflicting views of the human condition. That said, it is worth highlighting that, in his reply to Polanowska-Sygulska, Berlin adds the further thought that one's 'conception of man' is 'usually not too empirical'.[202] This is a revealing remark. As I discussed earlier, Berlin presents his value pluralist defence of negative liberty in distinctly empiricist terms, as grounded in his observations about '[t]he world that we encounter in ordinary experience'.[203] But he is also aware that no particular 'conception of man' automatically follows from a mere accumulation of empirical facts. To form such a conception one needs both empirical observation and some speculative thought. If one's political thought, based on one's 'conception of man', is to be plausible, one must strike the right balance between the empirical and the speculative.

With this in mind, it is worth recalling that Berlin repeatedly dismisses Arendt's political theory as 'metaphysical' in the pejorative sense: underpinned by nothing other than her 'transcendental' vision.[204] In other words, Berlin deems Arendt to have got the balance between the empirical and the speculative disastrously wrong. What is interesting about this harsh criticism is that it shows no regard for Arendt's own understanding of her theoretical enterprise. According to her, the phenomenological tradition to which she (somewhat ambiguously) belongs 'begin[s] with the smallest and seemingly most modest of things, with unpretentious "little things", with unpretentious words'.[205] This basic stance is discernible in virtually all of Arendt's writings, including her most theoretical work *The Human Condition*, whose aim is claimed to be 'very simple: it is nothing more than to think what we are doing.'[206] In short, what Berlin takes Arendt to be doing flatly contradicts her own account of what she is doing. This is a curious misrepresentation on Berlin's part. No less curious is his obliviousness to the similarity between his and her sceptical stances on theoretical system building devoid of an experiential basis. Whether he likes it or not, the following oft-cited words by Arendt strike a Berlinian note: 'What is the subject of our thought? Experience! Nothing else! And if we lose the ground of experience then we get into all kinds of theories. When the political theorist begins to build his systems he is also usually dealing with abstractions.'[207] Despite Berlin's claim to the contrary, Arendt is no less willing than he is to face reality as it is, unobstructed by excessively abstract, speculative or 'metaphysical' theories.[208]

The difference between Arendt and Berlin with regard to the significance of empirical experience for thought, then, does not concern the willingness or lack thereof to face reality as it is and reflect on 'the world that we encounter in ordinary experience'.[209] Rather, it concerns *what experiences* to draw on to undertake theoretical work, for there are numerous aspects of empirical reality one could look at, and various perspectives from which to look at them. Here again, Arendt's and Berlin's ideas display both important similarities and intriguing differences. On the one hand, they agree that the defining experience with which twentieth-century political theorists are confronted is the emergence of totalitarianism, and more specifically of the twin evils of Nazism and Stalinism. On the other hand, the two thinkers' perspectives on the empirical reality of totalitarianism starkly differ from each other, giving rise to a number of differences between their competing political theories. The next chapter tells this story—the story of how Arendt's and Berlin's rival theories of freedom, underpinned by their differing views of the human condition, reflect their conflicting understandings of the *unfreedom* and *inhumanity* of totalitarianism.

4

Inhumanity

IN APRIL 1943, Isaiah Berlin, then a staff member of the British Embassy in Washington, DC, received a copy of the latest issue of the *Menorah Journal*, a left-leaning, modernist Jewish periodical edited by Henry Hurwitz.[1] Included in the issue was Hannah Arendt's now celebrated essay, 'We Refugees'.[2] A mixture of report, memoir and polemic, the essay gave a vivid portrait of the predicament of Jewish refugees, illustrated by the author's first-hand account of the Gurs internment camp, where she had spent a few weeks in the summer of 1940. Whether Berlin read the essay is difficult to tell. He duly wrote a thank-you note to the journal editor, saying, 'I have read with much interest and profit the issue of the *Menorah Journal* which you sent me.'[3] This, needless to say, hardly amounts to evidence that Berlin actually read the essay, for it could be a pleasantry, merely acknowledging formally his gratitude to the sender. In fact, nowhere in the vast heap of Berlin's surviving papers do we find a reference to Arendt's semi-autobiographical piece. If he read this 'with much interest and profit' in 1943, he seems to have forgotten it later. Nevertheless, we have reason to believe that Berlin may indeed have found the essay informative, or would have found it so had he had the chance to read it. The reason is that he consistently drew a contrast between Arendt's philosophical and empirical works, and dismissed the former outright, while holding less harsh opinions on the latter. When the *Times Literary Supplement*, on the occasion of its seventy-fifth anniversary in 1977, asked him (and other writers) 'to nominate the most underrated and overrated books (or authors) of the past seventy-five years', it was *The Human Condition*, not *The Origins of Totalitarianism* or even *Eichmann in Jerusalem*, that Berlin nominated in the 'overrated' category.[4] Indeed, like his Oxford colleague Stuart Hampshire, Berlin considered *Origins* to be the least bad of all Arendt's books.[5]

Be that as it may, our protagonists' understandings of the crises of the twentieth century, culminating in Nazism and Stalinism and their genocidal policies, differed significantly from each other. They disagreed, among other things, over the definition of totalitarianism, its relative novelty, its goals and aspirations, its forms of oppression and domination and its paradigmatic patterns of emergence. In other words, they disagreed as to what the term 'totalitarianism' should denote; whether the denoted phenomenon had been unknown prior to the twentieth century; what it ultimately aimed at; how it deprived men and women of their freedom and humanity; and wherein lay its 'origins'. These points of disagreement were underpinned by the methodological differences between the two thinkers. Insistent on the power of ideas, Berlin on the one hand focused on the internal logic of totalitarian oppression, on how totalitarians *themselves* justified their behaviour. Dismissive of intellectual history, Arendt on the other hand attempted to identify a disparate set of elements that abruptly and contingently 'crystallised' into totalitarianism at a particular historical juncture. The choice of method and the substance of analysis were in a chicken-and-egg relationship: each thinker's unmediated, preliminary observations oriented him/her towards a specific approach, which in turn made the preliminary observations develop in a particular direction.

In his comprehensive study of post-war anti-totalitarian literature, Richard Shorten makes the important observation that different authors 'saw totalitarianism from different vantage points—concerns *closer to home*'.[6] I shall rely on this observation in this chapter, with the proviso that it applies more straightforwardly to Arendt than to Berlin. On the one hand, it is easy to tell what 'concerns closer to home' mean in Arendt's case. Her home was old Germany and Western and Central Europe before it was usurped by the Nazis; and her primary concern was to understand how the usurpers ruined 'the dignity of our [Western] tradition'.[7] On the other hand, it is more difficult to tell what 'concerns closer to home' mean in Berlin's case. His native home was Riga, occupied by the Nazis and the Soviet communists in succession. His adopted home, where he *felt* most at home, was Britain, which fought Nazi Germany during World War II and the communist East after it. Which variant of totalitarianism represented to Berlin 'concerns closer to home'? This is hard to tell. While Shorten is right to note that Berlin wrote more about Soviet totalitarianism than about its Nazi counterpart, it is hardly clear that the imbalance can be explained in terms of *proximity*. Berlin had little to say on the Nazi Holocaust, but the silence might well be because he was *too close* to, rather than too distant from, the crimes of the Nazis. After all, one is often lost for words when horror unfolds before one's eyes. On only one occasion, responding to an interviewer, did Berlin briefly mention the personal dimension of the Nazi Holocaust in public. He said, 'both my grandfathers, an uncle, an aunt, three cousins, were killed in Riga in 1941.'[8] Whatever one may think about the meaning of his public silence, it is unlikely that Berlin had little to say on the Nazi Holocaust because of distance. Nevertheless, Shorten's observation is still applicable to Berlin in one important respect: as far as his written and spoken words are concerned, 'it was Stalin's crimes, not Hitler's, that roused [Berlin's] most intense imaginative response.'[9] To overstate the matter a little, Berlin looked closely at the Soviet Union to form his theory of totalitarianism, whereas Arendt looked closely at Nazi Germany to form hers. The rest of this chapter will both substantiate and complicate this basic claim.

Defining Totalitarianism

First of all, consider the question of definition: what is totalitarianism? I shall begin with Arendt's answer, which is more original and more influential than Berlin's. According to her, totalitarianism is an unprecedented phenomenon—unknown, that is, prior to the emergence of Nazism and Stalinism. Twentieth-century totalitarianisms are so dissimilar from anything that might be considered comparable in the preceding centuries that they must be seen as a 'novel form of government'.[10] An attempt to explain totalitarianism by applying traditional concepts and categories such as tyranny, dictatorship and authoritarianism is likely to generate misunderstanding. As Arendt put it in retrospect, 'We had to learn everything from scratch, in the raw, as it were—that is, without the help of categories and general rules under which to subsume our experience.'[11] Arendt places particular emphasis on the uselessness of the concept of tyranny in understanding totalitarianism. Tyranny standardly refers to a lawless form of government in which power is exercised arbitrarily. By contrast, Arendt argues, totalitarianism is simultaneously a lawless and lawful government: it is lawless in that it dismisses the principle of the rule of law and defies all positive laws; but it is also lawful in that it strictly follows a purportedly 'higher' law, such as the law of nature in Nazism and the law of history in Stalinism. Totalitarianism is emphatically not an extreme form of tyranny. Rather, it is a categorically different phenomenon, which 'has exploded the very alternative [. . .] between lawful and lawless government, between arbitrary and legitimate power'.[12]

How, then, should we make sense of the 'shocking originality' of totalitarianism?[13] Arendt suggests an idiosyncratic conception of ideology as a key to understanding. In ordinary language, ideology may refer to a relatively vague and often inconsistent set of beliefs that influences political action and guides public policy. On this understanding, liberalism, conservatism, socialism and other such '-isms' are all ideologies, which are fluid, malleable and often internally inconsistent. The rigidity of totalitarian ideologies is an exception to the rule.[14] Arendt by contrast insists that ideology is inherently rigid, claiming that the term 'ideology' combines 'idea' and '-ology' and hence literally means 'the logic of an idea'.[15] This is a questionable claim. Pace Arendt, the literal meaning of the term 'ideology' is a *study of* ideas, as sociology is not a logic of society but a (systematic) study of it.[16] Regardless, she associates ideology with logic to highlight three important ways in which ideology imitates the consistency of (formal) logic, with disastrous political consequences. First, ideology attempts to explain all aspects of human life deductively from 'an axiomatically accepted premise' such as the professed 'law' of history or of nature. Next, starting from such a premise, ideology purports to provide 'the total explanation of the past, the total knowledge of the present, and the reliable prediction of the future'.[17] Third, when ideological explanation contradicts facts, its proponent does not concede deficiency but 'insists on a "truer" reality concealed behind all perceptible things'.[18] For example, if Jews are defencelessly slaughtered, antisemitic totalitarians interpret it not as evidence of their powerlessness but as a sign of their conspiratorial nature.

Arendt's conception of ideology has some resemblance to Karl Popper's idea of 'pseudo-science'. According to Popper, a scientific theory that purports to explain empirical phenomena must in principle be refutable by observable counterexamples. Conversely, if an allegedly scientific theory is not in principle open to empirical refutation, it must be considered 'pseudo-science'.[19] To cite a famous example, 'all swans are white' is a scientific proposition if and only if it may be refuted in principle by the observation of a non-white swan, provided that whiteness is not a definitional property of swans. Arendt's ideology resembles Popper's pseudo-science in that it too is not open to empirical refutation. Nevertheless, it differs from pseudo-science in that it does not leave reality as it is, but appeals to terror to make reality conform to its deductive logic. If, for example, a totalitarian ideology says 'all swans are white', the totalitarian regime will have all creatures that might challenge this proposition exterminated. Terror is the means by which totalitarianism remakes the world in its own ideological image.

It is worth noting here that Arendt identifies a specific *type* of terror—'total terror'—as essential for totalitarianism.[20] She observes that political terror conceptualised as the exercise of violence against political opponents has been known and repeatedly carried out in various regimes since ancient times. However, while terror in this sense has specifically targeted *opponents*, totalitarian terror is exercised over 'harmless citizens without political opinions'.[21] In tyranny, the ruler terrorises in order to instil fear into the ruled. In totalitarianism, by contrast, the ruler terrorises 'exclusively in accordance with the objective necessity of the natural or historical process'.[22] Fear under tyranny, as Peter Baehr succinctly puts it, 'offers people guidelines for their behaviour [...]; it suggests what to do and what not to do to stay out of trouble.' Terror under totalitarianism operates differently altogether. Men and women are deemed guilty not because of what they do or fail to do but because they belong to a 'wrong' category such as the Jewish 'race' or the bourgeois class.

'Their death sentence is pronounced by the tribunals of Nature or History, whose proxy is the totalitarian regime.'[23] Totalitarianism on Arendt's understanding is no longer rule by fear.[24] Ideology alone determines over whom terror is to be exercised, paying no attention whatsoever to victims' behaviour or feelings.

Arendt's discussion as thus outlined is well known. Few scholars, however, have seriously considered exactly how minimalist her conception of totalitarianism is.[25] According to Arendt, 'novel' totalitarianism should be distinguished not only from 'traditional' tyranny but also from its twentieth-century fascist cousins, including Mussolini's Italy.[26] Of course, the exclusion of fascist Italy from the totalitarian family is not a surprising claim today. Those who separate ('merely' fascist) Italy from (properly totalitarian) Germany and Russia are hardly a minority among recent scholars, though their view remains contested.[27] Nevertheless, the separation was more controversial in the immediate post-war period. For one thing, less was known about the similarity between Nazism and Stalinism. Moreover, the term 'totalitarian' (*totalitario*) had been used specifically to denote Italian fascism during the 1920s and 1930s, not least because Italian fascists themselves claimed the 'totalitarian' label to characterise their own commitment to totally guide citizens in both the public and private spheres.[28] Arendt insisted on abandoning this well-established earlier usage to reserve the 'totalitarian' label strictly for Nazism and Stalinism. According to her, Mussolini neither was a totalitarian 'nor even knew what totalitarianism meant', for fascist Italy had far greater similarity to the tyrannies of the past than to the Germany and Russia of the present.[29] To fail to see this, for her, is not only to misunderstand the nature of fascism but also to belittle the novelty of distinctly twentieth-century totalitarianism.[30]

More striking still is Arendt's repeated claim that Nazi rule in mid-1930s Germany was not yet 'a truly totalitarian rule.'[31] She is ambivalent as to exactly when Germany became fully totalitarian. For example, she suggests 1938 as the cut-off point on one page in *Origins* and 1942 on another page.[32] She is never able to pin down the precise date, though her suggested dates tend to indicate sometime around the end of the 1930s. Surprising corollaries follow.[33] If Arendt is right, Germany was not 'truly totalitarian' when the Nuremberg Laws were ratified and Jews stripped of their German citizenship in 1935, or when Hitler lied to the world to sign the Munich Agreement three years later, or when Jewish homes, shops and synagogues were destroyed on Kristallnacht on 9–10 November 1938. Nor was Nazism 'fully totalitarianized', according to some pages of *Origins*, when gassing by carbon monoxide as a method of mass killing was tested for the first time in autumn 1939; or when the Nazis invaded and occupied Denmark, Norway, the Netherlands, Belgium, Luxembourg and France; or even when three million German troops invaded the Soviet Union in a surprise attack on 22 June 1941. Arendt's inability to specify the precise cut-off point stems from her eminently sensible view that totalitarianism grew out of more familiar, 'traditional' precursors. Neither Hitler's movement nor Stalin's rule was totalitarian from the outset; each morphed into totalitarianism proper when it shed its traditional components to a sufficient degree. But Arendt has little to say when it comes to the question of the exact date by which the decisive morphing occurred, and the little she says is imprecise and inconsistent.

Isaiah Berlin does not share the strict limits Arendt sets on the extension of the concept of totalitarianism. On the contrary, *his* conception is highly expansive. Of course, he too sees Nazi Germany and Stalinist Russia as exemplars of totalitarianism. Nevertheless, unlike Arendt, he does not refrain from characterising mid-1930s Germany and 1920s Russia as totalitarian. Nor does he think, unlike Arendt, that Russia turned totalitarian because of Stalin; Russia under Lenin's leadership was, in Berlin's view, already totalitarian. The deeper point of disagreement, however, is that Berlin, unlike Arendt, does not consider totalitarianism to be categorically different from traditional forms of oppressive government. He often uses 'totalitarianism', 'tyranny', 'despotism', 'dictatorship' and 'authoritarianism' interchangeably. A series of corollaries follows. For example, he does not draw a strict line between Nazism and Stalinism on the one hand and their less violent cousins in twentieth-century Italy, Spain, Portugal, Greece and elsewhere on the other. He says, for example, that his theory of freedom was meant to be a weapon against both 'Soviet totalitarianism' *and* 'other forms of despotism of that period: Franco, Salazar, Mao and various fascist claims in the past about conferring "true liberty" upon their subjects'.[34] Similarly, while Berlin certainly considers the Great Terror of the late 1930s Soviet Union to be extraordinarily terrible, he does not (unlike Arendt) insist on its unprecedented nature. In terms of 'violence and [...] thoroughness', Berlin observes, it is comparable, if remotely, to the Spanish Inquisition and to the Counter-Reformation.[35] On his view, unlike Arendt's, the awfulness of totalitarianism is not a qualitative but quantitative matter.

More curious still is Berlin's reference to 'totalitarian Sparta' in his posthumously published essay 'The Birth of Greek Individualism'.[36] He calls Sparta totalitarian because it lacks diversity and is 'tightly organised' and 'militarised', at least in comparison to Athens.[37] This does not mean that Berlin considers Athens to be a proto-liberal democracy. On the contrary, as I discussed in Chapter 2, he finds Athens collectivist, moralistic, suffocating and *unfree* (in the negative sense). But he finds similar faults in Sparta *to a greater degree*, and applies the deliberately anachronistic term 'totalitarian' to the ancient city-state. This may seem implausible, but we should concede Berlin's consistency. He does not consider totalitarianism to be categorically different from traditional forms of oppressive government and is hence ready to characterise highly oppressive Sparta as 'totalitarian'.

Both Arendt's and Berlin's definitions of totalitarianism face the general problem of indeterminacy known as the sorites paradox. This in its classical form asks when grains of wheat turn into a heap, provided that a single grain does not constitute a heap and that adding another one does not turn a non-heap into a heap, either. A better-known version is the Bald Head, attributed, like the Heap, to Eubulides of Miletus:[38]

> Would you describe a man with one hair as bald? Yes. Would you describe a man with two hairs as bald? Yes. Would you describe . . . You must refrain from describing a man with a million hairs as bald, so where do you draw the line?[39]

Arendt's inability to determine the precise cut-off point for the emergence of totalitarianism involves a similar problem. When did Nazism develop into full-fledged totalitarianism if each of its excesses, such as the assassination of *one* liberal politician, the killing of *one* 'harmless citizen without political opinions' or the burning of *one* synagogue in itself did not make Nazism totalitarian? Where do we draw the line? Berlin circumvents this problem by adopting an expansive conception of totalitarianism. But he faces the return of the repressed: is it not *too* anachronistic to call Sparta totalitarian? If Sparta counts as totalitarian, should not Athens as well? What about Tudor England, Trump's America, and so on? It is as though Arendt was ready to call somebody bald if and only if no hair was left on his head, while Berlin was ready to do so when a few hairs fell from it.

The Concentration-Camp Society: Arendt on Totalitarianism

A further set of differences between Arendt's and Berlin's views of totalitarianism becomes clear as we turn to what each has to say about the goals and aspirations of totalitarianism, its forms of oppression and its patterns of emergence. The present section considers Arendt's view; the next turns to Berlin's.

The Emergence of Totalitarianism: A Pan-European Story

The basic tenet of Arendt's theory of totalitarianism is found in her magnum opus *The Origins of Totalitarianism* (1951), supplemented by several subsequent essays, most importantly 'Ideology and Terror', published in 1953. Incorporated into the later editions of *Origins*, this essay may be seen as Arendt's final word on totalitarianism—on *her theory* of totalitarianism, to be more precise. True, Arendt's subsequent writings complicate her theory in some respects, as I shall discuss shortly. But she never felt the need to revise the fundamentals of her theory formed by 1953. Let me examine those fundamentals first, followed by a further discussion of her post-1953 work.

As I have already observed, Arendt sees totalitarianism as a new type of regime and a new form of government. Yet it is an unusual type, in that it does not seek stability. It is first and foremost a *movement* aiming to translate, by means of total terror, an underlying 'law' postulated by a totalitarian ideology into reality. Whether it is the Nazi law of nature or the Stalinist law of history, ideological laws are dynamic because their chain of reasoning requires nothing but consistency. Thus, 'whoever says A must necessarily also say B and C and finally end with the last letter of the alphabet.'[40] For example, if Moscow asserts its technological superiority over the West, it ends up plotting the physical destruction of the Paris metro whose existence might undermine the initial assertion.[41] Such 'stringent logicality', Arendt writes, 'permeates the whole structure of totalitarian movements and totalitarian governments.'[42] Moreover, even when it comes to power, totalitarianism does not cease to move, but keeps mobilising domestically and expanding territorially. It indoctrinates citizens at home and disseminates propaganda abroad, never ceasing to find new 'objective enemies' to attack. As Margaret Canovan observes, 'The picture of totalitarianism in power presented by Arendt is very far from the familiar image of an omnipotent state with unified and coherent institutions. On the contrary, it is a shapeless, hectic maelstrom of permanent revolution and endless expansion.'[43]

A fierce critic of the determinist conception of history, Arendt analyses the success of totalitarian movements in the first half of the twentieth century in probabilistic terms.[44] While she repeatedly argues that this success was not inevitable, she also takes pains to specify a set of conditions under which it became *likely* in inter-war Europe. She identifies the rise of the 'masses', that is, atomised individuals with no sense of group membership, as the most important of such conditions.[45] While atomised individuals had always existed on the margins of modern society, they emerged in large numbers only in early twentieth-century Europe, as a result of the collapse of the traditional social structure. Arendt holds the destructive dynamism of the capitalist economy partly accountable for this change: the volatile forces of the capitalist market gradually made men and women insecure, rootless and disoriented.[46] But the turmoil of inter-war Europe was much more than the usual capitalist disorder. The decisive events in this context were World War I and the series of crises that followed, including revolutionary upheavals and civil wars between the political left and right; the dissolution of empires, founding of new nation-states and resulting ethnic cleansing and massive population transfers; and mass unemployment, hyperinflation and other economic disasters leading to the Great Depression. This set of events caused men and women to suffer comprehensive socio-economic disintegration, political disorganisation and in many cases geographical dislocation, depriving them of their identities. In Arendt's words, the masses in post-World War I Europe 'lost their home in the world'.[47] The worldless men and women so created proved to be the fervent supporters of totalitarian movements.

However, it was not only the old social and familial bonds that disappeared in the inter-war period. Gone also was a set of political institutions that had sustained the nation-state system during the nineteenth century, notwithstanding that system's internal volatility. The most important of such institutions was parliamentary democracy. This, as is well known, broke down most spectacularly in inter-war Germany. But the Weimar case was a part of the pan-European story, because no less than fourteen parliamentary democracies (including Germany), out of the twenty-six that had existed in the aftermath of the Treaty of Versailles, had collapsed by 1938.[48] Why did this happen? Arendt's basic diagnosis is simple but acute: nineteenth-century parliamentary democracy had been a mechanism to represent *class* interests; it therefore could not survive the demolition of the class system following the Great War. In the new Europe of the 1920s, parliamentary democracy was no longer useful, because citizens no longer had coherent class interests to represent. On the contrary, the continuing existence of the obsolete system made atomised men and women 'at best politically indifferent, or worse, brimming with resentment at the invisibility of their sufferings'.[49] This situation enabled cruel, mean and wicked 'mob men' like Hitler to mobilise disoriented mass men into a totalitarian movement.[50] Conversely, mass men were only too ready to submit themselves to the movement to acquire a sense of stability and restore self-respect. A totalitarian movement's demand for 'total, unrestricted, unconditional, and unalterable loyalty of the individual member' was met by the willingness on the part of the masses to reintegrate themselves 'into eternal, all-dominating forces'.[51] The consistency of totalitarian ideology proved especially appealing to the masses, who now found a stable world to escape into: the fictitious world of ideological lies.

Arendt's account of the emergence of totalitarianism raises an obvious question: if the rise of the masses was a pan-European phenomenon, why was it in Germany specifically that a totalitarian movement developed into a full-blown totalitarian regime? Unlike Berlin (as I shall discuss shortly), Arendt firmly rejects explanations attributing Nazism to 'Germany's national character and history'.[52] She insists that Bismarck was no different from other realist statesmen in modern Europe. Nor are German thinkers and writers to blame.

The writings of Hegel, Nietzsche and others are emphatically not responsible for 'what is happening in the extermination camps'.[53] Arendt's alternative explanation is purely circumstantial and largely demographic. It is based on the idea that a totalitarian movement cannot develop if it runs out of people to deport, dehumanise and kill. In this sense, the success of a totalitarian movement is dependent on a large population size. Thus, Arendt writes, 'semitotalitarian and totalitarian movements' in early twentieth-century Spain, Portugal, Italy, Romania, Hungary and elsewhere morphed into '*non*totalitarian dictatorships' because none of them had sufficient expendable human masses to sustain a totalitarian movement.[54] Nazi Germany, by contrast, conquered eastern territories early on to acquire the necessary population size. Herein lies the legacy of nineteenth-century imperialism to twentieth-century totalitarianism: territorial expansion is a lifeline for the movement. As Nazi Germany inherited this aspect of imperialism, Europeans' inhumanity to colonial subjects came home with a vengeance. In the age of empire, Britons invented a concentration camp to contain 'undesirable elements' in South Africa. In the age of extremes, Germans built concentration and extermination camps to dehumanise and mass-slaughter their fellow Europeans.[55]

Arendt's pan-European perspective on the rise of totalitarianism has an ambivalent bearing upon her analysis of the rise of Stalinism. On the one hand, her emphasis on the significance of an expendable population seems to apply to the Russian case relatively straightforwardly. Russia, she notes, had always had millions of human beings to expend domestically, while Germany had to conquer neighbouring countries to acquire a comparable population.[56] Russia thus satisfied one necessary condition for the growth of a totalitarian movement: a large population. On the other hand, it is doubtful if Arendt's argument regarding the masses, tied to her analysis of the breakdown of the nation-state system in inter-war Europe, has much explanatory power when applied to the Russian case. In fact, she herself has little to say on the pertinence of the rise of the masses to Stalinism, and the little she says shows signs of inconsistency. Sometimes she suggests that Russian agrarian society had always been a kind of atomised society, in that it lacked 'social stratification'.[57] But she sometimes suggests that 'Stalin [. . .] create[d] artificially that atomized society which had been prepared for the Nazis in Germany by historical circumstances'.[58] Both suggestions are questionable. The first sits oddly with the more nuanced analysis of the masses as a post-World War I phenomenon found elsewhere in Arendt's work. Similarly, the second suggestion does not explain how Stalin came to power in the first place without the existence of the masses, which Arendt elsewhere identifies as a precondition for the rise of a totalitarian movement. Facing these inconsistencies, some Arendt scholars have come up with ingenious, and sometimes acrobatic, interpretive strategies to minimise the significance of her Nazi-focused approach to totalitarianism.[59] While I appreciate the intellectual virtuosity of such interpreters, I see no reason why we should not be more candid. As Arendt herself was ready to concede,[60] she knew Nazi Germany far better than Stalinist Russia, and on several key occasions she drew too rigid an analogy between the German and Russian cases, at the expense of accuracy regarding the latter. Her 'masses' argument is one such occasion.

Living Corpses

Arendt is on a firmer footing when she proposes her idea of total domination to characterise the new type of domination that *both* Nazism *and* Stalinism aimed to achieve. Again, she contrasts 'traditional' tyranny with 'novel' totalitarianism to make her case. Under tyranny, subjects are not totally but partially dominated in that they are entitled to a degree of freedom in the private sphere. So long as they conform to the political order imposed by the regime, subjects of tyranny are by and large able to entertain free thought, enjoy family life and engage in professional activities. Under totalitarianism, by contrast, subjects are entitled to no such freedom: 'every aspect of their life' is dominated.[61] To achieve this goal, totalitarianism singles out two central human properties as targets of destruction: individuality and spontaneity. The former stands for that which makes each person unique and different from others; the latter, for the ability to do something on one's own initiative. Together, individuality and spontaneity give rise to the human capacity for doing something *unpredictable*. This capacity is the principal target of totalitarian destruction because it is fundamentally incompatible with the totalitarian ambition to remake the world according to the (predictable) logic of ideology. Totalitarianism is secure if and only if all subjects are deprived of their individuality and spontaneity and reduced to 'ghastly marionettes with human faces, which all behave like the dog in Pavlov's experiments, which all react with perfect reliability even when going to their own death'.[62] Or, to cite another metaphor Arendt repeatedly uses, total domination succeeds when human beings are transformed into 'living corpses'.

Arendt's repeated reference to *living* corpses is a telling one. Today, we tend to think of the mechanised production of dead bodies when we think about the Nazi Holocaust. The harrowing images of piled-up mutilated bodies and imposing crematoria loom large in our memory and imagination. Of course, Arendt does not neglect this aspect; she is aware that totalitarian terror ultimately led to 'death factories'.[63] Nevertheless, her main focus is on the inhuman conditions into which men and women were driven *before* they were finally killed. The 'camp administration', she writes, combined 'a regulated death rate and a strictly organized torture, calculated not so much to inflict death as to put the victim into a *permanent status of dying*.[64] As Peter Baehr notes, the *primary* purpose of the camps on Arendt's understanding is not killing per se, but to 'conduct an experiment on their hapless captives'.[65] It was neither the sheer number of the victims nor the modern, technological and instrumentally rational nature of mass killing that shocked Arendt most.[66] It was, rather, the progressive dehumanisation of victims. To put it differently, her focus is not so much on extermination camps, where new arrivals were *immediately* gassed, as on concentration camps, where many inmates were gradually forced to die of exhaustion, disease and malnutrition.[67] Arendt found the latter more shocking, because it represented a crime darker than mass killing itself: 'to eradicate the concept of the human being'.[68] It is this aspect of Nazi atrocity that she attempts to capture in her depiction of total domination as a step-by-step 'descent into Hell'.[69]

Arendt's own terminology is somewhat confusing to us today. Conforming to the terminological conventions of her time, she repeatedly speaks of 'concentration and extermination camps' and uses the word 'camps' as shorthand for both. As recent scholars such as Michal Aharony and Dan Stone have observed, however, Arendt in most cases means the former when she speaks of 'concentration and extermination camps'.[70] To be more precise, Arendt's main focus is not on the six death factories that operated in Nazi-occupied Poland between December 1941 and November 1944: Bełżec, Chełmno, Sobibór, Treblinka, and the extermination parts of Majdanek and Auschwitz. Rather, her focus is on the network of concentration camps across Europe and beyond, preceded by internment camps on the one hand and followed by extermination camps on the other. Among those numerous camps, Arendt was most familiar with Buchenwald, five miles north-west of Weimar, and Dachau, ten miles north-west of Munich. *Origins* in particular draws heavily on the first-hand accounts by David Rousset, Bruno Bettelheim and Eugen Kogon, who all survived Nazi concentration camps *inside* the German borders, not those in 'the East'.[71] As for Auschwitz, its significance for Arendt's theory of totalitarianism should not be exaggerated. True, this largest Nazi camp has come to occupy a central place in our memory of the Holocaust. Yet the author of *Origins* had limited information about it, and she was 'unsurprisingly [. . .] not familiar with Primo Levi's *Survival in Auschwitz*, first published in a print run of 2,500 copies in 1947'.[72] While her analysis of total domination has largely been confirmed by the subsequent literature on Auschwitz, Arendt herself mentions the camp only twice in passing in *Origins* and scarcely discusses it elsewhere in her work prior to *Eichmann in Jerusalem*. It is an anachronism to call *Origins* 'a view from Auschwitz'.[73]

Common Crimes

What *does* appear more prominently than Auschwitz in Arendt's theory of totalitarianism is the network of Soviet labour camps, known as 'the Gulag' in the West since the 1970s due to the publication (initially in Paris) of Aleksandr Solzhenitsyn's enormously influential *Gulag Archipelago*.[74] When Arendt wrote *Origins*, she had less information about the Gulag than about Dachau or Buchenwald. But she read what she could, including *The Dark Side of the Moon*, published anonymously by Faber & Faber in London in 1946.[75] Written by the extraordinary woman writer Zoë Zajdlerowa (alias Martin Hare), and equipped with a powerful preface by T. S. Eliot, the book was the first published record in the West of the experiences of Polish deportees in the Soviet Union in the early 1940s.[76] The enigmatic title echoed Arthur Koestler's characterisation of 'the vast land of Soviet reality' as being 'as remote from the Western observer as the dark side of the moon from the stargazer's telescope'.[77] Arendt juxtaposes her analysis of the available literature on the Soviet Union, such as *The Dark Side of the Moon*, with her extensive knowledge of German sources to present her taxonomy of concentration camps. She writes,

> Concentration camps can very aptly be divided into three types corresponding to three basic Western conceptions of a life after death: Hades, Purgatory, and Hell. To Hades correspond those relatively mild forms, once popular even in non-totalitarian countries, for getting undesirable elements of all sorts—refugees, stateless persons, the asocial and the unemployed—out of the way [. . .]. Purgatory is represented by the Soviet Union's labor camps, where neglect is combined with chaotic forced labor. Hell in the most literal sense was embodied by those types of camp perfected by the Nazis, in which the whole of life was thoroughly and systematically organized with a view to the greatest possible torment.[78]

Narrating the development of the camp system in this way, Arendt portrays Nazi total domination as *worse* than its Soviet counterpart. The two regimes *equally* created concentration camps as 'special laboratories' in which total domination was experimented with; yet it was in the Nazi camps that the laboratories of inhumanity reached unparalleled development and perfection.[79] While the two totalitarian regimes and the crimes they committed were comparable to each other, the Nazi variant was more advanced than the Stalinist one in essentials. This assessment justifies Arendt's methodology and her Nazi-focused approach to totalitarianism: if one hopes to grasp the essence of the new form of government, it is reasonable to look more closely at the exemplary German case than its further-from-ideal Russian counterpart.

It is worth emphasising here that Arendt does *not* attempt to analyse the so-called Final Solution in her work prior to *Eichmann in Jerusalem*.[80] To explain this specifically Nazi policy, she would not have needed to consider the Soviet Gulag as she did. Instead, she would have needed to examine mass killings by the Nazis in 'the East', that is, extermination camps proper on the one hand and mass killing by bullets and mobile gas vans in the occupied Soviet territory on the other. While *Eichmann* directly confronts the 'Final Solution', *Origins* and other earlier work focus on totalitarianism, and it is specifically for the sake of understanding this 'new form of government' that Arendt examines the institution of concentration camps. She does this not because the infernal institution was instrumental to totalitarian governance— on the contrary, she repeatedly insists on the uselessness or 'non-utilitarian character' of concentration camps: the enormous costs of camp administration vastly outweighed the little benefit the camps yielded.[81] Rather, on Arendt's reading, concentration camps were crucial in that they embodied the *ideal* of total domination. Outside the camps, total domination is achieved 'only imperfectly', because the secret police or the paramilitary can easily over- or under-inflict violence on targeted subjects.[82] In the former case subjects die, and in the latter they retain a measure of humanity. Either way, the victims are not totally dominated, in Arendt's sense of the term. Inside concentration camps, by contrast, camp administrators can inflict on inmates a desired level of violence necessary and sufficient for transforming them into living corpses. To the extent that the ultimate goal of totalitarianism is to transform *everyone* under its ever-expanding jurisdiction into living corpses, concentration camps are a purified microcosm of a larger totalitarian society. Conversely, the totally dominated 'new man' that the camp creates is 'the model "citizen" of a [future] totalitarian state'.[83] It is in this sense that Arendt characterises totalitarianism as a 'concentration-camp society'.[84]

Was Arendt right about the uselessness of concentration camps? Did the worth of the camps really consist in their symbolic power, not in their use-value, as she argued? Recent scholarship has a mixed answer to offer. First, contrary to the impression Arendt often gives, neither Nazism nor Stalinism excluded utilitarian considerations altogether when forming and reforming their respective camp policies. True, their intentions to extract economic benefits out of forced camp labour were often frustrated in reality for various reasons, such as the chaos and inefficiency of camp administration and the lack of experience, incentives and relevant skills among inmates. However, this does not mean that the totalitarian governments did not *attempt* to use concentration camps in a utilitarian manner. In the Soviet case, various scholars have identified economic factors as crucial to explaining the emergence and development of the Gulag, often drawing a parallel between slavery and the

Soviet forced labour system.[85] Although historians disagree as to exactly how significant economic factors were relative to others such as ideology and security, they at least agree that the desire to make use of 'remote resource-rich regions at a low cost of society's resources' was one 'constant' of Gulag administration.[86] While the Gulag often failed to generate use-value, it was not *meant* to be useless.

The story was rather different when it came to the Nazi case. Here economy was usually subordinate to racist ideology as the principal determinant in the development of the camp system. The primary function of the camps was to defeat the 'enemies of the state' in one way or another. To this extent Arendt's observation about the uselessness of concentration camps represents the Nazi reality better than its Soviet counterpart. Yet it also comes up against important counterevidence. First, according to the economic historian Peter Hayes, the overall balance sheet of the Nazi Holocaust was not a negative for the perpetrators. Considerable income was generated by the Nazis' exhaustive plundering, while expenditure was kept low by their relentless exploitation of the victims on the one hand and technical innovations on the other (the discovery of Zyklon as an effective substance for gassing lowered 'the average cost of murder per head' to 'less than one U.S. cent in 1942').[87] The Nazis ran the Holocaust as not only a 'self-financing' but sometimes even a 'profit-making enterprise'.[88] Moreover, economic considerations played an increasingly important role from late 1941, when the Nazis' military victory became less likely and their labour shortages more acute.[89] While Nazi camp policies were often inconsistent and their implementation disorderly, the Nazi leadership did make utilitarian efforts to lower the mortality rate among camp inmates and exploit their labour maximally so as to win the unwinnable war. They were in fact so desperately in need of manpower that in the spring of 1944 they began transporting Hungarian Jews to the Reich itself to boost war production, thereby compromising their key ideological principle of a *Judenfrei* Germany.[90] That this was a short-term tactical decision does not alter the fact that utilitarian calculation played a significant role at this stage of the Nazi camp development. In light of recent studies, then, Arendt's insistence on the 'non-utilitarian character' of concentration camps is at times exaggerated in the Nazi case as well as in the Soviet.[91]

Still convincing today, by contrast, is Arendt's claim that relying on a utilitarian explanatory framework could prevent us from seeing the mad, bizarre and nightmarish core of totalitarianism. Her claim is more than a call for a more balanced perspective. It is, rather, a demand to keep our eyes *focused* on the seemingly incomprehensible aspects of the camps that defy assimilation into a utilitarian framework, for it is in those aspects that the immoral heart of totalitarianism—its drive for total domination—manifests itself. Here

Arendt's argument becomes circular, albeit hermeneutically so. As we have seen, she proposes to reserve the term 'totalitarianism' for something that cannot be signified by tradition-bound terms such as 'tyranny', 'despotism' and 'dictatorship'. Recall here that 'totalitarianism' was a term that had been imported into the English language in the 1920s and gained currency only in the 1940s and 1950s. As a pioneer in popularising the new term, Arendt saw no point in using it unless something new could be signified by it. She thus encouraged us to distinguish between (properly) totalitarian and (merely) dictatorial aspects of Nazism and Stalinism, and to focus on the former to understand how totalitarianism differs from its traditional precursors. This approach allowed her to illuminate the originality of twentieth-century totalitarianism, which a utilitarian approach is likely to miss. Yet her approach has the downside of defining totalitarianism in peculiarly narrow terms in order to keep it *undiluted* by the remnants of traditional forms of oppressive government. As a consequence, she makes the questionable claim that neither Nazism nor Stalinism were 'fully totalitarian' through much of their violent, cruel and inhumane histories. But she was willing to make this trade-off. If it is impossible to draw an indisputable line between totalitarianism and its traditional precursors, she considers it *better* to draw too rigid a distinction than to blur it. If a degree of arbitrariness is unavoidable to achieve clarity, so be it. This is Hannah Arendt at her finest, determined to elucidate the unprecedented at all costs.

Stalinism, Marx and the 'Tradition'

Let me turn, finally, to Arendt's post-1953 work. What does this add to the theory of totalitarianism that she had formed by 1953? As is well known, immediately after completing *Origins*, she proposed to write a ninety-thousand-word monograph entitled 'Totalitarian Elements in Marxism' as a complementary volume.[92] According to the oft-cited research outline she submitted to the Guggenheim Foundation, she had been aware that Marxism was one of the important 'elements' of totalitarianism. But she had set this 'element' aside in *Origins* because it differed from all other 'elements', in that it alone did not originate from the 'subterranean currents in Western history' but, on the contrary, 'had behind it a respectable tradition'. The author of *Origins* feared that she might risk diminishing the 'shocking originality of totalitarianism' had she paid too much attention to Marxism. Hence the need to write a separate book afterwards—or so Arendt told the Guggenheim Foundation.[93] It is of course a matter of debate whether her research proposal truthfully represented her views; scholars may not always be candid when they are attempting to persuade a funding body.[94] Regardless, her request was approved, and she spent the next four years drafting various papers in preparation for the proposed book on Marxism.[95] This book failed to materialise. But the manuscripts she drafted were to serve as a basis for her mature work, in which her critical engagement with Marxism developed into a fundamental reconsideration of what she came to call the 'tradition': the canon of Western philosophy and political thought from Plato to Marx.[96] This development complicated the theory of totalitarianism that she had formed by 1953.

An important part of the complication was methodological.[97] As we have seen, Arendt in *Origins* largely *avoided* discussing philosophies, theories and ideas. Her approach sharply differed from those of Cold War liberals such as Berlin, Popper and Talmon, who traced the origins of twentieth-century totalitarianism back to the utopian philosophies of Marx, Hegel, Rousseau and Plato. It diverged no less sharply from Adorno and Horkheimer's approach in *The Dialectic of Enlightenment*, which explained totalitarianism in terms of Western rationality run amok.[98] Their numerous differences notwithstanding, liberals and critical theorists both told distinctly *intellectual* historical stories to account for the emergence of totalitarianism.[99] Arendt took an entirely different approach in *Origins*. She identified a complex set of sociological, institutional and demographic conditions under which nascent totalitarian movements contingently developed into full-fledged totalitarian regimes in twentieth-century Germany and Russia. Nevertheless, her methodological exceptionalism weakened in her post-*Origins* work. Her study of Marxism led her in the direction of intellectual history, consistent with her view that Marxism 'had behind it [the] respectable tradition' of Western philosophy and political thought. Furthermore, she was later to level the charge that the 'tradition' that had begun with Plato gave at least some assistance to totalitarians who attempted to destroy human plurality. Her work after 1953 appeared suspiciously similar to the intellectual historical works that she had resolutely rejected in *Origins*.

The similarity remained largely on the methodological level, however, for Arendt hardly revised the substance of her theory of totalitarianism in her post-1953 work. First of all, in her 'Totalitarian Elements' manuscripts, she painstakingly examined whether Marx's work might be said to have contributed to the subsequent rise of totalitarianism. Her answer was, on balance, negative, if deeply ambivalent. True, she was not willing to accept that Marx was totally innocent. His responsibility for Stalinism is certainly more substantive than, for example, Luther's alleged responsibility for Nazism. Yet it is practically impossible to demonstrate a causal link between a nineteenth-century philosopher's ideas and a twentieth-century political event. More importantly, Marx's self-nominated successors have to varying degrees appropriated and abused their master's ideas. 'Through Marxism', Arendt writes, 'Marx himself has been praised or blamed for many things of which he was entirely innocent.'[100] The figure Arendt singles out in this context is, of course, Stalin. In her view, Marxism before Stalin was not a totalitarian ideology; nor was the Soviet Union in Lenin's lifetime a totalitarian society. According to the 'Totalitarian Elements' manuscripts, as well as *Origins*, the 'decisive transformation' occurred only in the 1930s, under Stalin's leadership.[101] Soviet totalitarianism is a uniquely Stalinist-era phenomenon.

In her subsequent work, Arendt told a similar story about the relationship between the 'tradition' and totalitarianism.[102] On the one hand, she increasingly came to be convinced that the 'tradition' had been infected by anti-political biases, beginning with Plato's hostility to the *demos* that sentenced Socrates to death. Plato in fact emerges as an antihero in Arendt's post-1953 writings. She accuses him of abandoning the original meaning of politics as consisting in action and deliberation among equals, and replacing it with the rationalist conception of politics as rule by the competent few over the incompetent many. In so doing, Plato introduced an 'element of violence' into politics, for politics was now seen as a matter of coercion, although the means of coercion Plato himself was willing to use was not physical violence but the 'force' of truth (for the elite) and of myth (for the *demos*).[103] These anti-political 'Platonic' biases recurred throughout the 'tradition', at the end of which stands the figure of Karl Marx. While this historiography might sound like Cold War liberals' notion of the 'monist' roots of totalitarianism (discussed below), Arendt ultimately rejects it by insisting on the rupture between the 'tradition' and distinctly twentieth-century totalitarianism. In this respect, her 'tradition' is to totalitarianism as homophobic prejudices are to organised corrective rape.[104] The former is an important part of the cultural background from which the latter grows, but does not in itself generate the latter.

In addition, Arendt repeatedly insisted that the availability of new evidence since the early 1950s posed no fundamental challenge to her theory of totalitarianism. One such evidence was the Smolensk Archive: two hundred thousand pages of records from the Smolensk Region (*Oblast*) of the All-Union Communist Party, captured by the German army in 1941 and subsequently seized by the US army in 1945. The Harvard political scientist Merle Fainsod was the first to study the Archive, and his groundbreaking *Smolensk under Soviet Rule*, published in 1958, showed a Western audience for the first time the working of the Soviet Union from within.[105] Arendt conceded the significance of Fainsod's work, but did not find it revelatory. On the contrary, it tended to 'confirm what we [had known] before from less irrefutable sources'.[106] In fact, according to Arendt, the most remarkable feature of the Smolensk papers was 'the amount of information they *fail* to give us', as Fainsod's study forcefully demonstrated the general absence of 'reliable source and statistical material' in the Soviet Union.[107]

The situation was different, Arendt continued, in Nazi Germany, where reliable sources of information did exist. But there, too, newly available materials revealed little, because a fair sample of reliable sources had already been available by 1951, when *Origins* was published. Arendt recognised a pattern common to the Stalinist and Nazi sources: 'documentary material' that became available in recent years 'tended to confirm and to add to what had been known all along from prominent defectors and other eye-witness accounts'.[108] In other words, the fundamentals of totalitarianism had been known to the author of *Origins*, who had thoroughly studied then-available essential sources.[109] The conclusion Arendt reached in 1967 was the following: the 'original presentation' of her account of totalitarianism needed no 'substantial changes' in light of recent developments in scholarship.[110]

Arendt's unwillingness to modify the substance of her theory of totalitarianism is also discernible in her late occasional writings on the Soviet Union. While she was initially doubtful whether Stalin's death would bring about a fundamental change in the totalitarian regime,[111] she eventually came to realise that post-Stalinist Russia was no longer totalitarian in her sense of the term. 'In retrospect', she wrote in 1967, Stalin's death was followed by 'an authentic, though never unequivocal, process of detotalitarization'.[112] She backed this claim with evidence about recent developments under Khrushchev's leadership, including the liquidation of the police empire, the dismantling of concentration camps, the 'rich recovery of the arts', the disappearance of theatrical show trials and even the holding of a trial with hearings.[113] In short, total domination was no longer a goal after Stalin's death. Arendt was ambiguous as to why this 'detotalitarization' occurred, suggesting various possible explanations without drawing a clear conclusion. She was similarly unsure whether the 'detotalitarization' process could be reversed, mindful of the ways in which Stalin's purges came and went in his lifetime.[114] The details of Arendt's conjectures on post-Stalinist Russia are interesting, but they do not need to concern us in the present context.[115] The relevant point is that she kept her theory of totalitarianism unaltered when confronted with the new post-Stalinist reality. On her view, totalitarianism (by definition) must seek territorial expansion and total domination. Therefore, the Soviet Union *after* Stalin as well as before him could not be regarded as totalitarian.

Arendt reiterated a similar sense of confidence in her 'last public statement on Stalin and Stalinism', on 26 April 1972.[116] On this day she spoke in a seminar at Columbia University, convened under the title 'Stalinism in Retrospect'. Her aim was to reconsider Stalinism in light of three 'noteworthy' books by Russian authors recently made available to a Western audience.[117] These books were Roy Medvedev's *Let History Judge*, Nadezhda Mandelstam's *Hope against Hope* and a version of Aleksandr Solzhenitsyn's *The First Circle*.[118] The seminar took place in an intimate setting, with less than two dozen people attending. Arendt was more relaxed than usual, willing to explore provisional ideas, consider questions she was not quite able to answer and even show a sense of humour (which she is often said to have lacked).[119] In spite of her less guarded tone, however, her central message remained the same: none of the three books in question 'tell us anything "new", or anything that we did not know in principle'.[120] The only news was that the Russians themselves had known more about Stalin's crimes than was previously thought in the West. Whether Arendt unduly minimised the significance of the new literature is, of course, a matter for debate. But my present point is this: she remained confident to the very end that the theory of totalitarianism she had formed by the early 1950s had stood the test of time.

In spite of her confidence, however, Arendt's theory was contested and challenged by rival theories of totalitarianism in her lifetime, as it is today. One such theory was proposed by Isaiah Berlin.

The Totalitarian Mind: Berlin on Totalitarianism

Unlike Arendt, Berlin has little to say on either extermination or concentration camps. In fact, he has relatively little to say on the institutional aspect of totalitarianism. His main focus is on a set of ideas comprising the totalitarian mind; much of his energy is directed to analysing the ways in which totalitarians themselves *justify* oppression.[121] The first set of key ideas that Berlin preliminarily identified between the mid-1940s and the early 1950s were utopianism, scientism, paternalism, political violence and monism. Then, in the mid-1950s, he formed his concept of positive liberty, into which he integrated all of these key ideas comprising the totalitarian mind.

Utopianism

Let me begin with utopianism. By this Berlin means a faith in the possibility of realising an ideal society, in which all human problems, including normative ones, are solved once and for all. Utopian politics is not about providing piecemeal solutions to problems as they arise, such as when a government implements a tax reform to tackle inequality or when it introduces new visa rules to control migration. Rather, its aim is to provide what Berlin, obviously alluding to the Nazis, calls a 'final solution', after which everyone knows how he or she ought to live and is able to live as he or she should, both as an individual and as a member of society. One problem with this type of utopianism is that it raises the stakes of politics so high that it deprives men and women of their capacity for sensible cost–benefit analysis. In utopian politics, the benefits of realising an ideal society *always* outweigh the costs incurred in doing so. A further problem is that the goal of utopian politics is so far-fetched that its realisation is indefinitely postponed. The utopian goal, to cite George Crowder's apt characterisation, 'is not merely improvement but perfection, the complete realization of humanity's potential'.[122] A utopian struggle for such a goal continues so long as the complete realisation of humanity's potential remains unfulfilled, that is, in practical terms, in perpetuity. The costs of utopian politics thus accumulate indeterminately, while the promised delivery of the benefits is never accomplished. As Berlin succinctly puts it in a 1988 essay, 'if one really believes that such a [final] solution is possible, then surely no cost would be too high to obtain it: to make mankind just and happy and creative and harmonious for ever—what could be too high a price to pay for that? To make such an omelette, there is surely no limit to the number of eggs that should be broken—that was the faith of Lenin, of Trotsky, of Mao, for all I know of Pol Pot.'[123]

'Eggs' stand for human lives and an 'omelette' for a utopian society: these words by Berlin register his concern with the instrumental use of violence in utopian politics—the *breaking* of the eggs. Of course, one does not need to be a utopian to justify violence in politics. On the contrary, self-professed realists often appeal to the 'lesser evil' argument to that end. Violence is inherently undesirable, they argue, but it ought to be used in extreme circumstances so long as it is necessary for avoiding a greater evil. Nevertheless, while realists keep the stakes of politics low and set a fairly strict limit upon the degree of violence that could be used as a means towards an end politically, utopian cost–benefit analysis, and the gross exaggeration of estimated benefits that it entails, removes the limits altogether. It may be regrettable to murder a monarch and his family, starve an 'enemy' national group, send 'reactionaries' to labour camps and so on, but in the totalitarian mind these measures are always justified by the eventual gain which they are supposed to bring about: an ideal future society. Berlin cites Plekhanov's prophetic words to illustrate the utopian mentality: 'The safety of the revolution is the highest law.'[124] Plekhanov asserted this in theory; the Bolsheviks carried it out in practice.[125]

As his references to Plekhanov, Lenin, Trotsky, Mao and Pol Pot indicate, Berlin's critical discussion of utopianism is principally targeted at the left-wing variants of totalitarianism. But he apparently considered his 'utopian reading' of totalitarianism to be applicable to the right-wing variants, including Nazism.[126] While his comments on Nazism are limited and scattered, when asked to clarify his views Berlin tended to highlight the allegedly utopian aspect of Nazism. According to him, rank-and-file Nazis were not mad, irrational or pathological, but ignorant and misinformed.[127] If they supported or even took part in the persecution of Jews, for example, they did so because they were misled into believing that the elimination of the Jews was necessary for realising the utopian goals that the Nazi leadership postulated. The root cause of Nazi evil, on this account, was not inherent human perversity or cruelty, but misunderstanding or a lack of information.

It is worth asking an obvious question here: does Berlin's 'utopian' reading of Nazism do justice to reality? I doubt it. Consider a small sample of Nazi crimes. First: on 25 April 1938, a group of SA men entered a café in Vienna to 'force all the Jews inside to clean the café—with all the curtains drawn back so the crowd outside could watch. The SA ordered the Jews to move furniture, pile up chairs, wash the floors, and clean the silver. Moreover, they instructed the victims to chant insulting and humiliating words and demanded middle-aged un-athletic men to do knee-bending exercises and jump over tables and chairs.'[128]

Second: on 12 May 1942, an SS officer and Nazi filmmakers arrived in Warsaw ostensibly to shoot a scene at the ritual baths on Dzielna Street. Having gathered '20 Orthodox Jews with ear-locks and 20 upper-class women', the Nazis stripped them, made both sexes get into one ritual bath together and forced them 'into lewd and obscene acts imitating the sexual behaviour of animals'. The filmmakers recorded the scene to show the world 'how low the Jews ha[d] fallen in their morals, that modesty between the sexes ha[d] ceased among them and that they practice[d] sexual immorality in public'.[129]

Third: on 1 May 1943, in the stone quarry of the Buchenwald camp, SS officers 'bet each other six cigarettes or two glasses of beer apiece as to who could kill a prisoner in a given group by throwing stones from above. When their throwing marksmanship grew poor, they lost patience and simply started shooting. The result of this "pastime" was seventeen dead and wounded. "Shot while attempting to escape", as the official reports read. In every camp the number of such mass murders was legion.'[130]

The fact of these instances—of what Arendt called 'spontaneous bestiality'—does not mean that Nazism was a mere assemblage of base savageries.[131] As thinkers such as Zygmunt Bauman have highlighted (though with considerable exaggeration), Nazism certainly originated in part from instrumental rationality, technology and various aspects of modernity.[132] Nevertheless, sheer cruelty, hatred, malice, sadism and a perverse sense of 'fun' were widely observed across different facets of Nazi rule, and they have nothing to do with utopianism in Berlin's sense. The murderous game in which the camp guards in Buchenwald indulged surely made no contribution whatsoever to the realisation of humanity's potential. How would Berlin respond to this criticism? Henry Hardy's correspondence with Berlin gives us a clue. Expressing his reservations about Berlin's utopian reading of Nazism, Hardy told him, 'I bet that many of [the Nazis] simply hated Jews on no rational grounds, and didn't have qualms about acting accordingly; and, even if they did have false beliefs, would not have been impressed if their error had been pointed out to their satisfaction.'[133] Berlin's reply to Hardy is consistent but disappointing. He conceded the existence of evil and accepted that some 'evil people [. . .] do evil because it is evil'. Still, he defended his utopian reading of Nazism. In his view, most rank-and-file Nazis were 'ordinary non-evil Germans', who nevertheless committed crimes because they were misled into believing that persecution, genocide and so on were instrumental in realising 'the good life for Germans'.[134] For better or worse, Berlin believed that Nazi totalitarianism was no less utopian than its communist counterpart.

Scientism, Paternalism and Political Violence

Among the diversity of forms that utopianism may take, Berlin is chiefly concerned with that which claims to be supported by scientific knowledge. Soviet communism is the principal target of his criticism, as its architects, defenders and fellow travellers have often claimed that their politics is underpinned by historical materialism as the 'science of history'.[135] As is well known, Berlin expresses his doubts about the feasibility of a scientific history via his engagement with his contemporary and rival, the Marxist historian E. H. Carr.[136] Berlin also provides a sustained critique of 'scientism', the over-application of scientific methods to human problems, via his engagement with rationalist thinkers from Helvétius and Condorcet to August Comte and Karl Marx.[137] In essence, Berlin's position is one of striking a balance between the under- and overestimation of the power of science and of reason itself, based on the Kantian conviction that reason ought to be conscious of its own limits and refrain from trespassing beyond its proper boundaries. While he concedes that '[w]hat science can achieve must be welcomed', he expresses his doubts about 'the truth of Freud's dictum that while science cannot explain everything, nothing else can do'.[138] On this, if not on issues in political economy, Berlin disagrees with Karl Popper and agrees with Friedrich Hayek.[139] *Pace* Popper, there is no such thing as a 'unity of social and natural sciences'.[140]

Berlin's attack on scientism is not solely philosophical or methodological but also *moral* in nature. What is morally wrong with the utopian attempt to conscript science into politics? Berlin's answer is threefold. First, anticipating Arendt's concern in the post-*Origins* period,[141] Berlin warns of the sense of certainty that scientism breeds in the totalitarian mind. When utopians are convinced that their political programme is scientifically warranted, they feel entitled to dismiss voices of dissent as 'mere opinions', which are not only different from but also categorically inferior to 'scientific truth'. Berlin cites the words of the eighteenth-century physiocrat Le Mercier de la Rivière, which

Arendt also cites, to illustrate his point: 'Euclid is a veritable despot, and the truths of geometry which he has bequeathed to us are truly despotic laws.'[142] If, Berlin continues, 'we do not wish to escape from the truths of geometry, why from the truth of philosophers?'[143]

His second objection to scientism follows from this, and it concerns fanaticism. Not only do scientifically armed utopians dismiss their opponents' opinions in absolute terms. They also suppress their own 'doubts and scruples', assured by 'a fanatical faith' in what they regard as scientific truth.[144] Scientism thus *perverts* scientific rationality. It blinds and thwarts reasonableness, ignoring the fact that there is no finality to scientific truth, that science is and always will be an 'unended quest'.[145]

Berlin's final moral objection to scientism, which has been neglected in the literature, concerns the psychology of the utopians themselves. As they convince themselves to their own satisfaction of their epistemological superiority over their enemies, scientifically armed utopians lose their sense of responsibility and inflict self-harm on their own moral agency. This is the case because they effectively take flight from the burden of moral choice as they delude themselves into believing that all human problems, including those concerning how one *ought* to live, are scientific ones. It is one thing to join a socialist movement because one believes that this is what justice demands that one should do; it is quite another to join because one is (scientifically) convinced that it is what history dictates that one do. In the first case, one is acting as a moral agent; in the second, one is not.[146] Up to a point, Berlin's critique is a conventionally Humean attack on naturalistic fallacy: 'mere inspection of what happens in the world', Berlin writes, paraphrasing Hume, 'reveals no purpose, dictates no ends, establishes no "values"'.[147] But Berlin's critique is more than that, for given his conception of the human being as a choice-making creature, evading moral choice is not only an intellectual error, but amounts to a flight from the human condition itself. To 'refrain from choosing', Berlin said, 'would make you inhuman'.[148] If this is so, totalitarianism is the rule of the terrified *by the dehumanised.*

A further key component of the totalitarian mind is paternalism. Of course, paternalism in and of itself does not entail totalitarian politics. On the contrary, some liberals endorse a benign form of paternalism, arguing that the liberal state has the responsibility to discourage, if not prohibit, citizens from doing something harmful or otherwise unworthy of being done. For example, they think it reasonable for the liberal state to impose a high duty on tobacco products, to discourage smoking.[149] This type of paternalism does not bother Berlin. He is concerned with a different type that does not encourage or discourage, but forces and coerces. The initial image that Berlin evoked to illustrate his concern is an austere public school. In his June 1946 essay 'Why the

Soviet Union Chooses to Insulate Itself', he depicted Stalin as the old head-master, the Party as his office and Soviet citizens as schoolboys deemed inca-pable of independent thought and judgement.[150] As a school headmaster beats boys or has them beaten in order 'to make men out of callow boys', Stalin and his Party used force against Soviet citizens ostensibly to protect their own interests and promote their own wellbeing.[151] Torture was claimed to be good for the tortured, not for the torturer. Such was the perverse logic of totalitarian paternalism. By way of illustration, consider a Kolyma prisoner's recollections. Off the ship, he and other new arrivals were greeted by a camp guard, who said,

> Comrades! You have all committed various crimes against our just worker-peasant laws. Our great government has granted you the right to live, and a great opportunity—to work for the good of our socialist country and the international proletariat. You all know that in the Soviet Union work is a matter of honour, a matter of glory, a matter of valour and heroism, as was said by our great leader and teacher, Josef Vissarionovich Stalin. Our worker-peasant government and our own Communist party do not inflict punishment. We recognize no penal policy. You have been brought here to enable you to reform yourselves—to realize your crimes, and to prove by honest, self-sacrificing work that you are loyal to socialism and to our be-loved Stalin. Hurrah, Comrades![152]

In retrospect, Berlin's analogy between Stalinist Russia and a public school appears implausibly idyllic. After all, a school headmaster does not send his students to a forced labour camp. Nevertheless, when Berlin wrote his 1946 essay, in the immediate aftermath of World War II, Soviet Russia enjoyed rela-tive stability and openness after the devastating war, following the Great Ter-ror of the late 1930s. The future of the country was uncertain, and this provided some room for optimism. In this milieu, Berlin felt the need to challenge the more traditional image of the Soviet Union as a prison, which he believed to distort reality.[153] He made the following observation to support his analogy: as 'smoking and even rude language are tolerated' on special occasions in school life, restraints on Soviet citizens are sometimes relaxed, such as when the Red Army was let loose abroad after the defeat of the German army.[154]

The earlier prospect for the liberalisation of Soviet Russia had diminished by the end of the 1940s, when Berlin wrote a further and more systematic analysis of Stalinism. He now conceded the stability of the regime, finding little prospect for a short-term 'internal collapse', and likening the new phase of Russian history to a 'long, dark tunnel'.[155] In his January 1952 essay 'Genera-lissimo Stalin and the Art of Government', Berlin proposed to conceive of the post-war Stalinist stability not as quiet equilibrium but as a violently and yet regularly swinging 'pendulum', in which citizens had to follow the ever changing 'zig-zag' Party line by cautiously observing its recurring oscillation between 'Jacobin fanaticism' and post-revolutionary fatigue and apathy.[156] Stalin deliberately and skilfully kept society swinging to hold the system in 'the condition of permanent wartime mobilisation'.[157] Berlin no longer depicted Stalin as a patronising and yet sincere headmaster. He now depicted Stalin as a cruel, corrupt and cynical manipulator. Accordingly, he no longer portrayed Soviet paternalism in the benign image of a public school; he now evoked an alternative, and darker, image of a psychiatric hospital. A psychiatrist knows better than the patient him- or herself about the latter's condition and is professionally entitled to ignore the patient's own diagnosis. Likewise, Stalinist leaders saw themselves as having knowledge superior to that of citizens about the latter's condition, and thought that they were entitled to ignore citizens' own opinions about themselves. In his February 1952 lecture on 'Marxist versus Non-Marxist Ideas in Soviet Policy', Berlin observed that Russian Marxists since Lenin had regarded non-Marxist ideas 'rather as the psychiatrist regards the patient. [...] The patient will go on producing words, but the words aren't worth listening to as a description of the facts, only for the sake of a diagnosis.'[158] Backed by such 'scientific' certainty, those in power completely dismissed the egalitarian idea that everyone's opinion demands respect and deserves to be heard. By the same token, Berlin no longer depicted totalitarian citizens as disciplined schoolboys occasionally indulging in bad behaviour. He now depicted them as 'a passive, frightened herd', bullied into an 'unnatural [...] form of life'.[159]

If scientism justifies paternalism from above by assigning to the self-nominated elite epistemological *superiority* over the masses, a certain type of irrationalism justifies paternalism from below by stigmatising the masses as epistemologically *inferior* to the elite. Applied to politics, this type of irrationalism is likely to give rise to violence, because if the masses are deemed stupid, the elite are unlikely to try to persuade them but are prone to use force to coerce them into doing what the elite think they ought to do. According to Berlin, totalitarianisms of all stripes contain such irrationalist paternalism within themselves. His antihero in this context is Joseph de Maistre, about whom he began writing as early as the 1940s.[160] A deeply pessimistic thinker appalled by the chaos of the French Revolution, Berlin observes, Maistre regarded ordinary men and women as incurably wilful, ignorant and idiotic. Maistre thought that rational justification for legitimate authority was useless for, and irrelevant to, the masses; it is the terror of mysterious authority alone that could save ordinary men and women from their own idiocy. Berlin does not claim that Maistre's work, historically speaking, has had significant influence over later fascist or totalitarian movements. His suggestion, rather, is that Maistre's vision had an *affinity*, unmatched among his contemporaries', with the blood-spattered events of Berlin's time.[161] On Berlin's reading, Maistre is not so much a philosopher as a prophet, whose 'deeply pessimistic vision is the heart of the totalitarian-isms, both left and right, of our terrible century'.[162]

Observe Berlin's reference to the left, as well as the right, in the passage just cited. This indicates his conviction that communist totalitarianism is not a form of untainted ultra-rationalism, notwithstanding its alleged commit-ment to 'scientific' socialism. Rather, it is a mixture of rationalist and irratio-nalist components, the latter originating from Lenin's all-too-easy appeal to revolutionary violence. According to Berlin, communists from Marx to Ple-khanov still belonged to the world of Enlightenment rationalism. They at-tempted to persuade their enemies and educate the masses, in spite of their occasional rhetorical outbursts and flirtation with violent tactics. Lenin, by contrast, belonged to a different, more paranoiac world of the twentieth century. His method was above all coercion, believing that the 'masses were too stupid and too blind to be allowed to proceed in the direction of their own choosing'.[163] His dismissal of 'the function and value of the intellect' was less akin to his left-wing predecessors than to 'traditionalist, anti-rationalist right-wing thought', to which Maistre gave the most powerful expression.[164] To this extent, the divide between the political left and right broke down with Lenin. Like Maistre's mysterious authority, Lenin's revolutionary van-guard demanded 'uncritical worship' on the part of ordinary men and women, whom Lenin, like Maistre, considered to be 'wild, bad, stupid and unruly'.[165] While Berlin associates scientifically armed paternalism with left-wing totalitarianism, he sees irrationalist paternalism as a shared feature of left- and right-wing totalitarianisms.

Monism

Monism is the final major component of the totalitarian mind that Berlin iden-tified prior to formulating his concept of positive liberty. As critics have noted, his usage of the term is rather loose, assembling distinct claims under the generic 'heading of monism'.[166] Nevertheless, it is not difficult to specify the most fundamental meaning Berlin assigns to 'monism'. Ontological in na-ture, monism claims that the values human beings pursue and live by, such as liberty, justice, equality and courage, do not conflict with each other but form a frictionless whole. To this Berlin often adds a further, epistemological, mean-ing; namely, that the structure of human value is not only frictionless, but also intelligible, at least to the gifted few, if not to the stupid many. So defined, monism in its weak form recognises barriers between different values, but claims that the barriers can be offset, if not eliminated, as 'values may be ranked from superior to subordinate, or [. . .] the proper method or rule will permit us to arrive at the single correct resolution'.[167] A classic example of weak monism so conceived is utilitarianism, especially in its elegantly simple Benthamite form. This is ontologically monist in that it proposes the 'principle of utility' to be the ultimate 'standard of right and wrong'.[168] On this view, the pursuit of pleasure and the avoidance of pain is the fundamental principle that arbitrates each and every value conflict. Benthamite utilitarianism is also epistemologically monist in that it claims that pleasure and pain can be measured and compared, at least in principle. Whenever there is a conflict between multiple values, one is supposed to be able to settle it by an appeal to the two quantifiable 'sovereign masters' that allegedly govern humankind: pleasure and pain.[169]

Berlin certainly rejects utilitarianism and other forms of weak monism as false, for he holds the rival, pluralist, view, according to which different values are not always capable of being ranked or adjudicated to avoid conflict. But his chief target of criticism is *strong* monism, which he, in a manner reminiscent of Popper's 'enemies of the open society', associates with Plato, Rousseau, Hegel and Marx.[170] Strong monism claims that all human values *entail* each other, such that each and every element that constitutes the good, the true and the beautiful ultimately harmonises with the others to form a coherent whole. To cite Berlin's favourite metaphor: strong monists believe that the values men and women live by are like a 'jigsaw puzzle'. They fit together to form a coherent pattern, as the pieces of a jigsaw puzzle, if correctly arranged, form a complete picture.[171] Of course, 'disjected fragments' of a jigsaw puzzle may cause confusion so long as we are ignorant of their proper locations.[172] Similarly, multiple human values in our highly imperfect world may *appear* to conflict with each other, such as when a society fails to provide citizens with security without compromising their civil rights. Nevertheless, strong monists argue, all value conflicts are in principle soluble and will prove to be illusory in the long run, just as all fragments of a jigsaw puzzle are in principle capable of fitting together. In an ideal society, where a 'final solution' is implemented, everyone has an appropriate place and a proper role to play to be a part of the harmonious whole. Strong monism in this way guarantees the possibility of the 'complete realization of humanity's potential'.[173]

Like paternalism and scientism, monism does not in itself entail or necessarily lead to totalitarian politics. This is hardly surprising. In Berlin's view, political thought in the West, especially until the rise of romanticism in the late eighteenth century, has been predominantly monistic. If so, and if monism entailed totalitarian politics, Western political practice would have been more totalitarian than it had been. Nevertheless, Jonathan Allen overstates his case when he writes that 'the tie [Berlin draws] between monism and totalitarian politics' is not 'a logical or necessary connection' but 'a close—but still contingent—historical association'.[174] Allen is right to emphasise that the link *from* monism *to* totalitarianism is not a necessary one. For example, both Bentham's utilitarianism and Marx's theory of history are monistic in Berlin's sense; but one did not lead to totalitarian politics, while the other did. This conceded, however, the link *from* totalitarianism *to* monism is not equally contingent. On the contrary, Berlin believes that all totalitarian politics assume some form of monism.[175] He writes,

> One belief, more than any other, is responsible for the slaughter of individuals on the altars of the great historical ideals [. . .]. This is the belief that somewhere, in the past or in the future, in divine revelation or in the mind of an individual thinker, in the pronouncements of history or science, or in the simple heart of an uncorrupted good man, there is a final solution. This ancient faith rests on the conviction that all the positive values in which men have believed must, in the end, be compatible, and perhaps even entail one another.[176]

Whether left-wing or right-wing, totalitarians must, as a matter of logical necessity, assume the truth of monism, because otherwise their utopian aspiration for a 'final solution' would be unintelligible. If monism is untrue and human values do not form a frictionless whole, room for conflict is in principle ineliminable and the problem of how to live cannot be solved once and for all. Monism is a necessary condition for totalitarianism, and totalitarian politics a probable implication of monism.[177]

Positive Liberty Revisited

As I discussed in Chapter 2, it was only in the late 1950s that Berlin came to form his concept of positive liberty as the final component comprising the totalitarian mind. Two main factors account for the relatively late maturing of his thinking on this issue. First, it simply took time for Berlin to form a satisfactory conceptual apparatus to account for various concepts and conceptions of liberty/freedom. Second, and more importantly in the present context, he had not fully realised in the 1940s how central the idea of *freedom* was to totalitarians' justification for their oppressive behaviour. It was only in the early 1950s that Berlin came to see, as he would later put it, that 'Stalinist and communist patter about "true freedom"' was no mere rhetoric but 'cost innocent lives'.[178]

In its mature formulation, Berlin's positive liberty designates self-mastery. While this concept may be understood in different ways, all conceptions of positive liberty invariably entail a distinction between a higher and a lower self, between one that masters and the other that is mastered. Although such a division—the 'mythology of the real self'—could be individualist and politically harmless, it is inherently vulnerable to appropriation and abuse, and self-mastery is liable to be transformed into mastery by others. Berlin's antihero in this context, as I observed in Chapter 2, is Rousseau, whose notion of the general will encapsulates the 'grotesque and hair-raising paradox, whereby a man is told that to be deprived of his liberty is to be given a higher, nobler liberty'.[179] For Berlin, Rousseau is 'a madman with a system' and 'a highly consistent monomaniac'.[180] 'From Robespierre and Babeuf to Marx and Sorel, Lenin, Mussolini, Hitler and their successors', the Rousseauian robbing of freedom 'has played a major part in the great revolutions of our time'.[181]

Recent Rousseau scholars have vigorously repudiated Berlin's totalitarian reading of Rousseau. They accuse Berlin of anachronism, of projecting his own Cold War-era concerns onto the eighteenth-century figure, who thought and wrote in fundamentally different terms.[182] It is a matter of debate whether Berlin's recent critics are themselves guilty of anachronism; their desire to replace a totalitarian Rousseau with a liberal egalitarian Rousseau may be an expression of their own post-Cold War concerns.[183] Be that as it may, they are right to note that Berlin's critical remarks on Rousseau say more about Berlin than about Rousseau.[184] All of the key components of the totalitarian mind that Berlin identified by the mid-1950s meet in what he takes to be Rousseau's theory of liberty. In the first place, Berlin's Rousseau is utopian, professing to have found a theory of liberty so compelling that 'nobody need trouble to look for the solution again'.[185] He discovered a 'final solution'. Next, Berlin sees Rousseau as the bridge between Kant and Hegel, interpreting him as rationalist in a pejorative sense, that is, as someone who demands that a lower, irrational self be subordinated to its higher, more rational counterpart. This is short of full-fledged scientism, for which Berlin holds Marx accountable. Nevertheless, Rousseau's rationalism is, in Berlin's view, scientism in embryo, to the extent that it too demands that the oppressed should 'act in a way in which he would order himself to act' if he had known better.[186] Finally, Berlin's Rousseau is an arch-monist, who 'solved' by way of conceptual manipulation the conflict between the fundamental desire for liberty and the no less fundamental need for communal authority. His notion of the general will is nothing other than a device by which this value conflict is resolved with a 'sleight of hand'.[187] In short, Berlin's Rousseau is guilty of utopianism, rationalism (or proto-scientism), paternalism and monism; that is, of the main ideas comprising the totalitarian mind. His political thought played a decisive role in transforming hitherto harmless positive liberty into 'something close to a pure totalitarian doctrine'.[188]

The Power of Ideas 1: The Russian Paradigm

The last issue to consider in this chapter concerns Berlin's methodology. Why did he focus on totalitarian *ideas*, in stark contrast to Arendt's anti-intellectualist approach in *Origins*? Needless to say, it hardly answers the question to merely evoke Berlin's profession and say, 'because he was a historian of ideas'. This answer would be anachronistic as well as circular. When he began writing on totalitarianism in the mid-1940s, Berlin was not yet the full-fledged historian of ideas that he would later become. True, as early as 1939 he had published his first major work of intellectual history, *Karl Marx: His Life and Environment*. But he had also published essays in other genres, and the direction in which his work would develop in the future was at that point by no means predetermined. Berlin did not focus on totalitarian ideas because he was a historian of ideas; rather, his study of totalitarianism gradually turned him into a historian of ideas. It is worth recalling, additionally, that the intellectual historical approach was not the only option available at that time to those who were attempting to analyse totalitarianism and track its sources. Of course, this approach attracted an influential group of thinkers, including Talmon and Popper, whom Berlin admired.[189] Nevertheless, a no less powerful group of scholars, including Carl Friedrich and Zbigniew Brzezinski, was concurrently pioneering a sociological approach, directing their attention to the configuration of power in the totalitarian state.[190] Besides, as I have discussed, Arendt was inventing yet another approach, vocally expressing doubts about the merit of various intellectual historical approaches. Why, then, did Berlin choose to focus on the totalitarian *mind*?

Arguably the most important reason concerns Berlin's view of the national character of Russia.[191] According to him, Russians are endowed with an extraordinary enthusiasm for abstract ideas. 'One of the basic characteristics of the Russians', he observes, 'is the extreme rigour of their logic, greater than that of other nations, though it is true that they are sometimes apt to start with peculiar premises, and argue them through to a weird conclusion.'[192] This tendency was particularly strong among the educated minority, who tended to be sharply separated from the rest of Russian society due to the sheer size of the country, its mainly agrarian economy and the low level of literacy among the peasantry. Their sense of alienation was especially acute in the nineteenth century, when Russia's interaction with Western Europe dramatically increased. Immersed in Western science, literature and culture and yet not a part of the Western world, the educated minority oscillated between enthusiasm and envy, between admiration for the West and resentment towards it. Similarly, being part of Russia and yet somewhat disconnected from its traditional way of life, they held conflicting attitudes towards their compatriots in the agrarian countryside, sometimes idealising them, sometimes becoming frustrated by their passivity, ignorance and 'backwardness'. The educated minority thus felt both the West and Russia to be simultaneously close and distant. This complex dynamic nurtured among them a craving for *imported* ideas, which they studied with the utmost seriousness. The Russians, especially the elite, Berlin observes, 'absorb ideas from others and believe in them with a degree of passion nobody had begun to approach, and they always try to realise them in practice. When the facts prove obdurate, they simply try to bend the facts.'[193]

No other group embodied this distinctly Russian outlook better than the so-called 'intelligentsia'. A normative conception rather than a sociological one, the intelligentsia is much more than 'intellectuals' in the Western, let alone British, sense.[194] A 'necessary condition of membership' in this Russian group, Andrzej Walicki observes, is 'an ethical commitment to the struggle for progress, conceived as the liberation of the people from political and socio-economic oppression'.[195] The intelligentsia comprises radicals with utopian inclinations, often dreaming about revolutionary change and sometimes tempted by violent methods. Yet, anti-utopian though he is, Berlin does not condemn this group as mere fanatics. Quite the reverse: he admires their seriousness, moral integrity, passion for social reform and humanist outlook. In fact, some of his finest essays vividly portray the colourful personalities of some of the leading members of the intelligentsia, including Alexander Herzen, Vissarion Belinsky and Nikolay Chernyshevsky. Nowhere else are Berlin's fascination with human idiosyncrasies, his curiosity about the human drama and his playful sense of the human comedy exuded more markedly than from his essays on the Russian intelligentsia.

Nevertheless, Berlin's admiration for this group is by no means unlimited. He records their excesses, which include some of the major sins of which Berlin disapproves most.[196] For example, many members of the Russian intelligentsia regarded individual (or negative) liberty 'as a liberal catchword', willing to ignore the actual opinions of the peasants in whose name they acted.[197] They were, in Rousseauian terms, often inclined to force peasants to be free. Moreover, some of the intelligentsia resorted to physical violence. A dramatic example is 'the celebrated terrorist' Sergey Kravchinsky, who assassinated the head of the secret police in St Petersburg in 1878, before migrating to England.[198] But the problem Berlin identifies with the Russian intelligentsia is more than one of individual excesses such as Kravchinsky's. It is, rather, that their enthusiasm for ideas was prone to extremism, which gradually undermined their original humanist outlook and paved the way for Bolshevism. In effect, Berlin's story of the Russian intelligentsia is a tragic one. The early intelligentsia's moral integrity turned into Lenin's fanaticism; their intellectual seriousness into Lenin's dogmatism; and their passion for social reform into Lenin's indifference to the human costs deemed necessary for realising the communist goal. Such was the paradoxical legacy of the Russian intelligentsia, and of the Russian national character that they exemplified. 'Russians have', Berlin writes, 'a singular genius for drastically simplifying the ideas of others, and then acting upon them; our world has been transformed, for good and ill, by the unique Russian application of Western social theory to practice.'[199] This explains why Berlin's analysis of totalitarianism had to take the form of intellectual history. He accords prime importance to the role of ideas in accounting for the political disasters of the twentieth century because Berlin's archetypical totalitarians, the Bolsheviks, *themselves* were idea-driven fanatics.[200]

The Power of Ideas 2: From Russia to Germany

Berlin is ambiguous, however, as to whether Russia's enthusiasm for ideas was *sui generis* or merely extreme in comparative terms. Sometimes he appears to propose a Russian *exceptionalism*, indicating that the Russians are unique among the nations when it comes to their attitude towards ideas. Yet sometimes he suggests a more moderate Russian *extremism*, highlighting the nation's stronger interest in ideas and the greater willingness to apply them in practice *relative to* other nations. I do not think this tension is resolved in Berlin's work. Those two sides co-exist in his analysis. But his emphasis shifts towards the weaker, relational pole from his mid-career onwards, when he gradually formed his 'power of ideas' thesis. Challenging the Marxist preoccupation with the socio-economic structure, this thesis claims that the role of ideas in shaping *human* history—in Russia or elsewhere—is typically underestimated and demands greater attention. Berlin sometimes explains his convictions in terms of his 'Russianness', saying, 'To my Russian origins I think I owe my lifelong interest in ideas.'[201] But his chief source of inspiration in developing the 'power of ideas' thesis is Heinrich Heine and his fragments 'On the History of Religion and Philosophy in Germany'. In his characteristic manner, Berlin summarises and dramatises Heine's central message in a memorable proverbial form. 'Over a hundred years ago', Berlin writes, 'the German poet Heine warned the French not to underestimate the power of ideas: philosophical concepts nurtured in the stillness of a professor's study could destroy a civilisation.'[202] Berlin holds this to be true. That is why he studies *ideas* in order to understand the catastrophic destruction of civilisations in the twentieth century.

The reference to Heine supports Berlin's theory of totalitarianism in a two-fold manner. It allows him, first, to highlight the significance of ideas with great rhetorical force and, second, to forge the connection between Russia and Germany, between the left- and right-wing totalitarianisms. The poet's focus is on

Germany indeed. After calling Robespierre a mere 'hand of Jean-Jacques Rousseau',[203] Heine turns to the Germans, writing that

> the German revolution will not prove any milder or gentler because it was preceded by the 'Critique' of Kant, by the 'Transcendental Idealism' of Fichte, or even by the Philosophy of Nature. These doctrines served to develop revolutionary forces that only await their time to break forth and to fill the world with terror and with admiration. Then will appear Kantians [...] who will mercilessly upturn with sword and axe the soil of our European life in order to extirpate the last remnants of the past. There will come upon the scene armed Fichteans whose fanaticism of the will is to be restrained neither by fear nor by self-interest [...]. But most of all to be feared would be the philosophers of nature [...]. [T]here is aroused in [them] that ancient German eagerness for battle which combats not for the sake of destroying, not even for the sake of victory, but merely for the sake of the combat itself. [...] There will be played in Germany a drama compared to which the French Revolution will seem but an innocent idyll. [...] And the hour will come. As on the steps of an amphitheatre the nations will group themselves around Germany to witness the terrible combat.[204]

Berlin's discussion of Germany shares important parallels with Heine's, which he repeatedly cites. Of particular importance is Berlin's view that early modern Germany, like nineteenth-century Russia, suffered from a certain inferiority complex for a range of reasons, including relative inactivity during the Renaissance, the 'terrible devastation of the Thirty Years War', and the division of the German-speaking people into numerous principalities and territorial units.[205] French-inspired reforms by Frederick the Great solved some problems but exacerbated others. Again, as in Russia, a schism widened in Germany between the elite and the masses, between the Francophile king and his 'imported' French officials on the one hand, and humiliated and patronised ordinary Germans, 'particularly the traditional, religious, economically backward East Prussians' on the other.[206] Then came Napoleon's invasion, which completed the humiliation and incited 'the first great upsurge of nationalist passion' among the Germans.[207] By the late nineteenth century, Germany became a classic case of what Berlin describes as a 'bent twig' nation: a nation that has been subjected to so much external humiliation that 'when released it strikes uncontrollably against the source of deformity [...] like a twig deformed by an unnatural outside force'.[208]

The similarity between Germany and Russia ends there, however, for the Germans, unlike the Russians, did much more than develop imported ideas. They were indeed highly original inventors, whose tremendous creative energy found most vigorous expression in romanticism, understood by Berlin as an offshoot of the Counter-Enlightenment and a reaction to the Enlightenment rationalism that had been advocated by eighteenth-century French *philosophes*. As is often noted, Berlin's appraisal of romanticism is a highly ambivalent one. On the one hand, he is critical of its ultra-nationalist, irrationalist and sometimes antisemitic tendencies. On the other hand, he generously concedes the merits of its attack on certain superficial tendencies characterising overly optimistic Enlightenment rationalism. Berlin scholars have paid greater attention to the latter aspect, for they are naturally intrigued that the twentieth century's most celebrated liberal thinker should take inspiration from oft-demonised German romantics.[209] Yet my concern here is with the other, less striking side of Berlin's assessment of romanticism. Unlike Arendt, Berlin never denies the romantics' share of responsibility for the eventual rise of right-wing totalitarianism. In fact, he gives Hegel, Fichte and Nietzsche prominent places in his demonology of totalitarianism. Nor does Berlin deny the distinctively German character of National Socialism. Again unlike Arendt, Berlin agrees with the mainstream view of Hitler as a fanatical German nationalist, albeit of an exceptionally racist kind. Moreover, he uses the idea of 'bent twig' nationalism to understand inter-war Germany as well as post-Napoleonic Germany. The German twig was forcibly bent yet again at the end of World War I, when the salt of the Treaty of Versailles was added to the wound of the devastating military defeat. And this time the twig did more than swing back to strike the source of deformity. It exploded into National Socialism, asserting itself in the form of expansionism as well as wreaking vengeance on 'November Criminals' and their allegedly conspiratorial allies. If Arendt gives a resolutely international, pan-European account of the rise of Nazism, Berlin gives a distinctly national one.

Many historians have expressed reservations about Berlin's discussion of romanticism and the Counter-Enlightenment and their ostensibly German character. Some consider Berlin's stark contrast between the Enlightenment on the one hand and the Counter-Enlightenment and romanticism on the other to be exaggerated;[210] and others find his association of these two rival movements with France and Germany, respectively, crude and simplistic.[211] I do not intend to contribute to this debate here. My present purpose is to explain why Berlin's study of totalitarianism took the form of *intellectual* history. The answer must be clear by now. First, he considered the Bolsheviks to be idea-driven fanatics, who inaugurated the first full-fledged totalitarianism. Second, contradicting his occasional remarks on Russian exceptionalism, he believed ideas to be the prime motor of general human history. Finally, in the case of Germany, he offered historical and sociological explanations as to why romantic ideas should turn out to be particularly influential and explosive there, based on his un-Arendtian conviction that Nazism should be seen as a form of German nationalism. As I noted, there are internal tensions between Berlin's discussions of Russian, German and general histories, and his multiple reasons for taking an intellectual historical approach are not free of inconsistencies. Yet his choice of method was by no means a contingent product of his inner 'Russianness'. It was a considered choice by someone who was genuinely convinced of the role of ideas in causing political disasters.

Conclusion

In the late 1940s, Arendt and Berlin saw themselves as standing at different historical junctures. For Arendt, recovering from the traumatic loss of her German homeland, the threat of totalitarianism came to a tentative end with the conclusion of World War II. Her task now was to *look back* and ask, 'What happened? Why did it happen? How could it have happened?'[212] For Berlin, having returned from his life-changing visit to the Soviet Union in 1945–46, the menace of totalitarianism was only beginning to grow. His task now was to *look ahead* and contribute to the battle of ideas and ideologies, now fought between the two camps separated by the Iron Curtain. Needless to say, Arendt's and Berlin's assessments of the post-war predicament were both right. The defeat of Nazism and the beginning of the Cold War *both* constituted the hermeneutic horizon within which the two thinkers developed their respective ideas. But their perspectives *were* different, giving rise to two contrasting theories of totalitarianism. One saw totalitarianism as categorically different from its 'traditional' precursors and its contemporary fascist cousins; the other recognised no such discontinuity. One focused on social, economic and institutional factors to track the origins of totalitarianism; the other concentrated on ideational factors to tease out the internal logic of totalitarian oppression. One identified concentration camps as the heart of totalitarianism; the other identified utopianism, scientism, paternalism, monism and positive liberty as the key components comprising the totalitarian mind. One theory of totalitarianism was proposed by a German-Jewish refugee who arrived in New York as a stateless person in 1941; the other theory, by a Russian-Jewish émigré who, having had his cradle burned by the Bolsheviks, had embraced the good fortune of living in England since 1921.[213]

These differences were complicated, but they were to be complicated even further. A very different context abruptly opened up to bring Arendt and Berlin hermeneutically closer to each other in May 1960, when Adolf Eichmann was captured and brought to the State of Israel to be tried for his wartime crimes. As if the past had decided to burst into the present, the man who used to be known as 'the specialist on the Jewish question' in Nazi Germany now stood in a courtroom in the Jewish state that had not existed when his crimes were committed. The trial was extensively covered by the international media, and the history of the recent past began to generate an intense politics of memory. This series of events marked a new round of conflict between Arendt and Berlin. This time the clash centred not so much on history or politics, as on ethics. The geographical epicentre of the conflict shifted, too. The new twin epicentres were no longer Germany and Russia, on which this chapter has focused. Rather, they were Israel, where the Eichmann trial took place, and America, where the publication of Arendt's 'report' on the trial inaugurated a *Kulturkampf*. The next chapter considers this episode.

5

Evil and Judgement

IN THE EARLY morning of 4 March 1957, a man was shot outside his home in Tel Aviv. He died of his injury at a nearby hospital two days later. His name was Rudolf Kastner. Born in Cluj in present-day Romania in 1906, he was known for the controversial role he played during the Hungarian Holocaust. Forming an Aid and Rescue Committee in Budapest, Kastner and his associates entered ransom negotiations with some of the key members of the Nazi personnel, including Adolf Eichmann. They were Zionists, representing a tiny minority separate from both the dominant reformist community and its rival Orthodox counterpart in Hungary. Kastner himself was a 'foreigner', having moved to Budapest only in 1941 after Hungary annexed Northern Transylvania in August 1940.[1] An outsider to the local Jewish elite, he was not a member of the Judenrat, which the Nazis forced the Budapest Jews to establish in March 1944.[2] Nor was the Zionist-led Aid and Rescue Committee quite in a position to represent Hungarian Jewry as a whole. Yet they took initiatives to bring a halt to the unfolding catastrophe. Although their ambitious plan to save nearly a million Jewish lives in exchange for ten thousand trucks came to naught, their ransom negotiations resulted in the so-called 'Kastner train', arranged in exchange for a cash payment to the Nazis. On 30 June 1944, amid the rapid deportation of at least 434,351 Jews from Hungary to Auschwitz-Birkenau between 15 May and 8 July,[3] 1,684 souls, including Kastner's family members and relatives, boarded the train to leave Budapest.[4] They eventually found themselves in the safety of neutral Switzerland, thereby spared the fate of 564,507 Jews who perished in the Hungarian Holocaust.[5]

Notwithstanding the common epithet for the train, Kastner was by no means the only one involved in the ransom negotiations. Nor was Budapest the only place where such 'blood for goods' negotiations took place during World War II.[6] However, Kastner became an especially divisive figure in postwar Israel due to a pamphlet published in 1953. Written by Malkiel Grünwald, an amateur journalist and a member of the religious Zionist party, the pamphlet denounced what the author regarded as Kastner's wartime complicity in the destruction of Hungarian Jewry. It was also an attack on the governing Mapai party, of which Kastner was an important member. Kastner sued Grün-wald for libel, only to find himself on the defensive thanks to Grünwald's talented attorney, Shmuel Tamir. Judge Benjamin Halevi of the Jerusalem District Court accepted most of Grünwald's allegations, (in)famously accusing Kastner of 'selling his soul to the devil'. Kastner claimed that this was a gross miscarriage of justice, comparing himself to Alfred Dreyfus.[7] But his decision to appeal was to no avail. He was shot while he awaited the first hearing. The Supreme Court eventually overruled the previous verdict, but that happened only in January 1958—nine months after Kastner's death. His wartime conduct has remained divisive to this day.

Hannah Arendt discussed Kastner's wartime activities and his ultimate fate in post-war Israel in *Eichmann in Jerusalem*. She did so most extensively in the controversial seventh chapter of the book entitled 'The Wannsee Conference, or Pontius Pilate', in which she addressed various instances of 'cooperation' between some Jewish leaders and the Nazis. But Kastner also makes an appearance in Chapters 2, 3, 8 and 12, and Judge Halevi's accusation—that Kastner 'sold his soul to the devil'—is cited twice in *Eichmann in Jerusalem*.[8] This is a remarkable fact, because the Jerusalem court in 1961 mostly bypassed the Kastner affair. Involving the first political assassination in the independent State of Israel, this traumatic episode had occurred only a few years earlier and its memory was very much present among those confronting Eichmann in the courtroom.[9] Gideon Hausner, the attorney general and the chief prosecutor, was especially concerned by the risk that the Eichmann trial might re-run the whole Kastner affair. In fact, he requested in advance that his witnesses put the affair aside, 'since this was the trial of the exterminator and not of his victims'.[10] On this Arendt agreed. 'On trial are [Eichmann's] deeds', she wrote, and nothing else that the trial might symbolise.[11] Yet, directly challenging Hausner, she considered it necessary that the issue of Jewish cooperation in general and Kastner's case in particular should be tackled if Eichmann's crimes were to be put properly in perspective. Her intervention proved more successful than she had anticipated. Her Chapter 7 came to dominate the fierce controversy that *Eichmann in Jerusalem* provoked, and Arendt emerged, in the words of Deborah Lipstadt, as 'a more central character in the Eichmann story than Eichmann himself'.[12] There is certainly much more to Arendt's three-hundred-page book than the twenty-two-page chapter.[13] Nevertheless, Chapter 7 has overshadowed the rest of the book and decisively shaped Arendt's reputation and legacy ever since.

The aim of the present chapter is to examine the specifically moral aspect of the Arendt–Berlin conflict by way of considering the Eichmann controversy. As I noted in Chapter 2, Berlin's direct role in the controversy was to assist the publication of the English translation of the Arendt–Scholem exchange in *Encounter* magazine. Beyond this, however, he made critical remarks on *Eichmann in Jerusalem* in letters, conversations and interviews. At first glance, his comments appear to be thoroughly conventional and unoriginal. Like many others, he focused on the book's seventh chapter, while briefly expressing his doubts about Arendt's idea of 'the banality of evil'. He echoed many critics' remarks on *Eichmann in Jerusalem*: that Arendt was arrogant to pass judgement on the victims of the Shoah; that the tone of her criticism of the wartime Jewish leadership was malicious, heartless and utterly inappropriate; and that she was infected by a certain masochism and even self-hatred, demanding that Jewish victims 'take responsibility', while refraining from expecting the same from non-Jews. Such remarks might sound all too familiar to those who have followed the never-ending Eichmann controversy.[14] But they are more interesting than they might appear to be, when read in conjunction with Berlin's own work. This is the case because he reflected on moral conflict and moral dilemma more deeply than most other philosophers of his generation, arguably including Arendt. He has been credited for pioneering what came to be known as 'value pluralism', one of the most influential ideas in moral philosophy to emerge in the twentieth century.[15] As I shall show, Berlin fully relied on this idea to mount an attack on Arendtian ethics.[16]

The Eichmann Myths

Eichmann in Jerusalem continues to provoke impassioned debate even today, more than half a century after its original publication. As is often the case with emotionally charged debates in which participants project their own identities in various ways, the controversy has generated myths, which I would like to dispel at the outset before tackling more substantive issues. By 'myth' I mean misinformation about the book that falls outside the boundaries of interpretive flexibility. While *Eichmann in Jerusalem*, like other texts, is open to a number of interpretations, some claims made about the book are so devoid of textual support that they may be safely dismissed as misinformation. Five such myths are pertinent in the present context.

Myth 1 is the belief that Arendt was 'soft' on Eichmann. It partly stems from the fact that she firmly refused to characterise Eichmann as sadistic, perverted, megalomaniac or otherwise having abnormal psychological traits. She was well aware that some of the Nazi criminals had such traits. For example, she called Alfred Rosenberg a 'crackpot', Julius Streicher a 'sex criminal' and SA men in general 'beasts in human form'.[17] But she did not think Eichmann belonged to the same category. On the contrary, he was 'terribly and terrifyingly normal',[18] and this observation raised the question that animated the whole of *Eichmann in Jerusalem*: how should we account for the gap between the monstrosity of the Final Solution and the normality of the man who played a key role in it?[19] Of course, it is a matter of debate whether Eichmann was as normal as Arendt took him to be. Many recent studies have indeed challenged this aspect of her book.[20] But what is beyond dispute is that to characterise Eichmann as normal is *not*, in and of itself, to discount his criminality. It is, rather, to refuse to reduce Eichmann to a more familiar criminal type such as the sadist or the sex maniac. Contrary to Myth 1, Arendt explicitly wrote that Eichmann 'had at all times done his best to make the Final Solution final' and that he did so even during the last months of the war when many of his colleagues, including his superior Heinrich Himmler, were willing to abandon or at least suspend the extermination policy.[21] Moreover, conforming to her anti-consequentialist outlook, Arendt not only supported the Jerusalem court's decision to award Eichmann a capital sentence but also argued that the court ought to have placed a stronger emphasis on 'the element of retribution'.[22] In fact, *Eichmann in Jerusalem* ends with an extraordinary scene, in which the author imagines herself in the position of the presiding justice to announce *her* judgement directly addressed to Eichmann. What did she say? She clearly said, 'You must hang.'[23] She was hardly 'soft' on Eichmann.

Myth 2 is the belief that Arendt saw Eichmann as 'a small cog' in the machinery of the Final Solution. Many commentators are unhappy with this 'small cog' theory because this again seems to belittle Eichmann's criminality. The image of the small cog indeed suggests firstly that Eichmann played a minor role in the administration of the Final Solution, and secondly that he was replaceable by someone else who could function equally well as a small cog. These implications may indeed be problematic. But to accuse Arendt of subscribing to this theory is simply wrong. She did introduce the 'small cog' theory in *Eichmann in Jerusalem*, but that was because Eichmann's defence lawyer, Robert Servatius, used it as a defence strategy. And this she at once dismissed as false. While Eichmann's role, in Arendt's view, was cog-like to the extent that it mainly concerned the administration of the Final Solution rather than the conception of its fundamentals, she firmly rejected the 'small cog' theory, observing that Eichmann was not 'as small as the defense wished him to be'.[24] The fact that the defence's claim has been attributed to Arendt vindicates her lament that some critics of *Eichmann in Jerusalem* never bothered to read the book before criticising it.[25]

Nevertheless, it would be unfair to hold Arendt's critics accountable for the creation of *all* myths surrounding the Eichmann controversy. Unfortunately, Arendt herself had a share in generating Myth 3, according to which *Eichmann in Jerusalem* is no more than a trial report. Of course, the book *is* partly a trial report, and Arendt highlighted this aspect when she attempted to refute another myth—call this Myth 4—that her book is a philosophical treatise on evil.[26] As it happens, each of the opposing Myths 3 and 4 contains a degree of truth. *Eichmann* is a multifaceted book that indeed includes *both* a trial report *and* some philosophical reflections on the nature of evil. Also included is Arendt's attack on the chief prosecutor Hausner's attempt to give a 'general picture', to put Eichmann's crimes in perspective. She repeatedly dismissed this attempt as irrelevant to criminal justice, which she insisted was the sole goal of the Eichmann trial. Yet she did not quite think that contextualisation was altogether irrelevant. In fact, she proposed an alternative 'general picture' of her own, writing that 'no report on the Eichmann case, perhaps as distinguished from the Eichmann trial, could be complete without paying some attention to certain facts'.[27] Arendt thus introduced various facts in *Eichmann in Jerusalem* to contextualise the 'Eichmann case' *in her own way*. As Leora Bilsky observes, Arendt's challenge to Hausner concerned not so much *whether* a 'big picture' should be drawn as '*which* "big picture" to draw' as the most appropriate 'historical framework for the trial's story'.[28] In short, *Eichmann in Jerusalem* is more than a trial report.

Finally, Myth 5 is the belief that Arendt 'blamed the victim' instead of blaming the perpetrators. It would not be a myth if it were formulated a little differently, as follows: Arendt blamed *some* victims of the Shoah.[29] The difference might look pedantic, but much of the Eichmann controversy hinges on this deceptively insignificant-looking distinction. Highlighting the disquieting fact that some victims behaved less well than others,[30] Arendt challenged the prosecution's 'general picture' that not only assumed the unity of the Jewish victims but also neatly separated them from the German perpetrators.[31] In other words, contrary to Myth 5, Arendt differentiated between various Jewish victim groups and assessed them differently, instead of treating the Jewish victims as a coherent whole. She drew a particularly sharp contrast between the leadership and ordinary people, approvingly citing the following words of a Theresienstadt survivor: 'The Jewish people as a whole behaved magnificently. Only the leadership failed.'[32] Again, it is open to debate whether this contrast is too simplistic, whether the Jewish leadership 'failed' as Arendt claimed it did and whether the language of 'failure' is helpful in the first place in order to appreciate the role of the Jewish leadership in the context of the Shoah. What is beyond dispute is the inaccuracy of Myth 5—that Arendt blamed *the victim*—in its undifferentiated form.

One further point about Myth 5 is worth highlighting. As I discussed in Chapter 2, arguably the most controversial lines of *Eichmann in Jerusalem* concerned 'th[e] role of the Jewish leaders in the destruction of their own people' as 'the darkest chapter of the whole dark story'.[33] These and other select words from Chapter 7 have been frequently cited by Arendt's critics purportedly to give credence to Myth 5. What the critics do not usually tell us, however, is Arendt's own account of why she decided to write about 'the role of the Jewish leaders' more extensively than one might expect. She wrote,

> I have dwelt on this chapter of the story [...] because it offers the most striking insight into the totality of the moral collapse *the Nazis created* in respectable European society—not only in Germany but in almost all countries, not only among the persecutors but also among the victims.[34]

In Arendt's view, wartime Jewish leaders failed because they operated in an amoral world created by the Nazis. If they acted badly, that was because they had no choice but to act within the realms of possibility that had been demarcated by their enemies. True, Arendt accused some Jewish leaders of naivety and misjudgement, but she ultimately blamed the Nazis for creating the conditions under which those leaders were made to behave, in hindsight, in naive and self-destructive ways. Needless to say, this raises complicated questions concerning asymmetrical power. How much power could the Jewish leaders exercise in opposition to their Nazi oppressors? Were the oppressed entirely powerless? Or did they have some room to exercise agency? If the latter was the case, what *could* they do, exactly? Arendt's thoughts on these questions will be discussed shortly. My present point is this: although she blamed *some* Jewish victims of the Shoah, she placed the *ultimate* blame on the Nazis.

Berlin on *Eichmann in Jerusalem*: A First Look

Having dispelled some of the most common misunderstandings about *Eichmann in Jerusalem*, I would now like to turn to Isaiah Berlin's specifically moral objections to Arendt's 1963 book. His most substantive recorded comments on this issue appear in his 1992 interview with Steven Lukes. The relevant part is worth quoting in full:

> [W]hat does a Jew in the situation described by Miss Arendt do? You are a leader of some Jews in Lithuania. A Nazi official comes to you from the Gestapo and he says, 'You are in charge of the Jews here, they trust you, you manage their lives, you are the head man of the Jewish community, appointed by us. Give us their names and addresses, we wish to know this. Of course we could discover this without you, but it would take us longer, and that would be rather a nuisance for us. If you do this for us, we'll let you go, and you can take seventy-two other people with you. If you don't do it, you know what will happen, to you as well as to all the others.' You might say to yourself: 'how dare I, who am I to choose seventy-two people out of all these people to be saved?' Miss Arendt in effect said that you had no right

to sup with the devil: you should allow yourself to be shot, and that's that. I disagree. In my view there are four possible choices. One is that you say 'I am not playing your game'—in that case you are probably soon executed. The second choice is to commit suicide rather than talk to the Gestapo—at least you'll kill yourself—perfectly worthy, at least your conscience is clear—but perhaps not quite clear, because you might have saved seventy-two people. The third choice is to say, all right, I'll give you the names—and then you tell all the Jews that they must do everything they can to flee; and you know that once your act is discovered you are virtually certain to be killed, that the possibility of escaping is very small. The fourth choice is to accept: you get away, with seventy-two others. There was a man who did this. He was ultimately assassinated in Israel by a relative of one of those he left behind. What is the morally correct answer to this? There can be no question of any trade-off between any of these possibilities. In so extreme a situation, no act by the victims can (*pace* Miss Arendt) be condemned. Whatever is done must be regarded as fully justified. It is inexpressible arrogance on the part of those who have never been placed in so appalling a situation to pass judgement on the decisions and actions of those who have. Praise and blame are out of place—normal moral categories do not apply. All four choices—heroic martyrdom, and the saving of innocent lives at the expense of those of others, can only be applauded.[35]

These words are not from a written piece of work, but from an interview. As such they require some additional explanation. First, 'a leader of some Jews in Lithuania' does not signify any specific individual. It is a heuristic figure that Berlin uses in order to draw attention to the *type* of moral dilemma that confronted some victims of the Shoah, especially at the leadership level. This explains why he is not particularly concerned with the historical accuracy of the story of the tormented Jewish leader. In fact, every time he tells it, he tells a slightly different version. For example, the Jewish leader is located in Hungary in one telling, while he is located in Lithuania in others.[36] Similarly, the number of people he is permitted to take with him is seventy-two in Berlin's interview with Lukes cited above, but it is sixty-five in another telling, fifty-seven in another, and finally 'forty-seven [...], or a hundred and twenty, whatever you like' in yet another.[37] Berlin's lack of precision is not a weakness, however, for his narrative is not meant to be a report on any specific incident, but is a device to highlight an important *aspect* of the Shoah. Arguably, the lack of precision is part of his point, because the kind of moral dilemma Berlin discusses confronted a number of individuals and communities in Hungary, Lithuania, and elsewhere *across* Nazi-occupied territories. Indeed, one tragic feature of the Shoah is that we have no way of ever knowing how many victims were coerced into facing the agonising moral dilemma represented by Berlin's example before perishing, finally deprived of the capacity to bear witness to what had happened to them. It is this indeterminate group of victims that Berlin's Jewish leader is designed to signify.

Next, the 'man [...] ultimately assassinated in Israel' briefly discussed in the interview with Lukes is Rudolf Kastner. We know this because Berlin mentions Kastner's name in a different interview during which he tells the same story.[38] Berlin is, however, consistently confused about the identity of Kastner's assassin.[39] He believes that the assassin was Malkiel Grünwald, the author of the accusatory pamphlet that triggered the Kastner affair in post-war Israel. Grünwald was indeed 'a relative of one of those [Kastner] left behind' in Hungary, and his sense of grievance was an important factor motivating him to publish his pamphlet. By contrast, Kastner's real assassin, Ze'ev Eckstein, had no personal connections to the Hungarian Holocaust, and his motive for assassinating Kastner was not personal but political. For the purpose of this study we do not need to consider Eckstein's complicated life story, or various unanswered questions regarding the circumstances and background of the assassination.[40] Nor is it significant in the present context that Berlin confuses Grünwald with Eckstein, because the focus of Berlin's discussion of Kastner is on the latter's choice *during* the war, not his life and death afterwards. What matters at present is that Berlin considers Kastner's situation in the early 1940s to be an 'appalling' one, to which 'normal moral categories do not apply'. Whether Arendt agrees with this is what I am concerned with in this chapter.

Procedural Objections

Broadly speaking, two lines of objection are discernible in Berlin's critical comments on *Eichmann in Jerusalem*. The first one concerns *who* made the judgement, and *when* and *where* it was made; the second one concerns *what* judgement was made. The first is about the procedure of judgement; the second, the substance of it. Both lines of objection require some interpretive reconstruction on my part. I shall consider the first (procedural) objections in this section and the second (substantive) objections in the next.

Comparable Experience

Let me begin with Berlin's procedural objections. According to him, as 'someone who was sitting safely in New York', Arendt is emphatically not in a position to criticise the conduct of wartime Jewish leaders. She ought not to 'lecture to [victims of the Shoah] about what they should have done when threatened with deportation, death, etc.'[41] Berlin does not demand that observers such as Arendt should be completely silent. If they are inclined to praise or show sympathy for wartime Jewish leaders, they are entitled to do so. But if one is inclined to *blame* them, one ought, first of all, to reconsider. Even if one holds the same view afterwards, one still ought not to express it openly, so as to avoid victim-blaming.

Craig Taylor's recent work on moralism helps us understand this objection.[42] Generally speaking, moralism is a certain type of distortion of morality and it typically involves *excessive* moral judgement. For example, a father is being moral if he calmly tells his child to be quiet when the latter gets too excited in a quiet museum. He is moralising, or is guilty of moralism, if he scolds his child for this minor misbehaviour in a degrading and humiliating manner. To this elementary distinction Taylor adds a further dimension: even if it is not excessive or disproportionately punitive, a moral judgement can turn into a piece of moralism if it is expressed in an inappropriate context. In Taylor's words, 'morally judging another can be unreasonable even though the judgement is true: even though one is uttering a true proposition.'[43] Of course, Berlin did not think that Arendt's criticism of the wartime Jewish leadership contained a true proposition. As I shall elaborate shortly, he considered Arendt to be unduly judgemental and 'moralising' in the conventional sense of passing excessive moral judgement. But he also thought she was moralising in the less conventional sense to which Taylor draws attention. In Berlin's view, it was unreasonable for her to express moral judgement *regardless of* the truth or otherwise of the substance of her judgement.

To understand this objection further, consider Arendt's position in the early 1960s in comparison to Benjamin Halevi's position in the mid-1950s. As the judge of the Jerusalem District Court, Halevi had the formal mandate to express his judgement on Kastner's wartime conduct. Simply put, it was Halevi's job to judge. One may disagree with the substance of his judgement, as the subsequent Supreme Court ruling did. Or one may agree with it, as Halevi himself did even after the Supreme Court's ruling.[44] Regardless, Halevi was certainly in a position to judge, by virtue of his office. Arendt, by contrast, held no comparable office. She had somehow to authorise herself.[45] Were her qualifications, such as her expertise on Nazism, her reputation as a writer and her role as a trial reporter for the *New Yorker* sufficient to authorise her? Berlin thought not. In his view, she failed to see that she was not qualified to judge given her privilege—'the safety of New York'—vis-à-vis those about whom she wrote. This failure was a moral failure that amounted, in Berlin's words, to 'inexpressible arrogance'.

Berlin is, however, ambiguous as to precisely why in the early 1960s Arendt was not in a position to express her judgement. In his interview with Lukes, he suggested a lack of comparable experience as the reason. That she 'ha[d] never been placed' in a situation comparable to that of the tormented wartime

Jewish leaders disqualified her from expressing her judgement on them.[46] Taken literally, this is an implausible claim. We routinely form and express opinions on the decisions and actions of others in whose situations we have never been placed. Consider the well-known example from Jean-Paul Sartre's *Existentialism and Humanism*.[47] During the German occupation of France, Sartre tells us, a former student came to see him to seek advice on the moral conflict the young man was facing: whether to join the Free French forces in exile or to stay at home to look after a vulnerable mother deserted by her husband, a Nazi collaborator. To complicate the matter, Sartre's former student had a *motive* for joining the Gaullists: his brother had been killed by the German forces in a recent battle. The young man's patriotism was thus not an abstraction. It was as personal as his obligation to care for his mother. What, then, ought he to do? Sartre himself did not provide an answer, because he was an existentialist, that is, because he wanted to encourage his former student to exercise *his own* freedom to choose for himself. Sartre told him, 'You are free, therefore choose—that is to say, invent. No rule of general morality can show you what you ought to do: no signs are vouchsafed in this world.'[48] Unsurprisingly, Sartre's existentialist ethics has not persuaded everyone, and many readers of his classic work have expressed their opinions on what the young Frenchman ought to have done in that situation.[49] Most such readers have never been placed in it, but surely they are not thereby disqualified from expressing their opinions. Nor is it likely that Berlin would have objected to the use of Sartre's text in the safety of university classrooms at Oxford or elsewhere.[50] Why, then, did Berlin express such a strong objection to Arendt's discussion in *Eichmann in Jerusalem*?

Moral Dilemmas: Ordinary and Extreme

From a Berlinian perspective, the choice of Arendt's wartime Jewish leaders and that of Sartre's former student have something important in common. That is, they both face a moral dilemma in the strict sense of the term. This, as Lisa Tessman succinctly writes, is a situation in which:

1. there is a moral requirement to do A and a moral requirement to do B; and
2. one cannot do both A and B; and
3. neither moral requirement ceases to be a moral requirement as a result of the conflict.[51]

Sartre's former student is under two conflicting moral obligations: (A_1) to fulfil his patriotic duty, embodied by the figure of the deceased brother, and (B_1) to fulfil his family duty, embodied by the figure of the elderly mother.

Similarly, Arendt's wartime Jewish leaders were under two conflicting moral obligations: (A_2) to refuse to provide the Nazis with any assistance whatsoever, and (B_2) to do whatever one could to help Jewish victims. In both cases, A and B are incompatible. Furthermore, in both cases, the moral requirement to do A remains binding if one does B, and the moral requirement to do B remains binding if one does A. Thus, if the Frenchman decides to stay at home to look after his mother, he does what he is morally required to do, but his (other) obligation to join forces with his co-patriots is not thereby annulled. If, on the other hand, he decides to go abroad to fulfil his patriotic duty, he does what he ought to, but his (other) obligation, to look after his mother, is not thereby annulled, either. Likewise, if a Jewish leader decides to cooperate with a Nazi officer to save at least some innocent souls, he does what he is morally required to do, but his (other) obligation, to refuse categorically to cooperate with the Nazis, is not thereby annulled. If, by contrast, he decides to fulfil this latter obligation, his (other) obligation, to do whatever he could to help innocent Jews to survive, would not be thereby annulled, either. In Berlin's own terminology, both of the Frenchman's and the Jewish leaders' situations are 'tragic': two available options represent incompatible moral gains, and choosing either of the gains entails a loss of the other.

Why, then, does Berlin object specifically to Arendt's judgement? What is it that makes the choice of the Jewish leaders discussed in *Eichmann in Jerusalem* different from that of Sartre's former student discussed in *Existentialism and Humanism*? Of some help in answering this question is the little Berlin says in his interview with Lukes: the situation in which the Jewish leaders found themselves was 'so extreme' that it should not be considered by way of applying 'normal moral categories'. These remarks require some explanation. According to Berlin, moral dilemmas are part of ordinary human life, and most of us are at least occasionally confronted with a choice between competing options, each of which represents some good and yet neither of which normatively outweighs the other. A typical example would go something like this: a police officer is planning to attend her daughter's first piano recital after work at 6 p.m., but an unusual incident occurs at 4.30 p.m. and she is asked to be on duty for another few hours. This situation does not necessarily raise a moral dilemma, for the right course of action may be self-evident. For example, if the incident poses an existential threat to the police officer's community and her service is indispensable, her professional obligation overrides her family obligation (assuming that the recital still takes place). In this case, the police officer no longer faces a moral dilemma, for the requirement to do A (to fulfil her professional obligation and serve public safety) *cancels out* the moral requirement to do B (to attend her daughter's recital).[52] Conversely, if the incident is insignificant and someone else is able to serve in her stead, her professional obligation is outweighed by her family obligation, and in this case too a moral dilemma ceases to exist. But if the incident is moderately serious and the officer's service matters sufficiently, she may find the two obligations equally binding. This would be a dilemma more mundane than the one that confronted Sartre's Frenchman or the one that confronted Arendt's wartime Jewish leaders. Yet it is still a genuine moral dilemma from which there is no easy way out.

According to Berlin, finding oneself confronted with such dilemmas is part of what it is to live an ordinary human life. In his words, 'the ordinary resources of empirical observation and ordinary human knowledge [. . .] certainly give us no warrant for supposing [. . .] that all good things, or all bad things for that matter, are reconcilable with each other.'[53] Put differently, most of us occasionally have the experience of weighing conflicting normative reasons to choose between A and B, while knowing that neither option is satisfactory and that doing either, or neither, will cause us regret in one way or another. We can draw on such experiences to think about others' moral dilemmas, presumably including Sartre's former student's. Even if one has never been placed in the *same* situation as his, one is likely to have had *sufficiently similar* experiences to think about his moral dilemma, by virtue of living an 'ordinary' human life. Yet, Berlin seems to suggest, the situation of the wartime Jewish leaders was altogether different, in that it was so 'extreme' that what it is like to be in *their* situation is unimaginable to most of us. Consequently, Berlin argues, we ought to recognise and acknowledge that 'normal moral categories do not apply' to their situation. He echoes Scholem's rejoinder to Arendt: 'There were among them [in the Judenräte] many people in no way different from ourselves, who were compelled to make terrible decisions in circumstances that we cannot even begin to reproduce or reconstruct. I do not know whether they were right or wrong. *Nor do I presume to judge. I was not there.*'[54]

If this is a reasonable interpretation of Berlin's objection to Arendt, it immediately raises a question: wherein lies the boundary between 'extreme' and 'normal' situations? Surely, the situation in which Sartre's former student found himself was no ordinary situation. His brother had been killed by the German enemy and his mother had been abandoned by her husband, a Nazi collaborator. If we are entitled to draw on our ordinary experiences and use 'normal moral categories' to consider *this* situation, why are we not entitled to do the same to consider the wartime Jewish leaders' situation discussed in *Eichmann in Jerusalem*? Why does one situation count as 'extreme', while the other does not?

One answer might concern coercion. Sartre's Frenchman would not be punished by an external coercer if he evaded the dilemma he is facing. He would be unable to fulfil either of his moral obligations and to this extent might have qualms about his evasion, but the qualms come from within, not from without. Arendt's wartime Jewish leaders, by contrast, were coerced into facing a moral dilemma directly imposed by their oppressors; if they refused to choose they would be punished, perhaps by immediate execution, by their oppressors. Is this the decisive difference? Some of Berlin's remarks seem to support this hypothesis, that it is the existence of an identifiable oppressor or oppressors that separates 'extreme' from 'normal' situations. For example, he compares his Jewish leaders to 'people who are tortured'.[55] This, however, is an inadequate response, because it again raises a series of intractable questions. To begin with, external oppression can take many forms, and some are severer than others. If so, what specific forms of oppression would count as 'extreme'? Besides, what if a person who has experienced violent oppression—a torture survivor, for example—agrees with Arendt's judgement? Should we then conclude that the victim has not gone through a comparably extreme situation, perhaps because the particular torture inflicted on him or her was not severe enough? But this reasoning, apart from its obvious circularity, invites the boundary problem back, for we are again confronted with the question as to what standard we should use to determine what counts as 'extreme'. What separates 'extreme' from 'normal' situations remains ambiguous in Berlin's work.

'Safety of New York'

One may also ask whether Arendt's extraordinary life in fact furnished her with relevant experiences that gave her some insight into what Berlin called 'extreme' moral dilemmas. Consider her eight-day arrest and interrogation in Germany in 1933. The reason for the arrest was her illegal work for the Zionist Federation of Germany. But her mother was also arrested, because she happened to be with her daughter when the latter was found by the police. Interrogated in separate rooms, Hannah Arendt had to weigh two potentially conflicting obligations: to secure the safety of her mother and herself, and to keep information about her Zionist co-conspirators undisclosed. In the end, this conflict did not result in a genuine dilemma, for Arendt's interrogator turned out to be naive and inexperienced, and all she had to do to have herself released was to tell 'a string of lies'.[56] But this was not known to the captive when the interrogation began, and one wonders if the arrest, about which Arendt spoke rather lightheartedly in retrospect, gave her *some* insight into more serious moral dilemmas that confronted less fortunate victims.[57]

Consider, next, the issue of suicide. An indicator of the extremity of the wartime Jewish leaders' situation is that suicide presented itself to them as potentially the least bad option. As Berlin points out, the alternatives available

to them—such as being executed by the Nazis or forced into collaboration—
were so awful that killing oneself might reasonably be considered to be the best
available option. In this respect, the situation of Arendt's wartime Jewish leaders was far worse than that of Sartre's former student. The latter's situation may
have been agonising, but for him suicide was not even on the horizon. Arendt
was less fortunate. Of particular interest here is her letter to Gershom Scholem
dated 17 October 1941, in which she informed him of the devastating news that
their mutual friend Walter Benjamin had taken his life. Arendt and Benjamin
met regularly while they were exiled in France. As they sought ways to escape
Nazified Europe, they began hearing about 'the first suicide among those in
internment fleeing from the Germans'. This rumour petrified Benjamin. He
then talked repeatedly to Arendt about suicide: 'there was always "that" way
out.' To this she responded with 'energetic and emphatic objections that there
was still plenty of time before the situation became that desperate'. Arendt's
protest was, however, small consolation to her friend. Benjamin killed himself
on 27 September 1940.[58] In the meantime, Arendt also entertained the thought
of suicide while interned at a camp in Gurs in the summer of 1940.[59] Observe
her use of the first person plural in her 1943 essay 'We Refugees': '*We* are the
first nonreligious Jews persecuted—and *we* are the first ones who, not only in
extremis, answer with suicide.'[60] She survived after all, but she too had been
in a situation where suicide presented itself as potentially the least bad option.
Did this experience not give Arendt at least some insight into the 'appalling
situation' in which Berlin believed Arendt had never been placed?

It is anyone's guess what other relevant experiences Arendt might have
gone through during the turbulent period of her life between her departure
from Germany in 1933 and her arrival in America in 1941. Her life story is relatively well documented thanks to the magisterial biography by Elisabeth
Young-Bruehl. But we do not know all the details, and scholars keep unearth-
ing new information about Arendt's life as they look into various archives,
including new ones that did not exist when Young-Bruehl published her book
in 1982. What we do know is that Berlin's characterisation of the author of
Eichmann in Jerusalem as writing from 'the safety of New York' is one-sided.
Here it is worth considering a passage from the very opening chapter of *Eichmann*, in which the author subtly and in a measured tone announces her identity as a survivor. Arendt writes,

> The trial was supposed to show [the young and the uninformed] what it
> meant to live among non-Jews, to convince them that only in Israel could
> a Jew be safe and live an honorable life. [. . .] But in the audience there were
> hardly any young people, and it did not consist of Israelis as distinguished
> from Jews. It was filled with 'survivors', with middle-aged and elderly

people, immigrants from Europe, *like myself*, who knew by heart all there
was to know, and who were in no mood to learn any lessons and certainly
did not need this trial to draw their own conclusions.[61]

According to her later recollections, what Arendt intended to indicate in this
part of *Eichmann in Jerusalem* was that she had been 'in the audience, not of
reporters and journalists, but of "survivors" in the Jerusalem courtroom'.[62] This
assertion of the author's own identity, Leora Bilsky observes, is one of Arendt's
strategic moves to undermine the official framework of the trial, overseen by
Prime Minister Ben-Gurion, in which the figure of the victim is represented
as passive and powerless, in need of protection by the might of heroic Israelis.
In criticising this didactic aspect of the prosecution 'in a strong and direct
voice', Bilsky continues, Arendt challenges this victim/hero dichotomy and
'frustrate[s] readers' expectations of the passivity of survivors by offering her
own textual resistance'.[63] In other words, Arendt lets members of the audience
speak back to the lawyers in *Eichmann in Jerusalem*, whereas, according to the
official line, they are supposed to learn the moral of the trial quietly as the
prosecution stage-manages the courtroom drama *for them*. Arendt's assertion
of her identity is thus an attempt to claim her right to speak in opposition to
social norms and officially approved expectations. To extend Bilsky's analysis
further, it may also be seen as a pre-emptive strike at the criticism later levelled
at Arendt by her critics, including Berlin, who not only admires Scholem's
responsible silence but also follows his example: 'I do not [. . .] presume to
judge. I was not there.'[64] Arendt's pre-emptive response to this, subtly indicated by the disclosure of her identity as a survivor in the opening chapter of
Eichmann in Jerusalem, might be put as follows: 'I *was* there and have something to say.'

'A Degree of Shame'

Berlin was not, and did not see himself as, a survivor. Of course, he was by no
means unaffected by the Shoah, having had many of his relatives killed by the
Nazis in Riga in 1941. But his own safety was quite secure, and certainly much
securer than Arendt's. There is something paradoxical about his effort to highlight Arendt's 'safety' because, as far as the war years were concerned, it was
Berlin rather than Arendt who enjoyed the 'safety of New York' (and of Washington, DC, for that matter). The young Oxford philosopher witnessed a Nazi
officer at first hand as early as summer 1931 in Salzburg, which he was visiting
with his friends for the famous music festival. Unpleasant though it was, the
sight of the 'great corpulent creature in the official brown uniform, with a red
& black swastika on his sleeve' did not prevent Berlin from returning to the

annual festival in the Austrian city.[65] He made his last pre-war holiday visit to Salzburg as late as summer 1937, by which time Arendt had been in exile for four years. Once the war began, Berlin never set foot in continental Europe, except for two short stays at the Estoril Palace Hotel in neutral Portugal, where he stopped during his round trip between New York and Oxford.[66] As his return journey from Lisbon to New York in January 1941 was by sea, he gained sight of refugees heading for the United States on board. But he did so from the privileged position of his cabin, arranged by his friend John Foster, then working at the British Embassy in Washington.[67] This contrasted with Arendt's transatlantic travel four months later, also from Lisbon to New York, which she embarked on as a refugee with a ticket provided by the Hebrew Immigrant Aid Society.[68] True, as I observed in Chapter 2, Berlin did not idly wait for the war to end. On the contrary, he was eager to contribute to Britain's war effort, and he was filled with apprehension in the summer of 1940 when circumstances prevented him from throwing himself into war work.[69] Yet his was a 'Don's war', fought in the 'agreeable atmosphere' of the Survey Section of the British Embassy.[70] His main tasks consisted of gathering and analysing information on the one hand, and meeting and socialising with people of influence on the other. As Anne Deighton puts it, 'parties, gossip and chatter' were 'his forte in the [wartime] US'.[71] Strange though it may sound, his wartime work was not only fulfilling but often enjoyable. The same could not be said of Arendt.

Berlin might not have enjoyed his wartime experiences as much if he had been as informed as Arendt was about the catastrophe befalling European Jewry. By his own account, he was oblivious to the Shoah until 1944 or perhaps even 1945. As many commentators have noted,[72] this is surprising, because information about the mass killing of Jews in Europe had been publicly available in both Britain and the US since the spring of 1942. 'By June and July of 1942', Peter Hayes writes, 'the BBC and American newspapers were carrying fairly frequent reports of mass murder'.[73] Moreover, the Allies issued a widely reported joint declaration on 17 December 1942 to condemn the 'on-going bestial policy of cold-blooded extermination' by 'the German authorities'.[74] But archival evidence supports Berlin's professed lack of awareness during the war about what we today call the Holocaust.[75] If one examines his surviving papers archived in the Bodleian Library at Oxford, one would notice that his wartime geographical focus was not on Nazified Europe but on the United States, Britain and the Middle East. He paid close attention to the 'whereto' of the plight of European Jewry, not the 'wherefrom' of it. Needless to say, this by no means indicates that Berlin was indifferent to the Jewish plight. On the contrary, he did what he could to alleviate it, chiefly by challenging the strict migration quotas imposed by the British government on Jewish refugees trying to enter Palestine. Notwithstanding his reputation as 'a terrible fence-sitter',[76] he became a whistle-blower of sorts in 1943, leaking confidential information about the planned joint declaration by the British and American governments that, if published, would have dismissed the mounting opposition to the migration quotas as mere 'Zionist agitation'. Still, it remains true that Berlin paid little attention during the war to the unfolding catastrophe *inside* continental Europe—to his later regret and to some of his readers' disappointment.

In this context it is worth looking more closely at Berlin's *own perception* of his wartime conduct. He said in a 1988 interview,

> There is something [. . .] which I must confess with a degree of shame. I assumed from the very beginning that Hitler meant to inflict terrible sufferings on the Jews—he was a fiend and implacable, that was obvious. We all knew that Jews had been imprisoned, and some were killed, in concentration camps, from 1933 onwards. [. . .] After the invasion of Poland, I assumed that terrible things were happening to Jews, that they would be arrested, persecuted, tortured, perhaps killed, but none of us knew what was going on. Before the events of the Warsaw ghetto, no news came. We just assumed appalling horrors. Before 1944 I knew nothing about systematic extermination—the gas chambers. Nobody told me, in England or America; there was nothing about it in anything I read—perhaps that was my own fault. That makes me feel ashamed.[77]

Whether Berlin was right to feel ashamed is a matter of controversy that I do not wish to enter into here. Instead, in light of his 'confession' cited above, I would like to ask what went on in his psyche when Berlin expressed his anger at Arendt's audacity in expressing her critical opinions about the conduct of wartime Jewish leaders 'from the safety of New York'. Certainly, Berlin thought *he* was not entitled to criticise them. *He* was not there and did not presume to judge. But was Arendt equally unentitled? Was *she* not there, and ought *she* not to judge, either? I have already discussed Arendt's partial response to this question: she identified herself as a survivor. On the opening pages of *Eichmann in Jerusalem* she claimed, if calmly, that she too was there alongside other survivors, now confronting Eichmann in the Jerusalem courtroom.

But there is another aspect to Arendt's confidence in her right to speak about, and even to criticise, some of her fellow victims of the Shoah. This is discernible in her interview with Günter Gaus broadcast on the West German TV network ZDF in October 1964. Arendt explained how she had felt when she left Germany in 1933: 'I was arrested, and had to leave the country illegally [. . .] and that was instant gratification for me. I thought at least I had done something! At least I am not "innocent". No one could say that of me!'[78] In the pejorative sense used here, to be 'innocent' means to be a bystander. It is to keep one's head down and try to wait quietly until the trouble passes. Arendt held special disdain for this type of 'innocence', originating from her conviction that the Nazis' ascent to power was dependent on bourgeois passivity and liberal complicity. The 'respectable' Weimar centre hardly subscribed to the Nazi ideology, but they played a key role in letting the Nazis win, as they tolerated the Nazi movement until it was too late.[79] Arendt knew she had done better. The legal and illegal work she did for and with Zionists—the only group willing to 'defend themselves as Jews when attacked as Jews'—let her lose the irresponsible and ultimately suicidal 'innocence' of the bystander.[80] If she had a right to speak, then, that was not only because she was a survivor, but also because she survived honourably, with a loss of 'innocence'. A sense of self-assurance is shown, if implicitly, not only in her Gaus interview but also in many of her published works. These include *Eichmann in Jerusalem*, which contains harsh criticisms of 'innocent' bystanders, Jews and non-Jews alike. Arendt *earned* her right to speak—or so she thought.

Of course, that one has a right to speak does not mean that what one says is sensible or plausible. One can *both* appreciate Arendt's wartime activism *and* criticise what she had to say in *Eichmann in Jerusalem*.[81] Nevertheless, it seems likely that Arendt's self-assurance about her wartime past was a source of discomfort for Berlin, whose conscience had been troubled by his own. His sense of 'shame' was exacerbated in 1972, when the publication of his essay on 'Zionist Politics in Wartime Washington' in the Israeli paper *Ha'aretz* provoked a controversy over his wartime obliviousness to the Shoah and over the awareness (or lack thereof) of the Holocaust in wartime Washington more generally.[82] Needless to say, speculating on one's inner life is a risky business. But one does not have to be a psychoanalyst to see that Berlin's troubled conscience stiffened his attitude towards the outspoken survivor who wrote *Eichmann in Jerusalem*. A sense of shame silenced Berlin; it did not silence his 'bête noire'.[83]

This brings us to the important question of gender.[84] As many scholars have noted, the reaction that *Eichmann in Jerusalem* provoked would likely have been less violent had the author of the book not been a woman;[85] a woman, moreover, who challenged Israeli authority in charge of the Eichmann trial, mostly consisting of men, and who criticised the conduct of some wartime Jewish leaders, the majority of whom were men. Furthermore, Arendt was a woman writer who often adopted a 'masculine' persona, both in terms of her combative tone and her emphasis on agency.[86] The unsettling effect of this should not be discounted. Of course, the impact of implicit bias is notoriously difficult to measure, and those who consider the role of gender in the Eichmann controversy inevitably face the twin risks of overestimating and underestimating it. Nevertheless, gender undoubtedly played *some* role, and Jennifer Ring is undoubtedly right to make the following observation: 'To claim that gender cannot possibly have had anything to do with the response to [Arendt's] report on Eichmann is a denial of the first order.'[87] After all, women are not traditionally or 'normally' in a position to judge, and those, including Berlin, who dismissed Arendt as *unentitled* to judge were knowingly or unknowingly reaffirming traditional gender roles.[88] That Berlin appealed to Scholem's authority helps little in this context, for the latter's qualms about Arendt's 'right to criticise' have also been seen as 'a kind of gender rank pulling'.[89] Nor does it help that Berlin repeatedly called Arendt a 'bluestocking'—a somewhat pejorative term referring to educated and intelligent women, with sexist connotations.[90]

Berlin's sexism and gender bias, however, should not be overstated. True, some of his remarks are sexist by our twenty-first-century standards. But the same may be said of a large majority of thinkers and writers of his generation, including, unfortunately, Arendt. She not only showed little interest in feminist theory, but occasionally made remarks that would strike us today as sexist.[91] For example, she is reported to have given the following advice to William Phillips, editor of the *Partisan Review*, on how to deal with Simone de Beauvoir: 'The trouble with you, William, is that you don't realize that she's not very bright. Instead of arguing with her, [. . .] you should flirt with her.'[92] One could debate whether Berlin was more sexist than Arendt, or vice versa. Either way, his gender bias was to a large extent a shared feature of a generation. In fact, when it came to female intellectuals and academics, Berlin's attitude was relatively progressive, at least in comparison to his contemporaries at Oxford. He expressed open admiration for brilliant female scholars and writers such as Iris Murdoch and was fascinated by female (as well as male) geniuses, including Virginia Woolf and Anna Akhmatova. Furthermore, he praised the writer and Arendt's first literary executor Mary McCarthy as 'very observant [. . . ,] tough and clear and utterly honest'.[93]

Nevertheless, even if he was not a sexist reactionary, Berlin was not a feminist, either. As Nancy Hirschmann observes, he 'made no references to gender as a significant category for consideration in his theoretical writings'.[94] Similarly, it is unlikely that he took a moment to ask himself whether 'the fearful scandal about Miss Arendt's book' might have partly stemmed from the author's gender.[95] Unfortunately, when it came to Arendt, Berlin was not entirely free of misogynistic tendencies, whereby a woman's troubles are seen as originating in her own deficiencies rather than her enemies' and detractors' prejudices. While gender is but one factor in Berlin's impassioned objections to Arendt's *Eichmann*, it almost certainly fuelled his anger and contributed to his animosity towards her.

Substantive Objections

Berlin's critical remarks on *Eichmann in Jerusalem* do not only concern what I have called the 'procedure' of Arendt's judgement: whether Arendt was authorised or in a position to make normative judgements on the conduct of wartime Jewish leaders. He was also critical of the substance of Arendt's judgement. In his view, her criticism of the wartime Jewish leadership is objectionable *even if it were not inappropriate for her to criticise it*. What was the normative basis for this objection? And what would be an Arendtian response to it? To consider these questions it is useful to separate three issues from one another and examine each in turn: first, *whom* did Arendt criticise; second, *for what* did she criticise them; and third, why did she criticise them *in the way she did*?

Whom?

First, consider *whom* Arendt criticised. I have already shown that she distinguished between the Jewish people and the Jewish leadership, and directed her criticism exclusively at the latter. 'The Jewish people as a whole behaved magnificently. Only the leadership failed.'[96] I have also noted that the 'leadership' in this context encompassed a disparate group of people, including those who did not belong to a Judenrat, such as Kastner, as well as its various members, from Chaim Rumkowski in Łódź to Adam Czerniaków in Warsaw. Arendt's decision to group these diverse figures together under the generic category of the 'Jewish leadership' has attracted the charge of over-generalisation. That is, she has been criticised for ignoring important differences between these individuals with varying personal qualities and a diversity of circumstances under which they had to act. There is little doubt she generalised. The more difficult question, however, is whether she *over*-generalised, for Arendt's message was that a number of wartime Jewish leaders 'failed' alike, regardless of their personal or circumstantial differences. The 'failure' at issue is primarily a political one. Arendt did not deny that some, if not all, of the wartime Jewish leaders possessed admirable moral qualities.[97] Yet, she argued, even such men 'failed' to defy the Nazis as well as they could have.[98] That her criticism was political rather than moral does not make her criticism uncontroversial, however. On the contrary, it contained the highly divisive claim that the wartime Jewish leaders *ought to have done better* in the face of the Nazi threat. Berlin, for one, was not ready to accept this claim.

There is an important continuity between Arendt's criticism of the wartime Jewish leadership in Nazi-occupied territories on the one hand and her life-long polemic against modern Jewish leadership more broadly on the other. Her idiosyncratic brand of Zionism, purportedly inspired by Bernard Lazare, asserts itself here. As is well known, Arendt expressed strong scepticism towards 'parvenu' tendencies among the late eighteenth- and nineteenth-century Jewish elite. She was ready to concede their moral integrity up to a point; some of the elite wished to be accepted by 'respectable' gentile society out of a genuine desire to improve the general Jewish condition. But the downside of their ascent via the socio-economic path, according to Arendt, was that they tended to disengage from politics altogether. Her qualified support for Zionism ought to be understood against this background: Zionism made at least some Jews approximately 'political' in her sense of the term. Nevertheless, subsequent developments in Zionism were a disappointment to Arendt, as its leaders took the movement in the direction of diplomacy and *Realpolitik*. The democratic potential of the Zionist movement was thus frustrated, and many of the Zionist leaders came to be infected by the same inability to think and act politically as had characterised their 'parvenu' predecessors. It is this mindset, in Arendt's view, that resurfaced in the conduct of the wartime Jewish leaders. They tried to be accepted and protected by those in power, this time by the Nazis, at their peril. Shmuel Lederman succinctly summarises Arendt's frustration with *both* the pre-war *and* wartime Jewish leadership: 'the Judenräte [in Arendt's view] were but another example of Jewish leadership failing in their political understandings and judgments, resulting in numerous flawed calculations and decisions, albeit in a much more extreme situation and with disastrous consequences.'[99]

This criticism is based on Arendt's controversial view that, even in the ghettos, Jewish leaders 'had still a certain, limited freedom of decision and of action'.[100] Of course, they were far less free than their nineteenth-century 'parvenu' predecessors. But, according to Arendt, they still had freedom to the extent that they lived 'in an atmosphere of terror but not under the immediate pressure and impact of terror'.[101] She contrasted this with the conditions inside Nazi camps, where inmates were *totally* dominated, deprived absolutely of their freedom, and their agency reduced to nil. She consequently made the following remark that seems to run counter to her reputation as an arrogant moraliser:

> The well-known fact that the actual work of killing in the extermination centers was usually in the hands of Jewish commandos had been fairly and squarely established by witnesses for the prosecution—how they had worked in the gas chambers and the crematories, how they had pulled the gold teeth and cut the hair of the corpses, how they had dug the graves and, later, dug them up again to extinguish the traces of mass murder; how Jewish technicians had built gas chambers in Theresienstadt, where the Jewish 'autonomy' had been carried so far that even the hangman was a Jew. *But this was only horrible, it was no moral problem*.[102]

One way of characterising Arendt's view is that she divided the so-called 'privileged' Jews into two groups: members of Judenräte and other Jewish leaders
in the ghettos on the one hand, and Kapos (heads of labour squads) and other
prisoner-functionaries inside the concentration camps on the other.[103] In her
view, those in the former group are subject to normative judgement because
they 'had still a certain, limited freedom' and to this extent ought to be held
accountable for their conduct. No matter how difficult it may be, one ought
not to refrain from judging their decisions and actions because, Arendt professed, 'I do believe that we shall only come to terms with this past if we begin
to judge and to be frank about it.'[104] By contrast, 'privileged' Jews inside the
concentration camps ought not to be judged because they lived, so long as
they lived, 'under the immediate pressure and impact of terror' and enjoyed
no freedom whatsoever.[105] Arendt thus expressed a notable willingness to
withhold judgement. Where domination is total, morality talk is redundant.

Is this a sufficient response to Berlin's (and others') charge of Arendt's moralism in its substantive (as distinct from procedural) sense? Would he have
withdrawn his objection to Arendt had he paid greater attention to her neglected un-moralising comments on Jewish commandos in the concentration
camps? I doubt it. As is clear from the way he constructed his example of 'a
leader of some Jews in Lithuania', quoted earlier in this chapter, Berlin did not
accept the stark contrast Arendt drew between the ghettos, where 'a certain,
limited freedom' was supposedly available to victims, and the concentration
camps, where absolutely no freedom was available. On the contrary, Berlin saw
no qualitative difference between what in Arendt's terms would be 'oppression'
in the ghettos and 'total domination' in the concentration camps. In Berlin's
view, Jewish leaders in the ghettos emphatically did not have 'a certain, limited
freedom', because the options available to them were not meaningful ones.
Where all open doors lead to severe oppression, choosing which door to walk
through amounts to no free choice at all. Recall here that Berlin, referring to
Kastner, mentioned two specific *meaningless* options between which some Jewish leaders in the ghettos were coerced to 'choose': 'heroic martyrdom, and the
saving of innocent lives at the expense of those of others'.[106] The former was a
broadly deontological option; the latter, consequentialist. In Berlin's view,
doing either, or neither, of these would be *equally* bad. This does not necessarily
mean that Berlin was unable or unwilling to take sides on a general level in the
deontology/consequentialism divide in modern normative ethics.[107] It means,
rather, that the particular expression of this divide in the specific context of the
Nazi-controlled ghettos defied a clear-cut normative response. Hence Berlin's
approval of Scholem's silence: 'I do not presume to judge.'

As I discussed earlier in this chapter, Berlin considered tragic dilemmas in
the context of the Shoah to be 'extreme'. While he left considerable ambiguity

as to what the 'extreme' exactly meant and entailed, one could appreciate the kind of situation he had in mind by the following survivor testimony:

> To write about life in the ghetto . . . it would be wiser and more truthful to write about the death in the ghetto. . . . Every expression of human life, of joy, or of creativity disappeared completely. . . . Indifference, lack of feeling, not even desire for revenge, existed. . . . They ceased to have any will-power. . . . No sound of song, no laughter of children, could be heard in the ghettos. . . . Those who are sentenced to die do not smile.[108]

To this one could add the Berlinian observation that no freedom of choice or of action existed in the ghettos—that those who were sentenced to death do not freely choose, decide or act. Unlike Arendt, Berlin refused to draw a distinction between terrestrial ghettos and infernal camps; *both* constituted hell on earth. In his view, 'normal moral categories do not apply' to the extremity of the ghettos as well as to that of the concentration camps.[109] To say one was hell and the other was not, as Arendt tended to do, would be arbitrary.[110]

In her defence, some pages of Arendt's work may be interpreted as capable of responding to this Berlinian criticism. In *The Origins of Totalitarianism*, she had analysed an 'attack on the moral person' as an essential part of total domination, and described what in *Eichmann* she would call 'horrible' situations, where victims' conduct ought to be exempt from normative judgement. She wrote in *Origins*,

> When a man is faced with the alternative of betraying and thus murdering his friends or of sending his wife and children, for whom he is in every sense responsible, to their death; when even suicide would mean the immediate murder of his own family—how is he to decide? The alternative is no longer between good and evil, but between murder and murder. Who could solve the moral dilemma of the Greek mother, who was allowed by the Nazis to choose which of her three children should be killed?[111]

Arendt did not explicitly say that 'horrible' situations such as these could or did arise in the ghettos as well as in the concentration camps. Yet this is certainly a reasonable interpretation, which raises the well-known question of the consistency between *Origins* and *Eichmann* (as well as the internal consistency of *Origins*).[112] Did the early Arendt of *Origins* not imply that at least some victims in the ghettos were placed in so 'horrible' a situation that their conduct, no matter what they 'chose' to do, should be exempt from normative judgement, whereas the late Arendt of *Eichmann* categorically said that the victims in the ghettos (unlike those in the concentration camps) still enjoyed 'limited freedom' and to this extent their decisions and actions ought to be subject to normative judgement? In short, is there not fundamental disconti-nuity between the humane and sympathetic Arendt of *Origins* and the heart-less and judgemental Arendt of *Eichmann*?

This question does not need to be settled here. What needs to be high-lighted is that Arendt in and after *Eichmann in Jerusalem* continued to insist on the difference between limited freedom in the ghettos and absolute un-freedom in the concentration camps. In her considered opinion, there was indeed such a thing as 'a Jewish share in the guilt', and this concerned Jewish leaders' conduct *before* they were sent to a camp.[113] They were not 'merely helpless' but 'became in fact an important factor in the bureaucracy of de-struction'.[114] Arendt and Berlin agreed that one could not be blamed if one's freedom of choice was *absolutely* negated. But they disagreed as to whether such absolute negation occurred only inside the concentration camps, or outside them also.

For What?

Let us provisionally assume for the sake of argument that Arendt was right about wartime Jewish leaders' relative freedom in the ghettos. What, then, could they have done to respond to the Nazi threat? What specifically is it that they could have done but 'failed' to do with the 'limited freedom' they pur-portedly had? Arendt's answer is in two parts. First, the Jewish leaders did not fail to *resist*. It is crucial to note here that resistance in Arendt's sense requires a certain level of active confrontation. Of course, this is by no means the only plausible conceptualisation of resistance, and Arendt has been criticised for defining resistance in overly narrow terms.[115] For example, it might be more fruitful to understand resistance in the context of the Shoah as including *any* attempt—active or passive, violent or non-violent—at frustrating the Nazis' genocidal policy. My present purpose, however, is not to subject Arendt's ter-minology to critical scrutiny. Rather, it is to draw attention to its nuances to clarify what she saw as a failure on the part of the Jewish leaders. On Arendt's view, they did not fail to resist (in her sense) because the limitation to their freedom was such that they were simply not in a position to rebel, protest or otherwise actively fight back against their oppressors. It is for this reason that Arendt repeatedly criticised the prosecution in the Jerusalem courtroom for asking witnesses (read: survivors) wrong questions such as 'Why did you not rebel?' and 'Why did you not protest?'[116] These questions were 'cruel and silly', she argued, because they were based on 'a fatal ignorance of the conditions' in the ghettos.[117] The 'atmosphere of terror' that permeated the ghettos was so oppressive that resistance was, contrary to the prosecution's insinuation, no longer possible.

What, then, *could* the Jewish leaders have done with the limited freedom they purportedly had? The second part of Arendt's answer is 'non-participation'. She writes,

> [In the ghettos] there was no possibility of resistance, but there existed the possibility of *doing nothing*. And in order to do nothing, one did not need to be a saint, one needed only to say: I am just a simple Jew, and I have no desire to play any other role.[118]

Arendt contrasts individual non-participation with collective resistance. The latter stands for open action-in-concert such as civil disobedience which, according to her, was possible at the initial phase of total domination. Here, it should be recalled that 'total domination' in Arendt's sense *begins* with denaturalisation.[119] While it culminates in comprehensive dehumanisation in the concentration camp, the process of total domination starts when a group of people is singled out as belonging to a 'wrong' category, deprived of their citizenship and placed 'outside the normal penal system'.[120] This occurs in a pre-totalitarian society, whose degeneration into totalitarianism proper might be brought to a halt if robust action is taken by an alliance of victims (Jews, for example) and bystanders (Germans, for example). Arendt discusses Denmark as one country where such resistance qua solidaristic action took place. When the country was invaded by Nazi Germany in April 1940, the Danes openly protested at the German policy with respect to the 'Jewish question', blocking the implementation of anti-Jewish measures for two and a half years. Moreover, when the Nazis finally decided in autumn 1943 that Jews in Denmark should be deported immediately to Theresienstadt, the plan was leaked to the heads of the Jewish community.[121] Then, Jewish leaders in Denmark, 'in marked contrast to Jewish leaders in other countries' (Arendt), immediately communicated the news to the local Jewish population, and the majority of Danish Jews escaped and survived, as they found themselves surrounded by local Danes who were ready to help. Arendt was evidently moved by this Danish episode, characterising it as testifying to 'the enormous power potential inherent in non-violent action and in resistance to an opponent possessing vastly superior means of violence'.[122] This was the kind of resistance she wished to have seen more of during Europe's season of hell.

Arendt does not tell us under what conditions a Danish-style resistance could have occurred to block the Final Solution.[123] Nor, more importantly in the present context, does she clearly specify exactly when open resistance-in-concert ceased to be a possibility even in favourable conditions such as those in Denmark. Nevertheless, her general argument is clear enough: the possibility of collective resistance disappeared when the victim group was isolated from the rest of the society, the gates of the ghetto closed and 'an atmosphere of terror' reigned inside. No resistance qua political action could be taken beyond this point. At the same time, it was at this point that non-participation presented itself as a moral option. Arendt writes,

> There never was a moment [in the ghettos] when 'the community leaders' could have said, 'Cooperate no longer, but fight!' [. . .] Resistance, which existed but played a very small role, meant only: We don't want that kind of death, we want to die with honor.[124]

Whether one likes it or not, Arendt here expresses the profoundly un-Berlinian view that the options available to Jewish leaders in the ghettos were *not equally bad*. The worst option was cooperation with the likelihood of death without honour; less worse was non-participation with the likelihood of death with honour. Bernard Crick's appraisal is highly perceptive: the point of Arendt's non-participation was 'to demonstrate human freedom and dignity in defiance even of necessity, somewhat as the stoic faces death'.[125] It is worth highlighting in this context that Arendt, unlike Isaiah Trunk after her, did not clearly distinguish between partly voluntary 'collaboration' and thoroughly coerced 'co-operation'.[126] She was aware that some instances of cooperation were more coerced than others, but she did not formulate a terminological distinction to describe those differences. While she generally spoke about Jewish leaders' 'cooperation' rather than 'collaboration', she sometimes spoke of their 'collaboration' also, using the two terms interchangeably.[127] This coloured the conceptual lens through which she saw the matter. Closely associating cooperation with collaboration, Arendt saw non-participation as a radically different alternative to both. In fact, she effectively saw it as the only alternative that could save or could have saved victims' dignity and freedom, if not life, from destruction. Arendt's non-participation is akin to Nadezhda Mandelstam's scream:

> to scream when you are being beaten and trampled underfoot [. . .] is a concentrated expression of the last vestige of human dignity. It is a man's way of leaving a trace, of telling people how he lived and died. By his screams he asserts his right to live, sends a message to the outside world demanding help and calling for resistance. If nothing else is left, one must scream.[128]

Arendtian ethics, and the high degree of heroism that it appears to entail, has attracted furious criticism. In the eyes of her critics, it shows Arendt at her worst, as it seems to be rooted in her fantastical Grecomania, utterly inappropriate for thinking about real-world moral issues in the twentieth century.[129] This line of objection is best articulated by the Riga-born Jewish émigré political theorist Judith Shklar:

Why, [Arendt] asked, had the East European Jews not behaved like Homeric heroes? Why had they not resisted the Germans more courageously? Why had they contributed to their own destruction? Why had they left no gallant myth for us? All this in spite of the fact that she knew perfectly well that, while Eastern Jews might have made minor difficulties for the Germans, they never could have averted their doom.[130]

Confronted with strong criticisms such as the above, some Arendt scholars have accused her critics of distortion and misrepresentation.[131] This is an understandable reaction, for some critics who have accused Arendt of Grecomania have indeed caricatured her work a good deal. Yet it would be dishonest to deny the demandingness of Arendtian ethics. Again, Crick's candour is commendable: as a matter of fact, Arendt's discussion of non-participation contains 'a hard doctrine to swallow'.[132] That said, her critics such as Shklar are not entirely innocent of misrepresentation. In particular, they often exaggerate the connection between *The Human Condition* and *Eichmann in Jerusalem* to argue that Arendt applied a romantic existentialist ethic (purportedly found in *The Human Condition*) to wartime Jewish leaders' conduct, to reach disastrous conclusions (in *Eichmann*).[133] What is usually ignored by the critics is the important connection between *Eichmann* and Arendt's wartime writings prior to *The Human Condition*. *Eichmann* was by no means the first piece of writing in which Arendt defended the idea of death with honour. On the contrary, this had been repeatedly defended in her contributions to *Aufbau* during the 1940s, when she fervently argued for the formation of a Jewish army. Needless to say, she never made the ridiculous claim that a Jewish army, if formed, might defeat the Germans. Her point, rather, is that a Jewish army would allow Jews to retain or regain dignity and honour, even if they were defeated.[134]

The same idea is discernible in her appreciation of the Warsaw ghetto uprising. In her July 1944 piece 'Days of Change', she approvingly cited the following words from a Polish underground newspaper telling the story of the uprising that had recently been crushed: 'the passive death of Jews had created no new values; it had been meaningless; but [. . .] death with weapons in hand can bring new values into the life of the Jewish people'.[135] In her 1940s contributions to *Aufbau*, as in her 1960s comments on Judenräte, Arendt supported an act of defiance as not so much an effective strategy to defeat the enemy, as a performative statement on dignity and freedom. Like many members of the Zionist youth movements, Arendt wanted 'death with weapons in hand' to signal 'a message to Jews in the free world and humanity as a whole'.[136]

It is unlikely, however, that this Zionist source of Arendtian ethics would have impressed Isaiah Berlin. True, he shared Shklar's suspicion about Arendt's Grecomania,[137] and his irritation with Arendtian ethics might have been moderately softened had he been told that she was not as Grecophile as he thought she was. But his discontent with her did not only or even primarily stem from her purported Grecomania. As I discussed in Chapter 2, his brand of Zionism conflicted with hers, and he had *his* Zionist reasons to oppose the formation of a Jewish army. Just as she regarded the diplomatic 'Herzlian' Zionism he supported as ineffective, spineless and apolitical, he considered the 'fanatical' Zionism she supported during the war to be naive, irresponsible and counterproductive.[138] It made little difference to Berlin whether a martyr was a heroic Greek or a heroic Jew. The very idea of an honourable death attracted Berlin far less than Arendt. (This difference would resurface in their differing assessments of the 1956 Hungarian Revolution, as will be discussed in the next chapter.)

It is also worth asking whether Arendt's consistency on the issue of honourable death might be a vice rather than a virtue. Her opinions on this issue changed little between the early 1940s and the early 1960s, while the circumstances in which she expressed her opinions changed drastically over the same period. This raises a question to which Arendt paid little attention: is there not a difference between saying during the war 'Jewish leaders *ought to do* X' and saying in the 1960s 'Jewish leaders *ought to have done* X'? To put it more strongly, is there not a difference between saying 'A should do X' while A is alive on the one hand, and saying 'A should have done X' when A has already been murdered on the other? In the latter case, is it not more appropriate to utter a word of mourning and prayer than to issue a moral pronouncement? Notwithstanding her rejection of 'philosopher' as the name of her profession,[139] Arendt in this respect seems guilty of what she regarded as the philosopher's *déformation professionnelle*: the overvaluing of consistency at the expense of other, no less important, considerations.

This leads to Berlin's final point of disagreement with Arendtian ethics, and it concerns human psychology. Berlin shared with his friend Bernard Williams the fundamental conviction that 'philosophy, especially moral philosophy, is only as valuable or plausible or accurate as the psychology it incorporates'.[140] In other words, theories of morality are implausible to the extent that the psychological assumptions they tacitly make are untrue to men and women as they are rather than as we wish them to be. On this Arendt might have agreed in principle, for she criticised Kant's moral philosophy, and the excessive demands it imposes on men and women, as 'inhuman'.[141] But such 'inhumanity' was precisely what tainted Arendt's own critical remarks on the wartime Jewish leadership, in Berlin's view. Notwithstanding her effort to keep the Kantian absolute out of human affairs, she still demanded far too much from men and women, psychologically speaking. According to Berlin, a person does not have to be subjected to actual terror to lose his or her freedom; finding oneself 'in an atmosphere of terror' is enough for one to lose one's freedom *completely*.[142] Moreover, one does not need to be confined in a ghetto, let alone a concentration camp, to lose one's freedom. Berlin writes,

> If in a totalitarian State I betray my friend under threat of torture, perhaps even if I act from fear of losing my job, I can reasonably say that I did not act freely. Nevertheless, I did, of course, make a choice, and could, at any rate in theory, have chosen to be killed or tortured or imprisoned. The mere existence of alternatives is not, therefore, enough to make my action free (although it may be voluntary) in the normal sense of the word.[143]

Arendt emphatically does not share this view. If Berlin is right about the 'normal' usage of the word 'freedom', she is more than willing to dispute the convention. On her view, if one betrays one's friend for fear of losing one's job, one *should* be seen as having acted freely, if not entirely freely. Consequently, one ought to be held accountable for the decision one made and the action one took with the limited freedom one had. This means that we *are* perfectly entitled to blame a person for failing to do the right thing, such as sacrificing his or her job to save a friend. After all, according to Arendt, one of the key lessons to learn from the experience of Nazi Germany was that a number of 'normal' men and women became implicated in the Nazi system as they thought of little else except their own safety and security. Such 'normality' ought to be challenged, Arendt argues, together with the 'normal' sense of the term 'freedom' that excuses moral failures. This may be 'a hard doctrine to swallow', but she defends it.[144]

Arrogance?

The remaining question to ask in this chapter concerns Arendt's tone of criticism. Why did she criticise the wartime Jewish leadership with a tone that has struck many of her readers as arrogant, heartless and even 'self-hating'? As we have seen, Berlin shared in making all three of these charges. Not only did he repeatedly accuse Arendt of arrogance and heartlessness, but he also said to his friend Sam Behrman that the 'charges of self-hatred [against Arendt] seem to me to be valid'.[145] Is there anything to be said for this line of criticism?

Unfortunately, one explanation Arendt herself provided, most notably in her interview with Joachim Fest, served her little.[146] According to her, her style of writing reflected who she was rather than what she thought. While she did not want her work to cause personal offence, she was aware that *Eichmann in Jerusalem* and more specifically its often ironical style *had* hurt many people's feelings. She said, in a tone of resignation,

I'm obviously rather unpleasant in the eyes of a great many people. I can't do anything about that. What am I supposed to do? They just don't like me. The style in which people express themselves—well, that's something they themselves aren't aware of.[147]

It is certainly true that some of the venomous comments made during the Eichmann controversy were directed at the author rather than the book. It is also true that Arendt paid limited attention to her own style of writing. Generally speaking, she hardly calculated her readers' perception when writing a book or an essay. By her own account, 'I am not in the habit of thinking about the "impression" created by what I write [. . .]. I am content when I have found the word or the sentence which appears to me objectively adequate and appropriate.'[148] Nevertheless, *pace* Arendt, it is untrue that one's style of writing simply reflects who one is and therefore cannot be modified without a change of one's personality. On the contrary, when it comes to moral argumentation, the inability to choose an appropriate style or tone can itself be a moral failure. By the same token, choosing the wrong tone to criticise someone or something can be wrong even if the criticism contains a valid argument.[149] One wonders if Arendt was aware of this. When the second edition of *Eichmann in Jerusalem* appeared in 1965, only two years after its original publication, she took the opportunity to modify one particularly shocking sentence in order to *tone down* her criticism of the wartime Jewish leadership, perhaps in response to strong objections raised by her friends, including Scholem.[150] That is, she removed her earlier description of Rabbi Leo Baeck, a renowned leader of German Jewry who was sent to Theresienstadt in 1943, as the 'Jewish Führer'.[151] Needless to say, this does not mean that her personality changed between 1963 and 1965. It means, rather, that she came to realise that she had failed to choose the right tone to address the matter in the original edition of her book. She accordingly modified the text in 1965 without changing who she was. So much for her distinction between style and argument.

More revealing than this distinction are Arendt's scattered comments on the *vice of modesty* in *Eichmann in Jerusalem* and elsewhere.[152] The most important among those comments are found in Chapter 7 of the book. In this key chapter, she introduces an account, given by Eichmann himself, of how he finally got rid of his doubts about the Final Solution. The fateful day was 20 January 1942, when prominent Nazi officials, including Reinhard Heydrich and Heinrich Müller, met in Wannsee, thirteen miles from central Berlin. There, Eichmann, 'the déclassé son of a solid middle-class family', was admitted to the company of high-ranking German civil servants and Nazi dignitaries.[153] To Eichmann's surprise, they were all 'vying and fighting with each other for the honor of taking the lead' in the extermination policy. '"At that moment"'—Arendt cites Eichmann's recollections—'"I [Eichmann] sensed a kind of Pontius Pilate feeling, for I felt free of guilt." *Who was he to judge?* Who was he "to have [his] own thoughts in this matter?"'[154] On Arendt's reading, this was the moment when Eichmann finally transformed himself into a 'thoughtless' criminal. Thereafter Eichmann no longer 'thought what he was doing' and totally abstained from judging whether his conduct was good or bad, justified or unjustified. He became a new type of criminal, embodying 'the banality of evil'. Arendt observes, 'Each time he was tempted to think for himself, he said: Who am I to judge if all around me [...] think it is right to murder innocent people?'[155] In Arendt's terminology, Eichmann learned to be 'modest' at the Wannsee Conference.

Eichmann, however, was by no means the only one who had learned to be modest in Nazi Germany. On the contrary, the majority of the German popu-lation unquestioningly conformed to the new social norms that had come into being with Hitler's ascent to power, letting themselves become 'implicated in one way or another in the deeds of the regime as a whole'.[156] Of course, some modest people were more modest than others, and a handful of them played a key role in the Final Solution, while many did not. Regardless, they were all complicit. Arendt contrasted such a 'modest' many with the 'arrogant' few, who trusted their own judgement, formed their own opinions on good and evil and refused to be unthinkingly implicated in the Nazi system.[157] The 'abil-ity [of the arrogant few] to tell right from wrong had remained intact' amid the moral collapse in Nazi Germany.[158] They 'never doubted that crimes remained crimes even if legalized by the government'.[159] Such arrogant individuals in-cluded professionals, like Karl Jaspers, who preferred a career compromise to 'the "little formality" of entering the Nazi Party' or of swearing on Hitler's name.[160] They also included 'two peasant boys' who were executed after refus-ing to serve the SS, into which they had been drafted. Arendt insisted that the arrogant, including the executed peasant boys, 'were neither heroes nor saints'.[161] This may sound counterintuitive. But Arendt's point was that acts of arrogance were humanly possible, that one did not have to be superhuman to have the arrogance to think and judge for oneself. In fact, arrogant individuals 'could be found everywhere, in all strata of society, among the simple people as well as among the educated, in all parties, perhaps even in the ranks of the N.S.D.A.P. [Nazi Party]'.[162] To summarise, arrogance in Arendt's book is a virtue to be nurtured, while modesty is a vice that ruined many, including Adolf Eichmann.[163]

It is therefore supremely ironical that many of Arendt's critics, including Berlin, should have *accused* her of arrogance for writing a book that highlighted the importance of being arrogant. On this issue, Arendt and her critics genu-inely talked past each other: they understood arrogance very differently. In the case of Arendt and Berlin, the difference over arrogance was to some extent anchored in their differing views of Eichmann. Arendt thought Eichmann was neither a sadist nor a genocidal antisemite. Rather, he was a relatively normal bourgeois individual who 'had no motives at all' except for his own career.[164] Berlin, by contrast, had suspected a different side to Eichmann and eventually came to conclude that 'Eichmann deeply believed in what he did'.[165] But even more important than this difference over Eichmann's character was a larger disagreement between Arendt and Berlin as to whether the mass complicity in Nazi Germany and elsewhere in Europe might be accounted for by the concept of modesty and whether, by the same token, the virtue of arrogance might be an appropriate antidote to it. Berlin never understood the matter in those terms. For him arrogance was always a vice and Arendt had it in abundance. Arendt, by contrast, wished to live up to what she preached and was determined to carry the burden of 'arrogance' or, put differently, to retain the audacity to form and express unpopular opinions.

A little over a year before the publication of the first instalment of *Eichmann in Jerusalem* in the *New Yorker*, Arendt told her students, 'If you say to yourself in such [moral] matters: who am I to judge?—you are already lost.'[166] True, she did not foresee the intensity of the controversy that was to ensue in 1963. But even amid the ferocious furore she stuck to her guns, showing her apprehension and vulnerabilities only to her husband and her close friends. Her effort to remain 'arrogant' and unintimidated is nicely captured by an anecdote told by Norman Podhoretz. The two met soon after Podhoretz published a highly critical essay entitled 'Hannah Arendt on Eichmann: A Study in the Perversity of Brilliance'. Keeping her fighting spirit, Arendt wittily responded to her critic as follows: 'I may be brilliant, [...] but I am definitely not perverse.'[167] Her effort to keep her public persona proved to be highly successful—perhaps in the wrong way. She certainly impressed many readers with her 'arrogance'; not in her own positive sense, however, but in the conventional sense of being opinionated, inconsiderate and unable to listen to other people's sensible opinions. This is exactly what Berlin meant when he accused Arendt of 'the most terrible arrogance'.[168]

During the Eichmann controversy, Arendt's lifelong dispute with the Jewish leadership entered a new round. This time she called her opponents the 'Jewish establishment' and accused them of launching an organised campaign against her book. Their purported methods were lies and manipulation of public opinion; their goal, to create an 'image' of *Eichmann in Jerusalem* that would divert its readers' attention from the book itself. In Arendt's words, 'they say I said things I never said in order to prevent people from finding out what I really did say.'[169] Why would the 'Jewish establishment' do such a thing? According to Arendt, that was not only because she touched on highly sensitive issues or questioned the Israeli government's effort to use the Eichmann trial for political purposes. It was also because, she suspected, 'the Jewish leadership [. . .] has much more dirty laundry to hide than anyone had ever guessed'.[170] She did not specify what this 'dirty laundry' in truth was. But she made this allegation because she believed that the scale of the campaign against her would be inexplicable had there not been 'dirty laundry' to hide. Whether her suspicion was well founded need not concern us here. What is relevant is Arendt's disappointment at her fellow Jewish intellectuals, most of whom, in her view, succumbed all too easily to image-making by the 'Jewish establishment'. Arendt saw a parallel between the behavioural pattern of post-war Jewish intellectuals and that of pre-war German intellectuals. Just as the latter had quickly renounced their independent thought and judgement to align themselves with the new social norms in 1930s Germany, Jewish intellectuals in 1960s America and Israel promptly renounced their independent thought and judgement to 'jump on a bandwagon', accusing Arendt of saying things that she never said.[171] To her credit, Arendt expressed her criticism not in agentive but in structural terms. She did not say that her Jewish critics as individuals were especially naive, amoral or stupid. Her point, rather, was that the force of public opinion in modern times was such that even the finest minds, such as Scholem, could not avoid being compromised by it.[172]

It is in this context that Arendt made one of her few recorded remarks on Isaiah Berlin. As someone 'on the closest of terms with the government in Israel', she alleged, Berlin might have contributed his share to the manipulation of public opinion, especially in Britain.[173] It is not clear what she had in mind here. Perhaps, she was thinking about Berlin's role in bringing the Arendt–Scholem exchange to the attention of *Encounter* magazine. Or perhaps she was thinking about some other episode, or did not have anything specific in mind. No matter what the truth may be, Arendt in late 1963 expressed the suspicion that Berlin was more than an ordinary member of the party of the 'modest' many. He was, rather, a part of the 'Jewish establishment', who purportedly did their utmost to cover up inconvenient truths with lies and manipulative images. The conflict between Arendt and Berlin hit a new low during the Eichmann controversy.

Patriotism, Self-Criticism and Self-Hatred

Finally, Arendt's harshly critical tone of writing in *Eichmann in Jerusalem* must partly be accounted for by her Jewish identity. Again, some of the remarks she herself made during the controversy do little to illuminate the matter. Arguably the most problematic in this respect is her rejoinder to Scholem, who charged her with lacking *Ahabath Israel* or the 'love of the Jewish people'. (On this charge Berlin said, 'I think [Scholem] was perfectly right.'[174]) Her response to Scholem was twofold. First, she said that she indeed knew no such love, because she had never loved a collective entity and 'the only kind of love I know of and believe in is the love of persons'.[175] Second, she found the idea of loving a people suspect, as it might be abused and channelled into bad politics. Of these two responses, the first is better remembered. While it is indeed a clever and memorable response, however, it is a deeply defective one, for the simple reason that one of the key concepts in Arendt's political thought is *amor mundi*, or love of the world, and the world is no less a collective entity than is a nation or a people.[176] In other words, Arendt's first response to Scholem might have been plausible had their exchange been self-contained. But the exchange did not occur in a historical vacuum, and Arendt's own oeuvre negates her claim that collective entities cannot be an object of love. Contrary to what she told Scholem, she was perfectly capable of loving collective entities such as the world. If so, it may seem that Scholem was right after all: what she was unable to love was not collective entities in general, but the Jewish people in particular.

This would be a hasty conclusion to draw, however, because a very different line of argument is discernible in Arendt's second, rather confusing, response to Scholem. It begins with an eminently sensible but hardly original rejection of the 'love of a people' understood as blind and narcissistic attachment to a people. Then, she mentions patriotism, conceding, 'I can admit to you [...] that wrong done by my own people naturally grieves me more than wrong done by other peoples.'[177] Instead of elaborating on this issue, however, Arendt quickly changes topic, expresses her general doubts about 'the role of the "heart" in politics' and concludes this part of her response.[178] This move is unfortunate, because she bypasses the important question as to whether she considers patriotism, and more specifically a critical patriotism that entails 'opposition and criticism', to be a kind of love.[179] Does she accept the common idea of patriotism as the 'love of one's country'? This is an important question, because she perceives herself as a (highly) critical patriot.[180] Her professed source of inspiration is Bernard Lazare, and some of her descriptions of this 'great Jewish patriot' (Arendt) strike an autobiographical note.[181] For example, she writes,

> Lazare's criticism of his people was at least as bitter as Herzl's but he never despised them and did not share Herzl's idea that politics must be conducted from above. Faced with the alternative of remaining politically ineffective or of including himself among the élite group of saviors, he preferred to retreat into absolute isolation where, if he could do naught else, he could at least remain one of the people.[182]

Arendt hesitates to apply the term 'love' to characterise Lazare's critical patriotism. While she mentions Lazare's 'love for Jewry' in passing, she prefers in general to keep love out of politics, true to her response to Scholem.[183] Nevertheless, various terms related to love appear in her discussion of patriotism. They include 'devotion'. According to her, 'intense discontent [...] has always been the hallmark of true patriotism and of true devotion to one's people.'[184] Again, these words strike an autobiographical note, although they are meant to describe the sentiment, widespread among an earlier generation of European Jewry, awakened by the Dreyfus Affair.[185] Whether one calls it a love or not, it is Lazare-inspired 'devotion to one's people' that motivated Arendt's harsh criticism of the Jewish leadership. 'Their' failure is 'my' failure, too, for 'we' are bound together by our common peoplehood. It is in light of this idea that we should read the oft-cited passage from *Eichmann in Jerusalem*: 'To a Jew this role of the Jewish leaders in the destruction of their people is undoubtedly the darkest chapter of the whole dark story.'[186] These words are meant to be an attempt at self-criticism, anchored in Arendt's devotion to her people and their agentive capacity. Her conviction during the 1960s had hardly changed since 1942, when she wrote, 'Self-criticism is not self-hatred.'[187]

Arendt's is undoubtedly a tough devotion. It is reminiscent of a Freudian conception of fatherly love, nicely explicated by Erich Fromm in *The Art of Loving*:

> Fatherly love is conditional love. Its principle is 'I love you because you fulfil my expectations, because you do your duty, because you are like me.' [...] The negative aspect is the very fact that fatherly love has to be deserved, that it can be lost if one does not do what is expected. [...] The positive side is equally important. Since his love is conditional, I can do something to acquire it, I can work for it; his love is not outside of my control as motherly [i.e., unconditional] love is.[188]

Fromm went on to give his readers a sensible warning: 'be patient and tolerant, rather than threatening and authoritarian', or else fatherly love could misfire.[189] One could try to imagine what the Eichmann controversy might have been if Arendt had followed Fromm's advice. What would have happened if she had been more patient and tolerant, articulated her criticism of the wartime Jewish leadership in a more measured tone, and expressed her 'devotion' to her people less punitively, more compassionately—if you will, in a more 'motherly' fashion? What difference would that have made to the Western Holocaust consciousness that was only beginning to grow when *Eichmann in Jerusalem* was published? These questions are worth pondering, although the book's impact cannot be undone and the missed opportunity cannot be brought back.

What about the allegation of self-hatred? Is this utterly groundless, if Arendt's harsh tone of criticism is due to her refusal to be 'modest' on the one hand, and to her professed devotion to her own people on the other? Is she right to believe that 'self-criticism is not self-hatred'? Obviously, the answer depends on what one means by the loaded term 'Jewish self-hatred'. It is neither possible nor necessary to go into a full discussion of the term's complex history.[190] It is, however, worth noting that the term denotes various and often mutually conflicting ideas, and that at least some of its major meanings are inapplicable to Arendt. For example, if what is meant is a desire to flee from one's Jewishness, Arendt is emphatically not 'self-hating'. On the contrary, one of the key messages she iterated many times was that Jews should embrace their Jewishness, especially when this is perceived as a 'problem' by others. 'A human being can defend himself only as the person he is attacked as,' she wrote. 'A Jew can preserve his human dignity only if he can be human as a Jew.'[191] These are hardly the words of a 'self-hating Jew' in its escapist sense.

This, however, does not necessarily mean that *none* of the recognised meanings of the term 'Jewish self-hatred' are applicable to Arendt. Of particular relevance is its critical sense, that is, 'Jewish self-hatred' as a marker of the limits of Jewish self-criticism. One is said to be 'self-hating' in this sense if one's self-criticism goes too far, even if the motive for the self-criticism is an admirable one. As is well known, the risk of this usage of the term is that 'self-hatred' can be applied too indiscriminately to suppress self-criticism *altogether*. But this meaning of the term is still a legitimate one, at least when applied cautiously and prudently. Was Arendt a 'self-hater' in this sense, then? Her critics, including Berlin, thought she was. In their view, her relentless self-criticism, expressed on the pages of the *New Yorker* for all the world to see, went so far that it slid into self-hatred. Berlin got the impression that her overly self-critical attitude ultimately stemmed from her disillusionment with Zionism: Zionism was her God that failed and she could not forgive Him and His followers.[192] Arendt, needless to say, saw the matter differently. She thought her self-criticism was constructive and forward-looking, although she may have been half aware that she could go too far, such as when she called Leo Baeck a 'Jewish Führer'.

Who was right after all? Arendt and her supporters or her critics? Did she go too far in her criticism of the Jewish leadership? Or did she not trespass? No consensus has emerged more than half a century after the original controversy. Each side has said all there is to say more than once, and each has inflicted deep wounds on the other. Neither has been persuaded as a result, and the gap is likely to remain wide, forever. On this issue, if not on others, Berlin was right: 'I cannot conceive of any issue that could bring me to the same platform as Miss Hannah Arendt.'[193]

Conclusion

The Eichmann controversy was an important part of the conflict between Hannah Arendt and Isaiah Berlin, especially the latter's animosity towards the former. It was only after this controversy that Berlin began using 'Arendt' as a general noun to refer to something like perversity and deformation.[194] It is likely that he would not have seen Arendt as his 'real bête noire' had she not written *Eichmann in Jerusalem*. Nevertheless, it is also true that the Eichmann controversy was a part of a larger story; that it was not a stand-alone issue. This is true in three distinct senses. First, *chronologically*, Berlin's anger at *Eichmann in Jerusalem* was preceded by his political and philosophical disagreement with Arendt, and followed by his continuing enmity. The year 1963 marked a peak of his hostility towards her, rather than the beginning or the end of it. Second, *intellectually*, the specifically moral disagreement between the two thinkers that surfaced during the Eichmann controversy was tied to other differences. These included historical disagreement over the nature of totalitarian oppression and domination, and theoretical disagreement over freedom and its limits under highly oppressive conditions. Finally, *existentially*, the two thinkers' contrasting perspectives were inseparable from their differing life stories. Of particular relevance was the stark contrast between the sense of pride Arendt felt in her wartime deeds and the sense of shame Berlin felt about his obliviousness to the Shoah during the war. Given these multilayered differences, it is no wonder that the two could not agree with each other on many difficult issues raised by the Eichmann trial.

This, however, is not to say that our protagonists were always divided by unbridgeable differences. As we saw in previous chapters, they did not always disagree with each other, and even when they disagreed their differences could be subtle or moderate, rather than absolute and incommensurable. In fact, Arendt and Berlin are sometimes seen, for good reason, as belonging to the same group, in the scheme of things. Among those who have seen a resemblance between the two were dissidents in the communist East in the 1980s. Imagining a better future, some of them drew inspiration from the anti-totalitarian writings of *both* Arendt *and* Berlin. Were they right to see similarities in their political thought? Did the two thinkers' shared opposition to totalitarianism bring their ideas close to each other? It is to this question that I now turn.

6

Islands of Freedom

IN 1987, two years before the fall of the Berlin Wall, a slim volume entitled
Trójgłos o wolności (Three voices for freedom) was illegally published in Warsaw by a group of Polish dissidents associated with Solidarity. Included in this
107-page book were the Polish translations of Berlin's 'Two Concepts of Liberty' and Arendt's 'What Is Freedom?', alongside parts of Raymond Aron's
'Essai sur les libertés', also in translation.[1] The title of the samizdat volume was
a subtle one. It did not suggest or imply that the 'voices for freedom' spoke in
harmony. In fact, almost exactly when the volume appeared behind the Iron
Curtain, Isaiah Berlin, who was almost certainly unaware of its publication,
summarily expressed his dismissal of Arendt's political thought in a letter to
his Polish friend, the intellectual historian Andrzej Walicki.[2] He wrote, 'Miss
Arendt's dreams about ancient Athens mixed with Tocqueville, New England
Town Meetings, Quaker gatherings, mystical interpretations of Rousseau's
General Will—all that is not for me, and I am sure not for you.'[3]

These two episodes are worth considering in the light of *Isaac and Isaiah:
The Covert Punishment of a Cold War Heretic* by David Caute, published in
2013.[4] Like the present study, *Isaac and Isaiah* tells a story of Berlin and an
adversary: the Marxist historian Isaac Deutscher. As in the case of the Berlin–
Arendt conflict, the mutual dislike between Berlin and Deutscher was not
symmetrical, but stronger on Berlin's side. The philosopher had this to say of
the historian: 'I must tell you frankly that Deutscher is the only man whose
presence in the same academic community as myself I should find morally
intolerable. I will not dine at the same table as Deutscher.'[5] The 'only man' in
the quote is an exaggeration because, as we have seen, Berlin had almost identical things to say about Arendt (who was, of course, a woman, but this is irrelevant in the present context; by the 'only man' Berlin meant the only person). Berlin said, for example, 'my allergy vis-à-vis Miss Arendt is absolute and
her mere presence in a room gives me goose-flesh.'[6] Caute is thus right in
noting that 'Berlin's antipathy to Hannah Arendt [. . .] parallels closely—
though far from exactly—his aversion to Deutscher'.[7] If so, one crucial

difference between the two rivalries is worth highlighting: whereas the Cold War division between West and East accounted for much of the Berlin–Deutscher divide, it had little to do with the Berlin–Arendt divide. In fact, as the episode of the samizdat volume illustrates, the latter couple were on the same side in Cold War politics, although the versions of the 'West' they defended were in conflict with each other. In other words, the existence of the common enemy of totalitarianism did not turn Arendt and Berlin into allies. On the contrary, they conceptualised anti-totalitarian politics differently, not least because of their disagreement over liberty/freedom on the one hand and over totalitarianism and its evil on the other. Now that these points of disagreement have been examined in previous chapters, it is time to pull some of the central threads running through this book together to consider the following question. What kind of society or polity did Arendt and Berlin respectively defend as most accommodating to a genuinely free and human life?

In addressing this issue, one must keep in mind that neither Arendt nor Berlin considered the role of political theory to consist in the twin task of identifying a set of general normative principles that should govern society and teasing out their implications for public policy issues. This mode of political theorising, and the division between 'ideal' and 'non-ideal' theory that it presumes, became conventional only in the late twentieth century, when political theory came to isolate itself from neighbouring areas of scholarship to develop into a more or less independent and autonomous academic discipline. While the story of this development is beyond the scope of this book, it is worth recalling that both Arendt and Berlin belonged to an earlier generation, to whom our current understanding of political theory would have been alien. To complicate the matter further, both of our protagonists shared their generation's scepticism towards political blueprint-painting, which was, thanks to its close association with left-wing totalitarianisms, widely dismissed during the mid-twentieth century as irrelevant at best and disastrously counterproductive at worst.[8] Unlike later political theorists decisively influenced by John Rawls's *A Theory of Justice* (1971), both Arendt and Berlin constantly fused normative argument and empirical analysis, with the result that prescriptive ideas were often offered not as a straightforward normative theory but in the indirect form of suggestion and signalling.

With this in mind, this chapter compares Arendt's and Berlin's part-empirical, part-normative perspectives on England/Britain, the United States of America and revolutionary (1956) Hungary in order to tease out the important similarities and differences between the two thinkers' elusive visions of an ideal polity. More specifically, it first discusses Berlin's idealised representation of twentieth-century England/Britain as a model liberal society, followed by an analysis of his somewhat apologetic commentary on the country's imperialist past, compared to Arendt's highly critical commentary on it. Then, I turn to Arendt's idealised representation of the United States as a quintessentially modern, free republic, followed by an examination of her optimistic commentary on the country's turbulent late 1960s, compared to Berlin's highly pessimistic commentary on it. It will be demonstrated, on the one hand, that the two thinkers were undertaking parallel theoretical enterprises, in that each presented an idealised version of one specific country— England/Britain in Berlin's case and America in Arendt's—as a proxy for what a *human* society can ideally be. On the other hand, I show that their ideals conflicted with each other in several key respects, and that they disagreed on both normative and historiographical levels. If, as Berlin told Andrzej Walicki, Arendt's 'dreams' were not for him, Berlin's restatement of an old-fashioned liberalism was not for her, either. Finally, to complete my comparative study, the last section turns to an event of historic importance that could have created an 'island of freedom' (Arendt) in the midst of the totalitarian world: the Hungarian uprising against Soviet domination in 1956.[9] On the significance of this event Arendt's and Berlin's perspectives clashed yet again, throwing further light on some of my main arguments and findings in this chapter and this book as a whole.

Berlin's England

First, a note on terminology is in order. Berlin often uses 'England/English' as a synonym for 'Britain/British', as if to say that the latter were a mere extension of the former. This was a common, if not unquestionable, linguistic practice in his lifetime. Needless to say, it has become far more problematic today, when each of Britain's constituent nations is increasingly asserting its distinct identity, undermining Britons' identity as Britons to some extent. That said, my current goal is not to scrutinise Berlin's antiquated terminology or his Anglocentric bias. Rather, it is to examine the ideals which he takes England and Britain *alike* to stand for. Consequently, I accept his imprecise terminology when I discuss 'Berlin's England' in what follows, setting aside the issue of national differences within Britain for the sake of argument.

Berlin considers England (in this sense) to be a quintessentially liberal society.[10] This is testified to by many of his remarks, but the following from his autobiographical essay is particularly articulate and merits full citation:

> I confess to a pro-British bias. I was educated in England and have lived there since 1921; all that I have been and done and thought is indelibly English. I cannot judge English values impartially, for they are part of me: I count this as the greatest of intellectual and political good fortune. These

values are the basis of what I believe: that decent respect for others and the toleration of dissent are better than pride and a sense of national mission; that liberty may be incompatible with, and better than, too much efficiency; that pluralism and untidiness are, to those who value freedom, better than the rigorous imposition of all-embracing systems, no matter how rational and disinterested, or than the rule of majorities against which there is no appeal. All this is deeply and uniquely English, and I freely admit that I am steeped in it, and believe in it, and cannot breathe freely save in a society where these values are for the most part taken for granted.[11]

Berlin was a Russian-Jewish émigré and naturalised British citizen. As Michael Ignatieff suggests, his deep appreciation of English values and sensibilities may have stemmed from 'an exile's prerogative to love an adopted home with an absence of irony that is impossible for a native'.[12] Whether this is the case or not, Berlin certainly identifies himself closely with his adopted home, claiming to be unable to 'breathe freely' in a society that does not resemble England. No less remarkable is the proximity of the ostensibly 'English' values and sensibilities to the ones he defends in his theoretical work. If liberty and pluralism are at the heart of Berlin's work,[13] he, according to his own expressly 'biased' understanding, considers those ideas 'deeply and uniquely English'.

What (moral and political) goods, more precisely, does Berlin repeatedly associate with 'England'? Chief among them are: *individual liberty* conceptualised in negative terms as non-interference; *tolerance* towards others and their respective personal goals; *peace* and *stability* resulting from the fortune of England 'not [having been] invaded or seriously defeated for eight hundred years';[14] *decency* conceptualised primarily as the willingness to treat others humanely; and respect for *privacy* that allows men and women to do or to be (within limits) whatever they wish to do or to be. Those goods are tied to the liberal temperament of the English, who are, purportedly, immune to fanaticism or extremism; moderate; untidy, though by no means chaotic or anarchic; benevolent and well-meaning, if at times patronising; sober, empirical and commonsensical; and realistic, practical and piecemeal when tackling social and political problems. According to Berlin, England has been blessed with the historic fortune to connect the liberal goods and the liberal temperament organically to develop into a model liberal society. Liberalism, in his words, 'is essentially the belief of people who have lived on the same soil for a long time in comparative peace with each other. An English invention.'[15] Observe the use of the term 'soil', which also appears in Berlin's self-description. He says, for example, that he will never emigrate from England 'because we are what we are and can only live on the soil that we do'.[16] Similarly, he emphasises that 'by nature I *am* rooted, not rootless and cosmopolitan'—rooted, that is, in Oxford, England, Great Britain.[17] One may extend the organic metaphor and think of Berlin's liberal England in the image of a functional ecosystem: liberal goods are rooted in the fertile soil of liberal England, which is a natural habitat for liberals like Berlin himself.

It must be immediately noted that some liberal values are missing or marginalised in Berlin's liberal system. Consider progress and social welfare. Interpreted in evolutionary and organicist terms, these values were at the heart of the new liberalism of early twentieth-century Britain, finding its most succinct expression in L. T. Hobhouse's *Liberalism*.[18] This brand of liberalism not only developed its Millian predecessor in a new historical context but also contributed significantly to the subsequent rise of the welfare state in Britain.[19] Notwithstanding his express sympathy for 'New Dealism' and 'the welfare state under Attlee', however, Berlin gives little credit to the new liberal achievements; throughout his life, he was relatively unconcerned with socio-economic issues central to welfare thinking, including health, housing, employment and forms of industry. In fact, he hardly ever mentions key new liberal thinkers by name; on a rare occasion when he did so, Berlin said he 'was not deeply impressed [. . .] by Hobhouse'.[20] Similarly, while individual autonomy is integral to another important, perfectionist strand of liberalism, it does not feature prominently in Berlin's normative work. While he acknowledges the tradition of autonomy-based liberalism originating in Kant's moral philosophy, he presents himself as belonging to an alternative, negative liberty-based tradition represented by the Mill of *On Liberty*. Unlike liberal perfectionists such as Joseph Raz and Steven Wall,[21] Berlin does not consider it to be a legitimate part of the liberal state's job to encourage its citizens to live autonomously or otherwise perfect themselves; he believes that the liberal state should be non-partisan, if not strictly neutral, regarding citizens' personal decisions and their conceptions of the good. Thus, Berlin's liberal England represents a particular kind of liberalism, which is neither perfectionist nor reformist but distinctly *minimalist*. Its principal concern, as Jan-Werner Müller (with a nod to Judith Shklar) puts it, is 'to avoid a *summum malum*, not the realization of any *summum bonum*'.[22] To appropriate an image Arendt repeatedly evokes, Berlin's England is an 'island of freedom', conceptualised in negative terms, surrounded by non-liberal politics of various kinds from mild authoritarianism to Nazism and Stalinism. Berlin, like Arendt in this respect, considers the twentieth century to be a dark time and indeed 'the worst century there has ever been', characterised by the rise of totalitarianism, total wars and mass killing on an unprecedented scale.[23] On this menacing water floats Berlin's England, whose liberal tradition is historically unique and yet has universal normative appeal.

As I discussed in Chapter 4, two kinds of political menace appear prominently in Berlin's discussion of 'the worst century'. One is of a specifically

Bolshevik kind, whereby a small group of ideologically motivated fanatics use extra-legal means, especially terror, to seize power and establish a highly illiberal regime. This is one of the chief threats Berlin has in mind when he repeatedly refers to Heinrich Heine's 'power of ideas' maxim: 'philosophical concepts nurtured in the stillness of a professor's study could destroy a civilisation.'[24] Rousseau, Hegel, Marx and others came up with potentially explosive concepts, but it took the Bolsheviks to actually and physically destroy a civilisation. A mirror image of Berlin's fear is found in the words of Trotsky himself: 'Nothing great has been accomplished in history without fanaticism.'[25] To this type of threat Berlin's England is conveniently and rather suspiciously insusceptible. If the English are *by temperament* averse to fanaticism, extremism and cruelty, England must be exempt from the risk of a Bolshevik-style revolution or insurrection.

The second menace is of a distinctly right-wing kind, rooted in a specifically romantic nationalism. As is well known, Berlin does not regard nationalism as necessarily aggressive or inherently illiberal.[26] However, it can develop in these directions when, firstly, it entails a political demand for collective self-determination; secondly, the national community sets limits to the freedom of association and to the activities of other communities in civil society; thirdly, national values and allegiances are credited with moral supremacy over other group allegiances; and finally, the nation acquires a sense of mission that is considered so important that it justifies the removal of all impediments, by violent means if necessary.[27] Historically, Berlin argues, nations that have suffered from externally induced humiliation have been susceptible to this type of nationalism. As I discussed in Chapter 4, Berlin's celebrated 'bent twig' metaphor is meant to illustrate this point: an oppressed nation strikes at its oppressor as a twig 'deformed by an unnatural outside force' hits back at 'the source of deformity' at the moment of release.[28] The paradigmatic case of such 'bent twig' nationalism is, in Berlin's view, Germany after the Napoleonic invasion, strongly resenting the universalist pretensions of the French, while being acutely aware of its own cultural backwardness and political weakness.[29] A fierce critic of the determinist conception of history, Berlin concedes that German romantic nationalism did not need to develop into the militaristic nationalism of Wilhelm II; nor did this need to morph into National Socialism. However, Berlin (unlike Arendt in this respect) does not consider twentieth-century right-wing totalitarianism to be entirely unprecedented, marked by a fundamental break from its nineteenth-century, romantic nationalist precursor. The former could emerge out of the latter when combined with other ingredients such as utopianism and irrationalism under certain historical conditions. Again, Berlin's England is ideally insusceptible to this type of menace. Although the rise and fall of the British Empire yielded English nationalism and indeed 'English chauvinism', this was not comparable to its malicious and aggressive German counterpart.[30] Nor could it be, if Berlin is right, because, according to his 'bent twig' hypothesis, externally induced humiliation is a prerequisite for the rise of romantic nationalism. If so, fascism will not emerge in England, unless the country is invaded or seriously defeated in the future.

Berlin does not, however, consider the value of benign English nationalism to consist solely in its inability to develop beyond a certain limit. It also consists in its capacity for satisfying what he sees as one of the most basic human needs deeply ingrained in our nature: the need to belong. At issue here is a specifically *cultural* belonging. In Berlin's view, only in a group to which one has special cultural connections can one truly be at home and live a fulfilling life. He concedes that such a group does not need to be a nation; it could in theory be a voluntary association, a socio-economic class, and so on. In practice, however, the sense of *national* belonging, underpinned by a common language and shared memory, has proved stronger than other group allegiances. Berlin draws from this the conclusion that membership in a nation qua cultural group is *likely* to continue to best satisfy the human need to belong, at least in the foreseeable future.[31] Observe that Berlin's endorsement of nationality goes beyond Mill's functionalist argument that a 'feeling of common nationality' has the merit of generating political stability and sustaining 'free institutions'.[32] While Berlin broadly shares the Millian view, he ultimately defends nationality in intrinsic, rather than instrumental, terms. He follows Herder's conception of the nation as 'purely and strictly a cultural attribute' and considers the primary value of nationality to consist in its ability to provide a home for the collective life of a people.[33] This explains why the diversity Berlin wishes to see in society concerns individuals and their opinions, preferences and dispositions and does *not* extend to sub-national cultural communities; multiculturalist excess can undermine the special connections binding a people. Berlin claims that England is optimally diverse and animated by the right kind and degree of nationalism. While it is 'one of the least nationalist of all countries', Englishmen and Englishwomen are bonded by cultural and historical ties sufficiently rich that they do not feel surrounded by strangers.[34]

It is certainly true that Berlin reproduces some of the 'most self-approving myths' of England and its people.[35] But he does more than that: he does his share in *remoulding* the myths. Of particular relevance here is the way he narrates the British philosophical tradition. In terms of a general outlook, he observes, British philosophy (like English society) has essentially been empiricist: sober, cool-headed, commonsensical and anti-metaphysical. It began with Bacon and Hobbes, was developed by Locke, Berkeley and Hume, culminating in Bentham and Mill, and was succeeded in various ways by Berlin's (near) contemporaries such as Russell, Moore, Ayer and Austin.[36] Excluded from this narrative are, among others, British idealists such as T. H. Green,

F. H. Bradley and Bernard Bosanquet. Berlin certainly knows some of the idealists' work, not least because the Oxford of the late 1920s where he began his academic career was under their lingering influence.[37] However, he, like many of his empiricist contemporaries, often calls idealists 'English Hegelians' or 'Hegelians in England', underlining the foreignness of their 'Germanic' work to the presumably native British tradition. For example, in his best-known book on liberty, Berlin admires Green as 'exceptionally enlightened' and 'genuine[ly] liberal'; yet he ultimately portrays him as a follower of his German masters, prioritising positive liberty over the negative rival that has been defended by 'classical *English* political philosophers' and, of course, by Berlin himself.[38] Berlin in this way joins the early twentieth-century empiricists' attempt to undo what was done in British philosophy between Mill and Russell. Even Berlin's autobiographical recollections serve this purpose. Reading Bradley and Bosanquet as a student, he recalls, was like 'wandering in a very dark wood with broken light occasionally flickering through the branches'. Reading Moore's *Principia Ethica*, by contrast, gave the young Berlin the feeling of being 'transported' to 'an open, sunlit plain'.[39] British empiricism gently shines over Berlin's liberal England, to which idealists, as well as fanatics, extremists, terrorists, communists and fascists, do not belong.

To sum up, Berlin's England is not an impartial description of the country as it existed at a particular moment in time. Rather, it is a theoretical construct indicating what England *at its best can be*, embodying essential liberal values, an ideally liberal temperament and a long intellectual tradition simultaneously defending negative liberty and defying politically suspicious metaphysical thinking from Kant, Hegel and Marx through Green, Bradley and Bosanquet on one side and Nietzsche and Heidegger on the other. It is purportedly immune to the two worst manifestations of Berlin's fear: totalitarianism via a Bolshevik-style insurrection and totalitarianism via the hyperinflation of romantic nationalism. It is hardly surprising, then, that Berlin never seriously considered leaving England for either Israel (which he supported throughout his life) or America (where he thought his work could be better appreciated than in Britain). In fact, when Berlin was offered a full-time professorship by the City University of New York, he categorically said he did not have 'the slightest intention of leaving England for any purposes whatsoever'. He wished to remain in his adopted home, to which he was happily 'tied [...] by a thousand ties'.[40]

Debating British Imperialism

Berlin's narrative of England has a triadic temporal structure: (T1) the existence of a relatively homogeneous population in the distant past; (T2) the tolerant and overall happy co-existence of diverse groups of people, more or less conforming to the dominant English culture, in the post-war present; and (T3) the continuous flow of time connecting 'then' and 'now' as England organically developed from T1 to T2. A question naturally arises as to how the country's tumultuous events and dramatic changes, albeit no wholesale external invasion, fit into this narrative. While one could consider a number of such occasions, from the Reformation and the Civil War to late-twentieth-century migration and demographic changes, one issue stands out as particularly pertinent to this study: Britain's global expansion and imperial misadventures, especially during the latter half of the long nineteenth century when the Empire reached its zenith. How does this episode in British history square with Berlin's view of England as a quintessentially liberal society? Considering this question not only allows us to appreciate his normative ideas further; it also allows us to draw fascinating comparisons between the two protagonists of this book.

Isaiah Berlin and the Un-Englishness of British Imperialism

Berlin's view of Britain's imperial past is elusive and ambivalent. Unlike Arendt, he has no theory of imperialism. Nor, again unlike her, does he have much to say on the British Empire specifically. However, one thing that is clear is that he shows little sign of so-called 'imperial nostalgia'. This might be surprising, given his well-known admiration for Winston Churchill. His essay 'Winston Churchill in 1940' is said to border on hagiography,[41] and he indeed praises the statesman in such flattering terms as 'the saviour of his country, a mythical hero who belongs to legend as much as to reality, the largest human being of our time'.[42] But Berlin's Churchill is a formidable wartime leader, not an imperial hero. The philosopher hardly shares the statesman's hope of saving the crumbling Empire in one way or another. In fact, despite their surface similarity, Berlin's and Churchill's cases for a post-war Anglo-American alliance stemmed from different sources. While Churchill wanted to forge a closer alliance to continue the civilising project supposedly initiated by the English,[43] Berlin emphasised the significance of the alliance because he believed that post-war Britain's ability to 'preserve not merely an adequate standard of living, but life and liberty itself' was crucially dependent on the American superpower.[44] He expressed this realistic view on the BBC Third Programme in September 1949. Whether one liked it or not, Berlin pointed out, the Empire had been lost and lost for good, and post-war Britain would be powerless unless it acted with its friends and allies, most importantly with the United States. This assessment aggravated some of his listeners, who regarded Berlin's realism as mere defeatism. For example, an *Evening Standard* columnist accused the Oxford don of blindness to the prospect of imperial rejuvenation.

'Britain should ride out the storm alone,' the columnist wrote, 'placing her faith in the strength and the resources of the Empire. Why is Mr Berlin so blind to the attractions of this simple creed? The answer is as simple. He is not an Empire man.'[45] These remarks are true on a descriptive level. Berlin was indeed no 'Empire man'. In his view, 'the old paths to survival and recovery' had perished. To think otherwise in the late 1940s was delusional, amounting to a failure to 'realise that things are what they are and that their consequences are what they will be'.[46]

Delusion, however, was not a vice unique to the would-be resurrectors of the dying Empire in post-war Britain. In Berlin's view, it had infected Britain's foreign and imperial policies before, especially during the high imperialism of the late nineteenth century. Again, he does not have much to say on this issue, but the little he says shows his conviction that some of the empire-builders fooled themselves by over-earnestly embracing such notions as the 'white man's burden' and a civilising mission. This sobering view stems partly from his Herderian idea that each culture has its own centre of gravity and that no culture can claim *overall* superiority over others. This of course does not mean that specific practices within a culture ought not to be criticised externally. Nevertheless, it indicates that the high imperialist sense of civilisational superiority is a form of self-intoxication, a motley mix of ignorance, chauvinism and self-aggrandisement. Besides, Berlin's dismissal of Britain's high imperialist delusion is also informed by his empirical observations about the enduring power of nationalism. As he told his audience in New Delhi on the centenary of the Bengali poet Rabindranath Tagore's birth in 1961, one lesson to learn from twentieth-century decolonisation movements is the persistence of a nation's desire for self-rule, 'the fact that citizens of ex-colonial territories may prefer harsh treatment by their own kinsmen to even the most enlightened rule by outsiders'.[47] Britain's empire-builders' patronising hope—often well intentioned—of elevating 'lower' cultures by spreading a civilised (read: English) way of life strengthened and sometimes even awakened a sense of nationality on the part of the subordinated. To this extent the empire-builders were their own grave-diggers: imperial arrogance paved the way for the violent explosions of 'bent twig' nationalism.

Coming from Berlin, the charge of delusion levelled at Britain's empire-builders is not to be discounted. As we saw in Chapter 4, he tends to attribute the worst political disasters to delusional ideas, especially utopian ones. Yet delusion is not an intrinsic moral wrong, but a prudential error, albeit one that often results in moral wrongs. In spite of his sympathy for the nationalisms of small nations, underpinned by his Zionist commitment, Berlin, in contrast to Arendt, does not express strong *moral* indignation at modern European imperialism in general or its British variant in particular. For one thing, very much a man of his time in this respect, Berlin shows little interest in the debate over empire and imperialism.[48] His keen interest in the theoretical justifications for nationalism by Herder, Fichte, Maistre, Mazzini and others starkly contrasts with his lack of interest in the pros and cons of imperialism argued by Vitoria, Locke, Burke, Mill, Hobson, Lenin and Luxemburg, let alone Frantz Fanon and Aimé Césaire. This is partly due to the tacit assumption Berlin makes about the wrongness of imperialism: the wrongness consists primarily in unwanted rule over one nation by another. In other words, he sees imperialism through the lens of nationality. Imperialism is inherently wrong, on this view, to the extent that it violates the principle of national self-determination. This may of course be true, but one wonders what Berlin has to say about other evils and wrongs that go hand in hand with imperialism, such as racism and white supremacism, war and military conquest, murders, massacres and genocides, plunder and economic exploitation, theft of land and the forced displacement of native populations. On these Berlin has strikingly little to say, notwithstanding his acute concern with antisemitism and the specifically Jewish predicament. His silence gives some credence to Berlin's post-colonial critics' claim that the Anglo-Jewish philosopher's liberal political theory is compromised by his racial and colonial blindness.[49]

As for the British Empire more specifically, two aspects of Berlin's thought are worth highlighting. First, he holds the view—still common among Britons today—that British imperial rule was relatively benign, 'enlightened' and on balance even beneficial to the colonised.[50] Berlin thus echoes Karl Marx's quintessentially nineteenth-century notion of the civilising effect of capital, writing,

> It is not entirely correct to say that imperialism, or alien rule unwelcome to the ruled, has necessarily inflicted damage on these subjects. What I am thinking of is Karl Marx's very shrewd remark that the British in India have driven the Indians, by their rule, into three or four centuries of normal development from a totally agrarian society to a comparatively modern one. He adds, of course, that the British did not do this for the benefit of the Indians, but for their own benefit; nevertheless, he says that the idea that once upon a time there was a peaceful, rural society of contented peasants, free from the horrors of industrialism and modernisation, is a myth— that the brutality of the pre-British rulers of India was very great, and that the lot of the average Indian was in a sense greatly improved by British rule, whatever the motives of the British may have been.[51]

It is a matter of debate whether Berlin's somewhat antiquated sympathy for the civilising effect of British rule in India conflicts with his pioneering effort to defend Herderian cultural pluralism and egalitarianism. Should he not say, if he is to be consistently Herderian, that imperialism does *necessarily* inflict damage on the subordinated, although the damage may be mitigated or even sometimes overridden by the opposite, advantageous effects? Or, alternatively, should he not acknowledge in the spirit of pluralism that such balancing and calculation is impossible because cultural losses and socio-economic gains cannot be placed on a single scale? No matter what one may think about his consistency, it may be safely said that Berlin's understanding of British imperial history, like his understanding of liberal England, is a selective, charitable and not altogether impartial one. He certainly does not think (unlike Arendt, as we shall see shortly) that the British Empire is in some crucial respects a precursor to Nazi Germany.

Second, of even greater interest, is Berlin's view about the un-Englishness or perhaps even un-Britishness of British imperialism. If, as Berlin claims, the English tradition consists of empiricism, pragmatism, a piecemeal approach to politics and the like, some of the great heroes and villains of the Empire—dreamers and visionaries, martyrs and zealots, romantic adventurers and reckless warmongers—must be excluded from that tradition. Berlin's depiction of Disraeli in his late 1960s essay 'Benjamin Disraeli, Karl Marx and the Search for Identity' is especially telling in this context.[52] Berlin's Disraeli is a Jewish Disraeli, 'not in any ordinary sense an Englishman'.[53] He found himself in a hostile society, where his desire to be accepted and influential was met by deep-seated suspicion and prejudice. This, however, did not deter the ambitious, opportunistic and profoundly romantic writer and future prime minister. On the contrary, to satisfy his 'passionate desire to dominate [his] society', Disraeli fabricated his origins, invented the personality of a Jewish nobleman for himself, and 'half-hypnotised himself' into believing his own fiction, with the result that he acquired the confidence and ability to stand as an equal among his friends and enemies in the political class of Victorian Britain.[54] With no aristocratic ties, public school attendance or education at an ancient university, the young writer from London's Sephardi Jewish community turned himself into the Earl of Beaconsfield. Still, Berlin continues, Disraeli's ideas and fantasies remained foreign and 'Oriental', and they included his dreamy vision of the Empire. In fact, the Anglo-Jewish politician's imperial mystique is 'splendid but most un-English [. . .], romantic to the point of exoticism, full of metaphysical emotion, to all appearances utterly opposed to everything most soberly empirical, utilitarian, anti-systematic in the British tradition'.[55] This, however, does not mean that the imperial mystique stayed inside Disraeli's head. On the contrary, the politician successfully 'bound [his] spell on the mind of England for two generations'.[56] He did indeed remould the national consciousness, singlehandedly investing thitherto realistic, nononsense imperial rule with 'eastern splendours'.[57] Thus, Berlin's Disraeli is not only an outsider and a social climber but also a magician and a spellbinder. Before him, the Empire was an English system of rule; after him, it became an un-English cult, which lasted for 'two generations'.

This is the great-man theory of history at its extreme. Berlin makes Disraeli almost solely responsible for the late Victorian alliance between Tory conservatism and popular jingoism with a dash of fantastical and rather ridiculous Orientalism. It is indeed easy for historians to criticise Berlin for placing too strong an emphasis on one man's ability to shape a nation's destiny. From a normative theoretical perspective, however, the advantage of this great-man theory is that Berlin can keep his conception of Englishness uninfected by the worst episodes in imperial history. If the English were seized by imperialist zeal in the late nineteenth century, that was due not to a long-term development in England but to the spell cast by the foreign magician, 'the least Victorian of the Victorian age': Benjamin Disraeli.[58] Similarly, if some Englishmen behaved in a fervent, indecent and/or inhumane manner, for example when they combined scorched-earth tactics and concentration camps to fight the Boers in South Africa, that may be attributed to Disraeli's powerful and yet short-lived spell. In this respect, as in others, Berlin is not an Empire man. He saves Englishness from imperial mystique and its disastrous consequences. His historiography saves his island of freedom from its inner drive to morph into an empire of liberty.

Hannah Arendt and the (British) Imperialist Roots of Totalitarianism

Unlike Isaiah Berlin, Hannah Arendt has a theory of modern European imperialism. Hers, however, is not a stand-alone theory, but forms a part of her analysis of totalitarianism. In other words, she looks at the imperialist past from the vantage point of the post-totalitarian present. With this in mind, two aspects of her theory are worth highlighting. First, she identifies the years between 1884 and 1914—from the legitimation of European colonisation of Africa at the Berlin Conference to the beginning of World War I—as 'the age of Imperialism'.[59] This new imperialism must be distinguished from old 'empire building' dating back at least to ancient Rome. It is the former, not the latter, that brought about a fundamental break in Western history and laid the groundwork for 'coming catastrophes'.[60] Of course, Arendt is no less a historical anti-determinist than Berlin, and emphasises that twentieth-century totalitarianism was not a necessary outcome of the preceding imperialism. Nevertheless, as Karuna Mantena observes, Arendt thinks that imperial experiences such as racial domination, global expansion, administrative massacres and 'pacification' (read: rule by violence and terror) made twentieth-century

genocide, total domination and totalitarian terror 'experientially and conceptually possible if not inevitable'.[61] For this the entirety of *European* imperialism, rather than the particular imperialism of a single country, is responsible.
Most importantly in the present context, Arendt does not let British imperialism
claim innocence. She writes that the 'emergence of totalitarian governments
is a phenomenon within, not outside, our [read: European] civilization'.[62] The
British Empire is an important part of this disgraced civilisation, and *Origins*
attempts to document its rich and varied contributions to the rise of totalitarianism, especially the Nazi variant.

Second, Arendt characterises new imperialism as 'the first stage in the political rule of the bourgeoisie rather than the last stage of capitalism'.[63] This,
needless to say, is a challenge to the Marxist theory of imperialism most lu-
cidly articulated in Lenin's 1916/17 work *Imperialism, the Highest Stage of Capitalism*.[64] But her disagreement with Marxists, even with Lenin more specifically, is by no means total.[65] In fact, not only does she think, like Lenin, that
capitalism contains within itself a dynamic that gives rise to violent imperialist competition, but she also follows Lenin's (as well as Hobson's) lead in
highlighting the role of financial capital in the rise of imperialism.[66] A capitalist economy generates over-saving or, in Arendt's terminology, 'superficial
capital', which may be invested to create further superfluous capital. Historically speaking, opportunities for such investment were initially sought in the
domestic market, within the borders of the investor's nation-state. However,
the domestic opportunities were quickly exhausted and owners of superfluous capital began seeking further opportunities abroad. For this risky enterprise they sought state protection. This, according to Arendt, marked the
birth of imperialism. As the hitherto apolitical bourgeois class seized state
apparatuses to protect their business interests abroad, the aim of politics was
reconceptualised to follow the logic of financial investment: expansion for
expansion's sake.

So far, Arendt's analysis basically follows the classical Marxist theory of
imperialism. But the rest of the story she tells departs decisively from it, and
it concerns what she calls 'superfluous men' or 'the mob'. A by-product of the
relentless dynamism of capitalist economy, superfluous men are the unskilled,
unemployed and economically useless 'human debris' abandoned by bourgeois society.[67] Downtrodden in their home countries, they are resentful, reckless, cruel, 'hollow to the core' and ready to go anywhere to satisfy their
greed.[68] Yet one destination that they avoided, *pace* Marxist expectations, was
solidarity with other members of the international proletariat. Instead, they
followed wherever superficial capital was invested, plundering and profiteering
in far-off lands, while establishing themselves as members of the 'master race'.
South Africa turned out to be their exemplary destination. There, in alliance

with owners of superficial capital speculating in newly found gold and dia-
monds, superfluous men 'established the first paradise of parasites'.[69] This was
followed by similar 'paradises' replicated across the globe as the age of imperialism advanced. Contrary to Lenin's theory, the agents of new imperialism
were not monopoly capitalists attempting to 'share the world among themselves'.[70] Rather, they were the 'new alliance between the much-too-rich and
the much-too-poor', or between capital and the mob.[71]

It is within this general framework that Arendt discusses British imperialism. For the purpose of comparison with Isaiah Berlin, consider the key
players she focuses on to characterise British imperialism. Tellingly, parliamentary figures such as Disraeli and Gladstone appear only marginally in
her account. Given a more prominent place are overseas adventurers and
functionaries such as Cecil Rhodes, Lord Cromer and T. E. Lawrence, complemented by Joseph Conrad as the most perceptive chronicler of Europeans' experiences in Africa, and Rudyard Kipling as the author of the specifically British imperialist legend.[72] This selection of the dramatis personae
reflects Arendt's conviction that the moral heart of new imperialism is found
not in the home country but in the overseas territories. If one is to understand British imperialism, one ought to examine South Africa, Egypt and
India rather than the left bank of the River Thames. In fact, according to
Arendt, those in Westminster did little more than give post hoc justifications
for the behaviour of men on the spot acting, however presumptuously, in
the name of the Empire.

It is no coincidence, then, that Arendt's discussion of Benjamin Disraeli
appears not in the second 'Imperialism' part but in the first 'Antisemitism' part
of Origins. Anticipating Berlin's aforementioned essay on the subject, Arendt
presents a Jewish Disraeli, 'never a thorough Englishman and [...] proud of
the fact'.[73] Like Berlin fifteen years later, Arendt depicts Disraeli as a profoundly opportunistic social climber, a fabricator of an imagined Jewish history, a believer in his own fantasies and a 'wizard' who enchanted the British
society from which he was an outsider.[74] In fact, the two thinkers' portrayals
of Disraeli are so similar that it is hard not to suspect that Berlin wrote his essay
under Arendt's influence, although he may well have been too proud to concede such an influence or even to acknowledge the existence of Arendt's
work.[75] Be that as it may, what is important in the present context is one crucial *difference* between the two Disraelis. For Berlin, as we have seen, Disraeli
is an arch-imperialist, the greatest moulder of the late Victorian British national consciousness. For Arendt, by contrast, Disraeli is no more than a parvenu and a gifted charlatan, whose influence over Britain amounted to little
more than 'entertain[ing] a bored society with highly dangerous fairy-tales'.[76]
Of course, Disraeli was 'an English imperialist' as well as 'a Jewish chauvinist'.[77]

But the fate of the Empire did not lie in Disraeli's hands; it was in the hands of those who owned and invested superfluous capital. It is for this reason that Disraeli's story belongs to the first, 'Antisemitism', part of *Origins*. Although he makes brief and sporadic appearances in the second, 'Imperialism', part of the book, he does so not as an imperial statesman but only as a proto-theoretician of race, a British counterpart to Arthur de Gobineau, albeit a less serious one.[78]

In stark contrast to the marginality of Disraeli is the centrality of Rhodes, Cromer and Lawrence for Arendt's account of British imperialism. Rhodes's significance is easy to see. In her view, he is an archetype of the 'imperialist-minded businessman', for whom expansion is the only and ultimate aim of politics.[79] Arendt is particularly impressed by the story of Rhodes falling into despair when he realised that the stars he gazed at in the night sky were beyond his reach, beyond his capacity for conquest and exploitation. He lamented, 'I would annex the planets if I could.'[80] Arendt uses these megalomaniacal words as an epigraph to the 'Imperialism' part of *Origins*, for they perfectly capture the imperialist mindset: expansion for expansion's sake. As I noted in Chapter 4, she sees this mindset re-emerging as one of the pillars of totalitarianism in the form of the pursuit of global conquest in both Nazi and Stalinist ideologies. As Patricia Owens succinctly writes, paraphrasing Arendt, 'The totalitarian pursuit of global domination was presaged in the geographically unlimited search for imperial wealth.'[81]

Cromer's and Lawrence's significance lie elsewhere. They exemplify imperial service, an inadvertent precursor to totalitarian bureaucracy.[82] Well educated and sincere, they originated from what Arendt takes to be a deeply English 'tradition of dragon-slayers', deriving from Englishmen's inability to 'outgrow their boyhood ideals'.[83] Neither of them were hyper-efficient bureaucrats armed with instrumental rationality, pure and simple. Rather, they represented the Kiplingesque moral infants that imperial Britain was prone to produce, eager to travel to the four corners of the earth to meet 'exotic' natives, slay dragons for them and teach them 'something of the greatness of the Western world'.[84] Put more colloquially, they were superbly naive and sincere white kids filled with a messiah complex. Or, to use a different image, they were self-sacrificial missionaries whose gospel was England imagined as 'the supreme guarantee for humanity'.[85] Scarcely an Anglophile in the first place, Arendt expresses her profound contempt for such Englishmen, who in her opinion 'preserved *and* infantilized Western moral standards'.[86]

There is, however, more than one way of slaying dragons, and Arendt attempts to tease out differing legacies left by the two dragon-slayers, Cromer and Lawrence. The former's patriotism and devotion, on the one hand, gave rise to a novel conception of 'bureaucracy as a principle of foreign domination'.[87]

Henceforth, anticipating the desk murderers of Nazi Germany in some respects, imperial bureaucrats acted as de facto rulers of foreign territories with increasing levels of arbitrariness, aloofness, a lack of public accountability and tacit reliance on racial hierarchy.[88] Although calling Cromer a 'British Eichmann' would be inaccurate and anachronistic, his style of governance and administration made the Nazi officer's 'banal' evil 'conceptually and experientially possible if not inevitable'.[89] Lawrence, on the other hand, set an example for functionaries' total identification with the government they serve, which is supposed to embody occult forces of history. It is important to note here that Arendt's Lawrence is very different from the popular image of the desert-crossing romantic hero, represented most memorably in David Lean's film *Lawrence of Arabia*. Rather, Arendt's Lawrence is a nobody desperately in need of a role to play, a prototype of the totalitarian 'mass man' ready to identify himself wholly with a movement greater than himself. With Lawrence's self-annihilating service died 'the real pride of Western man': the Kantian conception of man as an end in himself.[90]

In short, according to Arendt, the moral core of British imperialism is megalomaniacal expansionism; its motor is the alliance of capital and the mob; its administrators are moral infants; and its most enduring legacies are bureaucratic domination and the thoroughly servile mentality of the functionary. To this skeletal outline she adds further analyses, identifying a range of proto-totalitarian elements discernible in British history, from the rich development of race thinking by the country's numerous Darwinists, eugenicists and polygenists to the philosophy of Thomas Hobbes understood as the true philosophy of the Rhodesian wealth-accumulating animal.[91] The details of this discussion are immaterial to the purpose at hand, for the contrast between Arendt and Berlin regarding British imperialism is already clear. For the Oxford philosopher, Britain's lapse into imperialist frenzy was a fleeting phenomenon. It was an exceptional instance of a tolerant, decent and liberal society acting out of character due to the spell cast by a foreign magician. For Arendt, by contrast, Britain's imperialist phase was an outcome of the country's long-term social developments and deep-rooted cultural trends, and its share of responsibility for the eventual rise of totalitarianism is no less significant than those of other European countries, including Germany. While she does not see British imperialism as worse than other imperialisms, she emphatically denies British exceptionalism—the idea, dear to Berlin, that Britain has somehow been immune to inhumanity in both its totalitarian and imperialist incarnations.[92] Here as elsewhere, Arendt tells a pan-European story, discounting the significance of national differences. Berlin disagrees. Highlighting the distinctiveness of each nation's character, he rescues Englishness from the negative legacy of Britain's high imperialism.

Arendt's America

Isaiah Berlin was by no means the only one among his contemporaries to idealise England and Britain as a model liberal society. Other key figures of so-called 'Cold War liberalism', such as Karl Popper and Raymond Aron, shared with Berlin a distinctly liberal Anglophilia, although they did not entirely agree with each other as to why England should be seen as a model liberal society.[93] Hannah Arendt emphatically did not belong to this group of political thinkers. She was prejudiced against liberalism, dismissive of English culture and had little time for British philosophy with the exception of Thomas Hobbes.[94] This, however, does not mean that she did not idealise any actually existing society, polity or country. On the contrary, she idealised one country a good deal, and that was the United States of America, which provided her with an adoptive home. To overstate a little, what America meant to Arendt approximated to what England meant to Berlin. As Berlin repeatedly referred to England to illustrate his normative ideas such as individual liberty and tolerance, Arendt time and again referred to America to illustrate her normative ideas.

Like Berlin's England, Arendt's America is claimed to have been blessed with the 'singular good fortune' to realise ideals of universal human appeal.[95] A set of historical conditions, such as the alleged absence of mass poverty and the grassroots tradition of local self-government, assisted the American endeavour to found a new free republic. As I shall elaborate shortly, however, the gap Arendt saw between the ideal of America—what America at its best could be—and the reality—what America happened to be at a given moment in Arendt's lifetime—was larger than the comparable gap Berlin saw in England. Her America was a somewhat schizophrenic entity, a free republic *in recurring crisis*. It was constantly pulled by various deleterious 'social' forces (in Arendt's sense of the term) unleashed by modernity, such as individualism, materialism and consumerism, while continually correcting itself by re-enacting what she called the 'revolutionary spirit'. America, for her, was a quintessentially *modern* republic, with all the contradictions characterising modernity itself. Yet it was, in her words, 'the *only* country where a republic at least still has a chance'.[96]

In Arendt's terminology, the revolutionary 'spirit' contrasts with the 'act' of revolution. The latter ended when the Americans liberated themselves from British rule and established a new political order, but that which inspired the act of revolution in the first place—the underlying spirit—had no need to vanish with the end of the act. On the contrary, it had to survive if the newly founded body politic was to last as a free republic. What specifically constitutes the 'spirit'? Chief among its components are: *political freedom* conceptualised as the exercise of the distinctly human capacity to act in the public realm and begin something new; the habit of forming *voluntary associations* to address matters of public concern in a pragmatic and non-partisan fashion; the awareness of, and a propensity for, *public happiness* (as distinct from private welfare) arising out of the enjoyable experience of 'discussions, [. . .] deliberations, and the making of decisions' over public business;[97] the *ambition to excel* accompanied by the desire to see the excellence of others working towards a shared political goal; and trust in the value of the *plurality of opinions* and the resulting opposition to the rule of unanimous public opinion. The revolutionary spirit so conceived is not a uniquely American spirit. It surfaced not only in revolutionary America but also in various moments of political upheaval such as France in 1848 and 1870–71, Russia in 1905 and 1917, Germany in 1918–19 and Hungary in 1956, when self-governing councils emerged spontaneously to form what she called 'a people's utopia'.[98] But the American Revolution was of special importance because, unlike the rest, it was neither externally suppressed nor descended into chaos, a civil war or a reign of terror. On the contrary, it reified itself into a written constitution, which thereafter served as the foundation of the new republic.

As Andrew Arato and Jean Cohen observe, Arendt's analysis of the American legal and political structure does not do justice to the complexity of competing constitutional principles that were present both at the moment of constitution-making and in subsequent US history; nor does her narrative of the American Revolution do justice to the 'competing interpretive perspectives' that deserve serious consideration.[99] Nevertheless, her discussion is of *theoretical* interest for the same reason as Berlin's commentary on England is of theoretical interest: it dramatises particular aspects of the American experience to imaginatively reconstruct the free republic at its best. In fact, she uses her narrative of America—what America once was—to criticise the actually existing America of her time from within. Much of Arendt's antidote to the ills of contemporary America consists in the *reclaiming* of what she takes to be older traditions of the republic.[100]

So understood, three features of Arendt's commentary on US history and institutions are worth highlighting. First, she sees the written Constitution as codifying the revolutionary spirit. The Supreme Court is 'a kind of Constitutional Assembly in continuous session' because the judges, by interpreting or decoding the Constitution, reanimate the revolutionary spirit that gave birth to the constitutional order in the first place.[101] Second, somewhat anachronistically reading Tocqueville into the history of revolutionary America, Arendt downgrades the populist current and underlines the anti-majoritarian current in both the written Constitution and the intentions of the Framers. She repeatedly highlights the Framers' worries about 'elective despotism', and presents both the Senate and the First Amendment as different institutional means of protecting dissenting minorities against the tyranny of the majority.[102]

Arendt's America is a republic of competing opinions. Finally, and also in a Tocquevillian spirit, Arendt highlights the importance of a broader political culture supporting democratic institutions. Of particular interest is her appraisal of citizens' *attachment* to the Constitution; a written constitution is critically defective if it is not 'understood, approved and beloved' in the country it is supposed to govern.[103] In short, the American legal and political structure institutionalises the revolutionary spirit and provides a basic framework whereby citizens have the opportunity to be 'a participator in the government of affairs'.[104]

Observe the difference between Arendt and Berlin on the underlying conditions that support the maintenance of their respective ideal polities. On the one hand, Berlin underlines the significance of *informal* institutions such as customs and conventions for the wellbeing of a liberal polity. More specifically, liberal politics depends on a set of favourable sociological conditions, including the liberal temperament of the populace and the relative cultural homogeneity that binds people through a common language and shared memory.[105] According to Arendt, on the other hand, a free republic depends not so much on 'customs, manners, and traditions' as on the more formal, and specifically 'legal systems that regulate our life in the world and our daily affairs with each other'.[106] Of course, Arendt does not overestimate the power of the laws, as seen in her emphasis on the extra-legal culture of people's attachment to the Constitution. However, 'culture' in this context refers to a Tocquevillian *political* culture, which differs from the Herderian *national* culture integral to Berlin's liberal England. Contrary to Berlin, Arendt believes that a free republic does not need to be anchored in nationhood or relative cultural homogeneity. Rather, it ultimately relies on citizens' mutual promises, including *written* promises, in the form of declarations, covenants and so on, that they will actively and continuously participate in public affairs.[107]

Like Berlin's liberal England, Arendt's American republic is claimed to have a built-in immune system defying the rise of totalitarianism. Here, it is worth recalling that the two thinkers have differing views on *how* totalitarianism paradigmatically emerges. Berlin's fear chiefly concerns two scenarios: the violent seizure of power by a small group of Bolshevik-like fanatics, and the romantic outburst of nationalism in reaction to external humiliation. Neither scenario worries Arendt as much. Her primary concern is with the Weimar-style degeneration of liberal democracy into paralysis and then into a power vacuum, which will be filled by a popularly supported totalitarian movement like Nazism. On her understanding, liberal democracy is inherently unstable and tends to feed its totalitarian enemies in two important ways. First, liberal democratic *society* increasingly releases men and women from traditional familial and social ties, thereby creating lonely, atomised and isolated

individuals. Second, a totalitarian movement can appropriate liberal democratic *institutions* to recruit members and supporters from the lonely mass so
created.[108] Thus, Arendt's chief worry concerns not fanaticism so much as
populism enhanced by modern mass society. Its mirror image is found in Hitler and Goebbels's May 1932 *praise* of elections: 'Voting, voting! Out to the
people. We're all very happy.'[109]

Nevertheless, Arendt does not believe that liberal democracies must of necessity repeat Weimar's failure. Their demise is averted so long as the deleterious forces of mass society are *overridden*. Her 'revolutionary spirit', at least in
the American context, plays precisely this role. Turning men and women into
active citizens instead of lonely individuals, it keeps the 'potentiality and [the]
ever-present danger' of a totalitarian takeover in America as it is: an *unrealised*
potentiality.[110] This aspect of Arendt's thought may be called a 'republicanism
of fear', which subverts the Berlinian primacy of negative liberty over its positive counterpart.[111] On her view, liberal democracy and the protection of
negative liberty it provides can collapse à la Weimar, *unless* citizens show the
willingness to exercise the political freedom to act and care for the human-
made world they inhabit. Negative liberty is in this sense dependent on political freedom, as much as the latter is dependent on the former. Inter-war Germans enjoyed a considerable degree of negative liberty and yet exercised
little—too little—political freedom. Arendt insists that post-war Americans
ought to act differently.[112]

Arendt is not sure, however, whether post-war Americans *do* as a matter of
fact act differently from inter-war Germans. In a series of essays published in
the late 1960s and early 1970s,[113] she diagnoses her adopted country with various political ills, which may be grouped under the familiar headings of 'individual', 'civil society' and 'state'. On the first level, US citizens were increasingly
yielding to the inclinations to delegate political freedom to elected representa-
tives, to embrace (negative) freedom *from* politics and retreat to the comfort
of privacy and the household, to seek happiness in the economic sphere of
consumption and production and to appropriate political institutions to pursue private interests rather than shared political goals ('[c]orruption and perversion [. . .] from below').[114] On the second level, of civil society, voluntary
associations had morphed into self-sustaining pressure groups, while extensively bureaucratised political parties served their own special interests. Finally, on the third level, of the state, the political class consisting of career politicians and their aides were withdrawing into the federal political capital;
public relations methods were infiltrating the sphere of governance to 'sell'
policies and 'buy' votes; and purported specialists equipped with social science techniques were being recruited in large numbers by the government to
tackle political problems as though these were managerial problems. In short,

Arendt sees 'the social' increasingly eclipsing all spheres of political life in America. Nevertheless, she does not claim that the country's revolutionary spirit has been irreparably lost; it has merely gone missing, albeit for a long time. She concedes that the republic has been chronically ill, but she insists that it needs and deserves citizens' loving care.

Furthermore, America's attraction for Arendt also consists of the republic's ability to inspire men and women to live a fulfilling life, as she conceptualises this. Ambiguities and hesitations notwithstanding, as I discussed in Chapter 2, she tends to defend the political way of life as more rewarding than other ways. In her view, one can neither realise one's full potential nor experience the happiness of living with and among others *unless* one exercises the distinctly human capacity to speak and act in the public realm. A human life lived with no political participation is, in Arendt's words, 'literally dead to the world; it has ceased to be a human life because it is no longer lived among men.'[115] Of course, she never supports the idea of *forcing* men and women into a particular way of life, no matter how good that way might be. Nor is she so naive as to expect everyone to show the courage to appear in public. But she wants free republics to 'assure [the politically active] of their rightful place in the public realm', to allow and encourage them to flourish, and she believes that such reassurance has by and large been provided in America.[116] This is what makes America especially appealing to Arendt. While it is true that the public happiness of participating in public affairs has largely given way to the private enjoyment of consumption and production in twentieth-century America, the former has never been completely forgotten. In fact, in Arendt's view, it underwent a renaissance in her own lifetime, when the new generation of young Americans came to respond to a series of crises confronting their republic. This generation is often called after one particular year that came to symbolise their experience: 'sixty-eighters'.

Debating the Revolutionary Spirit: America 1968

Arendt's comments on 1968 America reveal simultaneously her radical democratic ideas and her idiosyncratic view of the country's history. Moreover, 1968 serves as a fascinating point of comparison between Arendt and Berlin, because their responses to this year of turbulence could scarcely be more different. As it happens, their paths almost crossed physically in New York City in 1968. Arendt, as is well known, lived on the Upper West Side and paid close attention to the unrest in the city. Less familiar is the fact that Berlin then held a part-time visiting professorship at the City University of New York and spent nearly one year there in total between 1966 and 1971. But the parallel between the two thinkers ran further. Berlin was offered an honorary doctorate by

Columbia University and was scheduled to attend Commencement (the graduation ceremony) on 4 June 1968. In the meantime, Columbia students' protests escalated during the spring semester, and the university authorities decided to bring the police onto campus on 30 April, resulting in 712 arrests and 148 reported injuries.[117] Arendt was so curious about the rebellious youth that she visited the campus to see the upheaval for herself. Berlin paid no less attention from afar, wondering if the Commencement ceremony would take place as had been planned.

What were the two thinkers' responses? Consider Berlin first. In the late 1960s, he spoke, unsurprisingly, of the contrast between exhilarating and yet frightening New York/America and peaceful if somewhat dull Oxford/England.[118] He noted a worry in passing in May 1968: 'New York—the student riots—the slowly mounting mass of black anger—is terrifying.'[119] Nevertheless, he was not terrified enough to cancel his plan to attend the Columbia Commencement. He kept his head by portraying the situation in his characteristically humorous tone. A few days before Commencement, he wrote to his friend McGeorge Bundy, former security advisor to both Presidents Kennedy and Johnson,

> I propose to come [to Columbia] armed with a water-pistol, and if any militant student approaches me I shall rise up against him and say that the dons have turned, the worms fight back, and douse him. La Grande Peur, which is supposed to have seized everybody in 1791, or whenever it was, seems to be nothing compared to the terror of all professors before the slightest sign of student dissatisfaction. Why cannot the professors build barricades of their own?[120]

Berlin's tone is playful, but it is clear to which side he considered himself to belong: the university authorities. He regarded the hundreds of sixty-eighters filling the streets of New York—whom he called 'Christs'—with a mixture of curiosity, bewilderment, alarm and contempt. He regarded them as politically and intellectually worthless: they were 'all wild, all bearded, all very mad'.[121] In a less playful letter, Berlin denounced them as barbaric, crude, nihilistic, confused and 'complacently ignorant'.[122] This verdict was not solely due to his own taste for high culture. The sixty-eighters, even by their own account, were highly critical of the traditional liberal values and sensibilities Berlin cherished. To focus on the American case in particular, they wanted their fellow citizens, especially the older generation, to be less content with their government and to care more about the injustices it committed both at home and abroad. To be apolitical, in their view, was to endorse the status quo, amounting to complicity in the oppression of the Black population and the misadventure in Vietnam, among other things. Berlin disagreed. He considered the sixty-eighters' claims to be too naive, arguing that even Vietnam could not be understood in such unequivocal terms.[123] Nor was he impressed by their demand for greater democratic engagement, which was in his view moralistically curbing the sphere of privacy that men and women were entitled to enjoy. He was aware of his critics' perception of him as 'a kind of leader of a suicide squad of blind liberal reactionaries' and yet stood by his principles.[124] 'I long for some bourgeois stability,' he wrote, 'some protection against the turning of all private, inner, disinterested activity into screams and shouts and public issues.'[125] The sixty-eighters' primary vice, in Berlin's view, was their tendency to politicise everything—to be a political animal. A New York City filled with such animals was antithetical to Berlin's stable, orderly and tolerant liberal England. It reminded him of 'Rome in the very last years'.[126]

Arendt's response to the upheaval could scarcely have been more different. She noted the volatility of 'the country and the universities in particular' as early as November 1967, but from the outset she expressed clear sympathy for the rebellious youth.[127] She shared with them the basic sense that America was in moral as well as social and political crisis. Like them, she saw apathy and hypocrisy in the 'bourgeois stability' for which liberals like Berlin longed. Five months before the Columbia incident, she observed optimistically that as long as the police were kept off campus, 'things don't get out of hand, and the direction student opinion takes hardly ever drifts toward extremes'.[128] She remained firmly on the student side after witnessing the Columbia incident, criticising the university authorities as 'particularly dreadful'.[129] In her eyes, rebellious youth were not 'wild, bearded and mad Christs' or roaming ignorant barbarians. They were courageous citizens and carriers of the revolutionary spirit, fuelled by a sense of justice and undeterred by police brutality. Of course, she did not uncritically admire the sixty-eighters. She made differing judgements on their diverse practices, depending on their individual merits. Nor was she impressed by what she called the sixty-eighters' 'curious timidity in theoretical matters'.[130] In fact, she criticised their inclination to rely on clichéd slogans, often failing to 'recogniz[e] realities as such'.[131] Nevertheless, Arendt's overall view of the sixty-eighters was strikingly optimistic. The distinctive feature of this generation, she said, was 'its determination to act, its joy in action, the assurance of being able to change things by one's own efforts'.[132] The upheavals in New York, Chicago, Berkeley and elsewhere of her time were reminiscent of other moments of 'people's utopia'.[133] She wrote to Karl Jaspers,

> It seems to me that children in the next century will learn about the year 1968 the way we learned about the year 1848. [. . .] Things are in an extremely dangerous state here [in the United States], too; but I sometimes

think this is the only country where a republic at least still has a chance. And besides that, one has the feeling that one is among friends.[134]

The final sentence deserves special attention, because it indicates a sense of belonging, which is somewhat surprising, considering Arendt's life story. She spent her entire formative years in Germany and arrived in the United States in 1941 as a refugee and a thirty-six-year-old woman. She did not and could not become as socially and culturally American as Berlin, who migrated to England as an eleven-year-old boy, became socially and culturally English. Five years after her arrival in New York, Arendt composed in her native language arguably the saddest poem she ever wrote: 'Wohl dem, der keine Heimat hat; er sieht sie noch im Traum' (Happy is he who has no home; he still sees it in his dreams).[135] True, her legal homelessness ended on 10 December 1951, when she was granted the US citizenship that gave her a 'right to have rights', that is, 'the right of every human being to membership in a political community'.[136] But she never rid herself of a sense of loss, seeing herself as a 'German Jew driven from [her] homeland by the Nazis'.[137] Nevertheless, eventually, she came in a way to feel at home in America. That was not only because she cultivated a circle of close friends in her adopted country, but also because she found herself among fellow citizens who shared with her the willingness to act and work to preserve and improve the free republic that they had together inherited. Her true homeland may have remained the German language, but her political home was now America.[138] It is hard to avoid psychoanalytic imagery here: she found in the 1960s American republic a cure for the trauma that the Weimar Republic had inflicted on her in the 1930s.[139] It is telling that the term Arendt often uses to describe the sense one has when experiencing political freedom is 'public happiness'. Happy she did become, then, finding a home in America; she saw it before her eyes.

Freedom and/or Nationalism: Hungary 1956

When Hannah Arendt told Karl Jaspers in June 1968 that the United States was likely to be 'the only country where a republic at least still has a chance', she may well have had in mind another country where a chance of establishing a free republic had been brutally crushed a little over a decade earlier: Hungary.[140] For Arendt, the Hungarian Revolution of 1956 was simultaneously a testimony to human freedom and a missed opportunity: a nascent island of freedom destroyed by the flood of totalitarian violence. The significance of the event lay elsewhere to Isaiah Berlin's eye. For him, the Hungarian Revolution was first and foremost a nationalist movement, although it was also a struggle for freedom. The two thinkers' starkly contrasting perspectives on Hungary 1956 merit close examination.

A Stillborn Revolution

First, a brief overview of the Hungarian Revolution is in order. On the morning of 23 October 1956, two days after the election of Władysław Gomułka as first secretary of the Polish United Workers' Party, a group of students marched to the statue of Józef Bem in Budapest. The location of the gathering was well chosen. A Polish general who had led the Hungarian War of Independence in 1848–49, Bem symbolised the sense of solidarity that the Hungarian students felt for Poland's recent effort to assert autonomy and (limited) freedom from Moscow. Unidentified student orators read out the words of Sándor Petőfi, a Hungarian patriotic poet who had served as Bem's aide-de-camp:

> Our battalions have combined two nations,
> and what nations! Polish and Magyar!
> Is there any destiny that is stronger
> than these two when they are united?[141]

This peaceful gathering was followed by spontaneous demonstrations elsewhere in the city. The communist authorities attempted to calm the situation but their effort backfired. An intimidating speech by Ernő Gerő, the first secretary of the Hungarian Workers' Party, at 8 p.m. infuriated the protesters; and violence broke out when members of the much detested secret police, the Államvédelmi Hatóság, or AVH, opened fire to disperse the crowd gathering in front of a local radio station. Fighting soon spread all across the city, joined by members of the regular police and military as well as by students, workers and ordinary citizens. Meanwhile, protesters managed to pull down the imposing statue of Stalin in Heroes' Square. What began as a series of peaceful demonstrations quickly developed into a nationwide uprising.

This took everyone in the West, including the US intelligence community, by surprise.[142] The United States and its allies were utterly unprepared to provide any support for the Hungarians, except to continue their tough talk (and no action) on CIA-sponsored Radio Free Europe. Moscow, by contrast, had been better informed, better prepared, and acted swiftly. On 23 October, the Soviet forces that had been stationed in Hungary received mobilisation orders, joined by additional military divisions dispatched from Romania and the Carpathian Military Zone in Ukraine.[143] In spite of their impressive size, however, the Soviet forces were ill suited for the task at hand: a policing mission rather than regular warfare. They were defeated by poorly equipped Hungarian citizens turned guerrilla fighters, who were joined by Hungarian soldiers who had defected from the army, to the astonishment of the whole world. At the same time, local committees and councils spontaneously emerged across the country and legitimised themselves as de facto decision-making and administrative organs, mitigating the chaos and confusion that resulted from the loss of state authority.

The revolution seemed victorious by 29 October. Reformist Imre Nagy replaced Stalinist Gerő as prime minister, a ceasefire between the Hungarian and Russian forces was agreed, and a withdrawal of the Russian troops announced. The Nagy government began implementing, if slowly and rather reluctantly, some of the popular demands succinctly articulated as the 'Sixteen Points' that had effectively become 'the manifesto for the revolution'.[144] A mixture of euphoria, disbelief and hope swept across the country. The victory, however, proved to be short-lived. Nikita Khrushchev, who on the morning of 30 October had decided to let Hungary seek limited national autonomy following the Polish example, made a U-turn overnight.[145] Massive Soviet forces encircled Hungary over the next three days, while Soviet diplomats gave false reassurances to Nagy and his ministers to keep Hungary unprepared for the impending invasion. This time the Soviet operation was no longer a policing matter. The Soviet forces invaded Budapest early in the morning of 4 November and they effectively prevailed in three days—in time for the anniversary of the Russian Revolution on 7 November. Imre Nagy fled, was arrested and, in June 1958, executed. Meanwhile, under the new Moscow-sponsored premier János Kádár, more than a hundred thousand people were arrested and thirty-five thousand tried for 'counter-revolutionary acts'; nearly twenty-six thousand among them were sentenced to prison, and six hundred executed.[146] Some two hundred thousand people, or approximately two per cent of the country's total population, crossed the border to escape arrest and/or seek life elsewhere, in the West.[147]

What might have saved the stillborn revolution, or at least some of its achievements, was a US-led intervention. Many Hungarian rebels thought this was forthcoming, not least because Radio Free Europe gave the impression that the Americans were willing and ready to help, should there be a popular uprising against Soviet domination. But propaganda was one thing; reality, quite another. First of all, President Eisenhower was not willing to risk a third world war to save a country of less than ten million people. Furthermore, facing a presidential election on 6 November, he had little interest in escalating a Central European crisis, although he needed to sound tough enough to rebut criticisms by anti-communist hawks in his own party. Besides, quite unable to appreciate that some communists were better than others, the US government could not bring themselves to support Imre Nagy, despite his popularity in Hungary. Finally, the United States and its allies were entering a deep crisis as Britain and France made the disastrous decision to collude with Israel in the invasion of Egypt to seize the Suez Canal and protect their economic and geopolitical interests. Whether the outcome of the Hungarian Revolution might have been different if the United States, Britain and France had acted differently has been one of the greatest 'what if's' of the twentieth century.

Freedom and the Council System: Arendt on the Hungarian Revolution

Hannah Arendt followed the news from Hungary with keen interest. Her first surviving comments on the subject, made as early as 24 October 1956, suggest that she, like everyone else, did not quite foresee that the unfolding crisis would evolve into a world historic event. What she focused on at that time was the unmasking effect of the revolt. 'I just read that the Russian army has intervened in Hungary,' she wrote to her husband Heinrich Blücher. 'That's marvellous! Finally, finally they have to show their hands.'[148] In other words, Arendt was glad to see that the event in Hungary had exposed the fact that the so-called Soviet 'influence' over Central and Eastern Europe was nothing other than totalitarian domination. A couple of months later, when the revolution was aborted and 'order' restored on Moscow's terms, Arendt still spoke excitedly about Hungary, describing it as 'the best thing that has happened for a long time'.[149] This continuing sense of excitement was partly due to her view that the uprising 'still isn't over'—meaning, presumably, that the restored 'order' might not be rock-solid and could be challenged by subsequent developments in the country. Although Arendt was overly optimistic on this score, her excitement never waned, for she came to interpret the Hungarian Revolution as a monumental expression of freedom in her distinctly political sense of the term. She told Karl Jaspers that 'regardless of how it ends, it is a clear victory for freedom'. More specifically, she saw in Hungary 'the spontaneous appearance of a new governmental form *in nuce*, the council system'.[150]

Arendt elaborated this 'freedom and council' reading of the Hungarian Revolution in a forty-page essay entitled 'Totalitarian Imperialism: Reflections on the Hungarian Revolution', published in February 1958.[151] The essay is not so much a piece of political analysis as a eulogy honouring the Hungarian people's 'most glorious hour' that had come to an end.[152] It begins with a pronouncement that clearly expresses Arendt's anti-consequentialist conception of the political: the Hungarian Revolution 'was a true event whose stature will not depend upon victory or defeat; its greatness is secure in the tragedy it enacted.'[153] Read today, the essay is of interest for what it does *not* discuss as well as for what it does. Approximately half of the essay is devoted to analysing recent developments in the communist world in general and Soviet Russia in particular, as the author ponders the long-term impact of Stalin's death and the ensuing de-Stalinisation that gave rise to the Hungarian Revolution. When it comes to the uprising itself, Arendt exclusively focuses on the street level, presenting the event as an instance of 'Rosa Luxemburg's "spontaneous revolution"': 'a sudden uprising of an oppressed people *for the sake of freedom and hardly anything else*.'[154] In so doing, Arendt bypasses diplomacy and high politics altogether, in conformity with her view that the Hungarian Revolution was a rare instance of people's acting-in-concert *from below*. Consequently, her essay has nothing to say on Nagy's flawed but popularly supported leadership, or on the US's inability to provide substantive support for the rebels, or on the Suez Crisis, without which the Hungarian events might have taken a different course.

More tellingly, Arendt ignores or marginalises some of the important factors that did not fit into her 'freedom and council' reading of the revolution. Yet these were certainly at work on the streets, and Arendt was aware of them. One such factor was violence. While it is true that the revolution began as a peaceful protest and the rebels initially resorted to force as a means of self-defence, some of them inflicted extreme violence on captured AVH officers. This might be humanly understandable, given many Hungarians' justly felt anger at the secret police. After all, they were executing executioners. Nevertheless, the brutality of the violence against some of the captives was indisputable. Charles Gati, then a young journalist in Hungary, who eventually became a distinguished political scientist, can still 'recall how th[e] furious and frenzied crowd' not only lynched some AVH members but also 'took pleasure at the mutilation of dead bodies'.[155] Another journalist on the ground, Peter Fryer, gave some more details about this macabre 'pleasure' in his 1956 book:

> score upon score of secret police swung head downwards from the Budapest trees and lamp-posts, and the crowds spat upon them and some, crazed and brutalised by years of suffering and hatred, stubbed out cigarette butts in the dead flesh.[156]

We do not know how many AVH officers were lynched. The communist government that suppressed the uprising claimed in 1957 that 289 such deaths had been identified; a recent historical study dismisses this as mere 'propaganda' and proposes 'somewhere between 90 and 100' as the 'best estimate'.[157] Regardless of the exact number, photographs of dead AVH officers' bodies in various shapes and forms were shown widely in the international media, creating bad public relations for the Hungarian cause.[158] More importantly, news about the lynching of AVH officers, especially the killing of twenty-three of them at Republic Square on 30 October, 'stoked in Khrushchev's mind fears of [. . .] a "White Terror", after the violence carried out against Russian rebels by the White Army of imperial Russia during the civil war of 1917–23'.[159] In this way, the lynching inadvertently contributed to Moscow's fateful decision on 31 October to use military force to crush the revolution. While Arendt could not know Khrushchev's psyche, she certainly had access to some of the shocking photographs that frightened the Soviet leader. Given this, it may be safely assumed that Arendt made a deliberate choice in understating the significance of street violence when she wrote the following words in her 1958 essay: 'There were no crimes against life [. . .], for the few instances of public hanging of AVH officers were conducted with remarkable restraint and discrimination.'[160]

Similarly marginalised in Arendt's telling of the revolution is ordinary Hungarians' keen concern with the country's poor economic conditions. The centrality of this concern is hardly surprising. Hungary was on the brink of bankruptcy during the late 1940s, when the country, having fought a devastating war on the Axis side, was coerced into paying $300 million reparations (over six years) as part of the post-war settlement.[161] Then came the first five-year plan, launched in 1951. As manpower was forcibly transferred from agriculture to industry on a massive scale in a short span of time, the lives of 'several hundred thousand villagers' were catastrophically disrupted, while the macroeconomic outcome of the planned economy proved to be extremely volatile.[162] Such 'megalomaniac heavy industry projects' were subsequently moderated and the economy improved during Imre Nagy's first premiership. However, he was ousted in March 1955 for political reasons, leaving the country to face further economic uncertainties.[163] Small wonder, then, that the rebels' 'Sixteen Points' included demands that would belong, in Arendt's terminology, to the 'social' sphere as well as the 'political'. On the one hand, as Arendt highlights, the 'Sixteen Points' included distinctly political demands for free and fair elections, the right to fair trial, free speech, freedom of expression and a free press, and 'the immediate withdrawal of all Soviet troops from Hungary'.[164] On the other hand, although Arendt does not mention this, the list also included a series of economic demands, such as reform of the dysfunctional planned economy, a minimum living wage for workers, the rational use of agricultural produce and equal treatment between individual farmers and cooperatives.[165] In other words, pace Arendt, the goals of the revolution were not one but many, and they included the alleviation of poverty and economic hardships as well as 'freedom and hardly anything else'. To invoke Arendt's own theoretical framework, the Hungarian Revolution was more 'French' and less 'American' than she would have us believe.[166] Hungarians in 1956 wanted, in addition to freedom, a minimally functional economy undisturbed by disastrous central planning.

Arendt's discussion of the councils in revolutionary Hungary invites similar objections, albeit less unequivocally. Supposedly basing this on the UN Special Committee's 'Report on the Problem of Hungary',[167] Arendt identifies two types of council that emerged spontaneously from below: Revolutionary Councils fulfilling 'mainly political functions', and Workers' Councils handling 'economic life'. While she acknowledges that 'the dividing line between them was [not] unblurred', she separates the two rather neatly and directs her attention solely to 'the Revolutionary Councils and the political aspect'.[168] She then articulates, in a preliminary manner, her signature genealogy of the council system, connecting Hungary 1956 to its various forerunners across time and space.[169] On this account, there is nothing specifically Hungarian about the councils that emerged during the 1956 Revolution. On the contrary, what the Hungarian rebels created was 'the *same* organization which for more than a hundred years now has emerged whenever the people have been permitted [. . .] to follow their own political devices without a government (or a party program) imposed from above'.[170] In short, Arendt enthused over the Hungarian Revolution because this, and especially the Revolutionary Councils, purportedly brought forth the revolutionary spirit and established, if momentarily, 'islands of freedom' amid the sea of totalitarian and semi-totalitarian violence, rule and control.

Is this true? Does historical evidence support Arendt's claims? The answer seems mixed. For one thing, the distinction Arendt draws between the Workers' and Revolutionary Councils is a little too neat. Precisely because numerous councils and committees emerged spontaneously without central coordination, they varied quite widely from one another, giving themselves diverse names. Some of them were willing to work closely with Nagy's government; others, such as the fabled National Revolutionary Council led by József Dudás, presented themselves as an alternative to it.[171] To classify these diverse groups into *either* Workers' *or* Revolutionary councils is to simplify a good deal, and reflects more Arendt's pristine theory than the messy reality of the Hungarian Revolution. In fact, many of the actually existing councils in Hungary played multiple roles, setting themselves the tasks of revolutionary insurrection, defence and policing and the production and distribution of goods and resources, as well as political representation, political decision-making and the like. Which of these aspects was most central has been a matter of debate. It is worth noting in this context that the Hungarian philosopher Agnes Heller challenges Arendt's emphasis on the political. According to Heller, the Hungarian councils had their own distinct tradition that differed from their French and Russian counterparts. They had been 'basically an organization of self-management' and took political roles only circumstantially due to the breakdown of political authority.[172] Heller thus highlights a local tradition connecting the Hungarian councils of 1956 to their predecessors in the country's own past, instead of drawing international comparisons with various councils across Europe.[173] While there is no scholarly consensus as to which theorist's view comes closer to the empirical reality, it may be noted that Arendt's distinctly political reading of the Hungarian councils remains contested.[174]

Similarly, Arendt overlooks the nationalist dimension of the Hungarian Revolution. To look at the 'Sixteen Points' again, the list included a demand to restore national symbols instead of 'alien' (read: Russian) ones; a demand to recognise traditional national holidays; and a demand to replace the statue of Stalin with 'a monument commemorating the heroes and martyrs of the 1848–49 war of independence'.[175] In the words of the aforementioned UN Report, some of the rebels' demands were about 'national pride'.[176] Arendt completely ignores this aspect, despite her view that the UN Report is 'truly admirable'.[177] One possible explanation for this omission is that her analysis of Hungary has been coloured by her view of Zionism. As I described in Chapter 2, the tragic fate of Zionism, as she sees it, was that an honourable fight for freedom and dignity had degenerated into an ethno-nationalist struggle for sovereignty and self-determination within the framework of the nation-state system. If so, the last thing that Arendt wanted to see in Hungary may have been a replay of this 'bad dialectic of Jewish nationalism'.[178] Whether something like this crossed her mind or not, Arendt certainly downplays the role of nationalism in the Hungarian Revolution. Reading her essay, one does not learn that Petőfi's patriotic words had been read out, and the flags and ribbons of the Hungarian tricolour—red, white and green—were displayed everywhere in the country during the revolution. Nor does one learn that the chant often heard during the uprising struck a nationalist note: 'Russians go home!'[179] Nor, finally, does one learn that the rebel-controlled radio stations kept playing, as a desperate act of defiance, the Hungarian national anthem, when Budapest was seized by foreign invaders on 4 November. An un-Arendtian question suggests itself: is it not possible that, in the Hungarian capital in the autumn of 1956, a *national* anthem came to incarnate the *revolutionary* spirit? *Must* nationalism and political freedom conflict with one another?

Freedom and Nationalism: Berlin on the Hungarian Revolution

The Hungarian Revolution did not inspire Isaiah Berlin's imagination as it did Hannah Arendt's. Of course, it is hardly surprising that he did not publish an essay unequivocally supporting the Hungarian cause, for that would have endangered his relatives behind the Iron Curtain. He was aware that his 1945–46 visit to Soviet Russia had cost his relatives in the country dearly, and he was not going to repeat the mistake.[180] Paradoxically, one reason why Arendt could publish her influential essay on Hungary was that she, unlike Berlin, had been safely *disconnected* from the communist bloc. That said, what is striking is that Berlin had little to say on the Hungarian Revolution even in his private papers, not only from the late 1950s but also long after the event, when he could have said anything he liked without fearing the unintended consequences of his words. Despite his reputation as a Cold Warrior, Berlin had remarkably little to say on this major episode in Cold War history.

Why this silence? Part of the explanation is that Berlin was more concerned with Suez than with Hungary. After all, the former, unlike the latter, involved two countries that were central to Berlin's sense of who he was: Britain and Israel. He was keenly aware that both countries were under attack from all quarters during the Suez Crisis, and he rationalised their act of aggression (with France) against Egypt a good deal to excuse it. On 1 November, he wrote to none other than Clarissa Eden, the wife of the increasingly unpopular prime minister Anthony Eden, to say, 'I should like to offer the Prime Minister all my admiration and sympathy. His action seems to me very brave very patriotic and—I shd have thought—absolutely just.'[181] Of course, Berlin said this partly out of courtesy, though also because he had been unaware of the extent of Eden's duplicity in justifying a war on Egypt. Yet even as he came to learn more about the collusion between Britain, France and Israel, he was unwilling to condemn them and continued to sit on the fence, albeit with increasing discomfort. This annoyed many of his Oxford friends and colleagues, who felt that the Suez fiasco was 'literally the worst day of their lives' and indeed 'worse than Munich'.[182] One such friend, the eminent legal philosopher H.L.A. Hart, snapped when he heard about the announcement of the award of a knighthood to Berlin in 1957. 'What was it said to be for?', Hart wrote to his wife. 'Not attacking govt. during Suez?'[183] Hungary receded from view in Berlin's life amid the stormy debate over Suez in his social circle.

There is, however, another reason why Berlin did not enthuse over Hungary as Arendt did. That is, he came to see early on that the Hungarians were engaged in an unwinnable battle, that there was little the outside world could do to alter the outcome, and that those in Britain in particular could do almost nothing to influence the Central European event. This, needless to say, does not mean that Berlin did not morally support the Hungarian cause. He certainly did. Nevertheless, he was too much of a political realist to be optimistic about the Hungarian future. Moreover, he was not anti-consequentialist enough to echo Arendt's view that the greatness of the Hungarian Revolution would 'not depend upon victory or defeat'.[184] Contrary to this Arendtian sentiment, Berlin wanted the Hungarians to *win*, but he knew that they could not. He wrote to Arthur Schlesinger Jr. in November 1956 that

> even if we [i.e., the British] have been morally pure [. . .] our violent protests about Hungary would have made no difference. That the whole nineteenth century is filled with noble protests about martyred Poland or martyred Hungary or martyred Italy, and that the comfort from these

things to the martyrs themselves was less than nothing. There is a rumour that the United States would, but for Suez, have sent arms or men to Hungary. Unless they are prepared for genuine war against the Soviet Union, this would certainly not have helped. Clearly the Russians would have sent enough to crush the Hungarians whatever the resistance.[185]

Berlin saw that Hungary was in a genuinely tragic situation. The Hungarians' demands were just and yet they did not have the power to have them satisfied. The Soviet Union would not be persuaded to accept the just demands, and they would (and did) use force to suppress the dissent if (and when) it became excessive from Moscow's perspective. The only thing that could alter this fundamental power imbalance was international intervention, either by the United Nations or by the United States. Yet, here again, neither party could do much to assist the Hungarians. The United Nations was powerless because of the Soviet veto, the division (exacerbated by Suez) within the Security Council and the institution's general inability to mitigate international conflicts. The United States was no less powerless, because its leaders knew that their intervention would risk a third world war. Of course, they could in principle take this risk, following the maxim *Fiat justitia, ruat caelum*. But this would amount to a reckless gamble, and President Eisenhower was too sensible to take it. Berlin seems to have understood all this, and accepted reality as it was. He was exempt from an illusion that, according to Charles Gati, was widespread while the Hungarian event was unfolding. 'Too many Hungarians and Americans believed', Gati writes, 'that they would prevail because they were right.'[186] Berlin, the philosopher of value pluralism, did not believe this. He knew that might and right were different, and that the Hungarians could not prevail this time, no matter how right they were. Hence his lack of enthusiasm for the Hungarian Revolution.

This is not to say, however, that Berlin did nothing to alleviate the Hungarian tragedy. Although he knew he could do little, he did what he could, signing petitions and letters both during and after the stillborn revolution. Most notably, he signed with other scholars in Britain two statements, sent to Budapest in March 1961 and February 1962, respectively, to request the release of the Hungarian historian István Bibó, who had been given a life sentence in August 1958.[187] It is possible that the requests made some difference, for Bibó was indeed released under an amnesty on 27 March 1963.[188] Berlin was in this way willing to support small-scale interventions aimed at realistic goals. But he remained highly sceptical when it came to more ambitious plans. For example, when he heard that two undergraduates at Oxford, David Pryce-Jones and Jacob Rothschild, were thinking of travelling to Hungary as volunteers, he made an effort to dissuade them. He said,

I lectured them both on the fact that one must not take oneself so seriously, that undergraduates are undergraduates, that one must not ask oneself at every turn whether one is fulfilling one's purposes here or should be some- where else, and one must just carry on with whatever one is doing without feeling that the safety and happiness of the world depends upon one's posi- tion, or that one has some special calling or mission.[189]

This is a curious way of dissuading the two Oxford students, who, like other undergraduates elsewhere in Britain, felt special connections to Hungary pre- cisely because they were undergraduates.[190] They knew that the Revolution had been initiated by students in Budapest, joined by child volunteers still in secondary school.[191] 'In many parts of Budapest', as Victor Sebestyen writes, 'the revolution was a schoolkids' war.'[192] If so, why should British students be disqualified just because they were undergraduates? No matter what Berlin's answer may have been, he considered it silly that British students should feel that they could do something when even Eisenhower could do next to noth- ing. His profound disdain for the engagé students of 1968 had in this way been anticipated by his mild contempt for their predecessors in 1956.

One further aspect of Berlin's view of the Hungarian Revolution deserves consideration. Although this revolution does not appear prominently in his academic work, it does appear sporadically, and whenever it does it is pre- sented as a *nationalist* event of historic importance.[193] Here, it is worth reiterat- ing that Berlin thinks nationalism may take benign and humane forms as well as chauvinistic and aggressive ones; and it can be and often is a force for good, giving expression to the fundamental human need to belong. He never tires of emphasising how major political philosophers in the past dismissed nation- alism as irrational and epiphenomenal, only to be refuted by the reality of its endurance. Berlin's favourite target of criticism in this context is Karl Marx, whom he regards as an exemplary fool who grossly underestimated the power of nationalism. Of course, Berlin's reading of Marx is controversial, and he has been challenged by scholars who think that Marx's view of nationalism was more nuanced.[194] But Berlin was never persuaded by his critics, insisting that Marx and his orthodox followers had been blind to 'facts of history'.[195] Given this interpretation, it is hardly surprising that Berlin should have taken the most important lesson from Hungary 1956 to be the inhumanity of orthodox Marxism. In dismissing national consciousness altogether as irrational, com- munists from Marx and Engels to Lenin, Stalin and Khrushchev have failed to recognise the authenticity of the human need to belong. In Berlin's view, ex- pressed as early as 1957, 'recent events in Hungary, in Poland and elsewhere' provided 'evidence that the orthodox Marxist interpretation of national feeling and its lack of influence upon the working classes of a nation conspicuously no longer capitalist, contains fallacies that have proved tragic enough to many of those involved in them.'[196] Contrary to Arendt, Berlin does not think that the aspiration for national self-determination was secondary to the desire for freedom in revolutionary Hungary. In fact, it is the former that Berlin repeatedly highlights as the most significant legacy of the Hungarian Revolution. For him, this revolution first and foremost signified a nationalist movement.

It is worth highlighting here that Berlin repeatedly, if in passing, draws an analogy between Hungarian nationalism and Zionism.[197] The point of this analogy is not to use Zionism to illustrate the inherent contradictions of the nation-state system, as Arendt did. Rather, it is to highlight the legitimacy of both nations' demands: the Hungarians and the Jews are both morally entitled to demand self-determination, provided that they do not let nationalism slide into chauvinism, xenophobia and the like. Simply put, nationalism and freedom are incompatible for Arendt; they can be complementary for Berlin. In her view, crises and disasters of the early twentieth century had conclusively demonstrated that the principle of national self-determination would always be incompatible with the demographic complexity of Europe, Israel/Palestine and elsewhere, and what remained of the nation-state system after 1945 would be living on borrowed time. In Berlin's view, by contrast, nationalism should be given 'channels of productive self-expression', because the need to belong is a very basic human one, and national belonging has historically proved to be the only group allegiance that is rich enough to give its members 'indissoluble and impalpable ties of common language, historical memory, habit, tradition and feeling' to satisfy that need.[198] Separated from those 'ties', one cannot feel at home in the community to which one nominally belongs. Unfortunately, no comments by Berlin survive on the slogan repeatedly uttered in Hungary 1956: 'Russians go home!' It is, however, not too fanciful to imagine that this reminded him of an older slogan repeatedly heard in Palestine under the British mandate: 'British, go home!'[199] Nationalism has no place in Arendt's island of freedom. By contrast, if expressed in a benign and humane form, it has a very important role to play in that island's Berlinian counterpart.

Conclusion

'Hannah Arendt Blücher Born Hanover Germany Oct. 14, 1906 Died N.Y., N.Y. Dec. 4, 1975'. So says the epitaph on the tombstone of one of our protagonists, buried at the Bard College Cemetery in Annandale-on-Hudson. Seeing the long distance she travelled from the beginning to the end of her life, one might wonder if the sociologist Richard Sennett is right in saying that Arendt in America 'was somebody who was still living in Weimar Germany'. No matter how many years she spent in the United States, according to Sennett, she was in permanent exile; and no matter how famous she became, she never became a part of the 'American establishment'.[200] There is undoubtedly something to be said for this view. Yet, if one spends a little time inspecting Arendt's final resting place, strolling around and listening to various stories about her, one may begin to think that it might be appropriate that she should be buried there, after all. Right next to her tombstone is that of her husband Heinrich Blücher, who stayed with her for three decades. Hannah Arendt used to make an annual visit there, on the anniversary of her husband's death, to sit quietly and 'make the absent present' in her mind.[201] The small cemetery itself is reminiscent of vibrant New York intellectual life, as graves of deceased professors, writers and intellectuals are crammed into a limited space in a rather disorderly manner. Bard students often make a visit to the famed Professor Arendt's grave, sometimes 'praying for good grades on their *Eichmann in Jerusalem* papers'.[202] Her admirers also make a pilgrimage from afar, as evidenced by a number of pebbles, coins and hand-written notes left around the tombstone. When I visited in October 2014, one pebble that somebody had left showed an inscription of one of Arendt's key concepts, *amor mundi*. As she once told Karl Jaspers, it was in the United States that she came to understand this concept as a lived experience; that she came 'to truly love the world'.[203] Although the country typically failed to live up to her standards, America sometimes realised its potential, impressing her with 'the idea of the Republic' that it embodied with all its human imperfection.[204]

Isaiah Berlin is buried on the other side of the Atlantic, at the Wolvercote Cemetery in North Oxford. He too travelled from afar, from central Riga via Petrograd and London to the ancient university city. But in his case, unlike in Arendt's, it is hard to imagine where else he might have been buried. Many of the places that were central to his life are within short driving distance of the Wolvercote Cemetery. They include Corpus Christi College, where he began his life in Oxford in 1928; All Souls College, where he became the thinker that he was; his 'palatial Georgian residence in Headington', where he spent forty-one years of his life, until his death in 1997; and Wolfson College, where his legacy is firmly secured and institutionalised.[205] Portraits of Berlin hang in several Oxford colleges, and events celebrating his life and work are regularly held in the city, attended by his former students, friends, admirers and mostly sympathetic critics. In contrast to the Bard College Cemetery, Wolvercote is neatly divided into different sections, each representing a religion, a nationality, and/or a ritual style. Isaiah Berlin is buried in the Jewish section, next to his wife Aline, who passed away in 2014, at the age of ninety-nine. While different sections of the cemetery are clearly demarcated, they are not separated by walls or barriers. One may easily walk from one section to another, and if one does, one would see names of those with whom Berlin used to dine, gossip and argue, testifying to his remark that he is 'rooted' in his beloved Oxford, England, Great Britain.[206] If the human need to belong is as basic as Berlin claimed it to be, that need was met in his own life in this picturesque university town.

While the final resting places of our protagonists are in this way separated by the Atlantic Ocean, their books—the principal carriers of their legacies and afterlives—are often found close to each other in libraries and bookstores across the world. As books are typically displayed in an alphabetical order, Arendt's books are often placed just above Berlin's. It is not difficult to imagine how irritating this must have been to the Oxford don; and one could also imagine how the woman above might have shown her Olympian indifference to the irritated author below. Regardless of their unfortunate personal relations, however, we should feel fortunate that the writings of both are easily available to us today and that we are free to draw on them to develop our own ideas. That Arendt and Berlin often disagreed with each other means that they *together* left us with rich and heterogeneous resources to consider issues of common concern to them both: freedom, humanity and politics on the one hand, and unfreedom, inhumanity and the perversion of politics on the other. Once upon a time, as I mentioned at the beginning of this chapter, dissidents in communist Poland made use of those resources to imagine a free country in which they wanted to live. Our predicament in the twenty-first century is of course different. But the fact that both Arendt's and Berlin's lives and works continue to inspire political thinkers across the globe today indicates that their ability to help us imagine a better future has by no means been exhausted.[207]

7

Conclusion

THIS STUDY has been a testimony to William James's remark, 'The history of philosophy is to a great extent that of a certain clash of human temperaments.'[1] Hannah Arendt and Isaiah Berlin indeed had very different temperaments. She was brave, charismatic, upright, assertive, impulsive, tactless and argumentative; he was sceptical, ironical, humorous, charming, good-mannered and thin-skinned. She remained something of an outsider in her adopted home country; he became an indisputable member of the British elite. She liked to think of herself as a conscious pariah, an independent voice challenging the conformism of professional thinkers. He liked to think of himself as a pluralist fox, emphasising the importance of moderation and compromise in a world filled with fanatics and utopians. She kept an introspective *Denktagebuch*, or thought-diary, exemplifying the process of thinking she described as 'a dialogue between me and myself'. He was a socialite, said to be the greatest conversationalist since Denis Diderot,[2] leaving us with a vast heap of letters filled with gossip, curiosity, amiability, wit, mischief and an acute sense of the human comedy. In spite of her outsider status, or perhaps because of it, she was hardly in want of self-assurance. Despite his numerous honours and distinctions, he was often insecure and indecisive, constantly needing others to soothe his anxiety. She was often accused of arrogance; he, of cowardice. She professed to 'take great pleasure in a good fight'.[3] He professed to be 'very conformist' and to have 'never rebelled' in his life.[4]

In both Arendt's and Berlin's cases, it is difficult to separate temperament from experiences on the one hand and ideas on the other. She saw the fall of inter-war German parliamentarianism; he witnessed the violence of the Russian Revolution. The year 1933 taught her not so much the menace of a far-right movement per se as the danger of centralists' complacency coupled with the submissiveness of the masses; 1917 taught him the menace of the Bolsheviks' fanaticism and terror. Later on, she lived in the affluent post-war United States, where everyone seemed to her to be absorbed in the endless cycle of production and consumption. He visited the post-war Soviet Union, where he saw citizens bullied by an omnipotent state under a manipulative leader. Albeit in complicated ways, these experiential differences accounted for some of the major differences between our protagonists' ideas. She was deeply worried about institutional paralysis and political decay; he feared violent insurrection. She loathed bourgeois complacency; he abhorred extremism. She thought a revolution could be rejuvenating; he thought it likely to be destructive. She prized courage as a prime political virtue; he cherished tolerance. She wanted ordinary men and women 'to stop caring so much about ourselves or our souls, and start caring a lot more about our world';[5] he wanted patronisers of all stripes to stop interfering with other people's business. She defended active citizenship; he, liberal individualism.

If some experiences drove Arendt and Berlin apart, others brought them closer. Antisemitism played a significant role in shaping both of their identities. The rise of Nazism convinced them of the failure of assimilationism. Zionism presented itself not as an abstract theory, but as a viable political response to the crises confronting European Jewry during the first half of the last century. Both of them, just like their contemporary Raymond Aron, came to feel 'a sense of instability and anxiety that allow[ed] little space for leisurely pursuits' such as ontology and epistemology.[6] Migration was experienced very differently, Berlin's more peaceful and orderly than Arendt's. Yet some experiences were common to them both: acquisition of a new language, adjustment to an unfamiliar environment and a new way of life, appreciation of some aspects of the adopted home, coupled with a certain attachment to the culture, language and literature of the old world left behind. Both thinkers were multilingual Europeans in the Anglophone world, cultured cosmopolitans in the eyes of the less well travelled natives. She saw herself as 'a German Jew driven from [her] homeland by the Nazis'.[7] He saw himself as a Russian Jew fortunate enough to have been transplanted into British soil. While such (perceived) 'foreignness' caused them trouble and discomfort, it also boosted their reputation as intellectuals with broad horizons. She is said to have spoken with a 'central European accent that held lecture audiences spellbound'.[8] He is said to have spoken with an upper-class English accent gilded with 'a deep and lilting tone that sounded luxuriantly Eastern European'.[9]

Some things that connected Arendt and Berlin also deeply divided them. If Zionism brought them closer during the 1930s, it drove them apart by the end of the 1940s. Philosophy enchanted the two thinkers in their youth, but the versions of philosophy they were enthralled by were different. Heidegger and Jaspers inspired Arendt; they bored Berlin. Oxford philosophy failed to impress Arendt; Berlin was part of it. Both attended the Eichmann trial in Jerusalem; they could not disagree more on many of the difficult questions it raised. The gap between them was narrower when it came to the history of political thought. Here, too, however, a certain distance remained. She assumed that liberalism had already died by the mid-twentieth century; he gave it a new lease of life. She held the American Framers in great esteem; he never bothered to read the Federalist Papers.[10] She lamented freedom's retreat from the polis to the self in late antiquity; he welcomed the rise of a Hellenistic individualism accompanying the decline of the polis. These and other theoretical and historiographical differences manifested themselves in the two thinkers' contrasting perspectives on contemporary affairs. She held bourgeois liberalism partly accountable for the rise of Nazism; he underlined the centrality of Germany's 'bent twig' nationalism. The founding of the State of Israel reinforced her view that the nation-state system is inherently contradictory; it was for him 'a living witness to the triumph of human idealism and will-power'.[11] The Hungarian Revolution caused her much hope and optimism; by his calculation, the martyrdom it claimed outweighed the little gain it made. The sixty-eighters in America seemed to her like carriers of the country's dormant revolutionary spirit; they reminded him of the last days of Rome.

———

These individual points of agreement and disagreement, similarities and differences, have been discussed in detail in the previous chapters. Here, by way of conclusion, one overall theme that connects Arendt and Berlin is worth highlighting: their lives and works were hardly confined to academia, let alone one academic discipline. Needless to say, both made significant academic contributions, and some of their books and articles remain as 'must-reads' in several disciplines, including political theory, philosophy and intellectual history. But, *in addition to this*, Arendt had worked as an activist, a journalist, a social worker and a restorer of looted Jewish cultural artefacts; Berlin worked as a public servant, a diplomatic reporter on American public opinion and an analyst of Russian society, culture and politics; and both were, for want of a better word, intellectuals. Both sought to influence public opinion and public policy, albeit often through differing channels: writing for the people in Arendt's case, and speaking to policy-makers and public servants in Berlin's. Although they detached themselves fully from academia only for short periods, they both retained connections to friends and former colleagues in the 'real world', on whom they could and did rely when the need arose. True, the opportunity to build such connections came as much from circumstances as from voluntary choice and decision. It is entirely possible and perhaps even probable that Arendt would have continued her academic career as a fairly conventional, if exceptionally bright, German philosopher of her time if her life and world had not been catastrophically disrupted by the rise of Nazism. It is no less likely that Berlin would have stayed, uninterrupted, in Oxford as 'not a very political thinker', had his century turned out to be less violent, less totalitarian and less genocidal.[12] Still, once events of their century drove them out from the innocence of academic life, neither returned to it in its original, uneventful form.

A closely related connection between Arendt and Berlin was that both were direct witnesses of contemporary affairs. Witnesses, in the sense used here, contrast with scholars.[13] On the one hand, witnesses do not have the distance, impartiality and relative wealth of data available to scholars. On the other hand, they have the privilege of chronicling an event contemporaneously as it unfolds before their own eyes. Both of our protagonists witnessed some of the defining events of their times, sometimes writing a first rough draft of history, although they also wrote more polished drafts later. For example, Arendt wrote 'We Refugees' as a witness; she wrote *The Origins of Totalitarianism* as a scholar. Similarly, Berlin wrote some of his essays on Soviet Russia as a witness; he wrote others as a scholar. Of course, the difference between the two perspectives is a matter of degree. Both Arendt's and Berlin's most scholarly writings have in fact attracted the charge that they are 'not scholarly enough', that they lack the kind of impartiality, precision, rigour, footnotes and references expected of 'proper' academic research. This charge is partially valid, but it may also be read as a compliment. Both of our protagonists' works are characterised by the kind of immediacy, urgency, integrity and authority that are wanting in more detached scholarship. Neither Arendt's political theory nor Berlin's conformed to the Goethean rule that 'the tree of life is green but all theories are grey'.[14]

In retrospect, the lives and works of our protagonists strike us as embodying the Socratic maxim: true philosophy must be liveable. Or, more precisely, 'True philosophy is a harmony of speech and deed that is rooted in passion.'[15] While both Arendt and Berlin claimed to have abandoned philosophy, and indeed spent much of their time writing for a wider audience outside the community of academic philosophers, they remained philosophers in this Socratic sense, to the end of their lives. Both were entirely free from the kind of hypocrisy and inauthenticity characteristic of some philosophy faculty members across the world, then and now: preaching one thing and living a life that contradicts it.[16] Arendt was richly endowed with some of the virtues she commended in her theoretical work, such as courage, care for the world, opposition to the unanimity of public opinion and a passion for truth. Even her faults, such as tactlessness, moralism and demandingness, for which she has been attacked with much ferocity, are arguably derived from the positive qualities of her thought. Similarly, Berlin's personal qualities, both good and bad, were consistent with his theoretical outlook. They included decency, generosity, maturity and prudence on the one hand, and complacency, indecisiveness, cowardice and a status-quo bias on the other. One may feel greater sympathy for Arendt than for Berlin, or vice versa, depending on one's temperament and intellectual orientation. But we may all agree that each of them lived as a thinker should, on his/her own terms. Thanks to this 'harmony of speech and deed', both of our protagonists earn our highest respect and admiration. They strike us not only as brilliant minds but also as exemplars, even if the outlooks they exemplified differed from each other's.

Does this mean that our protagonists' works—or, rather, their mode of thinking, to the extent that a parallel may be drawn between them—is superior to that of their more institutionalised and professionalised descendants today, including, though not limited to, the hegemonic group consisting of neo-Kantians inspired by John Rawls's work? Does it matter that most contemporary philosophers and political theorists, unlike Arendt and Berlin, think and write in the tranquillity of academia, far from the corridors of power, far from the chaos of a 1917 Petrograd or a 1933 Berlin, and far from the fury of an Eichmann controversy? The answer that emerges from the preceding pages is a highly ambivalent one. On the one hand, as I have shown, there are many intellectual virtues that Arendt and Berlin shared and yet are not to be found in much academic work today. Of particular importance is our protagonists' shared determination to face up squarely to the most urgent challenges of their times and think them through, unhindered by intellectual cowardice and its twin, 'disciplinary boundaries'.[17]

On the other hand, this very strength had the downside to which recent academics, especially neo-Kantians, have been relatively immune: excessive mutual dependence between the normative and the empirical. Precisely because normative argument and empirical analysis were fused in both Arendt's and Berlin's works, each thinker's normative commitment systematically distorted his/her view of ongoing events, while his/her partial understanding of empirical reality unduly influenced his/her normative ideas. Many instances of this weakness have been documented in this study. For example, I have discussed how Arendt's theoretical commitment to political freedom and the council tradition distorted her perspective on the Hungarian Revolution; and how her conception of political freedom in the first place originated from her partial, Nazi-focused understanding of totalitarianism. Similarly, I have discussed how Berlin's defence of negative liberty was unduly influenced (as he himself later came to acknowledge) by his preoccupation with the Bolshevik model of totalitarian oppression; and how his embrace of England as a quintessentially liberal society coloured his perspective on Britain's present and its imperial past. In short, in both thinkers' cases, proximity to the 'real world' was a double-edged sword: what gave their works immediacy, urgency, integrity and authority also made them vulnerable to distortion, prejudice and rash judgement. This is a variation of the general problem that is endemic in non-idealised modes of political theorising: if one builds one's theory 'from below', beginning with a close examination of some concrete problem at hand rather than with an abstract model, then the resulting theory is likely to be too influenced by *that* particular problem, which may be currently urgent and yet may not be more significant than other problems in the long run. If Arendt's and Berlin's theories were not grey, the light that illuminated them nevertheless also did them damage.

Needless to say, this does not mean that Arendt's and Berlin's mode of thinking is necessarily inferior to its more scholarly and more detached alternatives today. Different approaches and perspectives—the view from nowhere, from here, from behind the veil of ignorance, from inside the real world and so on—all have their own disadvantages as well as advantages. If Arendt's and Berlin's works were alike tainted by distortion, prejudice and rash judgement, they were at the same time free from some of the major weaknesses of the work of many contemporary neo-Kantians, such as blindness to history, the inability to provide a guide to concrete action, the unwillingness to address issues outside their 'disciplinary boundaries' and the tendency unknowingly to smuggle unexamined assumptions and cultural biases into a purportedly idealised theory.[18] Methods of political theory and philosophy are like technologies in this respect: what solves the problems at hand gives rise to a different set of problems. If so, those who claim political thinking as their vocation will keep discovering, refining, discarding and rediscovering various ways of plying their trade, because no single way is a cure-all. Imperfect though they are, Arendt's and Berlin's writings are therefore likely to continue to inspire political theorists, philosophers and others for years to come, as they have done over the past several decades. This is certainly merited. Both thinkers' works are immensely rich and rewardingly complicated, packed with ideas that may be elaborated in a number of ways. None the less, they have significant shortcomings too, and those who draw inspiration from either or both are advised to tread carefully. They should resist yielding too easily to the suggestion contained in the seductive words that Plato gives to Socrates in the *Republic*: 'Do you think it is at all possible to admire something, and spend time with it, without wanting to imitate it?'[19]

ACKNOWLEDGEMENTS

I DO NOT know how many people became casualties of my obsessive talk about Hannah Arendt and Isaiah Berlin as I wrote this book over the past decade in Britain, France, Denmark and the USA. I am, however, aware that I owe a special debt of gratitude to the following individuals and institutions, without whose help and support I would have been unable to complete it.

I would like to thank Mark Lilla and Samuel Moyn, who back in 2010–11 kindly gave me feedback on a very crude outline for a comparative study of Arendt and Berlin. Little did I know that it would take ten years to turn that outline into a book! But I was fortunate to receive Lilla's and Moyn's comments at the very beginning and fully benefit from them as I worked on this book project.

I wrote a large part of the book at the University of Oxford between 2012 and 2018. I am incalculably indebted to my fellow Wolfsonian Henry Hardy, who not only helped me write this book in countless ways but also taught me more than I could ever describe through a number of conversations we have had over the past fifteen years or so. His infectious enthusiasm for Berlin's work has had a profound impact on me, and I hope this book repays some of the intellectual debt I owe him by way of contributing to Berlin scholarship.

I would like to thank my other friends and colleagues (formerly) at Oxford, including Roger Crisp, Jonathan Floyd, Roger Hausheer, Takuya Okada, Derek Penslar and Mark Pottle, who kindly read and gave me feedback on different parts of the manuscript. Thanks are also due to the president and fellows of Wolfson College for providing me with a home in Oxford, initially as a graduate student, and then as a junior research fellow and as a research fellow; to Anne Deighton, Christos Hadjiyiannis, Nicholas Hall, Gareth Hughes and Ana Martins for stimulating conversations; to Julian Savulescu for his unfailing support and encouragement; and to Abigail Green for letting me fellow-travel with an outstanding group of scholars at the Oxford Centre for Hebrew and Jewish Studies working on the 'Jews, Liberalism and Anti-Semitism' project in 2016–17. I am especially grateful to Arie Dubnov and Malachi Hacohen, with whom I discussed various issues in intellectual history, both at Oxford and (inevitably) online. In addition, a word of thanks is due to my doctoral supervisor Elizabeth Frazer. While this book is not based on the D.Phil. thesis that I wrote under her guidance, I could not have written it without the prior experience of completing the latter and figuring out, along the way, what kind of political theorist I wanted to be. Although I can no longer remember the names of all the individuals who shared their memories of, and anecdotes about, Isaiah Berlin with me at Oxford, I would like to record my heartfelt thanks to the late Bryan Magee, with whom I had many inspiring conversations at Wolfson.

Outside Oxford, I am indebted to many friends and colleagues from whom I learned much over the years I wrote this book. Special thanks go to my co-conspirators James Barry, Karin Fry, Jennifer Gaffney and Michael Portal for keeping me updated on the latest developments in Arendt studies; to those associated with the Hannah Arendt Circle, where I have had the pleasure of serving in various capacities; to Roger Berkowitz and his colleagues at the Hannah Arendt Center for Politics and Humanities at Bard College for hosting me in spring 2017; to Susumu Shimazono for hosting me at the University of Tokyo in 2012; and to Mark Lilla and the faculty and staff of the Institute for Human Rights and the Department of History at Columbia University for hosting me in 2010–11. Thanks are also due to Leroy Cooper, Wout Cornelissen, Tal Correm, Christian Emden, Allyn Fives, Olga Kirschbaum, Shmuel Lederman, Yasemin Sari and Ian Storey for lending me their expertise; to my editors at Princeton University Press for their commitment, patience and professionalism; to the three anonymous reviewers for the Press for their incisive comments and suggestions; and to my copyeditor Francis Eaves for his excellent work.

I drafted the final part of this book in France during my residency at the Paris Institute for Advanced Study. I cannot thank enough the Institute's director and staff members for providing me with the time, space and tranquillity to complete the manuscript. I presented parts of this book internally at the Paris Institute no less than three times, and received helpful feedback from some of my colleagues, including Adam Frank, Andrew Kahn, Gretty Mirdal, Penny Roberts, Joachim Savelsberg, Iain Stewart and Denis Walsh. Michelle-Irène Brudny was kind enough to meet me regularly in Paris (and once in Rouen), read several draft chapters and share her encyclopaedic knowledge of Arendt's life and work with me. This book would have been much worse had she not shown her heroic generosity. Thanks are also due to Mitchell Cohen for his insightful comments and enriching conversations; and to Alexis Butin, Gil Delannoi, Annabelle Lever, Johan Said and Judith Wechsler for giving me much food for thought.

Additionally, my warmest thanks go to Xiaofan Amy Li for keeping me sane over the years I wrote this book; to Joel Rosenthal and my former colleagues at Carnegie Council for Ethics in International Affairs for providing me with a home away from home in New York; and to my current colleagues at Aarhus University, including Bogdan Cristian Iacob and Mikkel Thorup, for their helpful comments on the penultimate manuscript. I am immeasurably indebted to Tatsuya Sakamoto, half-way across the globe in Tokyo, who introduced me to the world of ideas during my undergraduate years at Keio University and remains my mentor and interlocutor, and a singular source of inspiration. Thanks are also due to Tetsuji Uehiro for his support and encouragement; to Noboru Maruyama for placing his trust in me; to Shin Osawa for being my most reliable ally and *senpai*; and to Yohei Kawakami, Seiko Mimaki and Wang Qian for exchanging academic (and not so academic) gossip with me whenever I return to my home city. Last, but not least, I would like to thank my parents and sister in Tokyo for encouraging me to pursue my passion.

I have presented various parts of this book at Oxford, Paris II, the Paris Institute for Advanced Study, Sciences Po, Aarhus, Copenhagen, Bard College, Columbia University, Texas A&M, Keio University, Waseda University, the annual conference of the Political Studies Association in Brighton and the annual Hannah Arendt Circle conference at West Chester University. Thanks are due to Keith Breen and Annabelle Lever for acting as designated respondents in Brighton and Paris, respectively; and to Kazutaka Inamura and Naoyuki Umemori for hosting me at Waseda University. I am also grateful to Maria Dimova-Cookson, with whom I discussed our favourite topic—freedom—on both sides of the English Channel.

This book could not have been written without support by several funding bodies and charitable organisations. I am deeply grateful to the Uehiro Foundation on Ethics and Education in Tokyo for patiently supporting my work, showing blissful indifference to the overly utilitarian approach to academic funding that appears to be increasingly the norm in Japan as elsewhere. They encouraged me to write a book that I would not later regret, and I only hope that this book lives up to their expectations. Thanks are also due to the John Fell Oxford University Press (OUP) Research Fund for enabling my stay at Bard College; and to Wolfson College's Academic Fund for enabling my various research trips. This book has additionally benefited from the European Union's Horizon 2020 research and innovation programme under the Marie Skłodowska-Curie Grant Agreement No. 754513 and the Aarhus University Research Foundation, and from a EURIAS fellowship at the Paris Institute for Advanced Study (France), co-funded by Marie Skłodowska-Curie Actions, under the European Union's 7th Framework Programme for research, and from funding from the French State programme 'Investissements d'avenir', managed by the Agence Nationale de la Recherche (ANR-11-LABX-0027-01 Labex RFIEA+).

I would like to thank the following institutions and their staff members for their help with specific archival materials: Stevenson Library, Bard College (Hannah Arendt Collection); the Hannah Arendt Center at The New School University, and the Hannah Arendt Bluecher Literary Trust and its agent, George Borchardt, Inc. (Hannah Arendt Papers at the Library of Congress); the Bodleian Library, University of Oxford (Sir Isaiah Berlin Papers); the University Library, University of California, Santa Cruz (Norman O. Brown Papers); Birkbeck Library, University of London (Sir Bernard Crick Papers); the Arthur and Elizabeth Schlesinger Library on the History of Women in America, Harvard University (Elżbieta Ettinger Papers); Vassar College Libraries (Mary McCarthy Papers); the Howard Gotlieb Archival Research Center, Boston University Libraries (*Partisan Review* Collection); the John F. Kennedy Presidential Library and Museum, University of Massachusetts (Arthur M. Schlesinger Personal Papers); and the National Library of Israel (Gershom Scholem Papers). Special thanks are due to the Trustees of the Isaiah Berlin Literary Trust for giving me permission to cite Berlin's unpublished papers and to reproduce his report on *The Human Condition* by Hannah Arendt as an appendix.

The third and fifth chapters of this book incorporate materials, respectively, from Kei Hiruta, 'The Meaning and Value of Freedom: Berlin contra Arendt', *The European Legacy* 19:7 (2014), pp. 854–68, and Kei Hiruta, 'An "Anti-Utopian Age?": Isaiah Berlin's England, Hannah Arendt's America, and Utopian Thinking in Dark Times', *Journal of Political Ideologies* 21:1 (2017), pp. 12–29.

Finally, I feel obliged to acknowledge something I am not so keen to. While I was writing this book (as well as before that), I have been told more than a few times that those who have my skin colour, ethnicity or nationality are not entitled to do political theory or philosophy. The individuals thanked above are entirely free from such racist prejudices, so far as I can tell. I think it is rather ridiculous that I should feel grateful to them for not being racist, because one normally does not feel grateful to someone simply for not being depraved and contemptible. Nevertheless, having encountered many more racist bigots than I would ever have hoped to meet in my academic life, I cannot but feel grateful to those who behave decently in academia, at least in my discipline. So, thank you. Your decency means a lot to me.

APPENDIX

WHEN FABER & Faber was considering buying the UK publication rights of Hannah Arendt's *The Human Condition*, published in the United States by the University of Chicago Press in 1958, the British publisher asked Isaiah Berlin to review the book. He agreed and produced the following report (© The Trustees of the Isaiah Berlin Literary Trust 2020).

ISAIAH BERLIN TO FABER & FABER
n.d. [1958]

[Report on] *The Human Condition* by Hannah Arendt
I could recommend no publisher to buy the UK rights of this book. There are two objections to it: it will not sell, and it is no good. The author's reading has evidently been wide, but her comprehension has too often been incomplete. Indeed the suspicion grows, as one reads these pages, that her inadequate command of English (a language she appears to have learned only in mature years, as a refugee in America from Germany) has led her into many of the problems which she attempts to solve in these pages.

The first part of the argument of this book rests on the curious belief that the mean[ing] of the word 'labour' (or 'labor' as it appears in this American text) is somehow significantly different from the meaning of the word 'work'. This notion appears to have been prompted in the author's mind by a line in Locke about 'the labour of our body and the work of our hands'. Instead of seeing this as an attempt (one of the rare attempts) of that pedestrian stylist to embellish his prose with a little elegant variation, Dr Arendt sees it as the adumbration of a distinction in reality: a distinction which she here sets herself to elucidate.

'Labour', she believes, means those efforts which are necessary for the maintenance of the human species; 'work' means those efforts which go beyond the minimal demands of survival, and which yield the durable goods and furniture of the world. Taken as lexicographical definitions, these definitions are, of course, simply inaccurate. Presumably one must therefore take them as prescriptive or stipulative definitions. But even if they are thus accepted, they are found to lead, not to greater clarity, but to greater obscurity. In the later chapters of the book the categories of 'labour' and 'work' are supplemented by a third category of 'action'; action meaning not, as one might expect, doing things, but rather [as] being in some sort of quasi-personalist fusion with other people. This leads to such conclusions as the following (p. 230): 'The instrumentalization of action and the degradation of politics into a means for something else has of course never really succeeded in eliminating action, in preventing its being one of the decisive human experiences, or in destroying the realm of human affairs altogether.' The phrase 'of course' strikes an amusing note, does it not?

Subsidiary observations, as well as the central argument, illustrate the author's characteristic weakness. For example (p. 43), she writes: 'The unfortunate truth about behaviorism and the validity of its "laws" is that the more people there are, the more likely they are to behave, and the less likely to tolerate non-behavior.' This sentence had me completely foxed until I realised that the author was using the verb 'behave' in the sense of 'act civilly' and must therefore imagine that the word 'behaviorism' had something to do with civility!

A second example (p. 31): 'What all Greek philosophers, no matter how opposed to polis life, took for granted is that freedom is exclusively located in the political realm, that necessity is primarily a prepolitical phenomenon [. . .]'. It is perfectly true that, in thinking of political freedom, all Greek philosophers 'took for granted [. . .] that freedom is exclusively located in the political realm' (what else could they think?); but political freedom has nothing whatever to do with necessity; it is opposed to constraint. Necessity is opposed to free will, and is not a problem of political, but of metaphysical, philosophy. Once more the author has got tied up in a false antithesis.

Speaking of moral virtue, Dr Arendt says (p. 75) that 'the Christian demand to be good' is 'absurd'. Is it equally 'absurd' to demand that a book should be good? Let us hope she thinks so. Then she will not mind being told that her book is not good.

ABBREVIATIONS

AN ARABIC NUMERAL added to an abbreviation indicates the edition of the title. For example, *BPF3* is the third edition of *Between Past and Future*. Unless there is special reason to refer to an earlier edition, I use the latest and most easily accessible edition for readers' convenience.

Works by Hannah Arendt

BF. (with Mary McCarthy) *Between Friends: The Correspondence of Hannah Arendt and Mary McCarthy 1949–1975*, ed. Carol Brightman (New York: Harcourt Brace & Co., 1995)

BPF. *Between Past and Future: Eight Exercises in Political Thought*. 1st ed. under the title *Between Past and Future: Six Exercises in Political Thought* (New York: The Viking Press, 1961); 2nd ed. (New York: Penguin Books, 1968); 3rd ed. (New York: Penguin Books, 2006)

C. (with Karl Jaspers) *Correspondence 1926–1969*, ed. Lotte Kohler and Hans Saner, trans. Robert and Rita Kimber (New York: Harcourt Brace & Co., 1992)

CAS. (with Gershom Scholem) *The Correspondence of Hannah Arendt and Gershom Scholem*, ed. Marie Luise Knott, trans. Anthony David (Chicago: University of Chicago Press, 2017)

CR. *Crises of the Republic* (New York: Harcourt Brace Jovanovich, 1972)

DE. *Denktagebuch 1950 bis 1973, Erster Band*, ed. Ursula Ludz and Ingeborg Nordmann (Munich and Zurich: Piper Verlag, 2002)

DZ. *Denktagebuch 1950 bis 1973, Zweiter Band*, ed. Ursula Ludz and Ingeborg Nordmann (Munich and Zurich: Piper Verlag, 2002)

EIJ. *Eichmann in Jerusalem: A Report on the Banality of Evil* (London: Faber & Faber, 1963); revised and enlarged (2nd) ed. (New York: The Viking Press, 1965)

EU. *Essays in Understanding 1930–1954: Formation, Exile, and Totalitarianism*, ed. Jerome Kohn (New York: Harcourt, Brace & Co., 1994)

'Exchange'. (with Gershom Scholem) '"Eichmann in Jerusalem": An Exchange of Letters Between Gershom Scholem and Hannah Arendt', *Encounter* 22 (January 1964), pp. 51–56

HAP. Hannah Arendt Papers, Manuscript Division, Library of Congress, Washington, DC

HC. *The Human Condition* (Chicago: University of Chicago Press, 1958); 2nd ed. (Chicago: University of Chicago Press, 1998)

JW. *The Jewish Writings*, ed. Jerome Kohn and Ron H. Feldman (New York: Schocken Books, 2007)

LMT. *The Life of the Mind, Vol. 1: Thinking.* In *The Life of the Mind*, one-volume edition (New York: Harcourt Brace Jovanovich, 1978)

LMW. *The Life of the Mind, Vol. 2: Willing.* In *The Life of the Mind*, one-volume edition (New York: Harcourt Brace Jovanovich, 1978)

MID. *Men in Dark Times* (New York: Harcourt, Brace & World, 1968)

OR. *On Revolution* (New York: The Viking Press, 1963); 2nd ed. (New York: The Viking Press, 1965); 3rd ed. (New York: Penguin Books, 2006)

OT. *The Origins of Totalitarianism.* 1st UK edition under the title *The Burden of Our Time* (London: Secker & Warburg, 1951); 2nd ed. (New York: Meridian Books, 1958); 3rd ed. (New York: Harcourt Brace & World, 1979)

PP. *The Promise of Politics*, ed. Jerome Kohn (New York: Schocken Books, 2005)

RJ. *Responsibility and Judgement*, ed. Jerome Kohn (New York: Schocken Books, 2003)

TWB. *Thinking without a Banister: Essays in Understanding 1933–1975*, ed. Jerome Kohn (New York: Schocken Books, 2018)

Works by Isaiah Berlin

A. *Affirming: Letters 1975–1997*, ed. Henry Hardy and Mark Pottle (London: Chatto & Windus, 2015)

AC. *Against the Current: Essays in the History of Ideas*, ed. Henry Hardy (London: The Hogarth Press, 1979); 2nd ed. (Princeton: Princeton University Press, 2013)

B. *Building: Letters 1960–1975*, ed. Henry Hardy and Mark Pottle (London: Chatto & Windus, 2013)

CC. *Concepts and Categories: Philosophical Essays*, ed. Henry Hardy (London: The Hogarth Press, 1978); 2nd ed. (Princeton: Princeton University Press, 2013)

'Conversation'. (with Steven Lukes) 'Isaiah Berlin in Conversation with Steven Lukes', *Salmagundi* 120 (Fall 1998), pp. 52–134

CTH. *The Crooked Timber of Humanity: Chapters in the History of Ideas*, ed. Henry Hardy (London: John Murray, 1990); 2nd ed. (Princeton: Princeton University Press, 2013)

E. *Enlightening: Letters 1946–1960*, ed. Henry Hardy and Jennifer Holmes (London: Chatto & Windus, 2009)

F. *Flourishing: Letters 1928–1946*, ed. Henry Hardy (London: Chatto & Windus, 2004)

FIB. *Freedom and Its Betrayal: Six Enemies of Human Liberty*, ed. Henry Hardy (London: Chatto & Windus, 2002); 2nd ed. (Princeton: Princeton University Press, 2014)

KM. *Karl Marx: His Life and Environment* (London: Thornton Butterworth, 1939); 2nd ed. (London and New York: Oxford University Press, 1948); 3rd ed. (Oxford: Oxford University Press, 1963); 4th ed. (Oxford: Oxford University Press, 1978); 5th ed. as *Karl Marx* (without subtitle) (Princeton: Princeton University Press, 2013)

L. *Liberty*, ed. Henry Hardy (Oxford: Oxford University Press, 2002)

MSB. (see below)

PI. *Personal Impressions*, ed. Henry Hardy (London: The Hogarth Press, 1980); 2nd ed. (London: Pimlico, 1998); 3rd ed. (Princeton: Princeton University Press, 2014)

PIRA. *Political Ideas in the Romantic Age: Their Rise and Influence on Modern Thought*, ed. Henry Hardy (London: Chatto & Windus, 2006); 2nd ed. (Princeton: Princeton University Press, 2014)

POI. *The Power of Ideas*, ed. Henry Hardy (London: Pimlico, 2000); 2nd ed. (Princeton: Princeton University Press, 2013)

RR. *The Roots of Romanticism*, ed. Henry Hardy (London: Chatto & Windus, 1999); 2nd ed. (Princeton: Princeton University Press, 2013)

RT. *Russian Thinkers*, ed. Henry Hardy and Aileen Kelly (London: The Hogarth Press, 1978); 2nd ed. (London: Penguin Books, 2008)

SM. *The Soviet Mind: Russian Culture under Communism*, ed. Henry Hardy (Washington, DC: Brookings Institution Press, 2004); 2nd ed. (Washington, DC: Brookings Institution Press, 2016)

SR. *The Sense of Reality: Studies in Ideas and their History*, ed. Henry Hardy (London: Chatto & Windus, 1996); 2nd ed. (Princeton: Princeton University Press, 2019)

T. (see below)

TCE. *Three Critics of the Enlightenment: Vico, Hamann, Herder*, ed. Henry Hardy (London: Pimlico, 2000); 2nd ed. (Princeton: Princeton University Press, 2013)

UD. (with Beata Polanowska-Sygulska) *Unfinished Dialogue* (New York: Prometheus Books, 2006)

MSB and T. Some of Isaiah Berlin's unpublished papers cited in this book are archived under the overall shelfmark MS. Berlin as 'Papers of Sir Isaiah Berlin, 1897–98, with some family papers, 1903–72' in the Bodleian Library at the University of Oxford (for further details, see https://archives.bodleian.ox.ac.uk/repositories/2/resources/3284); others (or copies) are held by the Trustees of the Isaiah Berlin Literary Trust at Wolfson College, Oxford. Citations from the former are identified by 'MSB shelfmark/folio'; those from the latter are identified by 'T'. For example, 'Isaiah Berlin to Robert Silvers, 1 June 1966, MSB 279/14–15' means that the letter is in the Bodleian collection and catalogued as MS. Berlin 279, fols 14–15; and 'Isaiah Berlin to Norman Oliver Brown, 6 May 1991, T' means that the letter (or copy) is held by the Trustees of the Isaiah Berlin Literary Trust.

Works by Others

CIB. Ramin Jahanbegloo, *Conversation with Isaiah Berlin* (London: Peter Halban, 1991)

IBVL. Henry Hardy (ed.), The Isaiah Berlin Virtual Library, http://berlin.wolf.ox.ac.uk/index .html

MI Tapes. Michael Ignatieff, 'Michael Ignatieff's Biographical Interviews' (IBVL, 2017; last revised 6 March 2021), by tape number and page. Digitised versions of the original recordings are also available at the IBVL. Except where they have been checked by Henry Hardy for quotation purposes (indicated by bold type), the transcripts are currently imperfect. Consequently, those who wish to look into my citations are advised to consult the recordings. The transcripts and the recordings are both available via the IBVL, http://berlin.wolf .ox.ac.uk/lists/interviews/ignatieff/biographical-interviews/index.html, accessed 7 March 2021

PEE. The Papers of Elżbieta Ettinger, Folder 17.9, Correspondence: 'Berlin, Isaiah, 1992–1993', Arthur and Elizabeth Schlesinger Library on the History of Women in America, Radcliffe Institute for Advanced Study, Harvard University

NOTES

Chapter 1. Introduction

1. Arthur M. Schlesinger Jr., *Journals: 1952–2000* (London: The Penguin Press, 2007), 7 April 1977, p. 430.

2. Norman Oliver Brown to Isaiah Berlin, 6 April 1991. Norman O. Brown Papers. MS 35. Special Collections and Archives, University Library, University of California, Santa Cruz.

3. Samir al-Khalil [pseudonym for Kanan Makiya], *Republic of Fear: Saddam's Iraq* (London: Hutchinson Radius, 1989).

4. Ibid., p. 112, p. 115, p. 254.

5. Isaiah Berlin to Norman Oliver Brown, 6 May 1991, T.

6. Schlesinger, *Journals*, p. 430.

7. Berlin repeatedly used this phrase to criticise Arendt's work. For further discussion, see Chapter 2.

8. See Isaiah Berlin to Robert Silvers, 1 June 1966, MSB 279/14–15.

9. Jahanbegloo, *CIB*, p. 82.

10. Berlin to Brown, 6 May 1991.

11. Isaiah Berlin to Geza Vermes, 13 May 1982, T.

12. See McCarthy's letters to Arendt on 2 December 1952 (*BF*, p. 12), on 10 April 1953 (*BF*, p. 14) and on 14 June 1969 (*BF*, p. 239); and Arendt's letters to McCarthy on 4 February 1970 (*BF*, p. 254). See also Hannah Arendt to Karl and Gertrud Jaspers, 24 November 1963, *C*, p. 535.

13. For example, Arendt used Berlin's *Karl Marx: His Life and Environment* in her Spring 1955 lectures on the 'History of Political Theory' at the University of California, Berkeley; and in her Fall 1965 seminars on 'Selected Writings of Political Philosophers' at the New School for Social Research. She also used Berlin's essay 'Does Political Theory Still Exist?' in her 1963 lectures on 'Introduction into Politics' at the University of Chicago; and again in her Spring 1969 lecture on 'Philosophy and Politics: What is Political Philosophy?' at the New School for Social Research. See items 023969 (Berkeley 1955), 024345 (New School 1965), 023863 (Chicago 1963) and 023573 (New School 1969), in 'Subject File, 1949–1975, n.d.', HAP.

14. Those books are Isaiah Berlin, *KM2*; 'Montesquieu', *Proceedings of the British Academy* 41 (1955), pp. 267–96, reprinted in *AC2*, pp. 164–203; 'Introduction' to Franco Venturi, *Roots of Revolution: A History of the Populist and Socialist Movements in Nineteenth Century Russia*, trans. Francis Haskell (New York: Grosset & Dunlap, 1966), reprinted as 'Russian Populism' in *RT2*, pp. 240–72; a highly abridged version of 'Two Concepts of Liberty', in Anthony Quinton (ed.), *Political Philosophy* (London: Oxford University Press, 1967), pp. 141–52; and 'Introduction' to Alexander Herzen, *My Past and Thoughts: The Memoirs of Alexander Herzen*, trans. Constance

Garnett, ed. and abridged by Dwight Macdonald (New York: Knopf, 1973), reprinted as 'Herzen and his Memoirs' in *AC2*, pp 236–66.

15. Hannah Arendt, 'On Violence', *CR*, pp. 105–98, at p. 129, note 41. This reiterates a February 1966 entry of *Denktagebuch* (Arendt, *DZ*, XXV: 4, p. 654).

16. Seyla Benhabib, *Exile, Statelessness, and Migration: Playing Chess with History from Hannah Arendt to Isaiah Berlin* (Princeton: Princeton University Press, 2019).

17. Michael Ignatieff, *Isaiah Berlin: A Life* (London: Chatto & Windus, 1998), p. 135.

18. See Max Weber, *The Vocation Lectures*, ed. David Owen and Tracy B. Strong, trans. Rodney Livingstone (Indianapolis: Hackett Publishing, 2004).

19. Adam Kirsch, 'The Monist and the Pluralist', *The Wall Street Journal*, 19 July 2013, https://www.wsj.com/articles/SB10001424127887324348504578609523230589356, accessed 15 January 2020.

20. With the development of bioethics in the late twentieth century, some people today regard persons and human beings as distinct entities. In their view, some non-human animals such as chimpanzees and dolphins are persons; and some members of the human species, such as new-born infants, are non-persons. As this definitional debate did not occur early enough to influence Arendt's or Berlin's thought, and neither of them distinguished between persons and human beings, I follow their terminology and assume that all human beings are persons, and all persons human beings, in this book.

21. David Miller and Richard Dagger, 'Utilitarianism and Beyond: Contemporary Analytical Political Theory', in Terence Ball and Richard Bellamy (eds), *The Cambridge History of Twentieth-Century Political Thought* (Cambridge: Cambridge University Press, 2006), pp. 446–69, at pp. 446–47.

22. Of particular importance are various essays by Crick, including Bernard Crick, 'On Re-reading *The Origins of Totalitarianism*', *Social Research* 44:1 (1977), pp. 229–45; Bernard Crick, 'Hannah Arendt's Political Philosophy', in Robert Boyers (ed.), *Proceedings of History, Ethics, Politics: A Conference Based on the Work of Hannah Arendt* (New York: Empire State College, 1982), pp. 23–31; and Bernard Crick, 'Hannah Arendt and the Burden of Our Times', *The Political Quarterly* 68:1 (1997), pp. 77–84. See also Celso Lafer, 'Isaiah Berlin and Hannah Arendt', *Hannah Arendt Newsletter*, No. 1 (April 1999), pp. 19–24.

23. Chief among them are Steven E. Aschheim, *Beyond the Border: The German-Jewish Legacy Abroad* (Princeton: Princeton University Press, 2007), pp. 113–18; Ronald Beiner, *Political Philosophy: What It Is and Why It Matters* (Cambridge: Cambridge University Press, 2014), pp. xv–xxii; Benhabib, *Exile, Statelessness, and Migration*; David Caute, *Isaac and Isaiah: The Covert Punishment of a Cold War Heretic* (New Haven: Yale University Press, 2013), pp. 262–72; Joan Cocks, *Passion and Paradox: Intellectuals Confront the National Question* (Princeton: Princeton University Press, 2002), esp. pp. 71–91; Arie M. Dubnov, 'Can Parallels Meet?: Hannah Arendt and Isaiah Berlin on the Jewish Post-Emancipatory Quest for Political Freedom', *Leo Baeck Institute Year Book* 62 (2017), pp. 27–51; Kei Hiruta, 'The Meaning and Value of Freedom: Berlin contra Arendt', *The European Legacy* 19:7 (2014), pp. 854–68; Kei Hiruta, 'An "Anti-Utopian Age?": Isaiah Berlin's England, Hannah Arendt's America, and Utopian Thinking in Dark Times', *Journal of Political Ideologies* 22:1 (2017), pp. 12–29; Kei Hiruta, 'A Democratic Consensus?: Isaiah Berlin, Hannah Arendt, and the Anti-totalitarian Family Quarrel', *Think* 17:48 (2018), pp. 25–37; Jeremy Waldron, *Political Political Theory: Essays on Institutions* (Cambridge, MA: Harvard University Press, 2016); and Ilya Winham, 'After Totalitarianism: Hannah Arendt, Isaiah Berlin, and

the Realization and Defeat of the Western Tradition' (Ph.D. dissertation, University of Minnesota, 2015).

24. Berlin to Brown, 6 May 1991.

25. Isaiah Berlin to Martin Peretz, 22 November 1974, MSB 208/202.

26. Ramin Jahanbegloo, *Isaiah Berlin en toutes libertés: entretiens avec Isaiah Berlin*, trans. Gérard Lorimy (Paris: Éditions du Félin, 1991), published in English a year later as *CIB*.

27. Berlin repeatedly called Arendt his 'bête noire'. For further discussion, see Chapter 2.

28. Ignatieff, *Isaiah Berlin*. Also important was the publication of Berlin and Lukes, 'Conversation'.

29. Of particular importance is Seyla Benhabib, *The Reluctant Modernism of Hannah Arendt*, new ed. (Lanham, MD: Rowman & Littlefield, 2003), p. li note 6.

30. Berlin, *F, E, B, A*.

31. W. J. Mander, *British Idealism: A History* (Oxford: Oxford University Press, 2011), p. 11.

Chapter 2. A Real Bête Noire

1. Isaiah Berlin to Elżbieta Ettinger, 19 December 1992, PEE.

2. Berlin is duly mentioned in the Acknowledgements in Elżbieta Ettinger, *Hannah Arendt/Martin Heidegger* (New Haven: Yale University Press, 1995), p. ix.

3. Berlin to Ettinger, 19 December 1992; 29 September 1993; 5 November 1993, PEE.

4. Berlin to Ettinger, 14 January 1993, PEE. To my knowledge, the first surviving record of Berlin calling Arendt his 'bête noire' is Isaiah Berlin to Georges Nivat, 4 April 1985, MSB 220/50–52. He reiterates this in other letters, e.g., Isaiah Berlin to Norman Oliver Brown, 6 May 1991, T; and Isaiah Berlin to Leslie Lipson, 16 March 1993, T.

5. Sophie Loidolt, *Phenomenology of Plurality: Hannah Arendt on Political Intersubjectivity* (New York: Routledge, 2018), p. 25, p. 48 note 8.

6. Hannah Arendt, *Der Liebesbegriff bei Augustin: Versuch einer philosophischen Interpretation* (Berlin: Julius Springer, 1929), published in English with additional materials as *Love and Saint Augustine*, ed. and trans. Joanna Vecchiarelli Scott and Judith Chelius Stark (Chicago: University of Chicago Press, 1996).

7. Hannah Arendt, 'Original Assimilation', *JW*, pp. 22–28, at p. 22.

8. Hannah Arendt, '"What Remains? The Language Remains": A Conversation with Günter Gaus', *EU*, pp. 1–23, at p. 5.

9. Elisabeth Young-Bruehl, *Hannah Arendt: For the Love of the World*, 2nd ed. (New Haven: Yale University Press, 2004), p. 106.

10. See Arendt's essays from this period, 'The Professional Reclassification of Youth', 'A Guide for Youth: Martin Buber' and 'Some Young People Are Going Home', reprinted in *JW*, pp. 29–37.

11. Thence Blücher was sent to another internment camp in Villemalard. See Arendt and Blücher, *Within Four Falls: The Correspondence between Hannah Arendt and Heinrich Blücher, 1936–1968*, ed. Lotte Kohler, trans. Peter Constantine (New York: Harcourt, Inc., 2000), pp. 46–57.

12. For a study of *Aufbau*, see Peter Schrag, *The World of Aufbau: Hitler's Refugees in America* (Madison: The University of Wisconsin Press, 2019).

13. Irving Howe, *A Margin of Hope: An Intellectual Autobiography* (San Diego: Harcourt Brace Jovanovich, 1982), p. 270.

14. The Russian Revolution of 1905 also incited attacks on Jews and Social Democrats in Riga, but this wave of violence was over by the time of Isaiah Berlin's birth. His father, Mendel, recollected the few years between his son's birth and the outbreak of war as 'the happiest time of [his] life'. Mendel Berlin, 'For the Benefit of My Son', in Henry Hardy (ed.), *The Book of Isaiah: Personal Impressions of Isaiah Berlin* (Woodbridge: The Boydell Press, 2009), pp. 263–314, at p. 296.

15. Ibid., p. 304.

16. Michael Ignatieff, *Isaiah Berlin: A Life* (London: Chatto & Windus, 1998), p. 59.

17. This was to be followed by another honour of being elected, in autumn 1938, a fellow of New College, 'the first Jewish tutorial fellow since Samuel Alexander' (in other words, the second Jew to hold a college tutorial fellowship at Oxford). David M. Lewis, *The Jews of Oxford* (Oxford: Oxford Jewish Congregation, 1992), p. 62.

18. Ignatieff, *Isaiah Berlin*, p. 71.

19. Isaiah Berlin to Mendel Berlin, 10 September 1938, F, p. 282.

20. Isaiah Berlin to Marie Gaster, 3 January 1941, F, p. 357.

21. Collected and published as H. G. Nicholas (ed.), *Washington Dispatches 1941–1945: Weekly Political Reports from the British Embassy* (London: Weidenfeld & Nicolson, 1981).

22. Stefan Collini, *English Pasts: Essays in History and Culture* (Oxford: Oxford University Press, 1999), p. 195.

23. The precise number of their meetings remains ambiguous. In one letter, Berlin says he met Arendt 'on [. . .] four occasions' (Isaiah Berlin to Derwent May, 1 October 1986, A, p. 298); in another he says he met her 'not above three times' (Berlin to Ettinger, 5 November 1993). More typically, Berlin says he met Arendt 'a few' times. The ambiguity is largely due to the difficulty of determining what counts as a proper 'meeting'. Does mere presence in the same room count? As I shall show in this chapter, there were three occasions on which Arendt and Berlin 'met' in a sense more substantive than mere presence in the same room: New York in 1941, Harvard probably in 1949 and Harvard in 1967. The fourth, less significant, occasion that Berlin mentions in his letter to May (and omits in his letter to Ettinger) seems to be an informal meeting with Robert Silvers at an unknown coffee shop (MI Tape 19, p. 29). I know of no archival sources to give more information about this meeting.

24. Michael Ignatieff writes that Berlin and Arendt met in 1942, relying on a letter by Isaiah Berlin to Bernard Crick, 4 November 1963, T (Ignatieff, *Isaiah Berlin*, p. 253, p. 332). But I suggest late 1941 as more probable because: 1) Berlin identifies 1941 as the year of the meeting on most occasions (in other words, his letter to Crick is an exception to the rule); and 2) circumstantial evidence weighs in favour of my suggested date, as I shall show below.

25. See 'Chronology 1909–1946', in Berlin, F, pp. 695–701; and Berlin to Gaster, 3 January 1941, F, p. 356.

26. Young-Bruehl, *Hannah Arendt*, p. 164, pp. 171–72.

27. Ibid., p. 164.

28. See Ignatieff, *Isaiah Berlin*, pp. 117–18; and Arie M. Dubnov, *Isaiah Berlin: The Journey of a Jewish Liberal* (New York: Palgrave Macmillan, 2012), pp. 173–77.

29. Anne Deighton, 'Don and Diplomat: Isaiah Berlin and Britain's Early Cold War', *Cold War History* 13:4 (2013), pp. 525–40, at p. 539.

30. Olga Kirschbaum, 'Among Jews and Other European Peoples: Hannah Arendt (1924–1951)' (Ph.D. dissertation, Department of History, New York University, 2013), p. 280.

31. Isaiah Berlin to Chaim Weizmann, 25 February 1942, *F*, p. 396. Hannah Arendt to Waldemar Gurian, 27 March 1942, cited in Kirschbaum, 'Among Jews and Other European Peoples', p. 235.

32. Jochanan Ginat, 'Kurt Blumenfeld und der deutsche Zionismus', in Kurt Blumenfeld, *Im Kampf um den Zionismus: Briefe aus 5 Jahrzehnten* (Stuttgart: Deutsche Verlags-Anstalt, 1976), pp. 7–37.

33. Young-Bruehl, *Hannah Arendt*, p. 71; Hans Jonas, *Memoirs: Hans Jonas*, ed. Christian Wiese, trans. Krishna Winston (Lebanon, NH: Brandeis University Press, 2008), p. 179.

34. Young-Bruehl, *Hannah Arendt*, p. 71; and Hans Jonas, 'Hannah Arendt: An Intimate Portrait', trans. Brian Fox and Richard Wolin, *New England Review* 27:2 (2006), pp. 133–42, at p. 138.

35. One of the founders of the Keren Hayesod, Blumenfeld had been a member of its Board of Directors since 1933. Keren Hayesod-United Israel Appeal, Jerusalem (ed.), *Yehuda Kurt Blumenfeld. In Memoriam* (Jerusalem: The Jerusalem Post Press, 1964), p. 5.

36. See Henry Hardy's comments in Berlin, *F*, p. 93. Keren Hayesod was founded in London in 1920 and moved to Jerusalem in 1926.

37. Schocken and Arendt had known each other through Blumenfeld since the 1930s. See Anthony David, *The Patron: A Life of Salman Schocken, 1877–1959* (New York: Metropolitan Books, 2003), p. 191, pp. 342–60.

38. The essay was 'published in *YOUTH AND NATION*, the periodical of the Hashomer Hatzair'. Kurt Blumenfeld to Isaiah Berlin, 22 January 1945. MSB 112/14.

39. Berlin to Ettinger, 5 November 1993.

40. Jahanbegloo, *CIB*, p. 84.

41. Berlin to Crick 4 November 1963.

42. Hannah Arendt, 'Ceterum Censeo . . .' [26 December 1941], *JW*, pp. 142–44, at p. 143.

43. Ibid., pp. 143–44.

44. Ibid., p. 144; and Hannah Arendt, 'Who Is the "Committee for a Jewish Army"?' [6 March 1942], *JW*, pp. 146–49.

45. Derek J. Penslar, *Jews and the Military: A History* (Princeton: Princeton University Press, 2015), p. 193.

46. Young-Bruehl, *Hannah Arendt*, pp. 175–77; Kirschbaum, 'Among Jews and Other European Peoples', pp. 215–16.

47. Isaiah Berlin to Gershon Agronsky, 29 July 1942. MSB 110/20–27.

48. The guess is based on three pieces of available information: 1) the second meeting between Arendt and Berlin took place circa 1950; 2) Berlin was then staying in Lowell House at Harvard; and 3) he was recovering from the flu. For relevant information, MI Tape 19, p. 29; Isaiah Berlin to Hamish Hamilton, mid- to late December 1948, *E*, pp. 67–68; Isaiah Berlin to Sheila Newsome, 28 December 1948, *E*, p. 68; and Isaiah Berlin to Elena Wilson, 3 June 1949, *E*, p. 93.

49. Arthur M. Schlesinger Jr., *A Life in the Twentieth Century: Innocent Beginnings, 1917–1950* (Boston: Houghton Mifflin, 2000), pp. 281–82 and 295–96; MI Tape 23, p. 24.

50. See 'Chronology' in Berlin, *E*, p. 771.

51. Joshua L. Cherniss, *A Mind and Its Time: The Development of Isaiah Berlin's Political Thought* (Oxford: Oxford University Press, 2013), p. 72. Cherniss cites a letter from Schlesinger to Berlin, 2 October 1949: 'I only wish I had written after last [1948/49] winter rather than before, since I could then have plagiarized you more.'

52. MI Tape 23, p. 24.

53. Schlesinger, *A Life in the Twentieth Century*, p. 282. Schlesinger, who outlived Berlin by nearly a decade, spent the limited time available to him in the final years of his life to help Henry Hardy's editorial work on the publication of Berlin's letters, thereby contributing to the immortalisation of his deceased friend. See Henry Hardy, 'Preface: Drinks before Dinner', in Berlin, *F*, pp. xv–xxxv, at p. xxxi.

54. Oscar Handlin, 'The Study of Man: New Paths in American Jewish History: Afterthoughts on a Conference', *Commentary* 7 (January 1949), pp. 388–94, at p. 388.

55. Arthur M. Schlesinger Jr., *Journals: 1952–2000* (London: The Penguin Press, 2007), 7 April 1977, p. 430.

56. Arthur M. Schlesinger Jr., *The Vital Center: The Politics of Freedom* (Boston: Houghton Mifflin Co., 1949), p. 87; Hannah Arendt, 'The Concentration Camps', *Partisan Review* 15:7 (1948), pp. 743–63.

57. Young-Bruehl, *Hannah Arendt*, pp. 287–88; Richard H. King, *Arendt and America* (Chicago: University of Chicago Press, 2015), p. 99.

58. Schlesinger, *Journals*, p. 430.

59. Jahanbegloo, *CIB*, p. 84.

60. Anita Shapira, *Israel: A History* (London: Weidenfeld & Nicolson, 2014), p. 89.

61. See, e.g., ibid., p. 89; Walter Laqueur, *A History of Zionism* (London: Weidenfeld & Nicolson, 1972), pp. 545–49; and Aaron Berman, *Nazism, the Jews, and American Zionism* (Detroit: Wayne State University Press, 1990), pp 85–92.

62. E.g., Judith Butler, *Parting Ways: Jewishness and the Critique of Zionism* (New York: Columbia University Press, 2012), p. 36, pp. 145–46; Raluca Munteanu Eddon, 'Gershom Scholem, Hannah Arendt and the Paradox of "Non-Nationalist" Nationalism', *The Journal of Jewish Thought and Philosophy* 12:1 (2003), pp. 55–68; Amnon Raz-Krakotzkin, 'Binationalism and Jewish Identity: Hannah Arendt and the Question of Palestine', in Steven E. Aschheim (ed.), *Hannah Arendt in Jerusalem* (Berkeley and Los Angeles: University of California Press, 2001), pp. 165–80; Amnon Raz-Krakotzkin, 'Jewish Peoplehood, "Jewish Politics", and Political Responsibility: Arendt on Zionism and Partitions', *College Literature* 38:1 (2011), pp. 57–74.

63. E.g., Gil Rubin, 'From Federalism to Binationalism: Hannah Arendt's Shifting Zionism', *Contemporary European History* 24:3 (2015), pp. 393–414; William Selinger, 'The Politics of Arendtian Historiography: European Federation and *The Origins of Totalitarianism*', *Modern Intellectual History* 13:2 (2016), pp. 417–46, at pp. 426–27.

64. Norman Podhoretz, *Ex-Friends: Falling Out with Allen Ginsberg, Lionel & Diana Trilling, Lillian Hellman, Hannah Arendt, and Norman Mailer* (New York: The Free Press, 1999), p. 161.

65. Arendt, 'Zionism Reconsidered', *JW*, pp. 343–74.

66. E.g., Butler, *Parting Ways*; Elhanan Yakira, *Post-Zionism, Post-Holocaust: Three Essays on Denial, Forgetting, and the Delegitimation of Israel*, trans. Michael Swirsky (Cambridge: Cambridge University Press, 2010), pp. 220–302; Moshe Zimmerman, 'Hannah Arendt, the Early "Post-Zionist"', in Aschheim (ed.), *Hannah Arendt in Jerusalem*, pp. 181–93.

67. Arendt, 'Zionism Reconsidered', p. 343.

68. Richard J. Bernstein, *Hannah Arendt and the Jewish Question* (Cambridge, MA: The MIT Press, 1996), p. 104.

69. Arendt, *OT1*, p. 295. See also Shmuel Lederman, 'Parting Ways Too Soon: Arendt contra Butler on Zionism', *The European Legacy* 25:3 (2020), pp. 248–65, esp. pp. 253–54.

70. Berlin to Brown, 6 May 1991, emphasis added.

71. See Hardy's note in Isaiah Berlin, *L*, p. 92 note 2, updated online at IBVL, http://berlin .wolf.ox.ac.uk/published_works/l/corrections.html, accessed 30 September 2020

72. Forster's famous words are worth recalling here: 'I hate the idea of causes, and if I had to choose between betraying my country and betraying my friend, I hope I should have the guts to betray my country.' E. M. Forster, *Two Cheers for Democracy* (London: Edward Arnold & Co., 1951), p. 78.

73. Edward Said contends that Berlin ceased to be a liberal and was in fact 'fanatical' when it came to Israel and Zionism. He writes, '[W]here Israel was concerned [. . . Berlin] acted with the kind of unblinking zeal that fanatics of either the Right or the Left might have felt, but which in all his work on other subjects Berlin deplored. In that sense he was an organic intellectual for Israel.' Edward Said, *The End of the Peace Process: Oslo and After* (London: Granta, 2000), p. 221. See also Tariq Ali, *Conversations with Edward Said* (London: Seagull Books, 2006), p. 72. I hope to show in this study that Said's critical remarks fail to do justice to the complexity of the matter.

74. Ignatieff, *Isaiah Berlin*, p. 30.

75. MI Tape 2, pp. 6–7. See also Ignatieff, *Isaiah Berlin*, p. 27.

76. Jahanbegloo, *CIB*, p. 85.

77. Young-Bruehl, *Hannah Arendt*, pp. 121–22.

78. Winham suggests Arendt and Berlin probably met in Milan in September 1955 on the occasion of the international conference on 'The Future of Freedom' organised by the Congress for Cultural Freedom: Ilya Winham, 'After Totalitarianism: Hannah Arendt, Isaiah Berlin, and the Realization and Defeat of the Western Tradition' (Ph.D. dissertation, University of Minnesota, 2015), pp. 5–6. This is a reasonable guess but is untrue. Berlin was indeed in Italy between 12 and 17 September when the CCF conference took place; but he stayed in Santa Caterina Amalfi between 12 and 16 September, and then left for Milan to celebrate Rosh Hashanah, which fell on 17–18 September. Berlin explicitly said in a letter that he would not attend 'the exciting one [i.e., CCF conference] in Milan' (Isaiah Berlin to Morton White, 2 May 1955, MSB 289/60– 61. This part of the letter is unfortunately omitted from the published version in *E*, pp. 485–88). See, further, Berlin's postcards to Marie Berlin dated 12, 14 and 15 September 1955 (MSB 298/82, 85, 86), and his telegrams to her, dated 12, 14 and 18 September 1955 (MSB 298/81, 84, 87).

79. Berlin, *E*, p. 676 note 4.

80. Isaiah Berlin to Faber & Faber, '[Report on] *The Human Condition* by Hannah Arendt', no date [1958], reproduced in the Appendix of this book.

81. Bhikhu Parekh, 'Hannah Arendt's Critique of Marx', in Melvyn Hill (ed.), *Hannah Arendt: The Recovery of the Public World* (New York: St. Martin's Press, 1979), pp. 67–100; and Hanna Fenichel Pitkin, *The Attack of the Blob: Hannah Arendt's Concept of 'the Social'* (Chicago: University of Chicago Press, 1998). Parekh's critique concerns Arendt's distinction between work, action and labour. Pitkin's concerns Arendt's distinction between the social and the political.

82. Berlin to Faber & Faber, '[Report on] *The Human Condition* by Hannah Arendt'.

83. Ignatieff, *Isaiah Berlin*, p. 33. See Mendel Berlin, 'For the Benefit of My Son', p. 307.

84. Bernard Crick, 'Hannah Arendt and the Burden of Our Times', *The Political Quarterly* 68:1 (1997), pp. 77–84, at p. 78.

85. Seyla Benhabib, *The Reluctant Modernism of Hannah Arendt*, new ed. (Lanham, MD: Rowman & Littlefield, 2003), p. li, note 6.

86. Berlin, *E*, p. 676 note 4.

87. Jahanbegloo, *CIB*, pp. 81–85.

88. Benhabib, *Reluctant Modernism*, p. li note 6.

89. Berlin to Brown, 6 May 1991.

90. Benhabib, *Reluctant Modernism*, p. li note 6.

91. Isaiah Berlin to Meyer Schapiro, 28 January 1959, T.

92. E.g., Isaiah Berlin to Edmund Wilson, 26 January 1959, T; Berlin to Schapiro, 28 January 1959; Isaiah Berlin to Morton White, 6 February 1959, *E*, p. 676.

93. Berlin to Faber & Faber, '[Report on] *The Human Condition* by Hannah Arendt'; Berlin to White, 6 February 1959, *E*, p. 676; Berlin to Brown, 6 May 1991; Berlin to Ettinger, 19 December 1992. See also Jahanbegloo, *CIB*, pp. 82–83.

94. Berlin to Crick, 4 November 1963.

95. E.g., Dana R. Villa, 'Hannah Arendt: From Philosophy to Politics', in Catherine H. Zuckert (ed.), *Political Philosophy in the Twentieth Century: Authors and Arguments* (Cambridge: Cambridge University Press, 2011), pp. 108–25, at p. 119 note 21.

96. Isaiah Berlin to Anna Kallin, 27 July 1951, *E*, p. 234.

97. Jahanbegloo, *CIB*, p. 49; Isaiah Berlin to Bhikhu Parekh, 14 January 1983, MSB 218/10–11.

98. Berlin to White, 6 February 1959, *E*, p. 674.

99. Isaiah Berlin to Galen Strawson, 9 April 1982, *A*, p. 186; Berlin to Chiara Merlo, 9 April 1991, *A*, p. 411.

100. Isaiah Berlin to Morton White, 11 January 1955, T.

101. Isaiah Berlin to Hamilton Fish Armstrong, 1 February 1950, *E*, p. 168.

102. Edmund Husserl, *Logical Investigations*, 2 vols, ed. Dermot Moran, trans. J. N. Findlay (London: Routledge, 2001).

103. Loidolt, *Phenomenology of Plurality*, p. 7.

104. Ibid., p. 78.

105. Dermot Moran, *Introduction to Phenomenology* (London: Routledge, 2000), p. 83.

106. Hannah Arendt, 'What Is Existential Philosophy?', *EU*, pp. 163–93, at p. 166.

107. These lectures are now available in English as Martin Heidegger, *Plato's Sophist*, trans. Richard Rojcewicz and André Schuwer (Bloomington: Indiana University Press, 1997); *History of the Concept of Time: Prolegomena*, trans. Theodore Kisiel (Bloomington: Indiana University Press, 1985); and *Logic: The Question of Truth*, trans. Thomas Sheehan (Bloomington: Indiana University Press, 2010).

108. Theodore Kisiel, 'Rhetoric, Politics, Romance: Arendt and Heidegger 1924–26', in James E. Swearingen and Joanne Cutting-Gray (eds), *Extreme Beauty: Aesthetics, Politics, Death* (London: Continuum, 2000), pp. 94–109, at p. 98; Loidolt, *Phenomenology of Plurality*, pp. 171–72, p. 191 note 18. The most famous of those lectures, which Hans-Georg Gadamer, Hans Jonas, Leo Strauss and Karl Löwith, among others, attended, are now published as Martin Heidegger,

Basic Concepts of Aristotelian Philosophy, trans. Robert D. Metcalf and Mark B. Tanzer (Bloomington: Indiana University Press, 2009).

109. Arendt, '"What Remains? The Language Remains"', p. 2.

110. Hannah Arendt to Martin Heidegger, 28 October 1960, in Hannah Arendt and Martin Heidegger, *Letters 1925–1975*, ed. Ursula Ludz, trans. Andrew Shields (Orlando: Harcourt, Inc., 2004), p. 124.

111. Reprinted as 'Heidegger at Eighty' in Arendt, *TWB*, pp. 419–31.

112. Ibid., pp. 420–21.

113. Ibid., p. 420.

114. Ibid., p. 421.

115. See, e.g., the exchange between Wolin and Villa: Richard Wolin, 'Hannah and the Magician', *The New Republic* (15 October 1995), pp. 27–37; and Dana R. Villa, 'Apologist or Critic? On Arendt's Relation to Heidegger', in Aschheim, *Hannah Arendt in Jerusalem*, pp. 325–37.

116. The first part of Arendt's essay, her recollections of Heidegger as a teacher, is often cited in Heidegger scholarship to show the young philosopher's electrifying presence and his enormous influence over his students. See, e.g., John van Buren, *The Young Heidegger: Rumor of the Hidden King* (Bloomington and Indianapolis: Indiana University Press, 1994), p. 3; Theodore Kisiel, *The Genesis of Heidegger's Being and Time* (Berkeley and Los Angeles: University of California Press, 1993), pp. 15–16; and Richard Polt, *Heidegger: An Introduction* (Ithaca, NY: Cornell University Press, 1999), p. 20.

117. Arendt, 'Heidegger at Eighty', p. 423.

118. Ibid., p. 423, first emphasis is mine. See also Arendt, 'What Is Existential Philosophy?', p. 182.

119. On Ayer's own account, Berlin told him, circa 1933, 'Well look, Freddie, why don't you write a book before you lose your enthusiasm?' To this Ayer replied, 'I shan't lose my enthusiasm, but it's quite a good idea to write a book.' He thus began writing *Language, Truth and Logic*: Ted Honderich, 'An Interview with A. J. Ayer', in A. Phillips Griffith (ed.), *A. J. Ayer: Memorial Essays: Royal Institute of Philosophy Supplement 30* (Cambridge: Cambridge University Press, 1991), pp. 209–26, at p. 209.

120. A. J. Ayer, *Part of My Life* (London: Collins, 1977), pp. 130–34.

121. A. J. Ayer, *Language, Truth and Logic* (London: Victor Gollancz Ltd, 1938), p. 17.

122. Bradley's sentence is as follows: 'the Absolute enters into, but is itself incapable of, evolution and progress.' As those words are unlikely to be 'intended to express either a tautology or a proposition which was capable, at least in principle, of being verified', Ayer concludes, 'it follows that [Bradley] has made an utterance which has no literal significance even for himself.' Ayer, *Language, Truth and Logic*, p. 21 note 2.

123. See, most importantly, Isaiah Berlin, 'Verification', *Proceedings of the Aristotelian Society* 39 (1938–39), pp. 225–48, reprinted in *CC2*, pp. 15–40.

124. See Dubnov, *Isaiah Berlin*, pp. 53–76; and Cherniss, *A Mind and Its Time*, pp. 1–14.

125. Isaiah Berlin, 'Austin and the Early Beginnings of Oxford Philosophy', *PI3*, pp. 156–76, at p. 175.

126. Iris Murdoch, *The Sovereignty of the Good* (London: Routledge & Kegan Paul, 1970), p. 1.

127. A. J. Ayer to Isaiah Berlin, 2 February 1933, cited in Ben Rogers, *A. J. Ayer: A Life* (New York: Grove Press, 1999), p. 94.

128. Berlin to Merlo, 9 April 1991, *A*, p. 411.

129. Berlin to Ettinger, 5 November 1993.

130. Martin Jay, 'Walter Benjamin and Isaiah Berlin: Modes of Jewish Intellectual Life in the Twentieth Century', *Critical Inquiry* 43:3 (2017), pp. 719–37, at p. 731.

131. Arendt, *LMT*, p. 45.

132. Ibid.

133. Hannah Arendt, items 023805 and 023806 (materials related to her lectures on 'Introduction into Politics' at the University of Chicago in 1963), in 'Subject File, 1949–1975, n.d.', HAP.

134. See esp. Arendt, 'What Is Existential Philosophy?', 'Heidegger at Eighty', and Hannah Arendt, 'French Existentialism', *EU*, pp. 188–93.

135. Isaiah Berlin, 'The Trends of Culture', contribution to 'The Year 1949 in Historical Perspective', in *1950 Britannica Book of the Year* (Chicago/Toronto/London, 1950: Encyclopaedia Britannica, Inc.), pp. xxii–xxvii, reprinted as 'Three Years: Culture and Politics in the Mid Twentieth Century', IBVL, http://berlin.wolf.ox.ac.uk/published_works/singles/bib292.pdf, pp. 1–16, at p. 9, accessed 30 September 2020.

136. Frances Kiernan, *Seeing Mary Plain: A Life of Mary McCarthy* (New York: W. W. Norton & Co., 2000), p. 354.

137. Friedrich Nietzsche, *Twilight of the Idols, or, How to Philosophize with a Hammer*, trans. Duncan Large (Oxford: Oxford University Press, 1998), p. 43, p. 6.

138. Arendt cited in Podhoretz, *Ex-Friends*, p. 172.

139. She managed to name two Americans: William James and Charles Sanders Peirce (the latter with a 'maybe'): Larry May, 'Hannah Arendt: A Remembrance', *Arendt Studies* 1 (2017), pp. 13–22, at p. 15. See also an April 1970 entry of Arendt's *Denktagebuch*, in which she discusses 'the difficulties I have with my English readers' and writes about 'English "philosophy"' (note the quotation marks): Arendt, *DZ*, XXVII: 45, pp. 770–74.

140. Arendt, *OT3*, p. 139.

141. The literature on the divide is immense. See, e.g., Michael Friedman, *A Parting of the Ways: Carnap, Cassirer, and Heidegger* (Chicago and La Salle: Open Court, 2000); Peter E. Gordon, *Continental Divide: Heidegger, Cassirer, Davos* (Cambridge, MA: Harvard University Press, 2010); and Dermot Moran, 'Analytic Philosophy and Continental Philosophy: Four Confrontations', in Leonard Lawlor (ed.), *Phenomenology: Responses and Developments* (London: Routledge, 2014), pp. 235–66. For the implications of the analytic–Continental divide for political theory specifically, see, e.g., Clayton Chin and Lasse Thomassen (eds), 'Analytic and Continental Political Theory: An Unbridgeable Divide?', special issue of *European Journal of Political Theory* 15:2 (2016); and Jeremy Arnold, *Across the Great Divide: Between Analytical and Continental Political Theory* (Stanford: Stanford University Press, 2020).

142. The original remark goes as follows: 'I am not one of the "intellectuals who come from the German left". [. . .] If I can be said to "have come from anywhere", it is from the tradition of German philosophy.' Scholem and Arendt, 'Exchange', p. 53.

143. Bernard Williams, *Ethics and the Limits of Philosophy* (London: Fontana Press, 1985).

144. David Cesarani, *Eichmann: His Life and Crimes* (London: Vintage Books, 2005), pp. 25–34.

145. Doron Rabinovici, *Eichmann's Jews: The Jewish Administration of Holocaust Vienna, 1938–1945*, trans. Nick Somers (Cambridge: Polity, 2011), p. 63; Cesarani, *Eichmann*, pp. 67–71.

146. For Eichmann's attempt to downplay his share of responsibility during the interrogation and trial in Israel, see Bettina Stangneth, *Eichmann before Jerusalem: The Unexamined Life of a Mass Murderer* (London: The Bodley Head, 2014).

147. Testimony of Dieter Wisliceny, 3 January 1946, The International Military Tribunal for Germany, Nuremberg Trial Proceedings (Blue Set), Volume 4: Twenty-First Day to the Twenty-Ninth Day, http://avalon.law.yale.edu/imt/01-03-46.asp, accessed 5 June 2020.

148. See Uki Goñi, *The Real Odessa: How Perón Brought the Nazi War Criminals to Argentina* (London: Granta, 2003).

149. For Eichmann's Argentine years, see Stangneth, *Eichmann before Jerusalem*, pp. 103–360.

150. As early as October 1952, the German chancellor himself said as much in the Bundestag: 'In my opinion, we should call a halt to trying to sniff out Nazis.' Konrad Adenauer, cited in Stangneth, *Eichmann before Jerusalem*, p. 146.

151. Deborah E. Lipstadt, *The Eichmann Trial* (New York: Schocken, 2011), p. 7; Stangneth, *Eichmann before Jerusalem*, pp. 116–20, p. 139, p. 143, pp. 155–56, pp. 326–29, p. 351.

152. Cesarani, *Eichmann*, p. 14; Lipstadt, *The Eichmann Trial*, pp. 13–14.

153. The dramatic operation understandably became a subject of numerous books, articles and films of various kinds and differing qualities.

154. CBS, cited in Lipstadt, *The Eichmann Trial*, p. 24.

155. See the correspondence between Hannah Arendt and Karl Jaspers, *C*, pp. 410–34.

156. Isaiah Berlin to Teddy Kollek, 27 July 1960, *B*, p. 3.

157. Isaiah Berlin to Sam Behrman 28 May 1962, *B*, p. 93.

158. Isaiah Berlin to Aline Berlin, 27 March 1962, *T*. See also Berlin to Behrman, 28 May 1962.

159. Isaiah Berlin to Isaac [Stern?], 1 May 1962, MSB 383/18.

160. Isaiah Berlin to Rowland Burdon-Muller, 16 September 1960, MSB 269/155–62.

161. Berlin to [Stern?], 1 May 1962.

162. Lipstadt, *The Eichmann Trial*, pp. 24–31.

163. Raanan Rein, *Argentina, Israel, and the Jews: Perón, the Eichmann Capture and After*, trans. M. Grenzeback (Bethesda: University Press of Maryland, 2003), p. 217.

164. Hanna Yablonka, *The State of Israel vs. Adolf Eichmann* (New York: Schocken Books, 2004), p. 44.

165. Young-Bruehl, *Hannah Arendt*, p. 155, pp. 162–63.

166. See Jahanbegloo, *CIB*, pp. 19–23; and the exchange between Isaiah Berlin and Gershom Schocken, 5 and 6 November 1972, MSB 513/242, 252.

167. Hannah Arendt, 'Die wahren gründe für Theresienstadt', *Aufbau* 9:36 (3 September 1943), reprinted in English translation as 'The Real Reasons for Theresienstadt', in *JW*, pp. 191–92.

168. Arendt, *OT1*, p. 385 (*OT3*, p. 402).

169. For an overview of Arendt's relationship to the *New Yorker* editors, see Duncan Kelly, 'The *New Yorker* State of Hannah Arendt's Mind', in Fiona Green (ed.), *Writing for The New Yorker: Critical Essays on an American Periodical* (Edinburgh: Edinburgh University Press, 2015), pp. 209–27.

170. Hannah Arendt to Karl Jaspers, 2 December 1960, *C*, p. 409.

171. Hannah Arendt to Vassar College, 2 January 1961, cited in Young-Bruehl, *Hannah Arendt*, p. 329.

172. Hannah Arendt to Karl Jaspers, 23 December 1960, *C*, p. 417; Young-Bruehl, *Hannah Arendt*, 336.

173. Cesarani, *Eichmann*, p. 4.

174. Arendt, *EIJ2*, p. 117.

175. Anita Shapira, *Ben-Gurion: Father of Modern Israel* (New Haven: Yale University Press, 2014), p. 132.

176. Léon Poliakov, *Bréviaire de la haine. Le IIIᵉ Reich et les Juifs* (Paris: Calmann-Lévy, 1951), published in English as *Harvest of Hate: The Nazi Program for the Destruction of the Jews of Europe* (Syracuse, NY: Syracuse University Press, 1954); Raul Hilberg, *The Destruction of the European Jews* (Chicago: Quadrangle Books, 1961).

177. Arendt, 'The History of the Great Crime', *JW*, pp. 45–61.

178. Arendt, *EIJ2*, p. 125.

179. Yehuda Bauer, *Jews for Sale: Nazi–Jewish Negotiations, 1933–1945* (New Haven: Yale University Press, 1994); Bernard Wasserstein, *The Ambiguity of Virtue: Gertrude van Tijn and the Fate of the Dutch Jews* (Cambridge, MA: Harvard University Press, 2014).

180. Jacob Robinson, *And the Crooked Shall Be Made Straight: The Eichmann Trial, the Jewish Catastrophe and Hannah Arendt's Narrative* (New York: Macmillan, 1965).

181. Aron Zeitlin, cited in Richard I. Cohen, 'A Generation's Response to *Eichmann in Jerusalem*', in Aschheim (ed.), *Hannah Arendt in Jerusalem*, pp. 253–77, at p. 258; Leo Mindlin, 'During the week . . . as I see it', *The Jewish Floridian* (15 March 1963), p. A-10.

182. Luke Russell, *Evil: A Philosophical Investigation* (Oxford: Oxford University Press, 2014), p. 72.

183. E.g., Mark Lilla, 'Arendt and Eichmann: The New Truth', 'The Defense of a Jewish Collaborator' and 'Arendt and Eichmann' [Reply to Roger Berkowitz], in *The New York Review of Books*, 21 November, 5 December and 19 December 2013; John Gray, 'Blood on Their Hands', *Literary Review* 409 (May 2013).

184. Arendt, *EIJ2*, p. 252.

185. Arguably the clearest and most succinct statement of the meaning of the 'banality of evil' by Arendt is found in her 'Thinking and Moral Considerations', *RJ*, pp. 159–89, at pp. 159–60.

186. Hannah Arendt, 'The Eichmann Case and the Germans: A Conversation with Thilo Koch', *JW*, pp. 485–89, at p. 487, emphasis added.

187. For further discussion, see Young-Bruehl, *Hannah Arendt*, pp. 347–62; Richard I. Cohen, 'Breaking the Code: Hannah Arendt's *Eichmann in Jerusalem* and the Public Polemic: Myth, Memory and Historical Imagination', *Michael: On the History of the Jews in the Diaspora* 13 (1993), pp. 29–85; and Daniel Maier-Katkin, 'The Reception of Hannah Arendt's *Eichmann in Jerusalem* in the United States 1963–2011', *Zeitschrift für politisches Denken* 6:1/2 (2011), http://www .hannaharendt.net/index.php/han/article/view/64/84, accessed 5 June 2020.

188. Irving Spiegel, 'Hausner Criticizes Book on Eichmann', *The New York Times*, 20 May 1963, p. 12.

189. Hannah Arendt to Mary McCarthy, 20 September 1963, *BF*, p. 147.

190. Daniel Bell, 'The Alphabet of Justice: Reflections on *Eichmann in Jerusalem*', *Partisan Review* 30:3 (1963), pp. 412–29; Hans J. Morgenthau, 'Review of *Eichmann in Jerusalem*', *Chicago Tribune*, 26 May 1963; Mary McCarthy, 'The Hue and the Cry', *Partisan Review* 31 (1964),

pp. 82–94; and Dwight Macdonald, 'Arguments: More on Eichmann', *Partisan Review* 31 (1964), pp. 275–78.

191. Young-Bruehl, *Hannah Arendt*, p. 360.

192. Hannah Arendt, '"The Formidable Dr. Robinson": A Reply', *The New York Review of Books*, 20 January 1966, reprinted in *JW*, pp. 496–511.

193. King, *Arendt and America*, p. 217.

194. Isaiah Berlin to William Phillips, 7 May 1963, from the *Partisan Review* collection, Howard Gotlieb Archival Research Center at Boston University Libraries. The *Partisan Review* eventually published a scathing review by Lionel Abel. Like Berlin, Abel had held a low opinion of Arendt's work and in fact published a highly critical review of *Between Past and Future* prior to the publication of *Eichmann*. Yet, unlike Berlin, he did not decline the invitation to review *Eichmann* for the *Partisan Review*, which, according to Abel's retrospective explanation, 'must have been *expecting* a piece that would be very critical of Arendt'. Lionel Abel, *The Intellectual Follies: A Memoir of the Literary Venture in New York and Paris* (New York: W. W. Norton & Co., 1984), pp. 274–75. See Lionel Abel, 'Pseudo-Profundity', *New Politics* (Fall 1961), pp. 124–31; and Lionel Abel, 'The Aesthetics of Evil', *Partisan Review* 30:2 (1963), pp. 210–30.

195. Isaiah Berlin to Mary McCarthy, 7 August 1964. McCarthy 182.17, Archives and Special Collections, Vassar College Library. The part of the letter cited here is omitted in the published version in B, pp. 195–97.

196. This was suggested as highly likely by David Caute, *Isaac and Isaiah: The Covert Punishment of a Cold War Heretic* (New Haven: Yale University Press, 2013), pp. 268–69. Dubnov confirmed Caute's hypothesis with archival evidence in Arie M. Dubnov, 'Can Parallels Meet? Hannah Arendt and Isaiah Berlin on the Jewish Post-Emancipatory Quest for Political Freedom', *The Leo Baeck Institute Year Book* 62 (2017), pp. 27–51, at p. 28. See the entry dated 3 August 1963, 'Diaries of Gershom Scholem from different dates', The National Library of Israel, ARC. 4* 02 265.27.

197. Lotte Houwink ten Cate, '"Die Amerikanerin Scolds!": How the Private Friendship between Hannah Arendt and Gershom Scholem Went Public', *New German Critique* 46:1 (2019), pp. 1–14, at p. 12.

198. See the series of exchanges in Scholem and Arendt, *CSA*, pp. 205–19. See also Hannah Arendt to Karl Jaspers, 20 October 1963, *C*, p. 523.

199. John Mander to Hannah Arendt, 5 September 1963, cited in Cate, '"Die Amerikanerin Scolds!"', pp. 8–9.

200. Hannah Arendt to John Mander, undated [early September 1956], reprinted in Scholem and Arendt, *CSA*, pp. 217–18.

201. Arendt to Jaspers, 20 October 1963, *C*, p. 523.

202. Hannah Arendt to Karl and Gertrud Jaspers, 24 November 1963, *C*, p. 535.

203. Isaiah Berlin to Stephen Spender, 2 July 1963, T.

204. Maier-Katkin, 'The Reception of Hannah Arendt's *Eichmann in Jerusalem*', p. 2.

205. Isaiah Berlin to Sam Behrman, 27 August 1963, T.

206. Anonymous author [John Sparrow], 'Judges in Israel: The Case of Adolf Eichmann', *The Times Literary Supplement*, 30 April 1964, pp. 365–68; Caute, *Isaac and Isaiah*, p. 270. Incidentally, McCarthy called Sparrow's review 'a particularly nasty job and done by someone who was authentically stupid'. Mary McCarthy to Hannah Arendt, 9 June 1964, *BF*, p. 166.

207. Scholem and Arendt, 'Exchange', p. 51.

208. Isaiah Berlin to I. F. Stone, 13 February 1975, *B*, p. 592. See also Jahanbegloo, *CIB*, pp. 84–85; Isaiah Berlin to Geza Vermes, 13 May 1982, T; Berlin to May, 1 October 1986, *A*, pp. 299–300; and Berlin to Ettinger, 5 November 1993.

209. Gershom Scholem to Hannah Arendt, 28 January 1946, *CSA*, p. 42. See also Arendt to Scholem, 21 April 1946, *CSA*, pp. 47–50; and Scholem to Arendt, 6 November 1946, *CSA*, pp. 60–61.

210. See Steven E. Aschheim's excellent essay, 'Between New York and Jerusalem', *Jewish Review of Books* 4 (Winter 2011), pp. 5–8; and Amir Engel, *Gershom Scholem: An Intellectual Biography* (Chicago: University of Chicago Press, 2017), pp. 168–98.

211. Arendt wrote to Scholem that 'in your attacks on me, and after everything you wrote, you didn't accuse me of self-hatred' (Arendt to Scholem, 18 August 1963, *CSA*, p. 215).

212. E.g., Isaiah Berlin to Meyer Schapiro, 20 July 1967, *B*, p. 337; Berlin to Behrman, 19 July 1963, T.

213. Berlin to Behrman, 19 July 1963.

214. E.g., Berlin to Schapiro, 20 July 1967, *B*, p. 338; Isaiah Berlin to Robert Silvers, 19 March 1970, MSB 279/104–7.

215. Jonathan Haslam, *The Vices of Integrity: E. H. Carr, 1892–1982* (London: Verso, 1999), p. 247.

216. Young-Bruehl, *Hannah Arendt*, p. 410; Hannah Arendt to Karl Jaspers, 13 April 1967, *C*, p. 671.

217. Richard Pipes, *Struve: Liberal on the Left, 1870–1905* (Cambridge, MA: Harvard University Press, 1970).

218. Berlin and Pipes also met for dinner at All Souls on 14 June 1966. See Isaiah Berlin to Richard Pipes, 29 April 1966, T; and Berlin to Hugh Trevor Roper, 1 June 1966, T.

219. Isaiah Berlin to Richard Pipes, 20 April 1966, T.

220. Social Science Research Council, *Annual Report, 1967–1968* (New York: SSRC, 1968), p. 86.

221. Richard Pipes (ed.), *Revolutionary Russia* (Cambridge, MA: Harvard University Press, 1968).

222. Ibid., pp. 24–25.

223. Arendt, *OR3*, pp. 55–56, pp. 241–42, pp. 248–50, p. 257.

224. Pipes, *Revolutionary Russia*, p. 62.

225. To my knowledge, Winham is the only scholar who has analysed the interaction between Arendt and Berlin at the 1967 Harvard conference. See Winham, 'After Totalitarianism', p. 6.

226. Berlin to Ettinger, 19 December 1992.

227. Winham, 'After Totalitarianism', p. 6.

228. Isaiah Berlin to Martin Peretz, 22 November 1974, MSB 208/202.

229. Arendt to Jaspers, 13 April 1967, *C*, p. 671.

230. Arendt, 'Comment by Hannah Arendt on—"The Uses of Revolution" by Adam Ulam', in Pipes, *Revolutionary Russia*, pp. 344–51, at p. 344.

231. Schlesinger, *Journals*, p. 430.

232. Isaiah Berlin to Ursula Niebuhr, 27 April 1972, T.

233. Berlin to Peretz, 22 November 1974.

234. Zbigniew Pełczyński and John Gray, *Conceptions of Liberty in Political Philosophy* (London: The Athlone Press, 1984).

235. Isaiah Berlin to Zbyszek Pełczyński, 20 September 1983, T.

236. Jahanbegloo, *CIB*, p. 84.

237. Berlin to Brown, 6 May 1991.

238. Samir al-Khalil [pseudonym for Kanan Makiya], *Republic of Fear: Saddam's Iraq* (London: Hutchinson Radius, 1989). Arendt is mentioned in Chapter 4 and the Conclusion; Berlin in Chapter 7.

239. Berlin to Brown, 6 May 1991, emphasis added.

240. Isaiah Berlin to Pierre Vidal-Naquet, 17 February 1975, MSB 209/278.

241. See Celso Lafer's pioneering piece, 'Isaiah Berlin and Hannah Arendt', *Hannah Arendt Newsletter*, No 1 (April 1999), pp. 19–24.

Chapter 3. Freedom

1. Hannah Arendt, 'Freiheit und Politik. Ein Vortrag', *Die Neue Rundschau* 69:4 (1958), pp. 670–94. An English version of this piece appeared as 'Freedom and Politics: A Lecture', *Chicago Review* 14:1 (1960), pp. 28–46, now reprinted with small changes as 'Freedom and Politics, a Lecture', in *TWB*, pp. 220–44.

2. Hannah Arendt, 'What Is Freedom?', *BPF3*, pp. 142–69.

3. Ibid., p. 145.

4. Ibid., p. 149.

5. The first drafts were dictated on 29–30 August 1958. See Berlin, *E*, p. 783.

6. Martin Hollis, 'Preface', in Ian Forbes and Steve Smith (eds), *Politics and Human Nature* (London: Bloomsbury Academic, 2006 [1983]), pp. ix–x, at p. ix.

7. David Hackett Fischer, *Liberty and Freedom: A Visual History of America's Founding Ideas* (New York: Oxford University Press, 2005), p. 12.

8. David G. Ritchie, *Natural Rights: A Criticism of Some Political and Ethical Conceptions* (London: George Allen & Unwin Ltd, 1894), p. 135.

9. Hanna Fenichel Pitkin, 'Are Freedom and Liberty Twins?', *Political Theory* 16:4 (1988), pp. 523–52.

10. Arendt, *OR3*, pp. 19–20.

11. Kei Hiruta, 'Hannah Arendt, Liberalism, and Freedom from Politics', in Kei Hiruta (ed.), *Arendt on Freedom, Liberation, and Revolution* (Cham: Palgrave Macmillan, 2019), pp. 17–45, at p. 19. See also Pitkin, 'Are Freedom and Liberty Twins?', pp. 526–28.

12. Arendt, *OR3*, p. 267, emphasis added.

13. Hannah Arendt, '"The Freedom to Be Free": The Conditions and Meaning of Revolution', *TWB*, pp. 368–86, at p. 373, emphasis added. Similarly, 'to liberate' and 'to free' are used interchangeably in the same text, pp. 378–79.

14. John Rawls, *A Theory of Justice* (Cambridge, MA: Harvard University Press, 1971), p. 5; H.L.A. Hart, *The Concept of the Law* (Oxford: Clarendon Press, 1961), pp. 155–59.

15. Eric Margolis and Stephen Laurence, 'Concepts', *The Stanford Encyclopedia of Philosophy* (Summer 2019 edition), ed. Edward N. Zalta, https://plato.stanford.edu/archives/sum2019/entries/concepts/, accessed 15 January 2020.

16. I reject the cliché that 'theory' necessarily implies system building of an inflexible kind.

17. Joshua L. Cherniss, *A Mind and Its Time: The Development of Isaiah Berlin's Political Thought* (Oxford: Oxford University Press, 2013).

18. Isaiah Berlin, 'The Truro Prize Essay (1928)', reprinted in *F*, pp. 631–37.

19. Berlin, *KM1*, p. 135.

20. This body of work will be discussed in the next chapter.

21. Of particular relevance are Berlin's Mary Flexner Lectures on 'Political Ideas in the Romantic Age', delivered at Bryn Mawr College, Pennsylvania, in February and March 1952; and his BBC radio lectures on 'Freedom and Its Betrayal', broadcast in October and November 1952. The two lecture series, together with relevant materials, are now published as *PIRA2* and *FIB2*, respectively.

22. See the classic essay by A. Arblaster, 'Vision and Revision: A Note on the Text of Isaiah Berlin's *Four Essays on Liberty*', *Political Studies* 19:1 (1971), pp. 81–86.

23. Berlin himself is reported to have gone so far as to say that 'everything else' written by him 'is a footnote' to 'Two Concepts' (Berlin and Polanowska-Sygulska, *UD*, p. 119).

24. Isaiah Berlin, 'Two Concepts of Liberty', *L*, pp. 166–217, at p. 178, emphasis added.

25. Mario Ricciardi, 'Berlin on Liberty', in George Crowder and Henry Hardy (eds), *The One and the Many: Reading Isaiah Berlin* (New York: Prometheus Books, 2007), pp. 119–39, at p. 137.

26. Isaiah Berlin, 'Introduction', *L*, pp. 3–54, at p. 31.

27. Berlin, 'Two Concepts', p. 186.

28. Berlin, 'Introduction', p. 32.

29. Ibid.

30. Berlin, 'Two Concepts', pp. 169–70.

31. Berlin, 'Introduction', p. 45.

32. C. B. Macpherson, *Democratic Theory: Essays in Retrieval* (Oxford: Clarendon Press, 1973), p. 102.

33. Berlin, 'Two Concepts', p. 172.

34. Berlin, 'Introduction', p. 38.

35. E.g., Berlin and Polanowska-Sygulska, *UD*, passim; Jahanbegloo, *CIB*, pp. 40–42; Berlin and Lukes, 'Conversation', pp. 92–93.

36. E.g., George Crowder, *Isaiah Berlin: Liberty and Pluralism* (Cambridge: Polity Press, 2004), pp. 79–83; Beata Polanowska-Sygulska, 'Two Visions of Liberty: Berlin and Hayek', in *UD*, pp. 241–52.

37. See, most recently, Brian Caterino and Phillip Hansen, *Critical Theory, Democracy, and the Challenge of Neoliberalism* (Toronto: University of Toronto Press, 2019).

38. Berlin and Polanowska-Sygulska, *UD*, p. 154.

39. See, in particular, Berlin, 'Two Concepts', p. 177 note 1. Berlin's ambiguity on the numerical and qualitative aspects of negative liberty has given rise to a small academic industry. See, e.g., Ian Carter, *A Measure of Freedom* (Oxford: Oxford University Press, 1999); and Matthew H. Kramer, *The Quality of Freedom* (Oxford: Oxford University Press, 2003).

40. Berlin's critics here include Charles Taylor, 'What's Wrong with Negative Liberty', in his *Philosophy and Human Sciences: Philosophical Papers 2* (Cambridge: Cambridge University Press, 1985), pp. 211–29; and Nancy J. Hirschmann, 'Berlin, Feminism, and Positive Liberty', in Bruce Baum and Robert Nichols (eds), *Isaiah Berlin and the Politics of Freedom: 'Two Concepts of Liberty' 50 Years Later* (New York: Routledge, 2012), pp. 185–98.

41. Isaiah Berlin to Bernard Crick, 29 March 1966, *B*, p. 272.

42. Cherniss downplays this oscillation by calling it 'Berlin's [...] *occasional* practice' (*A Mind and Its Time*, p. 193, emphasis added). This is one of the interpretive moves Cherniss makes to present a neatly reconstructed Berlinian theory of liberty, in which non-interference and the ability to choose are categorically distinguished from each other. While his interpretive ingenuity is impressive, Cherniss makes Berlin's work look considerably more coherent than it in fact is. My reading of Berlin may be less charitable, but it is intended to be truer to his own words, including ambiguous and confusing ones.

43. Isaiah Berlin, 'From Hopes and Fear Set Free', *L*, pp. 252–79, at p. 271, emphasis added.

44. Berlin, 'Introduction', p. 39.

45. Berlin remained profoundly ambivalent towards positive liberty. In 'Two Concepts', he appears to have defended negative liberty against its positive rival. In some of his later interviews, he claimed that his intention had been different. But in a 1986 interview, he used the expressions 'liberty in my sense' and 'the negative sense' interchangeably (Berlin and Polanowska-Sygulska, *UD*, p. 42). I do not think his ambivalence was ever resolved.

46. Berlin, 'Two Concepts', p. 187.

47. Ibid., p. 194.

48. Ricciardi, 'Berlin on Liberty', p. 136.

49. Isaiah Berlin, 'Rousseau', *FIB2*, pp. 28–52, at p. 51.

50. Isaiah Berlin, 'Fichte', *FIB2*, pp. 53–79, at p. 66.

51. Berlin, 'Rousseau', p. 50. Brooke notes that some of the strong words of denunciation that Berlin uses against Rousseau are reserved for, apart from Rousseau, only Hitler. Christopher Brooke, 'Isaiah Berlin and the Origins of the "Totalitarian" Rousseau', in Laurence Brockliss and Ritchie Robertson (eds), *Isaiah Berlin and the Enlightenment* (Oxford: Oxford University Press, 2017), pp. 89–98, at p. 90.

52. Bertrand Russell, *History of Western Philosophy and Its Connection with Political and Social Circumstances from the Earliest Times to the Present Day* (London: George Allen & Unwin, 1946), p. 711, p. 667.

53. Berlin, 'Two Concepts', p. 198. I agree with Hampsher-Monk, who observes that the connection Berlin draws between positive liberty and totalitarian regimes is not conceptual but historical. See Ian Hampsher-Monk, 'Rousseau and Totalitarianism—with Hindsight?', in Robert Wokler (ed.), *Rousseau and Liberty* (Manchester: Manchester University Press, 1995), pp. 267–88, at p. 272.

54. Berlin and Lukes, 'Conversation', p. 92.

55. Michael Kenny, 'Isaiah Berlin's Contribution to Modern Political Theory', *Political Studies* 48:5 (2000), pp. 1,026–39, at p. 1,037.

56. Berlin, 'Introduction', p. 39.

57. Berlin, 'Two Concepts', p. 213, p. 182.

58. Ibid., p. 185.

59. See esp. Berlin, *PIRA2*.

60. Berlin and Polanowska-Sygulska, *UD*, p. 154.

61. Berlin's idea of value pluralism has given rise to a mini-industry in academia over the past few decades. In this book the idea will be discussed from a specific angle in Chapter 5, where the Eichmann controversy is considered. For more general discussions of Berlin's value

pluralism see, e.g., Crowder, *Isaiah Berlin*; George Crowder, *The Problem of Value Pluralism: Isaiah Berlin and Beyond* (London: Routledge, 2019); William Galston, *Liberal Pluralism: The Implications of Value Pluralism for Political Theory and Practice* (Cambridge: Cambridge University Press, 2002); John Gray, *Isaiah Berlin: An Interpretation of His Thought* (Princeton: Princeton University Press, 2013); and Steven Lukes, *Liberals and Cannibals: The Implications of Diversity* (London: Verso, 2003).

62. Berlin, 'Two Concepts', pp. 213–14.

63. Ibid., p. 216.

64. This aspect is highlighted in Gray's under-appreciated work *Isaiah Berlin*.

65. Berlin and Lukes, 'Conversation', p. 101. See also Berlin and Polanowska-Sygulska, *UD*, pp. 217–20.

66. Berlin and Lukes, 'Conversation', p. 101, emphasis added.

67. Isaiah Berlin, 'John Stuart Mill and the Ends of Life', *L*, pp. 218–51.

68. Berlin, 'Two Concepts', p. 175.

69. See, in particular, Isaiah Berlin, 'Conversations with Akhmatova and Pasternak' and 'Boris Pasternak', *SM2*, pp. 50–79 and pp. 80–84, respectively; and 'Meetings with Russian Writers in 1945 and 1956', *PI3*, pp. 356–432.

70. John Stuart Mill, 'On Liberty', in *On Liberty and Other Essays*, ed. John Gray (Oxford: Oxford University Press, 1991), pp. 1–128, at p. 72.

71. Ibid., p. 17.

72. Michael Freeden, *Ideologies and Political Theory: A Conceptual Approach* (Oxford: Clarendon Press, 1996), p. 146.

73. Or, in Alan Ryan's memorable words, Mill's liberty 'vacillates between Berlinesque negativism and Coleridgean positivism'. Alan Ryan, 'Freedom', *Philosophy* 40:152 (1965), pp. 93–112, at p. 101.

74. Berlin, 'Introduction', p. 39; Berlin and Polanowska-Sygulska, *UD*, p. 156, emphasis added.

75. See Cherniss, *A Mind and Its Time*, pp. 131–87.

76. Hannah Arendt, *Love and Saint Augustine*, ed. and trans. Joanna Vecchiarelli Scott and Judith Chelius Stark (Chicago: University of Chicago Press, 1996), esp. pp. 9–35.

77. See, e.g., Hannah Arendt, 'The Enlightenment and the Jewish Question' [1932] and 'Original Assimilation' [1932], reprinted in *JW*, pp. 3–18 and pp. 22–28, respectively.

78. See, in particular, her contributions to *Aufbau*, reprinted in *JW*, pp. 134–240.

79. I shall discuss this body of work in the next chapter.

80. Hiruta, 'Hannah Arendt, Liberalism, and Freedom from Politics', pp. 25–26.

81. Anthony Quinton (ed.), *Political Philosophy* (London: Oxford University Press, 1967), pp. 141–52.

82. Thanks are due to Roger Berkowitz and Helene Tieger for letting me examine the copy.

83. See esp. Cherniss, *A Mind and Its Time*, pp. 145–51.

84. Arendt, *DE*, IV: 17, p. 93.

85. Ibid., XVII: 10, pp. 404–5.

86. A copy of the German original, *Vom Wesen der Wahrheit*, is preserved in Bard College's Hannah Arendt Collection. A January 1968 entry in her *Denktagebuch* is devoted to this book by Heidegger (Arendt, *DZ*, XXV: 38, p. 675).

87. Martin Heidegger, *Vom Wesen der Wahrheit* (Frankfurt am Main: Vittorio Klostermann, 1943), p. 16; English translation as 'On the Essence of Truth', in Martin Heidegger, *Basic Writings*, ed. David Farrell Krell (London: Routledge Classics, 2011), pp. 59–82, at p. 73.

88. Arendt, *OR3*, p. 22.

89. Benjamin Constant, 'The Liberty of the Ancients Compared with That of the Moderns', in his *Political Writings*, ed. and trans. Biancamaria Fontana (Cambridge: Cambridge University Press, 1988), pp. 309–28; Arendt, *OR3*, p. 22.

90. Arendt, 'What Is Freedom?', p. 161.

91. Jeremy Waldron, *Political Political Theory: Essays on Institutions* (Cambridge, MA: Harvard University Press, 2016), pp. 290–307.

92. This is why Tim Gray's analysis of Arendt's political freedom as a 'status' conception is inadequate: Tim Gray, *Freedom* (Basingstoke: Macmillan, 1991), pp. 46–50.

93. Robert A. Dahl, *A Preface to Democratic Theory* (Chicago: University of Chicago Press, 1956); Gabriel Almond and Sidney Verba, *The Civic Culture: Political Attitudes and Democracy in Five Nations* (Princeton: Princeton University Press, 1963).

94. John Adams cited in Arendt, *OR3*, p. 137.

95. Arendt, *HC*, p. 52.

96. Ibid., p. 7.

97. Arendt, 'What Is Freedom?', pp. 151–52.

98. Ibid., p. 152.

99. Ibid., p. 152.

100. Ibid., p. 151. Or, in a different formulation (*HC*, p. 207): 'the "product" is identical with the performing act itself.'

101. Hannah Arendt, 'Totalitarian Imperialism: Reflections on the Hungarian Revolution', *The Journal of Politics* 20:1 (1958), pp. 5–43, at p. 5, p. 43.

102. Pettit is probably the most influential of the critics. See, e.g., Philip Pettit, *Republicanism: A Theory of Freedom and Government* (Oxford: Oxford University Press, 1997), p. 286; Philip Pettit, *On the People's Terms: A Republican Theory and Model of Democracy* (Cambridge: Cambridge University Press, 2012), p. 12; and Philip Pettit, 'Two Republican Traditions', in Andreas Niederberger and Philipp Schink (eds), *Republican Democracy: Liberty, Law and Politics* (Edinburgh: Edinburgh University Press, 2013), pp. 169–204, at p. 169. For an excellent study of Pettit's (mis)reading of Arendt, see Keith Breen, 'Arendt, Republicanism, and Political Freedom', in Hiruta (ed.), *Arendt on Freedom, Liberation, and Revolution*, pp. 47–78.

103. Berlin, 'Two Concepts', p. 187.

104. Hannah Arendt, *Lectures on Kant's Political Philosophy*, ed. Ronald Beiner (Chicago: University of Chicago Press, 1992).

105. I have discussed this issue further in Hiruta, 'Hannah Arendt, Liberalism, and Freedom from Politics', pp. 20–24. See also Joan Cocks, *On Sovereignty and Other Political Delusions* (London: Bloomsbury Academic, 2014) and Sharon R. Krause, *Freedom beyond Sovereignty: Reconstructing Liberal Individualism* (Chicago: University of Chicago Press, 2015).

106. Arendt, 'What Is Freedom?', p. 163.

107. Or, as Arendt herself puts it, approvingly paraphrasing Jaspers's conception of freedom, 'Only because I have not made myself am I free.' Hannah Arendt, 'What Is Existential Philosophy?', *EU*, pp. 163–93, at p. 184.

108. Quentin Skinner, 'A Third Concept of Liberty', *Proceedings of the British Academy* 117 (2003), pp. 237–68, at p. 242.

109. Thomas Hill Green, *Lectures on the Principles of Political Obligation* (London: Longmans, Green, 1941), pp. 17–18. Compare this to Arendt's characterisation of the political 'prior to the modern age' as follows: 'to be political meant to attain the highest possibility of human existence' (Arendt, *HC*, p. 64).

110. See esp. Arendt, *HC*, pp. 175–81.

111. Ibid., p. 176.

112. Ibid., p. 180.

113. Bonnie Honig, 'Arendt, Identity, and Difference', *Political Theory* 16:1 (1988), pp. 77–98, at p. 88.

114. Margaret Canovan, *Hannah Arendt: A Reinterpretation of Her Political Thought* (Cambridge: Cambridge University Press, 1992), esp. pp. 201–52.

115. The relevant literature is massive. See, e.g., Pettit, *Republicanism* and *On the People's Terms*, and Philip Pettit, *A Theory of Freedom: From the Psychology to the Politics of Agency* (Oxford: Oxford University Press, 2001); Skinner, 'A Third Concept of Liberty'; and Quentin Skinner, *Liberty before Liberalism* (Cambridge: Cambridge University Press, 1998).

116. Pettit, *Republicanism*, p. 27. See Quentin Skinner, 'Two Concepts of Citizenship', *Tijdschrift voor Filosofie* 55:3 (1993), pp. 403–19, at p. 411.

117. Jeremy Arnold, *Across the Great Divide: Between Analytical and Continental Political Theory* (Stanford: Stanford University Press, 2020), p. 100.

118. Arendt, *OR3*, p. 271.

119. See Skinner, 'Two Concepts of Citizenship', pp. 415–16.

120. Arendt, *OR3*, p. 271.

121. Dana R. Villa, *Public Freedom* (Princeton: Princeton University Press, 2008), p. 411.

122. Arendt, *OR3*, p. 210.

123. Ibid., p. 272.

124. Ibid., p. 23.

125. To cite Arendt's exact words: 'to *be* free and to act are the same', and 'to be human and to be free are one and the same' ('What Is Freedom?', p. 151, p. 166).

126. Arendt, *HC*, p. 58.

127. Ibid., pp. 10–11, p. 193.

128. I owe the term '*quasi*-transcendental' (emphasis added) to Sophie Loidolt, *Phenomenology of Plurality: Hannah Arendt on Political Intersubjectivity* (New York: Routledge, 2018), p. 122.

129. Berlin uses the terms 'human nature' and 'the human condition' interchangeably, and his conception of human nature is unequivocally empiricist and non-essentialist.

130. Arendt, *HC*, p. 9.

131. See Stephen Mulhall, *Philosophical Myths of the Fall* (Princeton: Princeton University Press, 2005). Here I disagree with Loidolt, *Phenomenology of Plurality*, p. 113, where she seems to let 'limits' stand for 'limitations' and consequently argues that the conditionality of Arendt's human condition is 'not to be understood as a "limit" [. . .] but rather as an *enablement*'. On my understanding, a limit encompasses *both* a limitation *and* an enablement.

132. Martin Heidegger, *Being and Time*, trans. John Macquarrie and Edward Robinson (Oxford: Blackwell, 1962), p. 294.

133. Stephen Mulhall, *Heidegger's Being and Time*, 2nd ed. (London: Routledge, 2013), p. 129.

134. Peter E. Gordon, *Continental Divide: Heidegger, Cassirer, Davos* (Cambridge, MA: Harvard University Press, 2010), esp. pp. 5–11.

135. See Arendt, *HC*, pp. 17–21, pp. 54–56, pp. 192–99, pp. 313–20.

136. Ibid., p. 9.

137. Ibid., pp. 177–78.

138. Ibid., p. 176.

139. Ibid., p. 177.

140. Arendt, 'What Is Freedom?', pp. 166–67; Arendt, *HC*, passim; Heidegger, *Being and Time*, pp. 290–91.

141. Arendt, *HC*, p. 97.

142. Ibid., p. 246.

143. Hannah Arendt, 'Concern with Politics in Recent European Philosophical Thought', *EU*, pp. 428–47, at p. 433.

144. Heidegger, *Being and Time*, p. 220.

145. Needless to say, the most systematic study of Arendt's conception of the social is Hanna Fenichel Pitkin, *The Attack of the Blob: Hannah Arendt's Concept of the Social* (Chicago: University of Chicago Press, 1998).

146. Arendt, 'Concern with Politics'; Hannah Arendt, 'Heidegger at Eighty', *TWB*, pp. 419–31.

147. Arendt, 'What Is Existential Philosophy?', p. 187, p. 178. In the same essay (p. 181), Arendt suggests a connection between Heidegger's philosophical solipsism and his later engagement with Nazism, observing that he 'd[rew] on mythologizing and muddled concepts like "folk" and "earth" in an effort to supply his isolated Selves with a shared, common ground to stand on.'

148. See the August 1970 entry in her *Denktagebuch*: Arendt, *DZ*, XXVII: 78, p. 793. This self-criticism is a part of Arendt's renewed engagement with Heidegger's work during the final eight years of her life. This was prompted by her meetings with Heidegger in the summer of 1967, when she travelled to Europe and Israel. Prior to these meetings that resulted in a 'new accord [. . .] between Arendt and Heidegger', the relationship between them had been poor for several years. According to Young-Bruehl, this was due to 'Heidegger's sharp reaction to the copy [Arendt] sent him of her German translation of *The Human Condition* in 1961'. Elisabeth Young-Bruehl, *Hannah Arendt: For the Love of the World*, 2nd ed. (New Haven: Yale University Press, 2004), p. 442.

149. Seyla Benhabib, *The Reluctant Modernism of Hannah Arendt*, new ed. (Lanham, MD: Rowman & Littlefield, 2003), p. 107; Richard J. Bernstein, 'Provocation and Appropriation: Hannah Arendt's Response to Martin Heidegger', *Constellations* 4:2 (1997), pp. 153–71, at p. 159.

150. Dana R. Villa, *Arendt and Heidegger: The Fate of the Political* (Princeton: Princeton University Press, 1996), p. 212, emphasis added.

151. Arendt, 'What Is Existential Philosophy?', p. 182. I owe the phrase 'phenomenology of plurality' to Loidolt, *Phenomenology of Plurality*.

152. Loidolt, *Phenomenology of Plurality*, pp. 170–71. See also Arendt, *DZ*, XXV: 17, p. 664.

153. Arendt, 'What Is Existential Philosophy?', p. 186. See also a related, and important, *Denktagebuch* entry dated August 1955: Arendt, *DE*, XXI: 68, pp. 549–50.

154. Arendt, *HC*, p. 7.

155. Waldron, *Political Political Theory*, pp. 290–93.

156. Judith Butler, *Notes Toward a Performative Theory of Assembly* (Cambridge, MA: Harvard University Press, 2015), p. 88.

157. Note that I am here drawing a distinction between (Millian) moral pluralism and (Berlinian) value pluralism. The former concerns the multiplicity of *conceptions of the good*, whereas the latter concerns the multiplicity of *goods* and their incompatibility and/or incommensurability. Mill and Rawls are both moral pluralists but neither is a value pluralist. Berlin, by contrast, is committed to both value and moral pluralism, although he is most famous for his (supposed) invention of value pluralism (hence the adjective 'Berlinian' value pluralism). See also Chapter 5 note 15 in this book.

158. Loidolt, *Phenomenology of Plurality*, p. 223.

159. Arendt, *HC*, p. 178.

160. Ibid., p. 176.

161. Ibid., p. 176. See also Arendt's high praise for Greek freedom in *DE*, IX: 6, p. 205.

162. Arendt, *HC*, p. 176.

163. Ibid.

164. Arendt, 'What Is Freedom?', p. 166.

165. Needless to say, the centrality of plurality for Arendt's political thought is highlighted in Canovan's seminal work, *Hannah Arendt*.

166. I have attempted a more systematic analysis of the concept of pluralism in political theory in Kei Hiruta, 'Making Sense of Pluralism' (D.Phil. thesis, University of Oxford, 2012).

167. Canovan, *Hannah Arendt*, p. 215 note 53.

168. See a revealing *Denktagebuch* entry dated August 1952: Arendt, *DE*, IX: 29, p. 223.

169. Loidolt, *Phenomenology of Plurality*, p. 69. See also pp. 101–5.

170. Villa, *Public Freedom*, p. 331, emphasis added. Other moral monist readings of Arendt include Ronald Beiner, *Political Philosophy: What It Is and Why It Matters* (Cambridge: Cambridge University Press, 2014), pp. xv–xxii; and Peter Lassman, *Pluralism* (Cambridge: Polity Press, 2011), pp. 152–53.

171. Hannah Arendt, 'Understanding and Politics (The Difficulties of Understanding)', *EU*, pp. 307–27, at p. 325 note 10; Berlin and Lukes, 'Conversation', p. 101.

172. Bernard Crick, *In Defence of Politics* (London: Weidenfeld & Nicolson, 1962).

173. Bernard Crick, *Freedom as Politics* (Sheffield: University of Sheffield, 1966).

174. Berlin, 'Introduction', pp. 34–35.

175. Isaiah Berlin to Bernard Crick, 29 March 1966, MSB 173/116–119. The part of the letter cited here is omitted from the published version in Berlin, *B*, pp. 271–75.

176. Aristotle, *Politics*, 1310a. Arendt cites from *Aristotle's Politics*, trans. Benjamin Jowett (New York: The Modern Library, 1943), p. 216; Berlin refers to William Lambert Newman, *The Politics of Aristotle*, vol. 3 (Oxford: Clarendon Press, 1887), pp. 501–2.

177. Arendt, 'What Is Freedom?', p. 146.

178. Ibid., p. 144.

179. Berlin to Crick, 29 March 1966, *B*, p. 274. Crick responded to Berlin's criticism on various occasions, including Bernard Crick, 'Hannah Arendt's Political Philosophy', in Robert Boyers, *Proceedings of 'History, Ethics, Politics: A Conference Based on the Work of Hannah Arendt'* (New York: Empire State College, 1982), pp. 23–31; 'Hannah Arendt and the Burden of Our Times', *The Political Quarterly* 68:1 (1997), pp. 77–84; and 'On Isaiah Berlin', in Bernard Crick, *Crossing Borders: Political Essays* (London: Continuum, 2001), pp. 163–73.

180. Isaiah Berlin, 'The Birth of Greek Individualism', *L*, pp. 287–321.

181. Ibid., p. 306.

182. Ibid., p. 287. Hellenism here stands for the period spanning from the death of Alexander (323 BCE) to the Roman annexation of Egypt (30 BCE).

183. Constant, 'The Liberty of the Ancients', p. 316.

184. Berlin, 'Introduction', p. 33.

185. Arendt, 'What Is Freedom?', p. 156.

186. Berlin refers to Epictetus's *Encheiridion*, whereas Arendt refers to his *Discourses*. But their understandings of Epictetus's conception of freedom are virtually identical. See Berlin, 'The Birth of Greek Individualism', p. 305; Arendt, 'What Is Freedom?', p. 146.

187. Berlin, 'The Birth of Greek Individualism', p. 306, pp. 318–19; Arendt, 'What Is Freedom?', p. 145.

188. Berlin, 'The Birth of Greek Individualism', p. 304.

189. Ibid., p. 321.

190. Arendt, 'What Is Freedom?', p. 145.

191. Ibid., p. 156.

192. Berlin, 'The Birth of Greek Individualism', p. 321.

193. Ibid., p. 312.

194. Ibid., p. 315.

195. Ibid.

196. Arendt, 'What Is Freedom?', p. 146.

197. Ibid., p. 144.

198. Ibid., pp. 163–64.

199. Arendt, *HC*, p. 41.

200. Berlin, 'John Stuart Mill and the Ends of Life', p. 221.

201. Berlin and Polanowska-Sygulska, *UD*, p. 44.

202. Ibid.

203. Berlin, 'Two Concepts', p. 213.

204. Isaiah Berlin to Mary McCarthy, 7 August 1964. McCarthy 182.17, Archives and Special Collections, Vassar College Library. The part of the letter cited here is omitted from the published version in *B*, pp. 195–97.

205. Arendt, 'What Is Existential Philosophy?', p. 166.

206. Arendt, *HC*, p. 5.

207. Arendt, 'Hannah Arendt on Hannah Arendt', *TWB*, pp. 443–75, at p. 449.

208. For further discussion, see Kei Hiruta, 'Value Pluralism, Realism and Pessimism', *Res Publica* 26:4 (2020), pp. 523–40.

209. Berlin, 'Two Concepts', p. 213.

Chapter 4. Inhumanity

1. From the *Menorah Journal* to Isaiah Berlin, 2 April 1943, MSB 110/163.

2. Hannah Arendt, 'We Refugees', *Menorah Journal* 31:1 (1943), pp. 69–77, reprinted in *JW*, pp. 264–74.

3. Isaiah Berlin to the editor of the *Menorah Journal*, 12 April 1943, MSB 110/174.

4. Isaiah Berlin, Contribution to 'Reputations Revisited', *The Times Literary Supplement*, 21 January 1977, p. 66. Berlin added a mischievous note in parentheses to say that the overrating applied to 'virtually all the work' by Arendt. But elsewhere he repeatedly expressed the view that *The Human Condition* is the worst of her oeuvre.

5. Stuart Hampshire, 'Metaphysical Mists', *The Observer*, 30 July 1978, p. 26.

6. Richard Shorten, *Modernism and Totalitarianism: Rethinking the Intellectual Sources of Nazism and Stalinism, 1945 to the Present* (Basingstoke: Palgrave Macmillan, 2012), pp. 16–17, emphasis added.

7. Arendt, *OT3*, p. ix.

8. Jahanbegloo, *CIB*, 21. See also Shlomo Avineri, 'A Jew and a Gentleman', in George Crowder and Henry Hardy (eds), *The One and the Many: Reading Isaiah Berlin* (New York: Prometheus Books, 2007), pp. 73–94, at pp. 91–92.

9. Michael Ignatieff, *Isaiah Berlin* (London: Chatto & Windus, 1998), p. 123.

10. Hannah Arendt, 'Ideology and Terror: A Novel Form of Government', *The Review of Politics* 15:3 (1953), pp. 303–27, which has been incorporated into *OT3*, pp. 460–79.

11. Hannah Arendt, 'Personal Responsibility under Dictatorship', *RJ*, pp. 17–48, at p. 25.

12. Arendt, *OT3*, p. 461.

13. Hannah Arendt, 'Project: Totalitarian Elements in Marxism', 1952, submitted to the John Simon Guggenheim Memorial Foundation, catalogued as 012649, 012650 and 012651 in 'Correspondence File, 1938–1976, n.d.', HAP.

14. Michael Freeden, 'Thinking Politically and Thinking about Politics: Language, Interpretation, and Ideology', in David Leopold and Marc Stears (eds), *Political Theory: Methods and Approaches* (Oxford: Oxford University Press, 2008), pp. 196–215, at p. 210.

15. Arendt, *OT3*, p. 469.

16. Besides this etymological inaccuracy, Arendt's claim about ideology is also questionable from a methodological perspective. Crick's critical remarks may be worth recalling here: '[Arendt's] pretentions can at times irritate: for example, a bad old Germanic habit of appearing to think that the original meanings of concepts should be returned to through philology.' Bernard Crick, 'Hannah Arendt and the Burden of Our Times', *The Political Quarterly* 68:1 (1997), pp. 77–84, at p. 79.

17. Arendt, *OT3*, p. 470.

18. Ibid., pp. 470–71.

19. Karl R. Popper, *The Logic of Scientific Discovery* (London: Hutchinson, 1959).

20. See Hannah Arendt, 'Mankind and Terror' [speech given on 23 March 1953], reprinted in *EU*, pp. 297–306; as well as Arendt, 'Ideology and Terror'.

21. Arendt, *OT3*, p. 322.

22. Ibid., p. 467.

23. Peter Baehr, *Hannah Arendt, Totalitarianism, and the Social Sciences* (Stanford: Stanford University Press, 2010), p. 73.

24. Dana R. Villa, *Politics, Philosophy, Terror: Essays on the Thought of Hannah Arendt* (Princeton: Princeton University Press, 1999), p. 182.

25. One outstanding exception is Peter Baehr, whose work guides much of my discussion in this chapter.

26. See, e.g., Arendt, *OT3*, pp. 308–9; Hannah Arendt, 'On the Nature of Totalitarianism: An Essay in Understanding', *EU*, pp. 328–60, at pp. 346–47.

27. For those who exclude Italy from the totalitarian family see, e.g., R.J.B. Bosworth, *The Italian Dictatorship: Problems and Perspectives in the Interpretation of Mussolini and Fascism* (London: Arnold, 1998); and Alexander de Grand, 'Cracks in the Façade: The Failure of Fascist Totalitarianism in Italy', *European History Quarterly* 21 (1991), pp. 515–35. Emilio Gentile is the most influential among those who argue that fascist Italy should be included in the totalitarian family. See, e.g., Emilio Gentile, 'Fascism and the Italian Road to Totalitarianism', *Constellations* 15:3 (2008), pp. 291–302.

28. Abbott Gleason, *Totalitarianism: The Inner History of the Cold War* (New York: Oxford University Press, 1995), esp. pp. 13–50.

29. Arendt, 'On the Nature of Totalitarianism', pp. 346–47.

30. Arendt's pioneering attempt was a part of the larger story in the evolution of the concept of totalitarianism. See Gleason, *Totalitarianism*; and Jeffrey C. Isaac, *Arendt, Camus, and Modern Rebellion* (New Haven: Yale University Press, 1992), pp. 37–45.

31. Arendt, *OT3*, p. 311.

32. Ibid., p. 419, pp. 409–10.

33. Here I build on Kei Hiruta, 'Value Pluralism, Realism and Pessimism', *Res Publica* 26:4 (2020), pp. 523–40, at p. 535.

34. Isaiah Berlin to W. J. Norman, 4 September 1991, MSB 227/242. See also Isaiah Berlin to Stephen Spender, 24 September 1968, MSB 283/120–21.

35. Isaiah Berlin, 'The Arts in Russia under Stalin', *SM2*, pp. 1–26, at p. 6.

36. Isaiah Berlin, 'The Birth of Greek Individualism', *L*, pp. 287–321.

37. Ibid., p. 301.

38. Diogenes Laertius, *Lives of Eminent Philosophers*, ed. Robert Drew Hicks (Cambridge, MA: Harvard University Press, 1925), Book 2: 108.

39. Dominic Hyde, *Vagueness, Logic and Ontology* (London: Routledge, 2016), p. 9.

40. Arendt, 'On the Nature of Totalitarianism', p. 355.

41. Arendt, *OT3*, p. 458.

42. Arendt, 'On the Nature of Totalitarianism', p. 355.

43. Margaret Canovan, 'Arendt's Theory of Totalitarianism', in Dana R. Villa (ed.), *The Cambridge Companion to Hannah Arendt* (Cambridge: Cambridge University Press, 2000), pp. 25–43, at p. 29.

44. This paragraph and the next draw on Kei Hiruta, 'Hannah Arendt, Liberalism, and Freedom from Politics', in Kei Hiruta (ed.), *Arendt on Freedom, Liberation, and Revolution* (Cham: Palgrave Macmillan, 2019), pp. 17–45, esp. pp. 29–30 and pp. 37–39.

45. I avoid the familiar term 'mass society' here because, in Arendt's lexicon, this refers to the type of consumerist society that she analyses in *The Human Condition*, rather than the 'society of the masses' that she discusses in *Origins*. Strikingly, she scarcely mentions 'mass society' in *Origins*. See Peter Baehr, 'The "Masses" in Hannah Arendt's Theory of Totalitarianism', *The Good Society* 16:2 (2007), pp. 12–18, at pp. 16–17.

46. This, needless to say, is a theme Arendt directly addresses in *The Human Condition*.

47. Arendt, *OT3*, p. 350.

48. Ira Katznelson, *Desolation and Enlightenment: Political Knowledge after Total War, Totalitarianism and the Holocaust* (New York: Columbia University Press, 2003), p. 14.

49. Robert Fine, *Political Investigations: Hegel, Marx, Arendt* (London: Routledge, 2001), p. 115.

50. Arendt, *OT3*, pp. 327.

51. Ibid., p. 323, p. 350.

52. Hannah Arendt, 'Approaches to the "German Problem"', *EU*, pp. 106–20, at p. 107.

53. Ibid., p. 108. For a further and excellent discussion of Arendt's dispute with historians holding specifically German characteristics to be accountable for the rise of totalitarianism, see William Selinger, 'The Politics of Arendtian Historiography: European Federation and the Origins of Totalitarianism', *Modern Intellectual History* 13:2 (2016), pp. 417–46.

54. Arendt, *OT3*, pp. 308–9, emphasis added.

55. Ibid., p. 440. Note that Arendt sees Jews as one of the European peoples.

56. Ibid., pp. 308–11.

57. Ibid., p. 313. See also p. 337.

58. Ibid., p. 318.

59. The most notable example is Bernard Crick, 'Arendt and *The Origins of Totalitarianism*: An Anglocentric View', in Steven E. Aschheim (ed.), *Hannah Arendt in Jerusalem* (Berkeley and Los Angeles: University of California Press, 2001), pp. 93–104.

60. See Hannah Arendt, 'Comment by Hannah Arendt', in Richard Pipes (ed.), *Revolutionary Russia* (Cambridge, MA: Harvard University Press, 1968), pp. 344–51, at p. 344.

61. Arendt, *OT3*, p. 456.

62. Ibid., p. 455.

63. Hannah Arendt, 'The Image of Hell', *EU*, pp. 197–205, at p. 198.

64. Hannah Arendt, 'Social Science Techniques and the Study of Concentration Camps', *EU*, pp. 232–47, at p. 238, emphasis added.

65. Peter Baehr, *Hannah Arendt, Totalitarianism and the Social Sciences*, p. 21.

66. Dan Stone, *The Holocaust, Fascism and Memory: Essays in the History of Ideas* (Basingstoke: Palgrave Macmillan, 2013), p. 50.

67. See Timothy Snyder, *Bloodlands: Europe between Hitler and Stalin* (London: The Bodley Head, 2000), pp. 380–83.

68. Hannah Arendt to Karl Jaspers, 17 December 1946, *C*, p. 69.

69. Richard J. Bernstein, *Hannah Arendt and the Jewish Question* (Cambridge, MA: The MIT Press, 1996), p. 88–100.

70. Michal Aharony, *Hannah Arendt and the Limits of Total Domination: The Holocaust, Plurality, and Resistance* (London: Routledge, 2015), p. 37; Dan Stone, *Concentration Camps: A Short History* (Oxford: Oxford University Press, 2017), pp. 38–39.

71. Aharony, *Hannah Arendt and the Limits of Total Domination*, pp. 37–61.

72. Baehr, *Hannah Arendt, Totalitarianism, and the Social Sciences*, p. 51.

73. Canovan, 'Arendt's Theory of Totalitarianism', pp. 26–29.

74. The term 'Gulag' was originally an abbreviation of the Stalinist-era administrative department *Glavnoye Upravleniye Ispravitelno-trudovykh Lagerey* (Chief administration of corrective labour camps). Later on it came to stand for a network of the Soviet camp system more broadly.

75. Anonymous author [Zoë Zajdlerowa], *The Dark Side of the Moon* (London: Faber & Faber, 1946).

76. For the background of publication, see 'Introduction' in Zoë Zajdlerowa, *Dark Side of the Moon: A New Edition*, ed. John Coutouvidis and Thomas Lane (New York: Harvester Wheatsheaf, 1989), pp. 1–46.

77. Arthur Koestler, *The Yogi and the Commissar* (London: Jonathan Cape, 1945), p. 146.

78. Arendt, *OT3*, p. 445.

79. Ibid., p. 392.

80. Needless to say, Arendt squarely tackles the issue of the 'Final Solution' in *Eichmann in Jerusalem*, which will be considered in the next chapter.

81. Arendt, 'Social Science Techniques and the Study of Concentration Camps', p. 233, p. 241.

82. Arendt, *OT3*, p. 456.

83. Ibid.

84. Ibid., p. 447.

85. For an overview of the rival approaches to the Gulag, see Wilson T. Bell, 'Gulag Historiography: An Introduction', *Gulag Studies* 2–3 (2009–2010), pp. 1–20.

86. Paul R. Gregory, 'Introduction to the Economics of the Gulag', in Paul R. Gregory and Valery Lazarev (eds), *The Economics of Forced Labor* (Stanford: Hoover Institution Press, 2003), p. 4.

87. Peter Hayes, *Why? Explaining the Holocaust* (New York: W. W. Norton & Co., 2017), p. 123.

88. Ibid., p. 132.

89. Marc Buggeln, *Slave Labor in Nazi Concentration Camps*, trans. Paul Cohen (Oxford: Oxford University Press, 2014), pp. 10–65.

90. Ibid., pp. 46–50; Kinga Frojimovics and Éva Kovács, 'Jews in a "Judenrein" City: Hungarian Jewish Slave Laborers in Vienna (1944–1945)', *The Hungarian Historical Review* 4:3 (2015), pp. 705–36.

91. Arendt herself may have changed her mind somewhat by the time she wrote *Eichmann in Jerusalem*. In this book, referring to Raul Hilberg's *The Destruction of the European Jews*, she highlights the economic use of slave labour within the camp system for German business. See Arendt, *EIJ2*, p. 79.

92. For a comprehensive study of this project, see Tama Weisman, *Hannah Arendt and Karl Marx: On Totalitarianism and the Tradition of Western Political Thought* (Lanham, MD: Lexington Books, 2013).

93. Arendt, 'Project: Totalitarian Elements in Marxism'.

94. Strangely, most Arendt scholars have read her correspondence with the Guggenheim Foundation as though her intention had not been to secure funding. It seems as if the contextualist revolution in intellectual history has never reached Arendt scholarship. See Quentin Skinner, *Visions of Politics, Volume 1: Regarding Method* (Cambridge: Cambridge University Press, 2002).

95. Elisabeth Young-Bruehl, *Hannah Arendt: For the Love of the World*, 2nd ed. (New Haven: Yale University Press, 2004), p. 279.

96. Arendt's unpublished (as well as published) papers from this period are now collected and published in an elegant volume: Hannah Arendt, *The Modern Challenge to Tradition: Fragmente eines Buchs*, ed. Barbara Hahn and James McFarland (Göttingen: Wallstein Verlag, 2019).

97. Dana R. Villa, *Public Freedom* (Princeton: Princeton University Press, 2008), p. 317.

98. Max Horkheimer and Theodor W. Adorno, *Dialectic of Enlightenment: Philosophical Fragments*, ed. G. S. Noerr, trans. E. Jephcott (Stanford: Stanford University Press, 2002).

99. The Cold War liberal approaches, though mostly limited to the case of Berlin, will be discussed later in this chapter. For Adorno and Horkheimer's approach compared to Arendt, see Seyla Benhabib, 'From "The Dialectic of Enlightenment" to "The Origins of Totalitarianism" and the Genocide Convention: Adorno and Horkheimer in the Company of Arendt and Lemkin', in Warren Breckman, Peter E. Gordon, A. Dirk Moses, Samuel Moyn and Elliot Neaman (eds), *The Modernist Imagination: Intellectual History and Critical Theory* (Oxford: Berghahn Books, 2009), pp. 299–330; Katznelson, *Desolation and Enlightenment*, esp. pp. 47–106; and Villa, *Public Freedom*, pp. 210–54.

100. Hannah Arendt, 'Karl Marx and the Tradition of Western Political Thought', *TWB*, pp. 3–42, at p. 4.

101. Ibid., pp. 5–6.

102. I have discussed Arendt's notion of 'the tradition' at some length in Hiruta, 'Hannah Arendt, Liberalism, and Freedom from Politics', pp. 20–24. For more detailed studies, see Villa, *Politics, Philosophy, Terror*, pp. 180–203; and Ilya P. Winham, 'After Totalitarianism: Hannah Arendt, Isaiah Berlin, and the Realization and Defeat of the Western Tradition' (Ph.D. dissertation, University of Minnesota, 2015), pp. 36–75.

103. See Hannah Arendt, 'What Is Authority?', *BPF3*, pp. 91–141, at esp. pp. 104–15.

104. Corrective rape is the practice of raping (perceived) lesbians to 'punish' them for their sexual orientation and to 'cure' them of lesbianism.

105. Merle Fainsod, *Smolensk under Soviet Rule* (London: Macmillan, 1958).

106. Arendt, *OT3*, p. xxxii.

107. Ibid., p. xxv, emphasis added; p. xxvi.

108. Ibid., p. xxix.

109. The sources include Arthur Koestler's *Scum of the Earth* (1941); Zoë Zajdlerowa's *The Dark Side of the Moon* (1947); Bruno Bettelheim's report on Dachau and Buchenwald (1946); Eugen Kogon's *Der SS Staat* (1946); David Rousset's *Les jours de notre mort* (1947) and *The Other Kingdom* (1947); and Edward L. Davis and Bruno Bettelheim, 'Copy of Document L-73', in US Office of Chief of Counsel for the Prosecution of Axis Criminality, *Nazi Conspiracy and Aggression* (Washington, DC: US Government Print Office, 1946), vol. 7, pp. 818–39.

110. Arendt, *OT3*, p. xxiv.

111. See Hannah Arendt, 'Totalitarian Imperialism: Reflections on the Hungarian Revolution', *The Journal of Politics* 20:1 (1958), pp. 5–43.

112. Arendt, *OT3*, p. xxv.

113. Ibid., pp. xxxvi–xxxvii.

114. Ibid., p. xxxvii.

115. For Arendt's tentative ideas on post-Stalinist Russia, see Peter Baehr (ed.), 'Stalinism in Retrospect: Hannah Arendt', *History and Theory* 54:3 (2015), pp. 353–66; and Peter Baehr, 'China the Anomaly: Hannah Arendt, Totalitarianism, and the Maoist Regime', *European Journal of Political Theory* 9:3 (2010), pp. 267–86.

116. Baehr, 'Stalinism in Retrospect', p. 355.

117. Ibid., p. 357.

118. Roy A. Medvedev, *Let History Judge: The Origins and Consequences of Stalinism*, ed. David Joravsky and Georges Haupt, trans. Colleen Taylor (New York: Knopf, 1971); Nadezhda Mandelstam, *Hope against Hope: A Memoir*, trans. Max Hayward (New York: Atheneum, 1970); Aleksandr I. Solzhenitsyn, *The First Circle*, trans. Thomas P. Whitney (New York: Harper & Row, 1968).

119. Arendt's perception of herself seems to have agreed with this commonly held view. She wrote to Karl Jaspers, in a letter dated 4 September 1947 (*C*, p. 99), that 'it's a pity that I can't write humor'.

120. Baehr, 'Stalinism in Retrospect', p. 357.

121. Cécile Hatier, 'Isaiah Berlin and the Totalitarian Mind', *The European Legacy* 9:6 (2004), pp. 762–82; Baehr, *Hannah Arendt, Totalitarianism, and the Social Sciences*, p. 13.

122. George Crowder, *Isaiah Berlin: Liberty and Pluralism* (Cambridge: Polity Press, 2004), p. 25.

123. Isaiah Berlin, 'The Pursuit of the Ideal', *CTH*2, pp. 1–20, at pp. 15–16.

124. Isaiah Berlin, 'Political Ideas in the Twentieth Century', *L*, pp. 55–93, at p. 70; 'Herzen and Bakunin on Individual Liberty', *RT*2, pp. 93–129, at p. 116. In the latter text 'the highest law' is replaced by 'the supreme law'.

125. Berlin, 'Political Ideas in the Twentieth Century', pp. 70–71.

126. Richard Shorten, 'Rethinking Totalitarian Ideology: Insights from the Anti-totalitarian Canon', *History of Political Thought* 35:4 (2015), pp. 726–61, at pp. 737–38.

127. Jahanbegloo, *CIB*, p. 38.

128. Ilana Fritz Offenberger, *The Jews of Nazi Vienna, 1938–1945: Rescue and Destruction* (Cham: Palgrave Macmillan, 2017), p. 40–41.

129. Zoë Waxman, *Women in the Holocaust: A Feminist History* (Oxford: Oxford University Press, 2017), p. 34.

130. Eugen Kogon, *The Theory and Practice of Hell: The German Concentration Camps and the System behind Them*, trans. Heinz Norden (London: Secker & Warburg, 1950), p. 93.

131. Arendt, *OT*3, p. 454.

132. Zygmunt Bauman, *Modernity and the Holocaust* (Cambridge: Polity, 1989).

133. Henry Hardy, *In Search of Isaiah Berlin: A Literary Adventure* (London: I. B. Tauris, 2018), pp. 253–54.

134. Ibid., p. 255.

135. Karl Marx with Friedrich Engels, *The German Ideology* (New York: Prometheus Books, 1998), p. 34.

136. See esp. Isaiah Berlin, 'The Concept of Scientific History', *CC*2, pp. 135–86; and 'Historical Inevitability', *L*, pp. 94–165.

137. See esp. 'Helvétius' and 'Saint-Simon', in *FIB*2, pp. 11–27 and pp. 113–41, respectively; and 'The Divorce between the Sciences and the Humanities', *AC*2, pp. 101–39.

138. Isaiah Berlin, 'Political Judgement', *SR*2, pp. 50–66, at p. 60, p. 61.

139. See Berlin's comments on Hayek in Berlin, *F*, pp. 541–42; *E*, p. 357; and *A*, pp. 423–28, p. 573.

140. Karl R. Popper, *The Poverty of Historicism* (London: Routledge & Kegan Paul, 1957); Friedrich A. von Hayek, 'Scientism and the Study of Society', *Economica* 9:35 (1942), pp. 267–91. See also Jan-Werner Müller, 'Fear and Freedom: On "Cold War Liberalism"', *European Journal of Political Theory* 7:1 (2008), pp. 45–64.

141. See, e.g., Hannah Arendt, 'Socrates', *PP*, pp. 5–39; 'Tradition and the Modern Age', *BPF*3, pp. 17–40; and 'Heidegger at Eighty', *TWB*, pp. 419–31.

142. Berlin, 'Helvétius', p. 26; Hannah Arendt, 'Truth and Politics', in *BPF3*, pp. 223–59, at p. 236.

143. Berlin, 'Helvétius', p. 26.

144. Berlin, 'Political Judgement', p. 54.

145. Needless to say, the idea of science as an unended quest is found in Karl R. Popper, *An Unended Quest*, revised ed. (London: Fontana, 1976).

146. This argument appears recurrently in Berlin's work from his *Karl Marx* to 'The Concept of Scientific History' and 'Historical Inevitability'.

147. Isaiah Berlin, *PIRA2*, p. 96.

148. Berlin and Lukes, 'Conversation', p. 101.

149. E.g., Joseph Raz, *The Morality of Freedom* (Oxford: Clarendon Press, 1986); Steven Wall, *Liberalism, Perfectionism and Restraint* (Cambridge: Cambridge University Press, 1998).

150. Isaiah Berlin, 'Why the Soviet Union Chooses to Insulate Itself', *SM2*, pp. 85–91.

151. Ibid. p. 88.

152. Vladimir Petrov, cited in Steven A. Barnes, *Death and Redemption: The Gulag and the Shaping of Soviet Society* (Princeton: Princeton University Press, 2011), p. 66.

153. Berlin, 'Why the Soviet Union Chooses to Insulate Itself', p. 88.

154. Ibid., p. 89. Writing in 1946, Berlin was unlikely to be aware of the scale of sexual violence that the Red Army committed as they advanced westwards at the end of the war (and afterwards). One wonders if Berlin would have modified or abandoned his metaphor of the schoolboys' rude behaviour had he known more about the Red Army's atrocious behaviour.

155. Isaiah Berlin, 'The Artificial Dialectic: Generalissimo Stalin and the Art of Government', *SM2*, pp. 92–111, at p. 110, p. 111. The essay was originally published under the pseudonym O. Utis in *Foreign Affairs* 30 (1952), pp. 197–214. The citations in this book are from *SM2*.

156. Berlin, 'The Artificial Dialectic', passim.

157. Ibid., p. 107.

158. Isaiah Berlin, 'Marxist versus Non-Marxist Ideas in Soviet Policy', reprinted in *SM2*, pp. 161–76, at p. 163.

159. Berlin, 'The Artificial Dialectic', p. 110, p. 107.

160. Isaiah Berlin, 'Joseph de Maistre and the Origins of Fascism', *CTH2*, pp. 95–177. According to Henry Hardy, Berlin began drafting this essay in the 1940s and continuously revised it until 1960. This means that his essay on Maistre may have been his 'first substantial essay on the history of ideas after his book on Karl Marx (1939)'. Hardy, *In Search of Isaiah Berlin*, p. 271 note 13.

161. On the difference between affinity and influence, see Shorten, *Modernism and Totalitarianism*, pp. 73–106.

162. Berlin, 'Joseph de Maistre and the Origins of Fascism', p. 130.

163. Berlin, 'Political Ideas in the Twentieth Century', p. 72.

164. Ibid., pp. 74–75.

165. Ibid., p. 73. Here I disagree with Crowder's interpretation of Berlin, which dissociates Lenin from irrationalism and associates him with a purely instrumental conception of violence. See Crowder, *Isaiah Berlin*, pp. 46–51.

166. Michael Kenny, 'Isaiah Berlin's Contribution to Modern Political Theory', *Political Studies* 48:5 (2000), pp. 1,029–39, at p. 1,029. See also Jason Ferrell, 'Isaiah Berlin on Monism', in Gene

Callahan and Kenneth B. McIntyre, *Critics of Enlightenment Rationalism* (Cham: Palgrave Macmillan, 2020), pp. 237–49.

167. Jonathan Allen, 'What's the Matter with Monism?', *Critical Review of International Social and Political Philosophy* 12:3 (2009), pp. 469–89, at p. 471.

168. Jeremy Bentham, *An Introduction to the Principles of Morals and Legislation*, ed. J. H. Burns and H.L.A. Hart (London: Athlone Press, 1970), p. 11.

169. Ibid.

170. Karl R. Popper, *The Open Society and Its Enemies*, 2 vols (London: Routledge & Kegan Paul, 1945).

171. E.g., Isaiah Berlin, *PIRA2*, p. 62; 'The Birth of Greek Individualism', p. 292; 'The Originality of Machiavelli', *AC2*, pp. 33–100, at p. 97; 'Vico and the Ideal of the Enlightenment', *AC2*, pp. 151–63, at p. 155; 'The Pursuit of the Ideal', p. 6; 'The Decline of Utopian Ideas in the West', *CTH2*, pp. 21–50, at pp. 28–29; 'European Unity and Its Vicissitudes', *CT2*, pp. 186–218, at p. 213; 'The Apotheosis of the Romantic Will: The Revolt against the Myth of an Ideal World', *CTH2*, pp. 219–52, at p. 223 and p. 251; *RR2*, passim; 'Herder and the Enlightenment', *TCE2*, pp. 208–300, at p. 269.

172. Berlin, *RR2*, p. 28.

173. Crowder, *Isaiah Berlin*, p. 25.

174. Allen, 'What's the Matter with Monism?', pp. 469–70.

175. The earliest clear statement of this view is found in Berlin's June 1949 lecture on 'Democracy, Communism and the Individual', reprinted in *POI2*, p. 276–84. See esp. p. 277.

176. Isaiah Berlin, 'Two Concepts of Liberty', *L*, pp. 166–217, at p. 212.

177. See Crowder, *Isaiah Berlin*, p. 4.

178. Berlin and Lukes, 'Conversation', p. 92.

179. Berlin, *PIRA2*, pp. 180–81.

180. Ibid., p. 170, p. 169.

181. Ibid., pp. 180–81.

182. E.g., Christopher Brooke, 'Isaiah Berlin and the Origins of the "Totalitarian" Rousseau', in Laurence Brockliss and Ritchie Robertson (eds), *Isaiah Berlin and the Enlightenment* (Oxford: Oxford University Press, 2017), pp. 89–98; J. Kent Wright, 'Rousseau and Montesquieu', in Helena Rosenblatt and Paul Schweigert (eds), *Thinking with Rousseau: From Machiavelli to Schmitt* (Cambridge: Cambridge University Press, 2017), pp. 63–91, at pp. 72–73.

183. For liberal egalitarian Rousseau see, e.g., Christopher Bertram, *Rousseau and the Social Contract* (London: Routledge, 2004); and Christopher Brooke, 'Rawls on Rousseau and the General Will', in James Farr and David Lay Williams (eds), *The General Will: The Evolution of a Concept* (Cambridge: Cambridge University Press, 2015), pp. 429–46.

184. See Céline Spector, *Au prisme de Rousseau: Usages politiques contemporains* (Oxford: Voltaire Foundation, 2011), pp. 51–71.

185. Isaiah Berlin, 'Rousseau', *FIB2*, pp. 28–52, at p. 39.

186. Berlin, *PIRA2*, p. 155.

187. Ibid., p. 142, p. 235.

188. Berlin, 'Two Concepts', p. 198.

189. Of particular importance are Popper, *The Open Society and Its Enemies*; Jacob L. Talmon, *The Origins of Totalitarian Democracy* (London: Secker & Warburg, 1952); and Jacob L. Talmon, *Political Messianism: The Romantic Phase* (London: Secker & Warburg, 1960).

190. Carl J. Friedrich and Zbigniew K. Brzezinski, *Totalitarian Dictatorship and Autocracy* (Cambridge, MA: Harvard University Press, 1956).

191. Hacohen's observation is acute: 'Like Ahad Ha-Am, the Russian Jewish founder of cultural Zionism, [Berlin] never doubted the existence of a "national character"—Jewish, Russian or English, and a primordial ethnicity was crucial in delineating it.' Malachi Haim Hacohen, 'Berlin and Popper between Nation and Empire: Diaspora, Cosmopolitanism and Jewish Life', *Jewish Historical Studies* 44 (2012), pp. 51–74, at p. 66.

192. Berlin, 'Marxist versus Non-Marxist Ideas in Soviet Policy', p. 162.

193. Ibid.

194. Andrzej Walicki, 'Berlin and the Russian Intelligentsia', in Crowder and Hardy (eds), *The One and the Many*, pp. 47–71, at p. 49.

195. Ibid.

196. Whether Berlin's perspective on the Russian intelligentsia was critical *enough* has been a matter of debate. See, e.g., Derek Offord, 'Isaiah Berlin and the Russian Intelligentsia', in Brockliss and Robertson (eds), *Isaiah Berlin and the Enlightenment*, pp. 187–202.

197. Isaiah Berlin, 'Russian Populism', *RT2*, pp. 240–72, at p. 245.

198. Isaiah Berlin, 'A Remarkable Decade', *RT2*, 130–239, at p. 143.

199. Isaiah Berlin, 'Epilogue: The Three Strands in My Life', *PI3*, pp. 433–39, at pp. 433–35.

200. My discussion responds to Caute and Lukes, both of whom criticise Berlin for exaggerating the role of ideas in accounting for political disasters. David Caute, *Isaac and Isaiah: The Covert Punishment of a Cold War Heretic* (New Haven: Yale University Press, 2013), p. 119; Steven Lukes, 'The Cold War on Campus', *Dissent* 61:1 (2014), pp. 71–75.

201. Berlin, 'Epilogue', p. 433.

202. Berlin, 'Two Concepts', p. 167.

203. Heinrich Heine, *Religion and Philosophy in Germany* (Albany: State University of New York Press, 1986), p. 106.

204. Ibid., pp. 158–161.

205. Isaiah Berlin, 'The Bent Twig: On the Rise of Nationalism', *CTH2*, pp. 253–78, at p. 261.

206. Ibid., p. 262.

207. Isaiah Berlin, 'Nationalism: Past Neglect and Present Power', *AC2*, pp. 420–48, at p. 442.

208. David Miller, 'Crooked Timber or Bent Twig?: Berlin's Nationalism', in Crowder and Hardy (eds), *The One and the Many*, pp. 181–206, at p. 182.

209. E.g., Gina Gustavsson, 'Berlin's Romantics and Their Ambiguous Legacy', in Joshua L. Cherniss and Steven B. Smith (eds), *The Cambridge Companion to Isaiah Berlin* (Cambridge: Cambridge University Press, 2018), pp 149–66.

210. E.g., Frederick Beiser, 'Berlin and the German Counter-Enlightenment', in Joseph Mali and Robert Wokler (eds), *Isaiah Berlin's Counter-Enlightenment* (Philadelphia: American Philosophical Society, 2003), pp. 105–16; Lawrence Brockliss and Ritchie Robertson, 'Berlin's Conception of the Enlightenment', in Brockliss and Robertson (eds), *Isaiah Berlin and the Enlightenment*, pp. 35–50.

211. E.g., Darrin M. McMahon, 'The Real Counter-Enlightenment: The Case of France', in Mali and Wokler (eds), *Isaiah Berlin's Counter-Enlightenment*, pp. 91–104; and (again) Brockliss and Robertson, 'Berlin's Conception of the Enlightenment'.

212. Arendt, 'Preface to Part Three: Totalitarianism' [1966], *OT3*, p. xxiv.

213. I owe the metaphor of the cradle burning to Caute, *Isaac and Isaiah*, p. 52.

Chapter 5. Evil and Judgement

1. Yehuda Bauer, *Rethinking the Holocaust* (New Haven: Yale University Press, 2001), p. 227.

2. Arendt mistakenly described Kastner as 'the most prominent member of the Hungarian Judenrat'. See Hannah Arendt, 'The Formidable Dr. Robinson: A Reply by Hannah Arendt', *JW*, pp. 496–511, at p. 506.

3. Randolph L. Braham, *The Politics of Genocide: The Holocaust in Hungary*, condensed ed. (Detroit: Wayne State University Press, 2000), pp. 152–53. During his Sassen interviews, Eichmann boasted about this deportation as follows: 'It was actually an achievement that was never matched before or since.' Eichmann cited in Bettina Stangneth, *Eichmann before Jerusalem: The Unexamined Life of a Mass Murderer* (London: The Bodley Head, 2014), p. 267.

4. The exact number of people who boarded the train remains unclear. See Leora Bilsky, *Transformative Justice: Israeli Identity on Trial* (Ann Arbor: The University of Michigan Press, 2004), p. 265 note 5.

5. Braham, *The Politics of Genocide*, pp. 251–53.

6. See Yehuda Bauer, *Jews for Sale?: Nazi–Jewish Negotiations, 1933–1945* (New Haven: Yale University Press, 1994).

7. Bilsky, *Transformative Justice*, p. 67.

8. Hannah Arendt, *EIJ2*, p. 42, p. 143.

9. See Bilsky, *Transformative Justice*, pp. 87–93.

10. Hausner cited in ibid., p. 90.

11. Arendt, *EIJ2*, p. 5.

12. Deborah E. Lipstadt, *The Eichmann Trial* (New York: Schocken, 2011), p. 149. Stangneth similarly observes that '[e]ver since *Eichmann in Jerusalem: A Report on the Banality of Evil* was published in 1963, every essay on Adolf Eichmann has also been a dialogue with Hannah Arendt': Stangneth, *Eichmann before Jerusalem*, p. xxii.

13. This fact has been emphasised by many scholars, including Dana R. Villa, *Public Freedom* (Princeton: Princeton University Press, 2008), pp. 303–4; Deirdre Lauren Mahony, *Hannah Arendt's Ethics* (London: Bloomsbury Academic, 2018), p. 34; and Michal Aharony, 'Why Does Hannah Arendt's "Banality of Evil" Still Anger Israelis?', *Haaretz*, 7 May 2019, https://www.haaretz.com/israel-news/.premium.MAGAZINE-why-does-hannah-arendt-s-banality-of-evil-still-anger-israelis-1.7213979, accessed 15 January 2020.

14. Note the suggestive title of a recent collection of essays on the Eichmann controversy: Richard J. Golsan and Sarah M. Misemer (eds), *The Trial that Never Ends: Hannah Arendt's Eichmann in Jerusalem in Retrospect* (Toronto: University of Toronto Press, 2017).

15. Whether Berlin invented value pluralism or (merely) rediscovered it has been a matter of much debate. Those who emphasise Berlin's novelty include John Gray, *Isaiah Berlin: An Interpretation of His Thought* (Princeton: Princeton University Press, 2013); and Jacob Levy, 'It Usually Begins with Isaiah Berlin', *The Good Society*, 15:3 (2006), pp. 23–26. Those who are sceptical of Berlin's novelty include Lauren J. Apfel, *The Advent of Pluralism: Diversity and Conflict in the Age of Sophocles* (Oxford: Oxford University Press, 2011); and Peter Lassman, *Pluralism* (Cambridge: Polity Press, 2011). Apfel argues that some classical writers anticipated value pluralism, while Lassman argues that some modern writers, most notably Max Weber, did so.

16. A useful overview of Arendt's specifically ethical thought is found in Mahony, *Hannah Arendt's Ethics*. Unfortunately, this book hardly addresses Arendt's critique of Judenräte,

ostensibly because this issue 'has been much discussed' elsewhere (p. 31). I beg to differ. While the issue has been 'much discussed' in terms of the volume of publications, it has not been addressed with an appropriate level of rigour and the subtlety demanded by the subject matter.

17. Arendt, *OT3*, p. 338, p. 454.

18. Arendt, *EIJ2*, p. 176.

19. Ibid., p. 54.

20. See, e.g., David Cesarani, *Eichmann: His Life and Crimes* (London: Vintage, 2005); Lipstadt, *The Eichmann Trial*; and Stangneth, *Eichmann before Jerusalem*. For a defence of Arendt on this issue, see Roger Berkowitz, 'Misreading "Eichmann in Jerusalem"', *The New York Times*, 7 July 2013, https://opinionator.blogs.nytimes.com/2013/07/07/misreading-hannah-arendts -eichmann-in-jerusalem/, accessed 15 January 2020.

21. Arendt, *EIJ2*, p. 146.

22. Bilsky, *Transformative Justice*, p. 160. See also Arendt, *EIJ2*, p. 287; and Hannah Arendt, '"As If Speaking to a Brick Wall": A Conversation with Joachim Fest', in *TWB*, pp. 274–90, at pp. 287–88.

23. Arendt, *EIJ2*, p. 279. Butler's comment on this part of *Eichmann in Jerusalem* is incisive: 'Through the rhetorical use of direct address, synthetic effect, and the equivocal doubling of a nameless voice, [Arendt] produces the textual image and sound of the judge who should have been but was not.' Judith Butler, *Parting Ways: Jewishness and the Critique of Zionism* (New York: Columbia University Press, 2012), p. 167.

24. Arendt, *EIJ2*, p. 58.

25. E.g., ibid., pp. 282–85; Hannah Arendt, 'The Eichmann Case and the Germans: A Conversation with Thilo Koch', *JW*, pp. 485–89, at pp. 486–87.

26. E.g., Arendt, *EIJ2*, p. 285; 'The Eichmann Case and the Germans', pp. 485–86; Hannah Arendt, 'Answers to Questions Submitted to Samuel Grafton', *JW*, pp. 472–84, at p. 482; Scholem and Arendt, 'Exchange', p. 55.

27. Arendt, *EIJ2*, p. 56. These words directly conflict with Arendt's later attempt to characterise *Eichmann* as little more than a report. She tells Scholem, for example, 'In my report I have only spoken of things which came up during the trial itself.' Scholem and Arendt, 'Exchange', p. 55.

28. Bilsky, *Transformative Justice*, p. 95, emphasis added.

29. Mahony, *Hannah Arendt's Ethics*, p. 33.

30. See esp. Arendt, *EIJ2*, pp. 119–20.

31. See Leora Bilsky, 'Between Justice and Politics: The Competition of Storytellers in the Eichmann Trial', in Steven E. Aschheim (ed.), *Hannah Arendt in Jerusalem* (Berkeley and Los Angeles: University of California Press, 2001), pp. 232–52.

32. Arendt, *EIJ2*, p. 284.

33. Ibid., p. 117.

34. Ibid., pp. 125–26, emphasis added.

35. Berlin and Lukes, 'Conversation', pp. 107–8.

36. Isaiah Berlin to Henning Ritter, 24 May 1993, *A*, p. 463.

37. Ibid.; MI Tape 19, p. 1 and MI Tape 29, p. 2.

38. MI Tape 19, pp. 1–3.

39. Ibid., p. 2 and MI Tape 29, p. 3.

40. For further discussion see, e.g., Ami Pedahzur and Arie Perliger, *Jewish Terrorism in Israel* (New York: Columbia University Press, 2011), esp. pp. 28–33; and Gaylen Ross (dir.), *Killing Kasztner: The Jew Who Dealt with Nazis* (2008; Brooklyn, NY: GR Films Inc, 2014), DVD, 2 discs.

41. Berlin to Ritter, 24 May 1993, *A*, p. 463.

42. Craig Taylor, *Moralism: A Study of a Vice* (Durham: Acumen, 2012).

43. Ibid., p. 2.

44. Michal Shaked, 'The Unknown Eichmann Trial: The Story of the Judge', *Holocaust and Genocide Studies* 29:1 (2015), pp. 1–38, at pp. 3–5.

45. In addition to Taylor's *Moralism*, I here draw on Robert K. Fullinwider, 'On Moralism', in C.J.A. Coady, *What's Wrong with Moralism* (Malden, MA: Blackwell Publishing, 2006), pp. 5–20.

46. Berlin and Lukes, 'Conversation', p. 108.

47. Jean-Paul Sartre, *Existentialism and Humanism*, trans. Philip Mairet (London: Methuen, 1948).

48. Ibid., p. 38.

49. The would-be advisors include Pierre Naville, whose discussion with Sartre is included in *Existentialism and Humanism*. According to Naville, Sartre's former student 'ought to have been answered. [. . .] I would most certainly have tried to arrive at a definite point of view [. . .]. Most certainly I would have urged him to do something' (*Existentialism and Humanism*, p. 69).

50. Berlin told Michael Ignatieff in 1988 that he had 'never read Sartre properly' (MI Tape 6, p. 17). But he read at least some of Sartre's work and acknowledged that 'he is a *very* clever man & his moral philosophy *is* what I think I ¾ believe'. Isaiah Berlin to Hamilton Fish Armstrong, 23 December 1954, *E*, p. 467.

51. Lisa Tessman, *When Doing the Right Things Is Impossible* (Oxford: Oxford University Press, 2017), p. 27.

52. To follow Tessman's terminology (ibid., p. 27), the police officer is still facing a 'moral conflict', which is a situation in which: 1) there is a moral requirement to do A and a moral requirement to do B; and 2) one cannot do both A and B.

53. Isaiah Berlin, 'Two Concepts of Liberty', in *L*, pp. 166–217, at p. 213.

54. Scholem and Arendt, 'Exchange', p. 52, emphasis added.

55. MI Tape 19, p. 3.

56. Elisabeth Young-Bruehl, *Hannah Arendt: For the Love of the World*, 2nd ed. (New Haven: Yale University Press, 2004), p. 106.

57. Her recollections of the arrest are found in Hannah Arendt, '"What Remains? The Language Remains": A Conversation with Günter Gaus', *EU*, pp. 1–23, at pp. 5–6.

58. Hannah Arendt to Gershom Scholem, 17 October 1941, *CAS*, pp. 5–9.

59. Young-Bruehl, *Hannah Arendt*, p. 154.

60. Hannah Arendt, 'We Refugees', *JW*, pp. 264–74, at p. 268, emphasis added.

61. Arendt, *EIJ2*, p. 8, emphasis added.

62. Arendt, 'Answers to Questions Submitted to Samuel Grafton', p. 474.

63. Leora Bilsky, 'In a Different Voice: Nathan Alterman and Hannah Arendt on the Kastner and Eichmann Trials', *Theoretical Inquiries in Law* 1:2 (2000), pp. 519–47, at p. 532.

64. Scholem and Arendt, 'Exchange', p. 52.

65. Isaiah Berlin to Charles Henderson, 14 August 1931, *F*, p. 27.

66. For this episode in Berlin's life, see Henry Hardy, 'Isaiah Berlin and James Bond at the Estoril Palace Hotel', presented at the Estoril Political Forum, 26 June 2018, https://www .youtube.com/watch?v=ykjgVYrIlho, accessed 15 January 2020.

67. MI Tape 14, p. 11.

68. Young-Bruehl, *Hannah Arendt*, p. 159.

69. Michael Ignatieff, *Isaiah Berlin: A Life* (London: Chatto & Windus, 1998) pp. 98–99.

70. 'Don's war' is Berlin's own expression, cited in Anne Deighton, 'Don and Diplomat: Isaiah Berlin and Britain's Early Cold War', *Cold War History* 13:4 (2013), pp. 525–40, at p. 529. The 'agreeable atmosphere' is also Berlin's own description in his 'Introduction by Isaiah Berlin', in H. G. Nicholas (ed.), *Washington Dispatches 1941–45: Weekly Political Reports from the British Embassy* (London: Weidenfeld & Nicolson, 1981), pp. vii–xiv, at p. x.

71. Deighton, 'Don and Diplomat', p. 532.

72. E.g., David Herman, 'Isaiah Berlin and the Holocaust: What Did Berlin Know? And When Did He Know It?', *Jewish Quarterly* 241 (Summer 2018), pp. 63–68; Michael Fleming, 'Isaiah Berlin and the Holocaust', *Dapim: Studies on the Holocaust* 32:3 (2018), pp. 206–25. See also the editors' note in Berlin, *B*, p. 510 note 1.

73. Peter Hayes, *Why? Explaining the Holocaust* (New York: W. W. Norton & Co., 2017), p. 281.

74. See Anthony Eden's reading of the joint declaration in the House of Commons in *Hansard*, House of Commons, vol. 385, cols 2,082–87, 17 December 1942, https://api.parliament.uk /historic-hansard/commons/1942/dec/17/united-nations-declaration, accessed 15 January 2020.

75. Berlin may have seen some of the mounting evidence of the destruction of European Jewry in 1942–43 but failed to recognise its significance at that time, possibly because of the institutional bias he shared with his colleagues in the Foreign Office. This possibility is suggested by Arie M. Dubnov, *Isaiah Berlin: The Journey of a Jewish Liberal* (New York: Palgrave Macmillan, 2012), pp. 172–73.

76. Herman, 'Isaiah Berlin and the Holocaust', p. 68.

77. Jahanbegloo, *CIB*, pp. 19–20.

78. Arendt, '"What Remains? The Language Remains"', p. 5.

79. Kei Hiruta, 'Hannah Arendt, Liberalism, and Freedom from Politics', in Kei Hiruta (ed.), *Arendt on Freedom, Liberation, and Revolution* (Cham: Palgrave Macmillan, 2019), pp. 17–45, at pp. 24–30.

80. Richard J. Bernstein, *Hannah Arendt and the Jewish Question* (Cambridge, MA: The MIT Press, 1996), p. 38. Bernstein's is a succinct summary of Arendt's own words, reiterated many times in various formulations.

81. Bernard Wasserstein's approach is exemplary in this respect. He is highly critical of Arendt and yet concedes that 'no one thinks of blaming Arendt for [ultimately] choosing to escape' from Nazified Europe. Bernard Wasserstein, *The Ambiguity of Virtue: Gertrude van Tijn and the Fate of the Dutch Jew* (Cambridge, MA: Harvard University Press, 2014), p. 240. See also Bernard Wasserstein, 'Blame the Victim', *The Times Literary Supplement*, 9 October 2009, pp. 13–14.

82. Isaiah Berlin, *Zionist Politics in Wartime Washington: A Fragment of Personal Reminiscence*, Yaacov Herzog Memorial Lecture (Jerusalem: Hebrew University of Jerusalem, 1972), reprinted

in Berlin, *F*, pp. 663–93. On the controversy that the publication (in Hebrew) of this text in *Ha'aretz* provoked, see Berlin, *B*, pp. 503–22.

83. To avoid misunderstanding: I am not suggesting that Berlin's silence on the Shoah may be accounted for *solely* by his sense of shame. There are certainly many other factors that must be taken into account, a particularly important one of which is proposed by Wasserstein. He writes, 'Berlin's public silence on the Nazi genocide, I would suggest, [arose] from deep scorn for the exploitation of the individual tragedies of millions for ulterior ends.' Bernard Wasserstein, *Isaiah Berlin, Isaac Deutscher and Arthur Koestler: Their Jewish Wars* (Amsterdam: Menasseh ben Israel Instituut, 2009), pp. 17–18.

84. I am not the first to address this aspect of the Arendt–Berlin conflict. See, e.g., Seyla Benhabib, *The Reluctant Modernism of Hannah Arendt*, new ed. (Lanham, MD: Lawman & Littlefield, 2003), p. li note 6; and David Caute, *Isaac and Isaiah: The Covert Punishment of a Cold War Heretic* (New Haven: Yale University Press, 2013), pp. 268–69.

85. Ring has written extensively on this issue. See Jennifer Ring, 'Hannah Arendt and the Eichmann Controversy: Cultural Taboos against Female Anger', *Women and Politics* 18:4 (1998), pp. 57–79; and Jennifer Ring, *The Political Consequences of Thinking: Gender and Judaism in the Work of Hannah Arendt* (Albany: State University of New York Press, 1997).

86. Bilsky, 'In a Different Voice', p. 540.

87. Ring, *The Political Consequences of Thinking*, p. 110.

88. An observation repeatedly made by scholars is worth recalling in this context: Raul Hilberg's *The Destruction of the European Jews*, on which Arendt relied heavily in her critique of Judenräte, did not attract nearly as strong a criticism as Arendt's book did. How much of this should be accounted for by gender, and how much by other factors, has been a matter of endless controversy.

89. Richard H. King, *Arendt and America* (Chicago: University of Chicago Press, 2015), p. 212.

90. See Berlin cited in Frances Kiernan, *Seeing Mary Plain: A Life of Mary McCarthy* (New York: W. W. Norton & Co., 2000), p. 354; and Isaiah Berlin to Derwent May, 1 October 1986, *A*, p. 300. Of course, 'bluestocking' was originally a non-pejorative term referring to a celebrated group of *salonnières* and their friends and associates in nineteenth-century London. But it came to acquire pejorative connotations fairly quickly, certainly before Berlin's lifetime.

91. One may recall another famous remark Arendt made during her interview with Günter Gaus: 'I always thought that there are certain occupations that are improper for women, that do not become them, if I may put it that way. It just doesn't look good when a woman gives orders. She should try not to get into such a situation if she wants to remain feminine.' Arendt, '"What Remains? The Language Remains"', pp. 2–3.

92. Arendt and McCarthy, *BF*, p. xiii.

93. Berlin in Kiernan, *Seeing Mary Plain*, p. 268.

94. Nancy J. Hirschmann, 'Berlin, Feminism, and Positive Liberty', in Bruce Baum and Robert Nichols (eds), *Isaiah Berlin and the Politics of Freedom: 'Two Concepts of Liberty' 50 Years Later* (New York: Routledge, 2012), pp. 185–98, at p. 185.

95. Isaiah Berlin to Stephen Spender, 2 July 1963, *T*.

96. Arendt, *EIJ2*, p. 284.

97. According to Arendt, 'one cannot claim that they [i.e., Jewish functionaries who cooperated during the Holocaust] were traitors. (There were traitors too, but that is irrelevant.)' Scholem and Arendt, 'Exchange', p. 54.

98. Arendt names male leaders only, but there were female leaders, too. Wasserstein's study of one female member of the Amsterdam Judenrat is a powerful, if implicit, rejoinder to Arendt's *Eichmann*. See Wasserstein, *The Ambiguity of Virtue*.

99. Shmuel Lederman, 'Hannah Arendt's Critique of the *Judenräte* in Context: Modern Jewish Leadership and Radical Democracy', *Holocaust and Genocide Studies* 32:2 (2018), pp. 207–23, at p. 214.

100. Scholem and Arendt, 'Exchange', p. 55. Arendt's view may have been influenced by her experience in the Gurs internment camp, where inmates were, on her observation, not totally dominated but fluctuated between despair and 'a violent courage to live'. Arendt, 'We Refugees', p. 268.

101. Scholem and Arendt, 'Exchange', p. 55.

102. Arendt, *EIJ2*, p. 123, emphasis added.

103. Needless to say, the 'privileged' Jew is a highly contested category and may be defined differently. Here I follow Adam Brown's definition, which includes 'privileged' Jews in both ghettos and camps. See Adam Brown, *Judging 'Privileged' Jews: Holocaust Ethics, Representation and the 'Grey Zone'* (New York: Berghahn, 2013).

104. Scholem and Arendt, 'Exchange', p. 55.

105. Ibid.

106. Berlin and Lukes, 'Conversation', p. 108.

107. It is not necessary to consider this issue fully in the present context. Simply put, however, Berlin rejected both deontology and consequentialism as incapable of doing justice to the complexity of moral life. But he tended to be more explicitly critical of consequentialism, not least because this has been appropriated by totalitarian leaders who justified short-term sacrifices ostensibly for long-term goals.

108. Bauer, *Rethinking the Holocaust*, p. 155.

109. Berlin and Lukes, 'Conversation', p. 108.

110. Yehuda Bauer may be implicitly criticising Arendt when he writes the following: 'Each Judenrat presided over a hell.' Bauer, *Rethinking the Holocaust*, p. 129.

111. Arendt, *OT3*, p. 452.

112. She writes, 'There are no parallels to the life in the concentration camps [. . .] all parallels create confusion and distract attention from what is essential' (*OT3*, p. 444). These words seem to indicate that, even in *Origins*, Arendt drew a sharp distinction between the situations in the ghettos and those in the camps.

113. Scholem and Arendt, 'Exchange', p. 55.

114. Hannah Arendt, 'The Destruction of Six Million: A *Jewish World* Symposium', *JW*, pp. 490–95, at p. 494.

115. See, most notably, Michal Aharony, *Hannah Arendt and the Limits of Total Domination: The Holocaust, Plurality, and Resistance* (London: Routledge, 2015).

116. Arendt, *EIJ2*, p. 11.

117. Ibid., p. 12. See also p. 283; Arendt, 'The Formidable Dr. Robinson', p. 496 and p. 508.

118. Scholem and Arendt, 'Exchange', p. 55.

119. See my discussion in Chapter 4.

120. Arendt, *OT3*, p. 447.

121. Involved in the leak were two Nazi officials, the Reich plenipotentiary Werner Best and his right-hand man Georg Ferdinand Duckwitz. Duckwitz was recognised as 'Righteous among the Nations' in 1971. Best's motive for facilitating the leak remains obscure.

122. Arendt, *EIJ*2, pp. 170–75.

123. Arendt is ambiguous on this issue. On the one hand, she writes that '[t]he story of the Danish Jews is *sui generis*' (Arendt, *EIJ*2, p. 171). On the other hand, she writes that 'the same thing happened in Bulgaria as was to happen in Denmark' (ibid., p. 187).

124. Arendt, 'Answers to Questions Submitted to Samuel Grafton', p. 481.

125. Bernard Crick, 'Hannah Arendt and the Burden of Our Times', *The Political Quarterly* 68:1 (1997), pp. 77–84, at p. 81.

126. Isaiah Trunk, *Judenrat: The Jewish Councils in Eastern Europe under Nazi Occupation* (Lincoln, NE: University of Nebraska Press, 1996), pp. 570–75.

127. E.g., Arendt, *EIJ*2, p. 11 and p. 143.

128. Nadezhda Mandelstam, *Hope against Hope* (London: The Harvill Press, 1999), pp. 42–43.

129. This line of criticism has a long history. See, e.g., Noël O'Sullivan, 'Hannah Arendt: Hellenic Nostalgia and Industrial Society', in Anthony de Crespigny and Kenneth Minogue (eds), *Contemporary Political Philosophers* (London: Methuen, 1976), pp. 228–51; Judith Shklar, 'Hannah Arendt as Pariah', *Partisan Review*, 50:1 (1983), pp. 64–77; and Richard Wolin, *Heidegger's Children: Hannah Arendt, Karl Löwith, Hans Jonas, and Herbert Marcuse* (Princeton: Princeton University Press, 2001), pp. 30–69.

130. Shklar, 'Hannah Arendt as Pariah', p. 75. There are many interesting parallels between Shklar's and Berlin's critical remarks on Arendt. A full study of Shklar's multilayered critical engagement with Arendt is wanting, but scholars have examined various aspects of it. See, e.g., Samantha Ashenden and Andreas Hess, 'Totalitarianism and Justice: Hannah Arendt's and Judith N. Shklar's Political Reflections in Historical and Theoretical Perspective', *Economy and Society* 45:3–4 (2016), pp. 505–29; Christof Royer, 'International Criminal Justice between Scylla and Charybdis: The "Peace Versus Justice" Dilemma Analysed through the Lenses of Judith Shklar's and Hannah Arendt's Legal and Political Theories', *Human Rights Review* 18:4 (2017), pp. 395–416; and Seyla Benhabib, *Exile, Statelessness, and Migration: Playing Chess with History from Hannah Arendt to Isaiah Berlin* (Princeton: Princeton University Press, 2018), esp. pp. 125–44.

131. Villa has arguably done more than any other Arendt scholar to defend Arendt from such misrepresentations. See, e.g., Dana R. Villa, *Politics, Philosophy, Terror: Essays on the Thought of Hannah Arendt* (Princeton: Princeton University Press, 1999), esp. pp. 61–86; and his *Public Freedom*, esp. pp. 302–37.

132. Crick, 'Hannah Arendt and the Burden of Our Times', p. 82.

133. Needless to say, whether one finds a romantic existentialism in *The Human Condition* has been a much contested issue, which I do not wish to discuss in detail in this book. (My short answer is, 'No.')

134. For further discussions, see Ruth Starkman, 'For the Honor and Glory of the Jewish People: Arendt's Ambivalent Jewish Nationhood', *The European Legacy* 28:2 (2013), pp. 185–96; and Tal Correm, 'Hannah Arendt on National Liberation, Violence, and Federalism', in Hiruta (ed.), *Arendt on Freedom, Liberation, and Revolution*, pp. 139–69.

135. Hannah Arendt, 'Days of Change', *JW*, pp. 214–17, at p. 217.

136. Bauer, *Rethinking the Holocaust*, p. 140.

137. Or, rather, Berlin suspected that Arendt's conception of 'participatory democracy' was 'derived from a totally imaginary vision of the Greek *polis*'. Berlin to May, 1 October 1986, *A*, p. 298.

138. Isaiah Berlin to Bernard Crick, 4 November 1963, T.

139. Arendt, '"What Remains? The Language Remains"', pp. 1–2.

140. This is a succinct summary by Jenkins of Williams's 'first guiding conviction'. Mark P. Jenkins, *Bernard Williams* (Chesham: Acumen, 2006), p. 3.

141. Hannah Arendt, 'On Humanity in Dark Times: Thoughts about Lessing', *MID*, pp. 3–31, at p. 27.

142. Scholem and Arendt, 'Exchange', p. 55.

143. Berlin, 'Two Concepts of Liberty', p. 177 note 1.

144. Crick, 'Hannah Arendt and the Burden of Our Times', p. 82.

145. Isaiah Berlin to Sam Behrman, 19 July 1963, T. See also Isaiah Berlin to William Phillips, 7 May 1963, from the *Partisan Review* collection, Howard Gotlieb Archival Research Center at Boston University Libraries; Berlin to Mary McCarthy, 7 August 1964, *B*, p. 196; and Berlin to Meyer Schapiro, 20 July 1967, *B*, p. 337.

146. Arendt, '"As If Speaking to a Brick Wall"'.

147. Ibid., p. 290.

148. Arendt, 'Answers to Questions Submitted to Samuel Grafton', p. 480.

149. I draw on Craig Taylor's *Moralism* here again.

150. Scholem and Arendt, 'Exchange', p. 52. See Michelle-Irène Brudny, 'Scholem and Arendt, from Berlin to Jerusalem or New York', *Arendt Studies* 3 (2019), pp. 215–21.

151. The first edition of *Eichmann* has the line, 'Dr. Leo Baeck, former Chief Rabbi of Berlin, who in the eyes of both Jews and Gentiles was the "Jewish Führer"'. Hannah Arendt, *EIJ1*, p. 105. The part beginning with 'who' is deleted in *EIJ2*.

152. This issue is extensively discussed in Barry Sharpe's neglected work *Modesty and Arrogance in Judgement: Hannah Arendt's* Eichmann in Jerusalem (Westport, CT: Praeger, 1999).

153. Arendt, *EIJ2*, p. 31.

154. Ibid., p. 114.

155. Arendt, 'Answers to Questions Submitted to Samuel Grafton', p. 480.

156. Hannah Arendt, 'Personal Responsibility under Dictatorship', *RJ*, pp. 17–48, at p. 33.

157. Arendt, *EIJ2*, p. 295.

158. Ibid., p. 104.

159. Hannah Arendt, 'Some Questions of Moral Philosophy', *RJ*, pp. 49–146, at p. 78.

160. Arendt, *EIJ2*, p. 104.

161. Ibid.

162. Arendt, *EIJ2*, p. 103.

163. The modesty/arrogance distinction is in many respects in parallel with the pariah/parvenu distinction that Arendt drew earlier in her career, most notably in Hannah Arendt, 'The Jew as Pariah: A Hidden Tradition', *JW*, pp. 275–97; and Hannah Arendt, *Rahel Varnhagen: The Life of a Jewess, First Complete Edition*, ed. Liliane Weissberg, trans. Richard and Clara Winston (Baltimore: Johns Hopkins University Press, 1997), pp. 237–59. The parallel is an interesting issue in its own right but is beyond the scope of this book.

164. Arendt, *EIJ2*, p. 287.

165. Jahanbegloo, *CIB*, p. 84. See also Isaiah Berlin to Leonard Schapiro, 29 December 1976, *A*, pp. 41–42.

166. Arendt cited in Young-Bruehl, *Hannah Arendt*, p. 339.

167. Norman Podhoretz, *Ex-Friends: Falling Out with Allen Ginsberg, Lionel & Diana Trilling, Lillian Hellman, Hannah Arendt, and Norman Mailer* (New York: The Free Press, 1999), p. 168.

168. Berlin to Ritter, 24 May 1993, *A*, p. 463.

169. Hannah Arendt to Karl Jaspers, 20 October 1963, *C*, p. 522.

170. Ibid., p. 524.

171. Ibid., p. 522.

172. See Hannah Arendt, 'The Destruction of Six Million', *JW*, pp. 490–95, at p. 493; Scholem and Arendt, 'Exchange', p. 54.

173. Hannah Arendt to Karl and Gertrud Jaspers, 24 November 1963, *C*, p. 535. See also Hannah Arendt to Mary McCarthy, 4 February 1970, *BF*, p. 254; Berlin to McCarthy, 7 August 1964, *B*, pp. 195–97; Isaiah Berlin to Arthur Schlesinger, 1 April 1977, T.

174. Isaiah Berlin to Elżbieta Ettinger, 29 December 1993, PEE.

175. Scholem and Arendt, 'Exchange', p. 54.

176. As pointed out by Judith Butler: Butler, *Parting Ways*, p. 135.

177. Scholem and Arendt, 'Exchange', p. 54.

178. Ibid.

179. Ibid.

180. For a more thorough discussion of Arendt's debt to Lazare, see Adi Armon, 'The "Origins of The Origins": Antisemitism, Hannah Arendt, and the Influence of Bernard Lazare', *Arendt Studies* 3 (2019), pp. 49–68.

181. Hannah Arendt, 'From Dreyfus Affair to France Today', *Jewish Social Studies* 4:3 (1942), pp. 195–240, at p. 239.

182. Ibid., p. 240.

183. Ibid., p. 240 note 109.

184. Ibid., p. 236.

185. Ibid.

186. Arendt, *EIJ2*, p. 117, emphasis added. See also Arendt, 'The Formidable Dr. Robinson', pp. 501–2.

187. Hannah Arendt (with Joseph Maier), 'Cui Bono?: Case against the *Saturday Evening Post*', *JW*, pp. 150–52, at p. 152.

188. Erich Fromm, *The Art of Loving* (New York: Open Road, 2013), pp. 72–73.

189. Ibid., pp. 73–74.

190. On this topic see, e.g., Paul Reitter, *On the Origins of Jewish Self-Hatred* (Princeton: Princeton University Press, 2012); Susan A. Glenn, 'The Vogue of Jewish Self-Hatred in Post-World War II America', *Jewish Social Studies* 12:3 (2006), pp. 95–136; and Sander L. Gilman, *Jewish Self-Hatred: Anti-Semitism and the Hidden Language of the Jews* (Baltimore: The Johns Hopkins University Press, 1986).

191. Hannah Arendt, 'A Way toward the Reconciliation of Peoples', *JW*, pp. 258–63, at p. 261.

192. Berlin writes, 'I cannot help thinking that her attitude to Zionists, and to some extent Jews, is somewhat like Koestler's towards Communists—there is something there which will go on punishing her & us for ever.' Berlin to McCarthy, 7 August 1964, *B*, p. 196.

193. Isaiah Berlin to Pierre Vidal-Naquet, 17 February 1975, MSB 209/278.

194. See my discussion in Chapter 2.

Chapter 6. Islands of Freedom

1. Hannah Arendt, Raymond Aron and Isaiah Berlin (the editors' and translators' names are unknown), *Trójgłos o wolności* (Warsaw: Wolna Spółka Wydawnicza Komitywa, 1987).

2. It is unlikely that Berlin was aware of the publication of *Trójgłos o wolności*.

3. Andrzej Walicki, *Encounters with Isaiah Berlin: Story of an Intellectual Friendship* (Frankfurt am Main: Peter Lang, 2011), p. 148.

4. David Caute, *Isaac and Isaiah: The Covert Punishment of a Cold War Heretic* (New Haven: Yale University Press, 2013).

5. Ibid., p. 4.

6. Isaiah Berlin to Ursula Niebuhr, 27 April 1972, T.

7. Caute, *Isaac and Isaiah*, p. 262.

8. This issue is discussed in Russell Jacoby, *Picture Imperfect: Utopian Thought for an Anti-Utopian Age* (New York: Columbia University Press, 2005). I have attempted to challenge some of Jacoby's claims in Kei Hiruta, 'An "Anti-utopian Age?": Isaiah Berlin's England, Hannah Arendt's America, and Utopian Thinking in Dark Times', *Journal of Political Ideologies* 22:1 (2017), pp. 12–29.

9. The image of an 'island of freedom' recurrently appears in Arendt's work. See, e.g., Hannah Arendt, 'Preface: The Gap between Past and Future', *BPF3*, pp. 3–15, at p. 6; 'What Is Existential Philosophy?', *EU*, pp. 163–87, at p. 186; and *OR3*, pp. 267–68.

10. This observation has been made by many authors, e.g., Michael Ignatieff, *Isaiah Berlin: A Life* (London: Chatto & Windus, 1998), p. 36; and Jan-Werner Müller, 'Fear and Freedom: On "Cold War Liberalism"', *European Journal of Political Theory* 7:1 (2008), pp. 45–64, at pp. 54–55. This chapter builds on their observations.

11. Isaiah Berlin, 'Epilogue: The Three Strands in My Life', *PI3*, pp. 433–39, p. 437.

12. Ignatieff, *Isaiah Berlin*, p. 36.

13. George Crowder, *Isaiah Berlin: Liberty and Pluralism* (Cambridge: Polity Press, 2004).

14. Jahanbegloo, *CIB*, pp. 101–2.

15. Berlin and Lukes, 'Conversation', p. 121.

16. Isaiah Berlin to Helen Gardner, 21 December 1965, *B*, p. 262.

17. Isaiah Berlin to John Sparrow, 14 March 1964, *B*, p. 190.

18. L. T. Hobhouse, *Liberalism* (London: Oxford University Press, 1911).

19. Michael Freeden, *Liberalism Divided: A Study in British Political Thought 1914–1939* (Oxford: Oxford University Press, 1986); Michael Freeden, *Ideologies and Political Theory: A Conceptual Approach* (Oxford: Clarendon Press, 1996), pp. 141–225.

20. Berlin and Lukes, 'Conversation', pp. 98–99, p. 91.

21. Joseph Raz, *The Morality of Freedom* (Oxford: Clarendon Press, 1986); Steven Wall, *Liberalism, Perfectionism and Restraint* (Cambridge: Cambridge University Press, 1998).

22. Müller, 'Fear and Freedom', p. 48.

23. Berlin cited in Ignatieff, *Isaiah Berlin*, p. 301.

24. See Henry Hardy, 'Editor's Preface', in Berlin, *POI2*, pp. xxv–xxxiii, at p. xxv.

25. Joshua Rubenstein, *Leon Trotsky: A Revolutionary Life* (New Haven: Yale University Press, 2011), p. 180.

26. Berlin sometimes distinguishes between 'national consciousness' and 'nationalism', the former designating a natural and benign sense of national belonging and the latter more narrowly the inflamed form of that feeling. But he does not consistently use the terminological distinction; nor does the dichotomy adequately capture the complexity of Berlin's analysis of the subject matter. I shall therefore use 'nationalism' in a broad sense and discuss various types of it without using the term 'national consciousness'.

27. My analysis is indebted to David Miller, 'Crooked Timber or Bent Twig?: Berlin's Nationalism', in George Crowder and Henry Hardy (eds), *The One and the Many: Reading Isaiah Berlin* (New York: Prometheus Books, 2007), pp. 181–206.

28. Ibid., p. 182.

29. E.g., Isaiah Berlin, 'Nationalism: Past Neglect and Present Power', *AC2*, pp. 420–48, at p. 442; 'A Note on Nationalism', *POI2*, pp. 301–11, at pp. 307–8; 'The Bent Twig: On the Rise of Nationalism', *CTH2*, pp. 253–78, at pp. 262–63.

30. Jahanbegloo, *CIB*, p. 102.

31. See esp. Isaiah Berlin, 'The Problem of Nationalism: A Dialogue with Stuart Hampshire, chaired by Bryan Magee', 1972, available at the IBVL (2006), http://berlin.wolf.ox.ac.uk/lists/nachlass/probnati.pdf, accessed 1 September 2020.

32. John Stuart Mill, 'Considerations on Representative Government', in *On Liberty and Other Essays*, ed. John Gray (Oxford: Oxford University Press, 1998), pp. 203–467, at pp. 427–34.

33. Isaiah Berlin, 'Herder and the Enlightenment', *TCE2*, pp. 208–300, at p. 256.

34. Berlin, 'The Problem of Nationalism', p. 3.

35. Ignatieff, *Isaiah Berlin*, p. 36.

36. E.g., Jahanbegloo, *CIB*, pp. 111–13; Isaiah Berlin, 'Appendix to the Second Edition', *CC2*, pp. 261–334, at pp. 288–89 and pp. 305–10.

37. See Arie M. Dubnov, *Isaiah Berlin: The Journey of a Jewish Liberal* (New York: Palgrave Macmillan, 2012), pp. 53–76; Joshua L. Cherniss, *A Mind and Its Time: The Development of Isaiah Berlin's Political Thought* (Oxford: Oxford University Press, 2013), pp. 1–14.

38. Isaiah Berlin, 'Introduction', *L*, pp. 3–54, at p. 42; 'Two Concepts of Liberty', *L*, pp. 166–217, at p. 180, p. 170, emphasis added.

39. Isaiah Berlin, 'England's Mistaken Moralist', *The Times Higher Education Supplement*, 15 October 1993.

40. Isaiah Berlin to Maurice Bowra, 3 December 1965, *B*, p. 259.

41. Dubnov, *Isaiah Berlin*, p. 188.

42. Isaiah Berlin, 'Winston Churchill in 1940', *PI3*, pp. 1–29, at p. 29.

43. See Michael Kenny and Nick Pearce, *Shadows of Empire: The Anglosphere in British Politics* (London: Polity Press, 2018), pp. 38–60.

44. Isaiah Berlin, 'The Anglo-American Predicament', *E*, pp. 743–48, at p. 747–48. This piece was originally published in the *Listener*, 29 November 1949, pp. 518–19. All citations in this book are from *E*.

45. 'Mr Berlin', *Evening Standard*, 5 October 1949, p. 4, cited in Berlin, *E*, p. 130.

46. Berlin, 'The Anglo-American Predicament', *E*, p. 748. These words, which Berlin liked to cite, are from Joseph Butler, *Fifteen Sermons Preached at the Rolls Chapel* (London: James & John Knapton, 1726), p. 136.

47. Isaiah Berlin, 'Rabindranath Tagore and the Consciousness of Nationality', *SR2*, pp. 316–37, at p. 327.

48. According to Pitts, substantial engagement with the question of empire and imperialism began only in the final two decades of the twentieth century in both political theory and intellectual history. Jennifer Pitts, 'Political Theory of Empire and Imperialism', in Sankar Muthu (ed.), *Empire and Modern Political Thought* (Cambridge: Cambridge University Press, 2012), pp. 351–87.

49. Barnor Hesse, 'Escaping Liberty: Western Hegemony, Black Fugitivity', *Political Theory* 42:3 (2014), pp. 288–313. It may be noted, however, that one does not automatically free oneself from racial and colonial blindness by merely saying *something* about evils and wrongs linked to imperialism and colonialism. Some contributors to the recent debate over 'what's wrong with colonialism' in Anglophone philosophy show varying degrees of such blindness, exacerbated by historical ignorance. For an overview of this debate, see Margaret Moore, 'Justice and Colonialism', *Philosophy Compass* 11:8 (2016), pp. 447–61.

50. The London-based pollster YouGov undertook a survey of the British public's attitude to the legacy of the Empire in 2014. The survey found, among other things, that 'most think the British Empire is more something to be proud of (59%) rather than ashamed of (19%)'; and that '[t]hough many (36%) are unsure, British people do tend to think that, overall, former British colonies are now better off for having been part of the empire, by 49–15%.' Will Dahlgreen, 'The British Empire is "Something to be Proud of"', 26 July 2014, https://yougov.co.uk/topics/politics/articles-reports/2014/07/26/britain-proud-its-empire, accessed 27 September 2019.

51. Isaiah Berlin to Geert Van Cleemput, 22 April 1996, *A*, p. 529; See also Berlin, 'Rabindranath Tagore', p. 328; and *KM5*, pp. 187–88.

52. Isaiah Berlin, 'Benjamin Disraeli, Karl Marx and the Search for Identity', *Transactions of the Jewish Historical Society of England* 22 (1968–69), pp. 1–20, reprinted in *AC2*, pp. 317–60. My references to this essay will be from *AC2*.

53. Ibid., p. 331. According to Cesarani, it was only in the early 1980s that Disraeli's biographers began discussing his Jewishness as a central theme. Berlin was a pioneer in this respect, though he was behind Arendt, as I shall discuss shortly. See David Cesarani, *Disraeli: The Novel Politician* (New Haven: Yale University Press, 2016), pp. 4–5.

54. Berlin, 'Benjamin Disraeli, Karl Marx and the Search for Identity', p. 330, p. 342.

55. Berlin, 'Winston Churchill in 1940', p. 12.

56. Ibid.

57. Berlin, 'Benjamin Disraeli, Karl Marx and the Search for Identity', p. 341.

58. Ibid., p. 346.

59. Arendt's usage of the term 'imperialism' is inconsistent. On the one hand, she sometimes uses it in a broad sense to refer to the 'Continental imperialisms' of the German and Slav pan-movements as well as the 'overseas imperialisms' of Britain, France, the Netherlands and so on. On the other hand, she sometimes uses 'imperialism' more narrowly, to refer solely to the 'overseas' type. In this chapter I focus on this narrow sense because pan-movements are largely irrelevant to British imperialism, which is an example of the overseas variety.

60. Arendt, *OT3*, p. 123.

61. Karuna Mantena, 'Genealogies of Catastrophe: Arendt on the Logic and Legacy of Imperialism', in Seyla Benhabib (ed.), *Politics in Dark Times: Encounters with Hannah Arendt* (Cambridge: Cambridge University Press, 2010), pp. 83–112, at p. 91.

62. Arendt, *OT3*, p 302.

63. Ibid., p. 138.

64. Vladimir Ilyich Lenin, 'Imperialism, the Highest Stage of Capitalism: A Popular Outline' [1916/1917] in his *Collected Works*, vol. 22 (Moscow: Progress Publishers, 1964), pp. 185–304.

65. Although my present focus is on Arendt's dispute with Lenin, a different and no less interesting story may be told about her critical engagement with another, and less orthodox, Marxist: Rosa Luxemburg. In fact, Arendt relies quite heavily on Luxemburg's theory of imperialism to challenge Lenin's theory. On this issue, see Seyla Benhabib, *The Reluctant Modernism of Hannah Arendt*, new ed. (Lanham, MD: Rowman & Littlefield, 2003), pp. 77–79. For a broader discussion of Arendt's debt to Luxemburg's theory of imperialism, see Philip Spencer, 'From Rosa Luxemburg to Hannah Arendt: Socialism, Barbarism and the Extermination Camps', *The European Legacy* 11:5 (2006), pp. 527–40.

66. Lenin himself expresses greater agreement with 'social liberal' Hobson than with 'un-Marxist' Kautsky. Lenin, 'Imperialism', pp. 269–70. See J. A. Hobson, *Imperialism: A Study* (London: James Nisbet, 1902).

67. Arendt, *OT3*, p. 150.

68. Ibid., p. 189.

69. Ibid., p. 151.

70. Lenin, 'Imperialism', p. 266.

71. Arendt, *OT3*, p. 155.

72. Mantena, 'Genealogies of Catastrophe', p. 89.

73. Arendt, *OT3*, p. 75. This is a quotation from Horace B. Samuel, *Modernities* (London: Kegan Paul, Trench, Trübner & Co., 1913), p. 58.

74. Arendt, *OT3*, pp. 68–79.

75. For nuanced analyses of the two Disraelis, see Joan Cocks, *Passions and Paradox: Intellectuals Confront the National Question* (Princeton: Princeton University Press, 2002), pp. 75–88; and Arie M. Dubnov, 'Can Parallels Meet? Hannah Arendt and Isaiah Berlin on the Jewish Post-Emancipatory Quest for Political Freedom', *The Leo Baeck Institute Year Book* 62 (2017), pp. 27–51, at pp. 39–44.

76. Arendt, *OT3*, p. 78.

77. Ibid., p. 74.

78. Ibid., p. 171, p. 175, p. 180, pp. 182–83.

79. Ibid., p. 144.

80. Ibid., p. 121, p. 124.

81. Patricia Owens, *Between War and Politics: International Relations and the Thought of Hannah Arendt* (Oxford: Oxford University Press, 2007), p. 61.

82. My reading here is especially indebted to Yehouda Shenhav, 'Beyond "Instrumental Rationality": Lord Cromer and the Imperial Roots of Eichmann's Bureaucracy', *Journal of Genocide Research* 15:4 (2013), pp. 379–99.

83. Arendt, *OT3*, p. 209, p. 211.

84. Ibid., p. 211.

85. Ibid., p. 182.

86. Ibid., p. 211.

87. Ibid., p. 185.

88. See Shenhav, 'Beyond "Instrumental Rationality"'.

89. Mantena, 'Genealogies of Catastrophe', p. 91.

90. Arendt, *OT3*, p. 220.

91. I have discussed Arendt's reading of Hobbes, and her critical view of 'bourgeois liberalism' more broadly, in Kei Hiruta, 'Hannah Arendt, Liberalism, and Freedom from Politics', in Kei Hiruta (ed.), *Arendt on Freedom, Liberation, and Revolution* (Cham: Palgrave Macmillan, 2019), pp. 17–45. See also Dubnov, 'Can Parallels Meet?', pp. 44–49; Liisi Keedus, 'Liberalism and the Question of the "Proud": Hannah Arendt and Leo Strauss as Readers of Hobbes', *Journal of the History of Ideas* 73:2 (2012), pp. 335–58; and Edgar Straehle, 'The Problem of Sovereignty: Reading Hobbes through the Eyes of Hannah Arendt', *Hobbes Studies* 32:1 (2019), pp. 71–91.

92. 'Indeed', Owens writes in support of Arendt's argument, 'more died in South Africa as a result of British actions than died in South West Africa as a result of German.' Owens, *Between War and Politics*, p. 65.

93. Müller, 'Fear and Freedom', pp. 54–55.

94. See my discussion in Chapter 2.

95. Arendt, *OR3*, p. 148.

96. Hannah Arendt to Karl and Gertrud Jaspers, 26 June 1968, *C*, p. 681, emphasis added.

97. Arendt, *OR3*, p. 110.

98. Hannah Arendt, 'Thoughts on Politics and Revolution: A Commentary', *CR*, pp. 199–233, at pp. 231–32. For a comprehensive study of the council system in Arendt's political thought, see Shmuel Lederman, *Hannah Arendt and Participatory Democracy: A People's Utopia* (Cham: Palgrave Macmillan, 2019).

99. Andrew Arato and Jean Cohen, 'Banishing the Sovereign?: Internal and External Sovereignty in Arendt', *Constellations* 16:2 (2009), pp. 307–30, at p. 314.

100. See Lisa Disch, 'How Could Hannah Arendt Glorify the American Revolution and Revile the French?: Placing *On Revolution* in the Historiography of the French and American Revolutions', *European Journal of Political Theory* 10:3 (2011), pp. 350–71.

101. Woodrow Wilson cited in Arendt, *OR3*, p. 192.

102. Arendt, *OR3*, pp. 155–56, pp. 217–21, pp. 229–30, p. 294 note 42; Hannah Arendt, 'Civil Disobedience', *CR*, pp. 49–102, at p. 92.

103. John Adams cited in Arendt, *OR3*, p. 137.

104. Thomas Jefferson, repeatedly cited in Arendt, *OR3*, pp. 117–22, pp. 207–73.

105. This means Waldron's recent criticism of Berlin's alleged neglect of political institutions is only partially valid: Jeremy Waldron, *Political Political Theory: Essays on Institutions* (Cambridge, MA: Harvard University Press, 2016), pp. 1–22 and pp. 274–89. It is valid to the extent that Berlin has little to say on formal institutions such as the role of the court; but it is invalid to the extent that Berlin has much to say on institutions broadly conceived as 'identifiable practices consisting of recognized roles linked by clusters of rules or conventions governing relations among the occupants of these roles'. Oran R. Young, *International Cooperation: Building Regimes for Natural*

Resources and the Environment (Ithaca, NY: Cornell University Press, 1989), p. 5. Young's is a standard definition of institutions in political science.

106. Arendt, 'Civil Disobedience', p. 79.

107. Ibid., pp. 85–87; Arendt, *OR3*, pp. 156–70.

108. See, in particular, Arendt, *OR3*, pp. 460–79.

109. Ian Kershaw, *Hitler 1889–1936: Hubris* (New York: W. W. Norton & Co., 1999), p. 367.

110. Arendt, *OT3*, p. 478.

111. This, needless to say, is an allusion to Judith N. Shklar, 'The Liberalism of Fear', in Nancy L. Rosenblum (ed.) *Liberalism and the Moral Life* (Cambridge, MA: Harvard University Press, 1989), pp. 21–38.

112. For further discussion, see Hiruta, 'Hannah Arendt, Liberalism, and Freedom from Politics'.

113. See esp. Arendt, *CR; TWB; OR3*, pp. 207–73; and Hannah Arendt, 'Home to Roost', in *RJ*, pp. 257–75.

114. Arendt, *OR3*, pp. 243–44.

115. Arendt, *HC*, p. 176.

116. Arendt, *OR3*, p. 271.

117. Columbia University Archives, Rare Book & Manuscript Library, '1968: Columbia in Crisis' (2011), https://exhibitions.cul.columbia.edu/exhibits/show/1968, accessed 1 February 2020.

118. E.g., Isaiah Berlin to Rowland Burdon-Muller, 26 January 1967, *B*, p. 322; Berlin to Elizabeth Hardwick, 6 November 1968, *B*, pp. 362–63; Berlin to Stephen Spender, 22 February 1967, MSB 283/87; Berlin to A. H. Halsey, 5 March 1968, MSB 179/99–100; Berlin to David Cecil, 21 March 1969, MSB 182/56–57.

119. Isaiah Berlin to Christopher Sykes, 11 May 1968, *B*, p. 347.

120. Isaiah Berlin to McGeorge Bundy, 31 May 1968, *B*, p. 350.

121. Berlin to Bowra, 2 April 1969, *B*, p. 381.

122. Isaiah Berlin to Anna Kallin, 1 October 1968, *B*, p. 360.

123. Isaiah Berlin to Brian Urquhart, 7 September 1966, *B*, pp. 311–12; Berlin to Burdon-Muller, 17 January 1968, *B*, p. 344. See also Berlin's contribution to Cecil Woolf and John Bagguley (eds), *Authors Take Sides on Vietnam: Two Questions on the War in Vietnam Answered by the Authors of Several Nations* (London: Peter Owen, 1967), pp. 60–62, reprinted in Berlin, *B*, pp. 601–2.

124. Isaiah Berlin to Alan Ryan, 25 November 1968, MSB 181/84.

125. Isaiah Berlin to Arthur Schlesinger, 6 June 1968, *B*, p. 352.

126. Berlin to Bowra, 2 April 1969, *B*, p. 381.

127. Hannah Arendt to Karl Jaspers, 25 November 1967, *C*, pp. 676–77. See also Hannah Arendt to Mary McCarthy, 21 December 1968, *BF*, pp. 230–31; Arendt, *DZ*, XXVI: 3, pp. 702–5.

128. Arendt to Jaspers, 25 November 1967, *C*, pp. 676–77.

129. Hannah Arendt to Gertrud and Karl Jaspers, 27 July 1968, *C*, p. 682. See also Arendt, *DZ*, XXVI: 13, pp. 710–12.

130. Hannah Arendt, 'On Violence', *CR*, pp. 103–98, at p. 125.

131. Arendt, 'Thoughts on Politics and Revolution', p. 211.

132. Ibid., p. 202.

133. Ibid., p. 231.

134. Arendt to Jaspers, 26 June 1968, C, p. 681.

135. Elisabeth Young-Bruehl, *Hannah Arendt: For the Love of the World*, 2nd ed. (New Haven: Yale University Press, 2004), p. 487.

136. Hannah Arendt, '"The Rights of Man": What Are They?', *Modern Review* 3:1 (1949), p. 34.

137. Arendt cited in Alfred Kazin, *New York Jew* (Syracuse, NY: Syracuse University Press, 1996), p. 218; reiterated in Hannah Arendt, 'On Humanity in Dark Times: Thoughts on Lessing', *MID*, pp. 3–31, at p. 17.

138. See Hannah Arendt, '"What Remains? The Language Remains": A Conversation with Günter Gaus', *EU*, pp. 1–23, at pp. 12–13; Amos Elon, *The Pity of It All: A Portrait of the German-Jewish Epoch, 1743–1933* (New York: Picador, 2002), p. 118.

139. Frank Mehring, '"All for the Sake of Freedom": Hannah Arendt's Democratic Dissent, Trauma, and American Citizenship', *Journal of Transnational American Studies* 3:2 (2011), pp. 1–32.

140. Arendt to Jaspers, 26 June 1968, C, p. 681.

141. Peter Fryer, *Hungarian Tragedy* (London: Dennis Dobson, 1956), p. 42.

142. For the role (or lack thereof) of the United States in the Hungarian Revolution I mainly rely on Charles Gati, *Failed Illusions: Moscow, Washington, Budapest, and the 1956 Hungarian Revolution* (Washington, DC: Woodrow Wilson Center Press, 2006).

143. According to Kramer, 'All told, some 31,500 Soviet troops, 1,130 tanks and self-propelled artillery, 380 armoured personnel carriers, 185 air defence guns, and numerous other weapons were redeployed at short notice' to restore 'order' in Hungary: Mark Kramer, 'The Soviet Union and the 1956 Crises in Hungary and Poland: Reassessments and New Findings', *Journal of Contemporary History* 33:2 (1998), pp. 163–214, at p. 185.

144. Victor Sebestyen, *Twelve Days: Revolution 1956* (London: Phoenix, 2007), p. 102. The 'Sixteen Points' have multiple versions. In this book I use the one reprinted as 'Document No. 24: The "Sixteen Points" Prepared by Hungarian Students, October 22–23, 1956', in Csaba Békés, Malcolm Byrne and János M. Rainer (eds), *The 1956 Hungarian Revolution: A History in Documents* (Budapest: Central European University Press, 2002), pp. 188–90.

145. See 'Document No. 49: Working Notes from the Session of the CPSU CC Presidium on October 30, 1956 (Re: Point 1 of Protocol No. 49)'; 'Document No. 50: "Declaration by the Government of the USSR on the Principles of Development and Further Strengthening of Friendship and Cooperation between the Soviet Union and Other Socialist States", October 30, 1956'; and 'Document No. 53: Working Notes and Attached Extract from the Minutes of the CPSU CC Presidium Meeting, October 31, 1956', in Békés, Byrne and Rainer (eds), *The 1956 Hungarian Revolution*, pp. 295–99, pp. 300–302 and pp. 307–10, respectively. See also William Taubman, *Khrushchev: The Man and His Era* (W. W. Norton & Co., 2003), pp. 294–99.

146. Kramer, 'The Soviet Union and the 1956 Crises in Hungary and Poland', p. 211.

147. András Lénárt and Thomas Cooper, 'Emigration from Hungary in 1956 and the Emigrants as Tourists to Hungary', *The Hungarian Historical Review* 1:3/4 (2012), pp. 368–96, at pp. 370–74.

148. Hannah Arendt to Heinrich Blücher, 24 October 1956, *Within Four Walls: The Correspondence between Hannah Arendt and Heinrich Blücher, 1936–1968*, ed. Lotte Kohler, trans. Peter Constantine (New York: Harcourt, Inc., 2000), p. 307.

149. Hannah Arendt to Karl Jaspers, 26 December 1956, C, p. 306.

150. Ibid.

151. Hannah Arendt, 'Totalitarian Imperialism: Reflections on the Hungarian Revolution', *The Journal of Politics* 20:1 (1958), pp. 5–43. This essay has multiple versions. I shall refer to the original version published in *The Journal of Politics*.

152. Ibid., p. 43.

153. Ibid., p. 5.

154. Ibid., p. 8, emphasis added.

155. Gati, *Failed Illusions*, p. 177 note 62.

156. Fryer, *Hungarian Tragedy*, p. 65.

157. Sebestyen, *Twelve Days*, p. 197.

158. The most famous in this genre is the series of photographs by John Sadovy, which appeared in a section entitled 'Hungarian Patriots Strike Ferocious Blows at a Tyranny', *Life* 41:20 (12 November 1956), pp. 34–43. In *Life* magazine, Sadovy's photographs were presented to illustrate the Hungarian rebels' bravery and righteous anger at oppressors; in some publications, especially in the Soviet Union, however, the same images were presented as evidence of the cruelty and brutality of the 'counter-revolutionaries'. For further discussion, see Isotta Poggi, 'The Photographic Memory and Impact of the Hungarian 1956 Uprising during the Cold War Era', *Getty Research Journal* 7 (2015), pp. 197–206.

159. Alex von Tunzelmann, *Blood and Sand: Suez, Hungary and the Crisis that Shook the World* (London: Simon & Schuster, 2016), p. 230.

160. Arendt, 'Totalitarian Imperialism', p. 28.

161. Laszlo G. Borhi, *The Merchants of the Kremlin: The Economic Roots of Soviet Expansion in Hungary, Working Paper No. 28* (Washington, DC: Woodrow Wilson International Center for Scholars, 2000), pp. 7–16.

162. Pál Germuska, 'Economic Growth and the Industrial Development Policy in Hungary, 1950–1975', in Christian Grabas and Alexander Nützenadel (eds), *Industrial Policy in Europe after 1945: Wealth, Power and Economic Development in the Cold War* (Basingstoke: Palgrave Macmillan, 2014), pp. 321–36, at p. 331.

163. Ibid., p. 325.

164. These are the fifth, eleventh, twelfth and first items in the 'Sixteen Points'.

165. These are the seventh, ninth and tenth items in the 'Sixteen Points'.

166. Needless to say, the contrast between these two models of revolution is found in Arendt's *On Revolution*.

167. The United Nations, General Assembly, Special Committee on the Problem of Hungary, *Report of the Special Committee on the Problem of Hungary: General Assembly Official Records: Eleventh Session, Supplement No. 18 (A/3592)* (New York: United Nations, 1957).

168. Arendt, 'Totalitarian Imperialism', p. 29.

169. Ibid., p. 28.

170. Ibid.

171. The National Revolutionary Council rejected Prime Minister Nagy's request, made between the two Soviet invasions, that the Hungarian people should surrender weapons and trust his government to rebuild socialist Hungary. The controversial leader of the Council, József Dudás, was executed in January 1957.

172. Agnes Heller and Stefan Auer, 'An Interview with Agnes Heller', *Thesis Eleven* 97:1 (2009), pp. 99–105, at pp. 104–5.

173. Ibid., pp. 104–5. A similar objection has been raised by McConkey, who criticises Arendt for 'entirely excluding the Hungarian Soviet Republic of 1919 from the record'. Mike McConkey, 'On Arendt's Vision of the European Council Phenomenon: Critique from an Historical Perspective', *Dialectical Anthropology* 16:1 (1991), pp. 15–31, at p. 23.

174. It may also be noted that Heller showed greater agreement with Arendt's reading of the Hungarian Revolution in her earlier work, co-authored with Fehér. See Ferenc Fehér and Agnes Heller, *Hungary 1956 Revisited: The Message of a Revolution—a Quarter Century After* (London: George Allen & Unwin, 1983), pp. 48–49 and pp. 97–115.

175. See the thirteenth and fourteenth items in the 'Sixteen Points'.

176. The United Nations, *Report of the Special Committee on the Problem of Hungary*, pp. 70–72.

177. Arendt, 'Totalitarian Imperialism', p. 23 note 11.

178. Cocks, *Passion and Paradox*, p. 85.

179. There is a consensus among witnesses and historians about the ubiquity of this chant. See, e.g., Gati, *Failed Illusions*, p. 13; Sebestyen, *Twelve Days*, p. 111, p. 113, p. 156; and Michael Korda, *Journey to a Revolution: A Personal Memoir and History of the Hungarian Revolution of 1956* (New York: Harper Collins, 2006), p. 94, p. 100.

180. The most tragic such human cost was in the case of Berlin's uncle, Leo. Caute writes (*Isaac and Isaiah*, p. 141), 'Uncle Leo had been arrested in 1952, at the time of the "Jewish doctors' plot". He was accused of belonging to a British spy ring which included his brother Mendel and his nephew Isaiah. [. . .] Leo was beaten, then confessed. Held in prison for over a year, he was released in February 1954. Walking in the streets of Moscow, weak and undernourished, he suddenly caught sight of one of his torturers crossing the road in front of him. He suffered a heart attack and died alone in the snowy streets.'

181. Isaiah Berlin to Clarissa Eden, 1 November 1956, *E*, p. 547.

182. Isaiah Berlin to Arthur Schlesinger, early/mid-November 1956, *E*. p. 557.

183. Nicola Lacey, *A Life of H.L.A. Hart: The Nightmare and the Noble Dream* (Oxford: Oxford University Press, 2004), p. 206.

184. Arendt, 'Totalitarian Imperialism', p. 5.

185. Berlin to Schlesinger, early/mid-November 1956, *E*. p. 557.

186. Gati, *Failed Illusions*, p. 220.

187. Iván Zoltán Dénes, 'Personal Liberty and Political Freedom: Four Interpretations', *European Journal of Political Theory* 7:1 (2008), pp. 81–98, at pp. 93–94.

188. For further discussion, see 'Introduction' by Dénes in István Bibó, *The Art of Peacemaking: Political Essays by István Bibó*, ed. Iván Zoltán Dénes, trans. Péter Pásztor (New Haven: Yale University Press, 2015), pp. 1–24.

189. Isaiah Berlin to Michel Strauss, 8 November 1956, *E*, p. 552–53.

190. Georgina Brewis, *A Social History of Student Volunteering: Britain and Beyond, 1880–1980* (New York: Palgrave Macmillan, 2014), pp. 165–69.

191. Pryce-Jones would have a distinguished career as a journalist and writer. He published a book on the Hungarian Revolution in 1969, and did not fail to underline the centrality of students' roles in the Hungarian event. See David Pryce-Jones, *The Hungarian Revolution* (London: Ernest Benn Limited, 1969), esp. pp. 61–103.

NOTES TO CHAPTER 7 265

192. Sebestyen, *Twelve Days*, p. 151.

193. E.g., Isaiah Berlin, 'European Unity and Its Vicissitudes', *CTH2*, pp. 186–218, at p. 207; 'The Bent Twig', pp. 267–70; and 'The Life and Opinions of Moses Hess', *AC2*, pp. 267–316, at p. 313.

194. Of particular importance are Andrzej Walicki, 'Marx, Engels and the Polish Question', *Dialectics and Humanism* 7:1 (1980), pp. 5–32; and Andrzej Walicki, *Philosophy and Romantic Nationalism: The Case of Poland* (Oxford: Clarendon Press, 1982), pp. 358–91. Berlin corresponded regularly with Walicki and the issue of Marx and nationalism recurred in their conversations. Despite Walicki's disagreement, however, Berlin never changed his mind on this issue. See Walicki, *Encounters with Isaiah Berlin*, esp. 66–67 and pp. 115–17.

195. Berlin, 'The Life and Opinions of Moses Hess', p. 313.

196. Ibid., p. 313.

197. E.g., Berlin, 'European Unity and Its Vicissitudes', p. 207; Isaiah Berlin to Andrzej Walicki, 2 March 1981, in Walicki, *Encounters with Isaiah Berlin*, pp. 121–22. See also Berlin, 'The Bent Twig', p. 268.

198. Berlin, 'A Note on Nationalism', p. 311; Berlin, 'The Counter-Enlightenment', *AC2*, pp. 1–32, at p. 16.

199. According to Berlin's friend Amos Oz, these were the first words that he, as 'a stone-throwing kid, a Jewish intifada kid', learned to say in English except for 'yes' and 'no'. Amos Oz, *How to Cure a Fanatic* (London: Vintage, 2012), p. 49.

200. Alan Macfarlane, 'Interview with Richard Sennett, Part 2 of 2', 24 April 2009, https://www.youtube.com/watch?v=sy4ecJukKBc, accessed 15 January 2020. A transcript of the relevant part is found in Ilya P. Winham, 'After Totalitarianism: Hannah Arendt, Isaiah Berlin, and the Realization and Defeat of the Western Tradition' (Ph.D. dissertation, University of Minnesota, 2015), p. 7.

201. Young-Bruehl, *Hannah Arendt*, p. 448

202. Sam Copeland, *Bardwatch*, 'Anti-Defamation League Condemns Treatment of Hannah Arendt's Grave', 21 February 2017, http://student.bard.edu/bardwatch/2017/02/21/anti-defamation-league-condemns-treatment-of-hannah-arendts-grave/, accessed 5 June 2020.

203. Hannah Arendt to Karl Jaspers, 6 August 1955, *C*, p. 264.

204. Hans Jonas cited in Richard H. King, *Arendt and America* (Chicago: University of Chicago Press, 2015), p. 1.

205. Caute, *Isaac and Isaiah*, p. 16.

206. Berlin to Sparrow, 14 March 1964, *B*, p. 190.

207. I have discussed one aspect of Arendt's and Berlin's continuing relevance in Kei Hiruta, 'A Democratic Consensus?: Isaiah Berlin, Hannah Arendt, and the Anti-totalitarian Family Quarrel', *Think* 17:48 (2018), pp. 25–37.

Chapter 7. Conclusion

1. William James, *Pragmatism: A New Name for Some Old Ways of Thinking* (London: Longmans, Green, and Co., 1907), p. 6.

2. *The Economist*, 'Chattering Classes', 19 December 2006, https://www.economist.com/special-report/2006/12/19/chattering-classes, accessed 15 January 2020.

3. The particular 'fight' that Arendt is referring to is one with 'sociologists, whom I've been irritating for years'. Hannah Arendt to Karl Jaspers, 21 December 1953, *C*, p. 235.

4. Berlin and Polanowska-Sygulska, *UD*, p. 194.

5. Dana R. Villa, *Public Freedom* (Princeton: Princeton University Press, 2008), p. 333.

6. Raymond Aron cited in Tony Judt, *The Burden of Responsibility: Blum, Camus, Aron, and the French Twentieth Century* (Chicago: University of Chicago Press, 1998), p. 171.

7. Arendt cited in Alfred Kazin, *New York Jew* (Syracuse, NY: Syracuse University Press, 1996), p. 218.

8. Norman Stone, *The Atlantic and Its Enemies: A History of the Cold War* (London: Allen Lane, 2010), p. 236.

9. Johnny Lyons, *The Philosophy of Isaiah Berlin* (London: Bloomsbury Academic, 2020), p. vii.

10. Malachi Haim Hacohen, 'Berlin and Popper between Nation and Empire: Diaspora, Cosmopolitanism and Jewish Life', *Jewish Historical Studies* 44 (2012), pp. 51–74, at p. 74.

11. Isaiah Berlin, 'The Origins of Israel', *POI2*, pp. 173–96, at p. 196.

12. Isaiah Berlin to Mendel Berlin, autumn 1935, IBVL, 'Supplementary Letters 1928–1946', p. 28, http://berlin.wolf.ox.ac.uk/published_works/f/l1supp.pdf, accessed 15 January 2020.

13. Here I build on Ash's distinction between the witness and the historian in Timothy Garton Ash, *We the People: The Revolution of '89* (Cambridge: Granta Books, 1990), pp. 11–24.

14. Johann Wolfgang von Goethe, *Faust Part One*, trans. David Luke (Oxford: Oxford University Press, 1987), p. 61.

15. Jacob Howland, *Kierkegaard and Socrates: A Study in Philosophy and Faith* (Cambridge: Cambridge University Press, 2006), p. 26.

16. Those who are guilty of such inauthenticity should accept a variation of the Socratic maxim, elegantly put by Howland (ibid., p. 26): 'one who loves philosophy so little that his actions are unfaithful to his best understanding does not deserve the name "philosopher".'

17. As I wrote in the Introduction, there is an odd disciplinary convention in Anglophone academia today, according to which political theorists ought *not* to address 'deep metaphysical questions' such as 'the human condition' (David Miller and Richard Dagger, 'Utilitarianism and Beyond: Contemporary Analytical Political Theory', in Terence Ball and Richard Bellamy (eds), *The Cambridge History of Twentieth-Century Political Thought* (Cambridge: Cambridge University Press, 2006), pp. 446–69, at pp. 446–47). This convention is odd in many ways, but one oddity that has come to light in the preceding pages is that two of the greatest political theorists of the last century, Arendt and Berlin, shared the opinion that the human condition is not a 'deep metaphysical question'. For Berlin, it is a part empirical, part speculative question, on which any thinking person cannot but ponder from time to time. For Arendt, considering the human condition is 'nothing more than to think what we are doing' (*HC*, p. 5). It is unclear how recent Anglophone scholars have come to make the questionable assumption that the human condition is a 'deep metaphysical question' that falls outside the discipline of political theory.

18. The most succinct statement of these objections to contemporary political theory is Raymond Geuss, *Philosophy and Real Politics* (Princeton: Princeton University Press, 2008).

19. Plato, *The Republic*, ed. G.R.F. Ferrari, trans. Tom Griffith (Cambridge: Cambridge University Press, 2000), p. 205.

INDEX

Abel, Lionel, 40, 227n194
Acton, 1st Baron (Lord Acton), 62
Adams, John, 67
Adenauer, Konrad, 34, 225n150
Adorno, Theodor W., 24, 29, 47, 103, 242n99
Aeschylus, 82
Aesop's Fables, 54, 58
Ahabath Israel. See under love
Aharony, Michal, 98
Aid and Rescue Committee (Hungary), 124
Akhmatova, Anna, 12, 63, 142
Allen, Jonathan, 114–15
Almond, Gabriel, 67
amor mundi. See under love
analytic–Continental divide, 32, 224n141
Anti-Defamation League, 40
antisemitism, 3, 10, 11, 20, 36, 90, 121, 155, 171, 200
Antisthenes, 83
Arato, Andrew, 179
Arendt, Hannah. *See also* camps; love
    arrest of, 3, 10, 14, 136, 140, 249n57
    arrogance, allegation of, 2, 9, 40, 42, 126, 130, 132, 144, 152, 154–55, 199 (*see also* arrogance)
    on Isaiah Berlin, 2–3, 30–31, 41, 65, 156, 215nn13–14
    as Berlin's 'bête noire', 2, 6, 9, 21, 32, 46, 141, 160, 217n4
    on British philosophy, 2, 31–32, 178
    and the council system, 179, 188–91, 203, 260n98
    death of, 2, 11, 45, 46, 196–97

    freedom, theory of, 49–50, 52, 64–80, 84–86, 181 (*see also* freedom)
    and German philosophy, 2, 25–27, 31–32, 224n142
    and Heidegger, 10, 26–27, 65–66, 73–77, 200, 223n116, 232n86, 235nn147–48 (*see also* Heidegger, Martin)
    on Hobbes, 2, 31–32, 177, 178, 260n91 (*see also* Hobbes, Thomas)
    on the human condition, 49, 50, 72–78, 80, 84–86, 234n125, 234n131, 266n17
    on the Hungarian Revolution, 68, 179, 185, 188–92, 193, 201, 203 (*see also under* revolution)
    on ideology, 89–91, 238n16 (*see also* ideology)
    on imperialism, 96, 173–77, 258n59, 259n65 (*see also* imperialism)
    'Introduction into Politics' (1963), lectures on, 30
    and a Jewish Army, 15, 18, 150, 151
    on the 'Jewish establishment', 3, 39, 155–56
    life of, 9–11
    on the mob, 95, 174–75, 177
    on natality, 50, 72–75, 78, 79, 80; and mortality, 73–74
    on non-participation, 148–50
    on Oxford philosophy, 30–31, 200
    and phenomenology, 10, 26, 76, 77, 85
    and pluralism, 78–80 (*see also* pluralism)

Arendt, Hannah (*continued*)
    on plurality, 50, 67, 75–77, 78, 79, 80,
        103, 179, 235n151, 236n165
    on resistance, 147–50
    self-hatred, allegation of, 42, 126,
        152, 158–59, 228n211
    on the sixty-eighters, 182–85, 201
    'Stalinism in Retrospect' (1972),
        seminar on, 105–6
    as a survivor, 137–38, 140, 141
    on totalitarianism, 5, 17, 87–106,
        117, 121, 122–23, 148, 160, 173–77,
        180–81, 203, 239n30, 240n53 (*see also*
        totalitarianism)
    on *vita activa* and *vita contemplativa*,
        79–80
    and Zionism, 9, 10, 14–16, 17–21, 136,
        141, 143–44, 150–51, 159, 192, 200,
        256n192 (*see also* Zionism)
Arendt, Hannah, works of: *Between Past and
    Future*, 11, 49, 227n194; 'The Concentration
    Camps', 17; 'The Concept of Love in
    Augustine', 10, 64; 'Days of Change', 150;
    Denktagebuch, 65, 199, 216n15, 224n139,
    232n86; *Eichmann in Jerusalem*, 2, 5, 9, 11,
    32–33, 37–42, 87, 98, 100, 123, 125–60, 197,
    227n194, 241nn80 and 91, 274n12, 248n23,
    248n27, 252n98, 254n151; 'Exchange' with
    Gershom Scholem (1963/64), 41, 42, 126,
    135, 156–57, 248n27 (*see also under* Berlin,
    Isaiah); 'Freedom and Politics', 48, 229n1;
    '"The Freedom to Be Free"', 51, 229n13;
    'Freiheit und Politik', 48, 64, 229n1;
    'Heidegger at Eighty', 26–27, 223n116; *The
    Human Condition*, 2, 9, 11, 22–25, 26, 29,
    40, 46, 49, 73, 85, 87, 150, 235n148, 238n4,
    239n45, 240n46, 253n133; 'Ideology and
    Terror', 93, 238n10; 'The Jew as Pariah',
    254n163; *The Life of the Mind*, 30, 79; *On
    Revolution*, 2, 11, 41, 43, 44, 49, 51, 263n166;
    The Origins of Totalitarianism, 1, 3, 9, 11, 18,
    22, 32, 37, 38, 41, 46, 49, 65, 87, 91, 93, 98, 99,
    100, 102–5, 109, 117, 146–47, 174–76, 202,
    239n45, 252n112; *Rahel Varnhagen*, 2,

254n163; 'To Save the Jewish Homeland',
18; 'Totalitarian Elements in Marxism',
102–4; 'Totalitarian Imperialism', 188–92,
263n151; 'We Refugees', 87, 137, 202 (*see also
under* Berlin, Isaiah); 'What Is Freedom?',
48, 81–82, 161; '"What Remains? Language
Remains"' (the 'Gaus interview'), 140, 141,
249n57, 251n91; 'Zionism Reconsidered',
18–19, 42
Aristippus, 83
Aristotle, 26, 31, 73, 77–78, 81–84 (*see also
under* freedom); *Nicomachean Ethics*, 26;
Politics, 81; *Rhetoric*, 26
Arnold, Jeremy, 71
Aron, Raymond, 161, 178, 200
arrogance, as a virtue, 154–55, 254n163. *See also
under* Arendt, Hannah
Aufbau, 11, 14, 18, 150
Athens, 78, 82, 92, 93, 161
Attlee, Clement, 165
Austin, J. L., 12, 30, 167
Austria: Holocaust in, 33. *See also* Salzburg;
Vienna
AVH (Államvédelmi Hatóság), 186, 189–90
Ayer, A. J., 12, 27–31, 167, 223nn119 and 122;
Language, Truth and Logic, 27–28, 30,
223n119

Bacon, Francis, 167
Baeck, Leo, 153, 159, 254n151
Baehr, Peter, 90, 98, 239n25
Balfour Declaration, 20
Bard College, 65, 232n86; Bard College
Cemetery, 196, 197
battle of Chaeronea, 83
Bauer, Yehuda, 38, 252n110
Bauman, Zygmunt, 108
Beauvoir, Simone de, 142
Behrman, Samuel Nathan, 152
Belinsky, Vissarion, 126
Bell, Daniel, 17, 40
Bem, Józef, 186
Ben-Gurion, David, 35, 36, 38, 138
Benhabib, Seyla, 23, 76

Benjamin, Walter, 10, 137
Bentham, Jeremy, 53, 61, 114, 115, 167
Berkeley, George, 28, 167
Berlin, Aline, 35, 197
Berlin, Isaiah
    on Arendt, 1–2, 6, 9, 15, 17–25, 29–30,
        32–33, 39, 40–47, 85, 87, 126, 129–60,
        161–63, 215n7, 217n27 (chap. 1),
        217n4 (chap. 2), 218nn23–24,
        238n4; on *Eichmann in Jerusalem*,
        2, 9, 32–33, 39, 40–42, 87, 126,
        129–60, 227n194; on *The Human
        Condition*, 2, 9, 22–24, 25, 29, 87,
        238n4; on *On Revolution*, 2, 41;
        on *The Origins of Totalitarianism*,
        9, 41, 87; on 'We Refugees', 87
    and the Arendt–Scholem exchange,
        41–42, 125–26, 135, 138, 145, 156–57
        (*see also under* Arendt, Hannah,
        works of)
    on the British Empire, 166–67,
        169–73, 177
    and British empiricism, 12, 27–31, 164,
        167–68, 172 (see also *empiricism*)
    and British idealism, 28–29, 167–68
        (*see also* idealism)
    as British public servant, 3, 12, 13–14,
        16, 22, 87, 139–40, 141, 201, 250n75
    death of, 6, 13, 46, 197
    on Eichmann, 35–36, 155 (*see also*
        Eichmann, Adolf)
    on England (and Britain), 162–69,
        172, 173, 177, 178, 179, 180, 184, 203,
        246n191
    freedom, theory of, 49–50, 52–64,
        84–86, 92 (*see also* freedom)
    and the Holocaust, 36, 88, 138–41, 160,
        251n83 (*see also* Holocaust)
    on the human condition, 49, 50,
        62–64, 80, 84–86, 110, 234n129,
        266n17
    on the Hungarian Revolution, 185,
        192–96, 201 (*see also under*
        revolution)

    on imperialism, 169–73 (*see also*
        imperialism)
    on Kant, 28, 48, 59–60, 61, 82, 116,
        165, 168 (*see also* Kant, Immanuel)
    life of, 11–13
    'metaphysical', on being, 2, 22,
        24–25, 28–29, 31, 41, 85, 168, 172
    and Mill, 19–20, 48, 53, 61, 63–64, 78,
        82, 165, 167–68, 171, 232n73, 236n157
        (*see also* Mill, John Stuart)
    on nationalism, 20, 120–22, 166–67,
        168, 170–71, 180, 185, 195–96,
        201, 257n26, 265n194 (*see also*
        nationalism)
    and the power of ideas, 83, 88, 117–22,
        166
    on the Russian intelligentsia, 117–19,
        246n196
    on Russia's 'national character', 119,
        246n191
    on Rousseau, 60, 61, 82, 103, 114, 116,
        161, 166, 231n51 (*see also* Rousseau,
        Jean-Jacques)
    on the sixty-eighters, 182–85, 195, 201
    and the Suez Crisis, 193–94 (*see also*
        the Suez Crisis)
    on totalitarianism, 5, 60, 61, 87–89,
        92–93, 106–23, 152, 160, 166, 168,
        180, 203, 231n53, 252n107 (*see also*
        totalitarianism)
    and Zionism, 13, 14–16, 17, 19–21,
        150–51, 159, 170, 196, 200, 221n73,
        256n192 (*see also* Zionism)
Berlin, Isaiah, works of: 'Benjamin Disraeli,
    Karl Marx and the Search for Identity',
    172, 175, 258n52; 'The Birth of Greek
    Individualism', 82, 83, 92; *Conversations with
    Isaiah Berlin* (with Ramin Jahanbegloo),
    6, 23, 46; 'Does Political Theory Still Exist?',
    30, 215n13; 'Epilogue: The Three Strands
    in My Life', 163; *Four Essays on Liberty*, 1,
    24, 53, 55, 65, 81, 168; 'Freedom and Its
    Betrayal', 230n21; 'Generalissimo Stalin
    and the Art of Government', 111, 244n155;

Berlin, Isaiah, works of (*continued*)
'Introduction' to *Roots of Revolution* (by
Franco Venturi), 3; 'Isaiah Berlin in
Conversation with Steven Lukes', 129–32,
134, 217n28, 246n200; 'Joseph de Maistre
and the Origins of Fascism', 244n160; *Karl
Marx*, 3, 12, 22, 53, 117, 215n13, 244nn146
and 160; 'Marxist versus Non-Marxist
Ideas in Soviet Policy', 112; 'Political Ideas
in the Romantic Age', 230n21; 'Political
Ideas in the Twentieth Century', 24–25;
'The Pursuit of the Ideal', 107; 'Two
Concepts of Liberty', 48, 49, 53, 61, 62, 64,
65, 82, 161, 215n44, 230n23, 231n45; 'Why
the Soviet Union Chooses to Insulate
Itself', 110–11; 'Winston Churchill in
1940', 169; 'Zionist Politics in Wartime
Washington', 141
Berlin, Leo (Lev Borisovich), 264n180
Berlin, Mendel, 11, 218n14, 264n180
Berlin Conference (1884–85), 173
Bernstein, Richard J., 76, 250n80
Bettelheim, Bruno, 106, 242n109
Bibó, István, 194
Bilsky, Leora, 128, 138
Bismarck, Otto von, 95
Blackstone, William, 66
Blücher, Heinrich, 10, 188, 196, 197, 217n11
Blumenfeld, Kurt, 14–16, 21, 219nn35 and 37
Bolshevism, 44, 118; Bolsheviks, 11, 107, 119,
121, 122, 166, 168, 180, 199
Bosanquet, Bernard, 28, 61, 168
Bradley, F. H., 28–29, 61, 168, 223n122
Brandeis, Louis, 15
Brown, Norman Oliver, 1, 2, 46
Brzezinski, Zbigniew K., 117
Bundy, McGeorge, 183
Burke, Edmund, 171
Butler, Joseph, 258n46
Butler, Judith, 78, 248n23

Cambridge, philosophy in, 28, 32
camps
    Arendt's taxonomy of, 99
concentration, 17, 93, 96–98, 99–101,
105, 106, 108, 122, 140, 144–47, 148,
152, 173, 214n91, 252nn103 and 112
extermination, 96–98, 100, 140
forced labour, 99, 100, 107, 111, 240n74
    (*see also* Gulag)
names of: Auschwitz, 36, 98, 99,
124; Bełżec, 98; Buchenwald, 98,
99, 108, 242n109; Chełmno, 98;
Colombes, 10; Dachau, 98, 99,
242n109; Gurs, 3, 10, 36, 87, 137,
252n100; Kolyma, 111; Majdanek,
98; Sobibór, 98; Theresienstadt,
144, 148, 153; Treblinka, 98;
Villemalard, 217n11
POW (Prisoner of War), 34
Camus, Albert, 31
Canovan, Margaret, 79, 94, 236n165
capitalism, 94, 174–75
Carnap, Rudolf, 28
Carneades, 82
Carr, E. H., 43, 109
Caute, David, 42, 161, 227n196, 246n200,
246n213, 264n180
Césaire, Aimé, 171
Cesarani, David, 37, 258n53
Cherniss, Joshua L., 52, 220n51, 231n42
Chernyshevsky, Nikolay, 118
Chrysippus, 82
Churchill, Winston, 169
CIA (Central Intelligence Agency), 16, 186
citizenship, 66, 68, 80, 82, 91, 148, 185, 200
civil war, 40, 94, 179; English, 169; as a
metaphor for the Eichmann controversy,
11, 32, 40, 42; Russian, 189
Cohen, Jean, 179
Cohn-Bendit, Erich, 10
Cold War, 61, 116, 122, 162, 193. *See also under*
liberalism
Collini, Stefan, 13
Columbia University, 105, 183–94
Commentary, 17
Committee for a Jewish Army (CJA), 16, 18
Comte, Auguste, 24, 109

Condorcet, Marquis de (Nicolas de Condorcet), 109
Conrad, Joseph, 23, 175
Constant, Benjamin, 53, 61, 66, 82
courage, 67, 113, 150, 182, 184, 200, 202, 252n100
court
    as an institution, 260n105
    Jerusalem District Court (*see also* Israel, the state of); and the Eichmann Trial, 35, 122, 125, 127, 138, 140, 147 (*see also under* Eichmann, Adolf); and the Kastner Trial, 125, 132 (*see also* Kastner, Rudolf)
    Supreme Court of Israel, 125, 132 (*see also* Israel, the state of)
    Supreme Court of the United States, 15, 179
Crates of Thebes, 83
Crick, Bernard, 2, 80–81, 84, 149, 150, 237n179, 238n16, 240n59
Cromer, 1st Earl of (Evelyn Baring), 175, 176–77
Crowder, George, 107, 244n165
Czerniaków, Adam, 143

Dagger, Richard, 5
Dahl, Robert A., 67
Deighton, Anne, 139
deontology, 145, 252n107
Derrida, Jacques, 27
Deutscher, Isaac, 161–62
Dilthey, Wilhelm, 26
Diogenes, 81–82, 83
Disraeli, Benjamin, 172–73, 175–76, 258n53, 259n75
domination, 3, 5, 67, 71, 88, 97, 160, 163, 173, 176, 177, 187, 188; total, 97–101, 105, 144–46, 148, 174, 252n100
Dreyfus, Alfred, 125; Dreyfus Affair, 158
Dubnov, Arie M., 41, 227n196, 250n75
Dudás, József, 199, 263n171. *See also* National Revolutionary Council

Eckstein, Ze'ev, 131
Eden, Anthony, 193, 250n74
Eden, Clarissa, 193
Egypt, 175, 187, 193, 237n182
Eichmann, Adolf, 11, 32–43, 122–23, 124–60, 203; capture of, 21, 34–35, 36, 122; 'normality' of, 126–27, 155; as a 'small cog', 33, 127; 'thoughtlessness' of, 11, 39, 154; trial of, 11, 32–37, 122–23, 124–60, 200, 225n146, 248n27 (*see also under* court). *See also under* Berlin, Isaiah
Eisenhower, Dwight D., 187, 194, 195
Eliot, T. S., 107
empiricism, 2, 12, 24, 27–32, 85, 167–68, 172, 234n129. *See also under* Berlin, Isaiah
Encounter, 41, 42, 126, 156
Epictetus. *See under* freedom
Epicurus, 81, 82; epicureanism, 82, 83–84
Ettinger, Elżbieta, 9, 217n2
Eubulides, 93
Evening Standard, 169
evil, 'banality' of, 39, 126, 154, 177, 226n185

Faber & Faber, 22–24, 99, 209
Fainsod, Merle, 43, 104
Fanon, Frantz, 171
fascism, 91, 92, 112, 122, 167, 168, 239n27
Federalist Papers, 201
Ferro, Marc, 43
Fest, Joachim, 152
Fichte, Johann Gottlieb, 61, 120, 121, 171
'Final Solution', 33, 100, 106–7, 114–15, 116, 127, 148, 153–54, 241n80. *See also* Holocaust
Forster, E. M., 221n72
Foster, John Galway, 139
Franco, Francisco, 92
Freeden, Michael, 63
freedom. *See also under* Arendt, Hannah; Berlin, Isaiah
    of the ancients, 82
    Aristotle and, 81 (*see also* Aristotle)
    in classical Greece, 82–84
    Epictetus on, 82, 237n186
    existentialist', 133

freedom (*continued*)
    as free will, 48
    Heidegger on, 65–66 (*see also*
        Heidegger, Martin)
    and Hellenism, 82–84 (*see also*
        Hellenism)
    'islands' of, 161, 163, 165, 173, 185, 191,
        196, 256n9
    liberty and, 50–51, 229n13
    Mill on, 63–64, 78, 82, 165, 232n73
        (*see also* Mill, John Stuart)
    of the moderns, 66, 82
    negative, 48, 49–50, 51, 52, 53–64, 68,
        69, 72, 80–84, 85, 92, 118, 164, 165,
        168, 203, 230n39, 231nn42, 45
        and 73; Arendt and, 51, 65–66, 72,
        181; and its conditions, 54–55; and
        neo-republican liberty, 71–72; and
        political freedom, 50, 68, 69,
        71–72, 80–84, 181
    neo-republican: and negative liberty,
        71–72; and political freedom, 50,
        70–72
    political, 48, 50, 64, 66–84, 178, 181,
        185, 188–92, 201, 203, 233n92,
        234n125; and negative liberty, 50,
        68, 69, 71–72, 80–84, 181; and
        neo-republican liberty, 50, 70–72;
        and positive liberty, 50, 69–70;
        and self-disclosure, 70, 77–78, 80;
        and self-realisation, 68, 69–70,
        72, 77–78, 80, 182
    from politics, 72, 84, 181
    positive, 49–50, 53, 58–64, 65–66, 82,
        92, 106, 113, 115–16, 122, 168, 181,
        231nn45 and 53; and the mythol-
        ogy of the real self, 59–60, 116;
        and political freedom, 50, 69–70
    and sovereignty, 69, 233n107
    under totalitarianism, 97, 144–52,
        160 (*see also* totalitarianism)
Freiburg, 32
Freud, Sigmund, 109, 158
Friedrich, Carl J., 117

Fromm, Erich, 24, 158
Fryer, Peter, 189

Gati, Charles, 189, 194, 262n142
Gaus, Günter, 140, 141, 249n57, 251n91
gender, 25, 251n91; and the Eichmann
    controversy, 141–42, 251n88
Gentile, Emilio, 239n27
Gerő, Ernő, 186, 187
Gladstone, William Ewart, 175
Glazer, Nathan, 17
Gobineau, Arthur de, 176
Goldmann, Nahum, 40
Gomułka, Władysław, 186
Gordon, Peter E., 74
Gray, John, 46, 232n64, 247n15
Great War. *See* World War I
Green, Thomas Hill, 28, 61, 167–68
Grünwald, Malkiel, 124–25, 131
Gulag, 99, 100–101, 240n74. *See also* camps
Gurian, Waldemar, 14

Ha'aretz, 141, 250n82
Hacohen, Malachi Haim, 246n191
Halevi, Benjamin, 38, 125, 132
Hamann, Johann Georg, 29
Hampshire, Stuart, 12, 87
Handlin, Oscar, 17
Hardy, Henry, 6, 22, 108–9, 220n53, 244n160
Hart, H.L.A., 30, 51, 193
Harvard University, 1, 13, 16, 43–45, 104,
    218n23, 219n48, 225n228
Hausner, Gideon, 40, 125, 128
Hayek, Friedrich A., 47, 55, 109
Hayes, Peter, 101, 139
Hegel, G.W.F., 28, 50, 60, 61, 69, 96, 103, 114,
    116, 121, 166, 168
Heidegger, Martin, 9, 10, 24, 25–31, 168, 200,
    223n116, 235n148; Arendt's appropriation of,
    26, 73–77, 235n147 (*see also under* Arendt,
    Hannah); *Being and Time*, 76; on freedom,
    65–66; *On the Essence of Truth*, 65, 232n86,
    233n87
Heine, Heinrich, 119–20, 166

Hellenism, 82–84, 201, 237n182. *See also under* freedom

Heller, Agnes, 191, 264n174

Helvétius, Claude-Adrien, 109

Herder, Johann Gottfried, 167, 171

Herodotus, 82

Herzen, Alexander, 118

Herzl, Theodor, 157

Heydrich, Reinhard, 153

Hilberg, Raul, 38, 241n91, 251n88

Himmler, Heinrich, 37, 127

Hirschmann, Nancy, 142

Hiruta, Kei, 236n166, 242n102, 256n8, 260n91, 265n207

Hitler, Adolf, 15, 35, 60, 89, 91, 92, 95, 116, 121, 140, 154, 181, 231n51

Hobbes, Thomas, 2, 31–32, 40, 48, 53, 61, 167, 177, 178, 260n91. *See also under* Arendt, Hannah

Hobhouse, L. T., 165

Hobson, J. A., 171, 174, 259n66. *See also under* imperialism

Hollis, Martin, 49

Holmes, Jennifer, 6, 22

Holocaust, 2, 33, 36, 38–39, 88, 97–98, 100–101, 124–60, 251n83, 251n97. *See also* 'Final Solution'; *under* Berlin, Isaiah

Honig, Bonnie, 70

Hook, Sidney, 17

Horkheimer, Max, 47, 103, 242n99

Houwink ten Cate, Lotte, 41

Hume, David, 28, 110, 167

Hurwitz, Henry, 87

Hussein, Saddam, 1

Husserl, Edmund, 10, 24, 25–26, 27, 28

idealism (philosophy), 120; British, 28–29, 167–68 (*see also under* Berlin, Isaiah)

ideology, 19, 20, 44, 89, 94, 95, 97, 101, 104, 122, 141, 176. *See also under* Arendt, Hannah

Ignatieff, Michael, 6, 164, 218n24, 249n50

Ihud, 18

imperialism: British, 163, 168–77, 203, 258n59; European, 170, 173, 174, 177;

German, 177, 258n59; Hobson on, 174, 259n66; Lenin on, 174–75, 259nn65–66; Luxemburg on, 259n65; Marx on, 171; Marxist theory of, 174–75; nostalgia about, 169; wrongness of, 171, 258n49. *See also under* Arendt, Hannah; Berlin, Isaiah; totalitarianism

India, 171, 175

individualism, 55, 61, 78, 83, 84, 178, 200, 201

individuality, 63, 70, 75, 78, 80, 84, 97

Israel, the State of, 2, 11, 17, 19, 21, 34–36, 41, 122–23, 124–25, 130–31, 137–38, 141, 156, 168, 187, 193, 196, 221n73, 225n146, 235n148; founding of, 18, 19, 201. *See also under* court

Jabotinsky, Vladimir, 16

Jahanbegloo, Ramin, 6, 23, 46

James, William, 199, 224n139

Jaspers, Karl, 10, 24, 25, 29, 31, 35, 37, 43, 45, 77, 154, 184, 185, 188, 197, 200, 233n107, 243n119

Jewish Cultural Reconstruction, Inc., 11

Johnson, Lyndon B., 183

Jonas, Hans, 14, 222n108

Kádár, János, 187

Kant, Immanuel, 26, 27, 28, 48, 50, 59, 60, 61, 69, 77, 82, 116, 120, 151, 165, 168; *Critique of Judgement*, 77

Kastner, Rudolf, 38, 124–25, 131, 132, 143, 145, 247n2; 'Kastner train', 124, 247n4. *See also under* court

Kazin, Alfred, 17, 40

Kennan, George, 43–44

Kennedy, John F., 16, 183

Keren Hayesod, 14, 15, 219n35, 219n36

Khrushchev, Nikita, 105, 187, 189–90, 195

Kierkegaard, Søren, 26, 31, 61

Kipling, Joseph Rudyard, 175

Koestler, Arthur, 99, 242n109, 256n192

Kogon, Eugen, 98, 242n109

Kravchinsky, Sergey, 118

Kristallnacht, 91

Lawrence, T. E., 175–77; *Lawrence of Arabia* (film), 177

Lazare, Bernard, 143, 157–58, 255n180

Lederman, Shmuel, 144

Le Mercier de La Rivière, Pierre-Paul, 109

Lenin, Vladimir Ilyich, 44, 60, 82, 92, 104, 107, 112, 113, 116, 118–19, 171, 174–75, 195, 244n165, 259n65–66. *See also under* imperialism

Levi, Primo, 98

Levinas, Emmanuel, 25

liberalism, 19–20, 55, 61, 72, 78–79, 89, 110, 163, 165, 171, 178, 183–84, 201; Cold War, 16, 103, 104, 178, 194, 242n99, 260n91; and libertarianism, 55

Lipsky, Louis, 15

Lipstadt, Deborah E., 125

Locke, John, 28, 31, 167, 171

Loidolt, Sophie, 25, 234nn128 and 131, 235n151

love: fatherly and motherly, 158; of the Jewish people (*Ahabath Israel*), 42, 156–58; patriotism as, 157–58; of the polis, 82 (*see also* polis, Greek); of the world (*amor mundi*), 157, 197

Lukes, Steven, 129–31, 132, 134, 246n200. *See also under* Berlin, Isaiah, works of

Luther, Martin, 103

Luxemburg, Rosa, 171, 189, 259n65. *See also under* imperialism

Macdonald, Dwight, 17, 40

Maier, Joseph, 18

Maistre, Joseph de, 112–13, 171, 244n160

Makiya, Kanan (pseud. Samir al-Khalil), 46; *Republic of Fear*, 1, 46, 229n238

Mandelstam, Nadezhda, 105, 149; *Hope against Hope*, 105

Mander, John, 41

Mantena, Karuna, 173

Mao Zedong, 92, 107

Marburg, 10, 26, 32

Marx, Karl, 12, 22, 50, 53, 60, 61, 65, 69, 103–4, 109, 113, 114–15, 116, 166, 168, 171, 195, 224n160, 265n194. *See also under* imperialism

Mazzini, Giuseppe, 171

McCarthy, Mary, 2, 17, 40, 41, 142, 227n206

McTaggart, John M. E., 28–29

Medvedev, Roy A., 105

Menorah Journal, 87

Merleau-Ponty, Maurice, 24, 25

Mill, John Stuart, 20, 24, 31, 48, 53, 61, 63–64, 78, 165, 167–68, 171, 232n73, 236n157; *On Liberty*, 63, 82, 165. *See also under* Berlin, Isaiah; freedom

Miller, David, 5

modesty, 153–55, 156, 159, 254n163

monism, 78–79, 81, 84, 104, 106, 113–15, 116, 122, 236n170

Montesquieu, Charles-Louis de Secondat, 48, 66

Moore, G. E., 2, 28–29, 30, 167, 168

moral dilemma, 38, 126, 129–37, 145–46, 151–52. *See also under* pluralism

Morgenthau, Hans, 40

Moses, Siegfried, 40

Mossad, 34–35

Müller, Heinrich, 153

Müller, Jan-Werner, 165

Munich Agreement, 12, 91, 193

Murdoch, Iris, 29, 142

Mussolini, Benito, 91, 116

Nagy, Imre, 187, 189, 190, 191, 263n171

Napoleon Bonaparte, 120, 166

National Revolutionary Council (Hungary), 191, 263n171. *See also* Dudás, József

National Socialism. *See* Nazism

nationalism: English, 166–67; German, 120–22, 166–67, 201 (*see also under* Nazism); and the Hungarian Revolution, 185, 192, 195–96; Jewish, 15, 18, 192 (*see also* Zionism); Russian, 43–44. *See also under* Berlin, Isaiah

Naville, Pierre, 249n49

Nazism, 5, 33, 37, 47, 65, 86, 87–109, 121–22, 132, 165, 166, 174, 176, 180, 200, 201, 235n147; and German nationalism, 95, 121–22, 166, 201; and Stalinism, 5, 47, 86, 87, 89, 91, 92, 97, 102, 165; and utopianism, 107–9 (*see also* utopianism)

neoliberalism, 55. *See also* liberalism
Neurath, Otto, 28
New Yorker, 37, 39, 132, 155, 159, 225n169
Niebuhr, Reinhold, 15
Nietzsche, Friedrich, 26, 31, 96, 121, 168
Nuremberg Laws, 91
Nuremberg trials, 33

Oakeshott, Michael, 47
Owens, Patricia, 176, 260n92
Oxford, 11–13, 21, 22, 23, 28, 29, 32, 43, 46, 48, 87, 133, 139, 142, 165, 183, 193, 194–95, 197–98, 202, 218n17; All Souls College, 12, 42, 197, 228n218; Bodleian Library, 139; Corpus Christi College, 11, 197; New College, 11, 218n17; philosophy in, 12, 28, 30–31, 168, 200; Wolfson College, 13, 197; Wolvercote Cemetery, 197

Palestine, 10, 11, 14, 18, 20, 38, 140, 196
Parekh, Bhikhu, 23, 221n81
Partisan Review, 40, 142, 227n194
Pasternak, Boris, 12, 63
paternalism, 106, 109, 110–13, 114, 116, 122
patriotism. *See under* love
Peirce, Charles Sanders, 224n139
Pełczyński, Zbigniew, 46
Penslar, Derek J., 15
Petőfi, Sándor, 186, 192
Petrograd (St Petersburg), 3, 11, 20, 118, 197, 203
Pettit, Philip, 50, 70, 233n102
phenomenology, 2, 10, 24, 25–26, 28, 30, 31, 76, 77, 85, 235n151. *See also under* Arendt, Hannah)
Phillips, William, 31, 40, 142
Pipes, Richard, 43–44, 228n218; *Revolutionary Russia*, 43, 44
Pitkin, Hanna F., 23, 50, 221n81, 235n145
Plato, 26, 31, 82, 83, 103, 104, 114, 204; *The Republic*, 204; *The Sophist*, 26,
Plekhanov, Georgy V., 107, 113
pluralism: Arendt and, 79–80; cultural, 171–72; moral, 78–80, 236n157;

ontological, 79; political, 79; value, 62–63, 80, 84, 85, 114, 126, 164, 194, 199, 231n61, 236n157, 247n15 (*see also* moral dilemma)
Podhoretz, Norman, 31, 155
Polanowska-Sygulska, Beata, 84–85
Poliakov, Léon, 38
polis, Greek, 81–84, 201, 254n137. *See also under* love
Pol Pot, 107
Popper, Karl R., 90, 103, 109, 114, 117, 178, 244n145
Pottle, Mark, 6
Pryce-Jones, David, 194–95, 264n191

Quine, W.V.O., 30
Quinton, Anthony, 65

Radio Free Europe, 186, 187
Rand, Ayn, 79
Rawls, John, 30, 51, 72, 162, 203, 236n157
Raz, Joseph, 165
Reichstag Fire (27 February 1933), 10
Ritchie, David G., 50
revolution, in philosophy, 25–32
revolution (revolutionary upheavals), political, 94, 107, 113, 116, 118, 120, 166, 189, 200
    American (1775–83), 68, 178, 179, 190, 263n166
    French (1789), 112, 120, 190, 263n166
    French (1848), 179
    French (1870–71), 179
    German (1918–19), 179
    Hungarian (1956), 68, 151, 162, 179, 185–96, 201, 203, 262n142, 264nn174 and 191 (*see also under* Arendt, Hannah; Berlin, Isaiah; nationalism); 'Sixteen Points' by Hungarian Students, 187, 190, 192, 262n144, 263n164–65, 264n175
    Russian (1905), 179, 218n14
    Russian (1917), 3, 11, 20, 43–44, 179, 187, 199; 1967 conference on, 43–45, 228n225
    spirit of, 178–80, 181, 182, 184, 191, 192, 201

Rhodes, Cecil John, 175, 176, 177
Riesman, David, 24
Riga, 11, 20, 88, 138, 149, 197, 218n14
Ring, Jennifer, 142, 251n85
Robespierre, Maximilien, 116, 120
Robinson, Jacob, 38, 42
Rosenberg, Alfred, 126
Rosenberg, Harold, 17
Rousseau, Jean-Jacques, 48, 60, 61, 82, 103,
   114 116, 118, 120, 161, 166, 231n51, 245n183
   (*see also under* Berlin, Isaiah); *The Social
   Contract,* 60
Rousset, David, 98, 242n109
Rothschild, Jacob, 194–95
Rovere, Richard H., 17
Rumkowski, Chaim, 143
Russell, Bertrand, 2, 28, 30, 31, 60, 83, 167,
   168; *History of Western Philosophy,* 83
Russell, Luke, 39

Said, Edward, 221n73
Salazar, António de Oliveira, 92
Salzburg, 138–39
Sartre, Jean-Paul, 24, 25, 29, 31, 133–35, 137,
   144, 249nn49–50; *Existentialism and
   Humanism,* 133–35, 249n49
Sassen, Willem, 34, 247n3
Schapiro, Leonard, 43
Schlesinger, Arthur, Jr., 1, 16–17, 45, 193,
   220nn51 and 53
Schlick, Moritz, 28
Schocken, Salman, 15, 219n37
Scholem, Gershom, 40, 41, 42, 126, 135, 137,
   138, 142, 145, 153, 156–58, 228n211, 248n27.
   See also under Arendt, Hannah, works of;
   Berlin, Isaiah
scientism, 106, 109–10, 112, 114, 116, 122
Sebestyen, Victor, 195
Sennett, Richard, 196
Servatius, Robert, 127
sexism. *See* gender
Shklar, Judith N., 149–50, 165, 253n130,
   261n111
Shoah. *See* Holocaust

Shorten, Richard, 88
Skinner, Quentin, 50, 70
slavery, 65, 66, 78, 100, 241n91
Smolensk Archive, 104
Socrates, 83, 104, 204
Solzhenitsyn, Aleksandr I.: *The First Circle,*
   105; *The Gulag Archipelago,* 99
Sophocles, 82
Sparrow, John, 42, 227n206
Sparta, 82, 92–93
Spender, Stephen, 42
Stalin, Joseph, 24, 60, 82, 89, 92, 96, 104,
   105–6, 111–12, 186, 188, 192, 195
Stalinism, 5, 12, 47, 61, 63, 86, 87, 89, 91, 92, 94,
   96–97, 99, 100, 102–5, 111–12, 115, 165, 176,
   187, 240n74; and Nazism, 5, 47, 86, 87, 89,
   91, 92, 97, 102, 165
Stangneth, Bettina, 225nn146 and 149, 247n12
Stoicism, 59, 82–84; Stoics, the, 48, 54, 58,
   60, 61, 69, 82, 83, 149
Stone, Dan, 98
Strauss, Leo, 47, 222n108
Strawson, P. F., 30–31
Streicher, Julius, 126
Suez Crisis, 187, 189, 193, 194. *See also under*
   Berlin, Isaiah
suicide, 3, 58, 69, 130, 136–37, 146, 184

Tagore, Rabindranath, 170
Talmon, Jacob L., 103, 117
Talleyrand, Charles-Maurice de, 19
Taylor, Craig, 132, 254n149
terror, 47, 90, 112, 120, 151, 166, 173, 179, 183, 199;
   atmosphere of, 144, 147, 149, 152; Great
   Terror (in the Soviet Union), 92, 111;
   terrorists, 44, 118, 168; total (totalitarian),
   90–91, 94, 97, 144–45, 174; white, 189.
   See also violence
Tessman, Lisa, 133, 249n52
Thucydides, 82
Times Literary Supplement, 17, 42, 87
Tocqueville, Alexis de, 53, 61, 80, 161, 179
tolerance (toleration), 63, 158, 164, 178, 200;
   and England, 164, 168, 177, 178, 184

totalitarianism, 3, 4, 5, 17, 37, 60, 61, 62, 65, 86, 87–123, 148, 152, 160, 162, 163, 165, 166, 168, 180–81, 185, 188, 191, 203, 231n53, 239n27, 239n30, 240n53; definitions of, 89–93; and imperialism, 96, 173–77. See also under Arendt, Hannah; Berlin, Isaiah; freedom

total war, 47, 165

Treaty of Versailles, 95, 121

Trójgłos o wolności (Three Voices for Freedom), 161, 162, 256n2

Trotsky, Leon, 24, 107, 166

Trunk, Isaiah, 149

tyranny, 62, 72, 89, 90, 91, 92, 97, 102; of the majority, 179; tyrants, 60, 61

Ulam, Adam, 43, 45

United Nations, the, 36, 194; 'Report on the Problem of Hungary', 190, 192

utopianism, 103, 106–10, 115, 116, 118, 122, 166, 170, 199. See also under Nazism

Venturi, Franco, 3

Verba, Sidney, 67

Vico, Giambattista, 29

Vienna: persecution of the Jews in, 33, 108; philosophy in, 28–29, 32

Vietnam War, 183–84

Villa, Dana R., 76, 80, 253n131

violence, 15, 49, 90, 92, 100, 104, 106, 107, 109, 112–13, 118, 148, 173, 185, 186, 189–90, 191, 199, 218n14, 244n165; sexual, 242n104, 244n154. See also terror

Vitoria, Francisco de, 171

Waldron, Jeremy, 77, 260n105

Walicki, Andrzej, 118, 161, 163, 265n194

Wall, Steven, 165

Wannsee Conference, 125, 153–54

Warsaw, 108, 143, 161; ghetto uprising in, 140, 150

Wasserstein, Bernard, 38, 250n81, 251n83, 252n98

Weber, Max, 247n15

Weizmann, Chaim, 12, 14, 15

Wilhelm II, Kaiser, 166

Williams, Bernard, 32, 151, 254n140

Winham, Ilya, 44, 221n78, 228n225, 265n200

Wise, Stephen, 15

Wisliceny, Dieter, 33

Wittgenstein, Ludwig, 28

Woolf, Virginia, 142

World War I, 11, 26, 94–95, 96, 121, 173, 190, 218n14

World War II, 1, 3, 10, 12, 13, 15, 16, 33, 34, 38, 64, 88, 101, 111, 122, 124–68, 169, 244n154

World War III, prospect of, 187, 194

Young-Bruehl, Elisabeth, 43, 137

Youth Aliyah, 10, 21

Zajdlerowa, Zoë (pseud. Martin Hare), 99, 241n76, 242n109

Zeno of Citium, 92

Zionism, 9, 10, 13–16, 17–21, 24, 25, 124, 140, 141, 143–44, 150–51, 159, 170, 192, 196, 200, 221n73, 246nn191–92; anti-, 18; Biltmore, Extraordinary Zionist Conference (May 1942) in, 18–19, 21; post-, 15, 18; World Zionist Organization, 10, 40; Zionist Federation of Germany, 10, 14, 136; Zionist Organization of America, 13, 19. See also under Arendt, Hannah; Berlin, Isaiah

Zweig, Arnold, 10

A NOTE ON THE TYPE

This book has been composed in Arno, an Old-style serif typeface in the classic Venetian tradition, designed by Robert Slimbach at Adobe.